Constantinople and Old and New

This substantial account of Constantinople -- or Istanbul as it is known today -- is both a history and a guide to that magnificent and fabled metropolis where east and west have met for many centuries. Written in 1915 when, as Stamboul, the city was the last stop on the Orient Express, it is illustrated with many rare period photographs. This book for the general reader evokes all the colour and richness of the ultimate oriental city, ancient capital of the Byzantine and Ottoman empires, captured on the brink of modernization in the first years after the revolution. The author describes everyday life in the city, - the features of permanent interest such as mosques, gardens, fountains, the traces of Byzantium and the quays of the Golden Horn as well as the feasts, customs, festivals and holidays that once enlivened Constantinople but are now only a memory. The work concludes with an account of the revolution and of the effects of World War I on the city. This is a portrait of the Istanbul that all travellers hope to find - and still can, in the pages of this book.

H.G. DWIGHT was a private American scholar and resident of Venice and Constantinople at the beginning of this century.

THE KEGAN PAUL TRAVELLERS SERIES

A Year Amongst the Persians
Edward Granville Browne

Constantinople and Istanbul Old and New
H. G. Dwight

Tahiti
George Calderon

Cruise of the Snark
Jack London

In the South Seas
Robert Louis Stevenson

Six Months in Hawaii
Isabella Bird

Korea and Her Neighbours
Isabella Bird

Photograph by Alinari Brothers, Florence

Sultan Mehmed II, the Conqueror

From the portrait by Gentile Bellini in the Layard Collection

CONSTANTINOPLE AND ISTANBUL
OLD AND NEW

H. G. DWIGHT

Routledge
Taylor & Francis Group
LONDON AND NEW YORK

First published 2002 by Kegan Paul Limited

2 Park Square, Milton Park, Abingdon, Oxfordshire OX14 4RN
52 Vanderbilt Avenue, New York, NY 10017

Routledge is an imprint of the Taylor & Francis Group, an informa business

First issued in paperback 2019

Distributed by:
Turpin Distribution
Columbia University Press

British Library Cataloguing in Publication Data
Dwight, H. G.
Constantinople old and new. - (Kegan Paul travellers series)
1.Istanbul(Turkey) – Description and travel 2.Istanbul (Turkey) – History
I.Title
949.6'18

Library of Congress Cataloging-in-Publication Data
Applied for.

ISBN 13: 978-0-7103-0721-7 (hbk)
ISBN 13: 978-1-138-99164-4 (pbk)

OF HIS BOOK

A NUMBER of years ago it happened to the writer of this book to live in Venice. He accordingly read, as every good English-speaking Venetian does, Mr. Howells's "Venetian Life." And after the first heat of his admiration he ingenuously said to himself: "I know Constantinople quite as well as Mr. Howells knew Venice. Why shouldn't I write a 'Constantinople Life'?" He neglected to consider the fact that dozens of other people knew Venice even better than Mr. Howells, perhaps, but could never have written "Venetian Life." Nevertheless, he took himself and his project seriously. He went back, in the course of time, to Constantinople, with no other intent than to produce his imitation of Mr. Howells. And the reader will doubtless smile at the remoteness of resemblance between that perfect little book and this big one.

Aside, however, from the primary difference between two pens, circumstances further intervened to deflect this book from its original aspiration. As the writer made acquaintance with his predecessors in the field, he was struck by the fact that Constantinople, in comparison with Venice and I know not how many other cities, and particularly that Turkish Constantinople, has been wonderfully little "exploited" — at least in our generation and by users of our language. He therefore turned much of his attention to its commoner aspects — which Mr. Howells in Venice felt, very happily, under no obligation to do. Then the present writer found himself more and more irritated by the patronising or contemptuous tone of the West toward the East, and he made it rather a point — since in art one may choose a point of view — to dwell on the picturesque and admirable side of Constantinople. And soon after his return there took place the revolution of 1908, whose various consequences have attracted so much of international notice during the last five years. It was but natural that events so moving should find some reflection in the pages of an avowed impressionist. Incidentally, however, it has come about that the Constantinople of this book is a Constantinople in transition. The first chapter to be written was the one called "A Turkish Village." Since it was originally put on paper, a few weeks before the revolution, the village it describes has been so ravaged by a well-meaning but unilluminated desire of "progress" that I now find it impossible to bring the chapter up to date without rewriting it in a very different key. I therefore leave it practically untouched, as a record of the old Constantinople of which I happened to see the last. And as years go by much of the rest of the book can only have a similar documentary reference.

At the same time I have tried to catch an atmosphere of Constantinople that change does not affect and to point out certain things of permanent interest — as in the chapters on mosque yards, gardens, and fountains, as well as in numerous references to the old Turkish house. Being neither a Byzantinist nor an Orientalist, and, withal, no expert in questions of art, I realise that the true expert will find much to take exception to. While in matters of fact I have tried to be as accurate as possible, I have mainly followed the not infallible Von Hammer, and most of my Turkish translations are borrowed from him or otherwise acquired at second hand. Moreover, I have unexpectedly been obliged to correct my proofs in another country, far from books and from the friends who might have helped to save my face before the critic. I shall welcome his attacks, however, if a little more interest be thereby awakened in a place and a people of which the outside world entertains the vaguest ideas. In this book, as in the list of books at its end, I have attempted to do no more than to suggest. Of the list in question I am the first to acknowledge that it is in no proper sense a bibliography. I hardly need say that it does not begin to be complete. If it did it would fill more pages than the volume it belongs to. It contains almost no original sources and it gives none of the detailed and classified information which a bibliography should. It is merely what I call it, a list of books, of more popular interest, in the languages more commonly read by Anglo-Saxons, relating to the two great periods of Constantinople and various phases of the history and art of each, together with a few better-known works of general literature.

I must add a word with regard to the spelling of the Turkish names and words which occur in these pages. The great difficulty of rendering in English the sound of foreign words is that English, like Turkish, does not spell itself. For that reason, and because whatever interest this book may have will be of a general rather than of a specialised kind, I have ventured to deviate a little from the logical system of the Royal Geographical Society. I have not done so with regard to consonants, which have the same value as in English, with the exception that *g* is always hard and *s* is never pronounced like *z*. The gutturals *gh* and *kh* have been so softened by the Constantinople dialect that I generally avoid them, merely suggesting them by an *h*. *Y*, as I use it, is half a consonant, as in *yes*. As for the other vowels, they are to be pronounced in general as in the Continental languages. But many newspaper readers might be surprised to learn that the town where the Bulgarians gained their initial success during the Balkan war was not Kîrk Kiliss, and that the second syllable of the first name of the late Mahmud Shefket Pasha did not rhyme with bud. I therefore weakly pander to the Anglo-Saxon eye by tagging a final *e* with an admonitory *h*, and I illogically fall back on the French *ou* — or that of our own word *through*. There is another vowel sound in Turkish which the general reader will probably give up in despair. This is uttered with the teeth close together and the tongue near the roof of the mouth, and is very much like the pronunciation we give to the last syllable of words ending in *tion* or to the *n't* in *needn't*. It is generally rendered in foreign languages by *i* and sometimes in English by the *u* of *sun*. Neither really expresses it, however, nor does any other letter in the Roman alphabet. I have therefore chosen to indicate it by î, chiefly because the circumflex suggests a difference. For the reader's further guidance in pronunciation I will give him the rough-and-ready rule that all Turkish words are accented on the last syllable. But this does not invariably hold, particularly with double vowels — as in the name Hüsséïn, or the word *serái*, palace. Our common *a* and *i*, as in *lake* and *like*, are really similar double vowel sounds, similarly accented on the first. The same rules of pronunciation, though not of accent, apply to the few Greek words I have had occasion to use. I have made no attempt to transliterate them. Neither have I attempted to subject well-known words or names of either language to my somewhat arbitrary rules. Stamboul I continue so to call, though to the Turks it is something more like Îstambol; and words like *bey*, *caïque*, and *sultan* have long since been naturalised in the West. I have made an exception, however, with regard to Turkish personal names, and in mentioning the reigning Sultan or his great ancestor, the Conqueror, I have followed not the European but the Turkish usage, which reserves the form Mohammed for the Prophet alone.

This is not a book of learning, but I have required a great deal of help in putting it together, and I cannot close this prefatory note without acknowledging my indebtedness to more kind friends than I have space to name. Most of all I owe to Mr. E. L. Burlingame, of *Scribner's Magazine*, and to my father, Dr. H. O. Dwight, without whose encouragement, moral and material, during many months, I could never have afforded the luxury of writing a book. I am also under obligation to their Excellencies, J. G. A. Leishman, O. S. Straus, and W. W. Rockhill, American ambassadors to the Porte, and especially to the last, for cards of admission, letters of introduction, and other facilities for collecting material. Among many others who have taken the trouble to give me assistance of one kind or another I particularly wish to express my acknowledgments to Arthur Baker, Esq.; to Mgr. Christophoros, Bishop of Pera; to F. Mortimer Clapp, Esq.; to Feridoun Bey, Professor of Turkish in Robert College; to H. E. Halil Edhem Bey, Director of the Imperial Museum; to Hüsseïn Danish Bey, of the Ottoman Public Debt; to H. E. Ismaïl Jenani Bey, Grand Master of Ceremonies of the Imperial Court; to H. E. Ismet Bey, *Préfet adjoint* of Constantinople; to Kemaleddin Bey, Architect in Chief of the Ministry of Pious Foundations; to Mahmoud Bey, Sheikh of the Bektash Dervishes of Roumeli Hissar; to Professor Alexander van Millingen; to Frederick Moore, Esq.; to Mr. Panayotti D. Nicolopoulos, Secretary of the Mixed Council of the Œcumenical Patriarchate; to Haji Orhan Selaheddin Dedeh, of the Mevlevi Dervishes of Pera; to A. L. Otterson, Esq.; to Sir Edwin Pears; to Refik Bey, Curator of the Palace and Treasury of Top Kapou; to E. D. Roth, Esq.; to Mr. Arshag Schmavonian, Legal Adviser of the American Embassy; to William Thompson, Esq.; to Ernest Weakley, Esq.; and to Zia Bey, of the Ministry of Pious Foundations. My thanks are also due to the editors of the *Atlantic Monthly*, of *Scribner's Magazine*, and of the *Spectator*, for allowing me to republish those chapters which originally came out in their periodicals. And I am not least grateful to the publishers for permitting me to change the scheme of my book while in preparation, and to substitute new illustrations for a large number that had already been made.

HAMADAN,
6th Sefer, 1332.

CONTENTS

CONTENTS

ILLUSTRATIONS

CONSTANTINOPLE OLD AND NEW

I, a Persian and an Ispahani, had ever been accustomed to hold my native city as the first in the world: never had it crossed my mind that any other could, in the smallest degree, enter into competition with it, and when the capital of Roum was described to me as finer, I always laughed the describer to scorn. But what was my astonishment, and I may add mortification, on beholding, for the first time, this magnificent city! I had always looked upon the royal mosque, in the great square at Ispahan, as the most superb building in the world; but here were a hundred finer, each surpassing the other in beauty and in splendour. Nothing did I ever conceive could equal the extent of my native place; but here my eyes became tired with wandering over the numerous hills and creeks thickly covered with buildings, which seemed to bid defiance to calculation. If Ispahan was half the world, this indeed was the whole. And then this gem of cities possesses this great advantage over Ispahan, that it is situated on the borders of a beautiful succession of waters, instead of being surrounded by arid and craggy mountains; and, in addition to its own extent and beauty, enjoys the advantage of being reflected in one never-failing mirror, ever at hand to multiply them. . . . "Oh! this is a paradise," said I to those around me; "and may I never leave it!"

—J. J. Morier, "*The Adventures of Hajji Baba of Ispahan.*"

CONSTANTINOPLE OLD AND NEW

I

STAMBOUL

If literature could be governed by law — which, very happily, to the despair of grammarians, it can not — there should be an act prohibiting any one, on pain of death, ever to quote again or adapt to private use Charles Lamb and his two races of men. No one is better aware of the necessity of such a law than the present scribe, as he struggles with the temptation to declare anew that there are two races of men. Where, for instance, do they betray themselves more perfectly than in Stamboul? You like Stamboul or you dislike Stamboul, and there seems to be no half-way ground between the two opinions. I notice, however, that conversion from the latter rank to the former is not impossible. I cannot say that I ever really belonged, myself, to the enemies of Stamboul. Stamboul entered too early into my consciousness and I was too early separated from her to ask myself questions; and it later happened to me to fall under a potent spell. But there came a day when I returned to Stamboul from Italy. I felt a scarcely definable change in the atmosphere as soon as we crossed the Danube. Strange letters decorated the sides of cars, a fez or two — shall I be pedantic enough to say that the word is really *fess?* — appeared at car windows, peasants on station platforms had something about them that recalled youthful associations. The change grew more and more marked as we neared the Turkish frontier. And I realised to what it had been trending when at last we entered a breach of the old Byzantine wall and whistled through a long seaside quarter of wooden houses more tumble-down and unpainted than I remembered wooden houses could be, and dusty little gardens, and glimpses of a wide blue water through ruinous masonry, and people as out-at-elbow and down-at-the-heel as their houses, who even at that shining hour of a summer morning found time to smoke hubble-bubbles in tipsy little coffee-houses above the Marmora or to squat motionless on their heels beside the track and watch the fire-carriage of the unbeliever roll in from the West.

I have never forgotten — nor do successive experiences seem to dull the sharpness of the impression — that abysmal drop from the general European level of spruceness and solidity. Yet Stamboul, if you belong to the same race of men as I, has a way of rehabilitating herself in your eyes, perhaps even of making you adopt her point of view. Not that I shall try to gloss over her case. Stamboul is not for the race of men that must have trimness, smoothness, regularity, and modern conveniences, and the latest amusements. She has ambitions in that direction. I may live to see her attain them. I have already lived to see half of the Stamboul I once knew burn to the ground and the other half experiment in Haussmannising. But there is still enough of the old Stamboul left to leaven the new. It is very bumpy to drive over. It is ill-painted and out of repair. It is somewhat intermittently served by the scavenger. Its geography is almost past finding out, for no true map of it, in this year of grace 1914, as yet exists, and no man knows his street or number. What he knows is the fountain or the coffee-house near which he lives, and the quarter in which both are situated, named perhaps Coral, or Thick Beard, or Eats No Meat, or Sees Not Day; and it remains for you to find that quarter and that fountain. Nevertheless, if you belong to the race of men that is amused by such things, that is curious about the ways and thoughts of other men and feels under no responsibility to change them, that can see happy arrangements of light and shade, of form and colour, without having them pointed out and in very common materials, that is not repelled by things which look old and out of order, that is even attracted by things which do look so and therefore have a mellowness of tone and a richness of association — if you belong to this race of men you will like Stamboul, and the chances are that you will like it very much.

You must not make the other mistake, however, of expecting too much in the way of colour. Constantinople lies, it is true, in the same latitude as Naples; but the steppes of Russia are separated from it only by the not too boundless steppes of the Black Sea. The colour of Constantinople is a compromise, therefore, and not always a successful one, between north and south. While the sun shines for half the year, and summer rain is an exception, there is something hard and unsuffused about the light. Only on certain days of south wind are you reminded of the Mediterranean, and more rarely still of the autumn Adriatic. As for the town itself, it is no white southern city, being in tone one of the soberest. I could never bring myself, as some writers do, to speak of silvery domes. They are always covered with lead, which goes excellently with the stone of the mosques they crown. It is only the lesser minarets that are white; and here and there on some lifted pinnacle a small half-moon makes a flash of gold. While the high lights of Stamboul, then, are grey, this stone Stamboul is small in proportion to the darker Stamboul that fills the wide interstices between the mosques — a Stamboul of weathered wood that is just the colour of an etching. It has always seemed to me, indeed, that Stamboul, above all other cities I know, waits to be etched. Those fine lines of dome and minaret are for copper rather than canvas, while those crowded houses need the acid to bring out the richness of their shadows.

Stamboul has waited a long time. Besides Frank Brangwyn and E. D. Roth, I know of no etcher who has tried his needle there. And neither of those two has done what I could imagine Whistler doing — a Long Stamboul as seen from the opposite shore of the Golden Horn. When the archæologists tell you that Constantinople, like Rome, is built on seven hills, don't believe them. They are merely riding a hobby-horse so ancient that I, for one, am ashamed to mount it. Constantinople, or that part of it which is now Stamboul, lies on two hills, of which the more important is a long ridge dominating the Golden Horn. Its crest is not always at the same level, to be sure, and its slopes are naturally broken by ravines. If Rome, however, had been built on fourteen hills it would have been just as easy to find the same number in Constantinople. That steep promontory advancing between sea and sea toward a steeper Asia must always have been something to look at. But I find it hard to believe that the city of Constantine and Justinian can have marked so noble an outline against the sky as the city of the sultans. For the mosques of the sultans, placed exactly where

From an etching by Ernest D. Roth

A Stamboul street

their pyramids of domes and lance-like minarets tell most against the light, are what make the silhouette of Stamboul one of the most notable things in the world.

Of the many voyagers who have celebrated the panorama of Constantinople, not a few have recorded their disappointment on coming to closer acquaintance. *De gustibus* . . . I have small respect, however, for the taste of those who find that the mosques will not bear inspection. I shall presently have something more particular to say in that matter. But since I am now speaking of the general aspects of Stamboul I can hardly pass over the part played by the mosques and their dependencies. A grey dome, a white minaret, a black cypress — that is the group which, recurring in every possible composition, makes up so much of the colour of the streets. On the monumental scale of the imperial mosques it ranks among the supreme architectural effects. On a smaller scale it never lacks charm. One element of this charm is so simple that I wonder it has not been more widely imitated. Almost every mosque is enclosed by a wall, sometimes of smooth ashler with a pointed coping, sometimes of plastered cobblestones tiled at the top, often tufted with snapdragon and camomile daisies. And this wall is pierced by a succession of windows which are filled with metal grille work as simple or as elaborate as the builder pleased. For he knew, the crafty man, that a grille or a lattice is always pleasant to look through, and that it somehow lends interest to the barest prospect.

There is hardly a street of Stamboul in which some such window does not give a glimpse into the peace and gravity of the East. The windows do not all look into mosque yards. Many of them open into the cloister of a *medresseh*, a theological school, or some other pious foundation. Many more look into a patch of ground where tall turbaned and lichened stones lean among cypresses or where a more or less stately mausoleum, a *türbeh*, lifts its dome. Life and death seem never very far apart in Constantinople. In other cities the fact that life has an end is put out of sight as much as possible. Here it is not only acknowledged but taken advantage of for decorative purposes. Even Divan Yolou, the Street of the Council, which is the principal avenue of Stamboul, owes much of its character to the tombs and patches of cemetery that border it. Several sultans and grand viziers and any number of more obscure persons lie there neighbourly to the street, from which he who strolls, if not he who runs, may read — if Arabic letters be familiar to him — half the history of the empire.

Of the houses of the living I have already hinted that they are less permanent in appearance. Until very recently they were all built of wood, and they all burned down ever so often. Consequently Stamboul has begun to rebuild herself in brick and concrete. I shall not complain of it, for I admit that it is not well for Stamboul to continue burning down. I also admit that Stamboul must modernise some of her habits. It is a matter of the greatest urgency if Stamboul wishes to continue to exist. Yet I am sorry to have the old wooden house of Stamboul disappear. It is not merely that I am a fanatic in things of other times. That house is, at its best, so expressive a piece of architecture, it is so simple and so dignified in its lines, it contains so much wisdom for the modern decorator, that I am sorry for it to disappear and leave no report of itself. If I could do what I like, there is nothing I should like to do more than to build, and to set a fashion of building, from less perishable materials, and fitted out with a little more convenience, a *konak* of Stamboul. They are descended, I suppose, from the old Byzantine houses. There is almost nothing

Divan Yolou

Arabic about them, at all events, and their interior arrangement resembles that of any *palazzo* of the Renaissance.

The old wooden house of Stamboul is never very tall. It sits roomily on the ground, seldom rising above two storeys. Its effect resides in its symmetry and proportion, for there is almost no ornament about it. The doorway is the most decorative part of the façade. Its two leaves open very broad and square, with knockers in the form of lyres, or big rings attached to round plates of intricately perforated copper. Above it there will often be an oval light filled with a fan or star of swallow-tailed wooden radii. The windows in general make up a great part of the character of the house, so big and so numerous are they. They are all latticed, unless Christians happen to live in the house; but above the lattices is sometimes a second tier of windows, for light, whose small round or oval panes are decoratively set in broad white mullions of plaster. For the most original part of its effect, however, the house counts on its upper storey, which juts out over the street on stout timbers curved like the bow of a ship. Sometimes these corbels balance each other right and left of the centre of the house, which may be rounded on the principle of a New York "swell front," only more gracefully, and occasionally a third storey leans out beyond the second. This arrangement gives more space to the upper floors than the ground itself affords and also assures a better view. If it incidentally narrows and darkens the street, I think the passer-by can only be grateful for the fine line of the curving brackets and for the summer shade. He is further protected from the sun by the broad eaves of the house, supported, perhaps, by little brackets of their own. Under them was stencilled of old an Arabic invocation, which more rarely decorated a blue-and-white tile and which nowadays is generally printed on paper and framed like a picture — "O Protector," "O Conqueror," "O Proprietor of all Property." And over all is a low-pitched roof, hardly ever gabled, of the red tiles you see in Italy.

The inside of the house is almost as simple as the outside — or it used to be before Europe infected it. A great entrance hall, paved with marble, runs through the house from street to garden, for almost no house in Stamboul lacks its patch of green; and branching or double stairways lead to the upper regions. Other big halls are there, with niches and fountains set in the wall. The rooms opening out on either hand contain almost no furniture. The so-called Turkish corner which I fear is still the pride of some Western interiors never originated

A house in Eyoub

anywhere but in the diseased imagination of an upholsterer. The beauty of an old Turkish room does not depend on what may have been brought into it by chance, but on its own proportion and colour. On one side, covering the entire wall, should be a series of cupboards and niches, which may be charmingly decorated with painted flowers and gilt or coloured moulding. The ceiling is treated in the same way, the strips of moulding being applied in some simple design. Of real wood-carving there is practically none, though the doors are panelled in great variety and the principle of the lattice is much used. There may also be a fireplace, not set

A house at Aya Kapou

off by a mantel, but by a tall pointed hood. And if there is a second tier of windows they may contain stained glass or some interesting scheme of mullioning. But do not look for chairs, tables, draperies, pictures, or any of the thousand gimcracks of the West that only fill a room without beautifying it. A long low divan runs under the windows, the whole length of the wall, or perhaps of two, furnished with rugs and embroidered cushions.

Other rugs, as fine as you please, cover the floor. Of wall space there is mercifully very little, for the windows crowd so closely together that there is no room to put anything between them, and the view is consciously made the chief ornament of the room. Still, on the inner walls

The house of the pipe

may hang a text or two, written by or copied from some great calligraphist. The art of forming beautiful letters has been carried to great perfection by the Turks, who do not admit — or who until recently did not admit — any representation of living forms. Inscriptions, therefore, take with them the place of pictures, and they collect the work of famous calligraphs as Westerners collect other works of art. While a real appreciation of this art requires a knowledge which few foreigners possess, any foreigner should be able to take in the decorative value of the Arabic letters. There are various systems of forming them, and there is no limit to the number of ways in which they may be grouped. By adding to an inscription its reverse, it is possible to make a symmetrical figure which sometimes resembles a mosque, or the letters may be fancifully made to suggest a bird or a ship. Texts from the Koran, invocations of the Almighty, the names of the caliphs and of the companions of the Prophet, and verses of Persian poetry are all favourite subjects for the calligrapher. I have also seen what might very literally be called a word-picture of the Prophet. To paint a portrait of him would contravene all the traditions of the cult; but there exists a famous description of him which is sometimes written in a circle, as it were the outline of a head, on an illuminated panel.

However, I did not start out to describe the interior of Stamboul, of which I know as little as any man. That, indeed, is one element of the charm of Stamboul — the sense of reserve, of impenetrability, that pervades its Turkish quarters. The lattices of the windows, the veils of the women, the high garden walls, the gravity and perfect quiet of the streets at night, all contribute to that sense. From the noisy European quarter on the opposite bank of the Golden Horn, where life is a thing of shreds and patches, without coherent associations and without roots, one looks over to Stamboul and gets the sense of another, an unknown life, reaching out secret filaments to the uttermost parts of the earth. Strange faces, strange costumes, strange dialects come and go, on errands not necessarily too mysterious, yet mysterious enough for one who knows nothing of the literature of the East, its habits, its real thought and hope and belief. We speak glibly of knowing Turkey and the Turks — we who have lived five or ten or fifty years among them; but very few of us, I notice, have ever known them well enough to learn their language or read their books. And so into Stamboul we all go as outsiders. Yet there are aspects of Stamboul which are not so inaccessible. Stamboul at work, Stamboul as a market-place, is a Stamboul which welcomes the intruder — albeit with her customary gravity: if a man buttonholes you in the street and insists that you look at his wares you may be sure that he is no Turk. This is also a Stamboul which has never been, which never can be, sufficiently celebrated. The Bazaars, to be sure, figure in all the books of travel, and are visited by every one; but they are rather sighed over nowadays, as having lost a former glory. I do not sigh over them, myself. I consider that by its very arrangement the Grand Bazaar possesses an interest which can never disappear. It is a sort of vast department store, on one floor though not on one level, whose cobbled aisles wander up hill and down dale, and are vaulted solidly over with stone. And in old times, before the shops or costumes of Pera were, and when the *beau monde* came here to buy, a wonderful department store it must have been. In our economic days there may be less splendour, but there can hardly be less life; and if Manchester prints now largely take the place of Broussa silk and Scutari velvet, they have just as much colour for the modern impressionist. They also contribute to the essential colour of Constantinople, which is neither Asiatic nor European, but a mingling of both.

A last fragment of old Stamboul is walled in the heart of this maze, a square enclosure of deeper twilight which is called the *Bezesten*. Tradition has it that the shopkeepers of the *Bezesten* originally served God as well as mammon, and were required to give a certain amount of time to their mosques. Be that as it may, they still dress in robe and turban, and they keep shorter hours than their brethren of the outer bazaar. They sit at the receipt of custom, not in shops but on continuous platforms, grave old men to whom it is apparently one whether you come or go, each before his own shelf and cupboard inlaid with mother-of-pearl; and they deal only in old things. I do not call them antiques, though such things may still be picked up — for their price — in the *Bezesten* and out of it, and though the word is often on the lips of the old men. I will say for them, however, that on their lips it merely means something exceptional of its kind. They could recommend you an egg or a spring lamb no more highly than by calling it *antika*. At any rate, the *Bezesten* is almost a little too good to be true. It might have been arranged by some Gérome who studied the exact effect of dusty shafts of light striking down from high windows on the most picturesque confusion of old things — stuffs, arms, rugs, brasses, porcelain, jewelry, silver, odds and ends of bric-à-brac. In that romantic twilight an antique made in Germany becomes precious, and the most abominable modern rug takes on the tone of time.

The real rug market of Constantinople is not in the Bazaars nor yet in the *hans* of Mahmoud Pasha, but in the Stamboul custom-house. There the bales that come down from Persia and the Caucasus, as well as from Asia Minor and even from India and China, are opened and stored in great piles of colour, and there the wholesale dealers of Europe and America do most of their buying. The rugs are sold by the square metre in the bale, so that you may buy a hundred pieces in order to get one or two you particularly want. Burly

Turkish porters or black-capped Persians are there to turn over the rugs for you, shaking out the dust of Asia into the European air. Bargaining is no less long and fierce than in the smaller affairs of the Bazaars, though both sides know better what they are up to. Perhaps it is for this reason that the sale is often made by a third party. The referee, having first obtained the consent of the principals to abide by his decision — "Have you content?" is what he asks them — makes each sign his name in a note-book, in which he then writes the compromise price, saying, "Sh-sh!" if they protest. Or else he takes a hand of each between both of his own and names the price as he shakes the hands up and down, the others crying out: "*Aman!* Do not scorch me!" Then coffees are served all around and everybody departs happy. As communications become easier the buyers go more and more to the headquarters of rug-making, so that Constantinople will not remain indefinitely what it is now, the greatest rug market in the world. But it will long be the chief assembling and distributing point for this ancient trade.

There are two other covered markets, both in the vicinity of the Bridge, which I recommend to all hunters after local colour. The more important, from an architectural point of view, is called Mîssîr Charshî, Corn or Egyptian Market, though Europeans know it as the Spice Bazaar. It consists of two vaulted stone streets that cross each other at right angles. It was so badly damaged in the earthquake of 1894 that many of its original tenants moved away, giving place to stuffy quilt and upholstery men. Enough of the former are left, however, to make a museum of strange powders and electuaries, and to fill the air with the aroma of the East. And the quaint woodwork of the shops, the dusty little ships and mosques that hang as signs above them, the decorative black frescoing of the walls, are quite as good in their way as the *Bezesten*. The Dried Fruit Bazaar, I am afraid, is a less permanent piece of old Stamboul. It is sure to burn up or to be torn down one of these days, because it is a section of the long street — almost the only level one in the city — that skirts the Golden Horn. I hope it will not disappear, however, before some etcher has caught the duskiness of its branching curve, with squares of sky irregularly spaced among the wooden rafters, and corresponding squares of light on the cobblestones below, and a dark side corridor or two running down to a bright perspective of water and ships. All sorts of nuts and dried fruits are sold there, in odd company with candles and the white ribbons and artificial flowers without which no Greek or Armenian can be properly married.

This whole quarter is one of markets, and some of them were old in Byzantine times. The fish market, one of the richest in the world, is here. The vegetable market is here, too, at the head of the outer bridge, where it can be fed by the boats of the Marmora. And all night long horse bells jingle through the city, bringing produce which is sold in the public square in the small hours of the morning. Provisions of other kinds, some of them strange to behold and stranger to smell, are to be had in the same region. In the purlieus of Yeni Jami, too, may be admired at its season a kind of market which is a specialty of Constantinople. The better part of it is installed in the mosque yard, where cloth and girdles and shoes and other commodities meet for the raiment of man and woman are sold under awnings or big canvas umbrellas. But other sections of it, as the copper market and the flower market, overflow beyond the Spice Bazaar. The particularity of this Monday market is that it is gone on Tuesday, being held in a different place on every day of the week. Then this is a district of *hans*, which harbour a commerce of their own. Some of these are hotels, where comers from afar camp out in tiers of stone galleries about an open court. Others are places of business or of storage, and, as the latter, are more properly known by the name *kapan*. The old *Fontego* or *Fondaco dei Turchi* in Venice, and the *Fondaco dei Tedeschi*, are built on the same plan and originally served the same purpose. The Italian word *fondaco* comes from the Arabic *fîndîk*, which in turn was derived from the πανδοχεῖον of Constantinople. But whether any of these old stone buildings might trace a Byzantine or Venetian ancestry I cannot say. The habit of Stamboul to burn up once in so often made them very necessary, and in spite of the changes that have taken place in business methods they are still largely used. And all about them are the headquarters of crafts — wood-turning, basket-making, amber-cutting, brass-beating — in alleys which are highly profitable to explore.

One of the things that make those alleys not least profitable is the grape-vine that somehow manages to grow in them. It is no rarity, I am happy to report. That grape-vine is one of the most decorative elements of Stamboul streets; and to me, at least, it has a whole philosophy to tell. It was never planted for the profit of its fruit. Vines allowed to grow as those vines grow cannot bear very heavily, and they are too accessible for their grapes to be guarded. They were planted, like the *traghetto* vines in Venice, because they give shade and because they are good to look upon. Some of them are trained on wires across the street, making of the public way an arbour that seduces the passer-by to stop and taste the taste of life.

Fortunately there are special conveniences for this, in places where there are vines and places where there are not. Such are the places that the arriving traveller sees from his train, where meditative citizens sit cross-legged of a morning over coffee and tobacco. The traveller continues to see them wherever he goes, and never without a meditative citizen or two. The coffee-houses indeed are an essential part of Stamboul, and in them the outsider comes nearest, perhaps, to intimacy with that reticent city. The number of these institutions in Constantinople is quite fabulous. They have the happiest tact for locality, seeking movement, strategic corners, open prospects, the company of water and trees. No quarter is so miserable or so remote as to be without one. Certain thoroughfares carry on almost no other form of business. A sketch of a coffee-shop may often be seen in the street, in a scrap of sun or shade, according to the season, where a stool or two invite the passer-by to a moment of contemplation. And no *han* or public building is without its facilities for dispensing the indispensable.

I know not whether the fact may contribute anything to the psychology of prohibition, but it is surprising to learn how recent an invention coffee-houses are, as time goes in this part of the world, and what opposition they first encountered. The first coffee-shop was opened in Stamboul in 1554, by one Shemsi, a native of Aleppo. A man of his race it was, an Arab dervish of the thirteenth century, who is supposed to have discovered the properties of the coffee berry. Shemsi returned to Syria in three years, taking with him some five thousand ducats and little imagination of what uproar his successful enter-

That grape-vine is one of the most decorative elements of Stamboul streets

prise was to cause. The beverage so quickly appreciated was as quickly looked upon by the orthodox as insidious to the public morals — partly because it seemed to merit the prohibition of the Koran against intoxicants, partly because it brought the faithful together in places other than mosques. "The black enemy of sleep and of love,"

A water-side coffee-house

as a poet styled the Arabian berry, was variously denounced as one of the Four Elements of the World of Pleasure, one of the Four Pillars of the Tent of Lubricity, one of the Four Cushions of the Couch of Voluptuousness, and one of the Four Ministers of the Devil — the other three being tobacco, opium, and wine. The name of the drug may have had something to do with the hostility it encountered. *Kahveh*, whence *café* and coffee, is a slight modification of an Arabic word — literally meaning that which takes away the appetite — which is one of the names of wine.

Süleïman the Magnificent, during whose reign the *kahveji* Shemsi made his little fortune, took no notice of the agitation against the new drink. But some of his successors pursued those who indulged in it with unheard-of severity. During the sixteenth and seventeenth centuries coffee-drinkers were persecuted more rigorously in Constantinople than wine-bibbers have ever been in England or America. Their most unrelenting enemy was the bloody Mourad IV — himself a drunkard — who forbade the use of coffee or tobacco under pain of death. He and his nephew Mehmed IV after him used to patrol the city in disguise, *à la* Haroun al Rashid, in order to detect and punish for themselves any violation of the law. But the Greek taverns only became the more popular. And the latter sultan was the means of extending the habit to Europe — which, for the rest, he no doubt considered its proper habitat. To be sure, it was merely during his reign that the English made their first acquaintance of our after-dinner friend. It was brought back from Smyrna in 1652 by a Mr. Edwards, member of the Levant Company, whose house was so besieged by those curious to taste the strange concoction that he set up his Greek servant in the first coffee-house in London. There, too, coffee was soon looked upon askance in high places. A personage no more strait-laced than Charles II caused a court to hand down the following decision: "The Retayling of Coffee may be an innocente Trayde; but as it is used to nourysshe Sedition, spredde Lyes, and scandalyse Greate Menne, it may also be a common Nuisaunce." In the meantime an envoy of Mehmed IV introduced coffee in 1669 to the court of

Louis XIV. And Vienna acquired the habit fourteen years later, when that capital was besieged by the same sultan. After the rout of the Turks by John Sobiesky, a vast quantity of the fragrant brown drug was found among the besiegers' stores. Its use was made known to the Viennese by a Pole who had been interpreter to a company of Austrian merchants in Constantinople. For his bravery in carrying messages through the Turkish lines he was given the right to establish the first coffee-house in Vienna.

The history of tobacco in Turkey was very much the same. It first appeared from the West in 1605, during the reign of Ahmed I. Under Mourad IV a famous pamphlet was written against it by an unconscious fore-runner of modernity, who also advocated a mediæval Postum made of bean pods. Snuff became known in 1642 as an attempt to elude the repressive laws of Sultan Ibrahim. But the habit of smoking, like the taste for coffee, gained such headway that no one could stop it. Mahmoud I was the last sultan who attempted to do so, when he closed the coffee-houses for political reasons in 1730.

There is, it is true, a coffee habit, whose abuse is no less demoralising than that of any other drug. But it is so rare, and Stamboul coffee-houses are so different from American or even most European cafés, that it is hard to imagine their causing so much commotion. Nothing stronger than coffee is dispensed in them — unless I except the *nargileh*, the water-pipe, whose effect is wonderfully soothing and innocent at first, though wonderfully deadly in the end to the novice. The tobacco used is not the ordinary weed but a much coarser and stronger one, called *toumbeki*. Smoking is the more germane to coffee-shops, because in the Turkish idiom you drink tobacco.

You may also drink tea, in little glasses, as the Persians do. And to desecrate it, or coffee either, with the admixture of milk is an unheard-of sacrilege. But you may content yourself with so mild a refreshment as a bit of

"Drinking" a *nargileh*

rabat locoum, more familiar to you, perhaps, as Turkish Delight, and a glass of water.

The etiquette of the coffee-house, of those coffee-houses which have not been too much infected by Europe, is one of their most characteristic features. I have seen a newcomer salute one after another each person in a crowded coffee-room, once on entering the door, and again on taking his seat, and be so saluted in return — either by putting the right hand on the heart and uttering the greeting *merhaba*, or by making the *temenna*, that triple sweep of the hand which is the most graceful of salutes. I have also seen the entire company rise on the entrance of an old man, and yield him the corner of honour. As for the essential function of the coffee-house, it

Fez-presser in a coffee-house

has its own traditions. A glass of water comes with the coffee, and a foreigner can usually be detected by the order in which he takes them. A Turk sips his water first. He lifts his coffee-cup, whether it possess a handle or no, by the saucer, managing the two in a dexterous way of his own. And custom favours a rather noisy enjoyment of the cup that cheers, as expressing appreciation and general well-being. The current price for a coffee, in the heart of Stamboul, is ten *para* — something like a penny — for which the waiter will say: "May God give you blessing." Mark, too, that you do not tip him. I have often been surprised to be charged no more than the tariff, although I gave a larger piece to be changed, and it was perfectly evident that I was a foreigner. That is an experience which rarely befalls a traveller even in his own land. It has further happened to me to be charged nothing at all, nay, to be steadfastly refused when I persisted in attempting to pay, simply because I was a traveller, and therefore a "guest."

Altogether the habit of the coffee-house is one that requires a certain leisure. Being a passion less violent and less shameful than others, I suppose, it is indulged in with more of the humanities. You do not bolt coffee as you bolt the fire-waters of the West, without ceremony, in retreats withdrawn from the public eye. Neither, having taken coffee, do you leave the coffee-house. On the contrary, there are reasons why you should stay — and not only to take another coffee. There are benches to curl up on, if you would do as the Romans do, having first neatly put off your shoes from off your feet. There are texts and patriotic pictures to look at, to say nothing of the wonderful brass arrangements wherein the *kahveji* concocts his mysteries. There is, of course, the view. To enjoy it you sit on a low rush-bottomed stool in front of the coffee-shop, under a grape-vine, perhaps, or a scented wistaria, or a bough of a neighbourly plane-tree; and if you like you may have an aromatic pot of basil beside you to keep away the flies. Then there are more active distractions. For coffee-houses are also barber shops, where men cause to be shaved not only their chins but different parts of their crowns, according to their countries; and a festoon of teeth on a string or a suggestive jar of leeches reminds you how catholic was once the art of the barber in other parts of the world. There is also the resource of games — such as backgammon, which is called *tavli* and played in Persian, and draughts, and cards. They say, indeed, that bridge came from Constantinople. There is a club in Pera which claims the honour of having communicated that passion to the

Playing *tavli*

Western world. But I must confess that I have yet to see an open hand of the long narrow cards you find in a coffee-house.

The great resource of coffee-houses, however, is the company you meet there. The company is better at certain hours than at others. Early in the day the majority of the habitués may be at work, while late in the evening they will have disappeared altogether. For Stamboul has not quite forgotten the habits of the tent. At night it is a deserted city. But just before and just after dark the coffee-houses are full of a colour which an outsider is often content to watch through lighted windows. They are the clubs of the poorer classes. Men of a street, a trade, or a province meet regularly at coffee-houses kept often by one of their own people. So much are the humbler coffee-houses frequented by a fixed clientèle that the most vagrant impressionist can realise how truly the old Turkish writers called them Schools of Knowledge. Schools of knowledge they must be, indeed, for those capable of taking part in their councils. Even for one who is not, they are full of information about the people who live in Stamboul, the variety of clothes they wear, the number of dialects they speak, the infinity of places they come from. I am at the end of my chapter and I cannot stop to descant on these things — much less on the historic guilds which still subsist in the coffee-house world. The guilds are nearly at the end of their chapter, too. Constitutions and changes more radical are turning them into something more like modern trade-unions. Their tradition is still vivid enough, though, for it to be written, as in the laws of Medes and Persians, that no man but one of Iran shall drive a house-builder's donkey; that only a Mohammedan Albanian of the south shall lay a pavement or a southern Albanian who is a Christian and wears an orange girdle shall lay railroad ties; that none save a landlubber from the hinterland of the Black Sea may row a caïque or, they of Konia peddle *yo'ourt*, or ——

It is no use for me to go on. I would fill pages and I probably would not make it any clearer how clannish these men are. Other things about them are just as interesting — to the race of men that likes Stamboul. That first question, for instance, that comes to one on the arriving train, at the sight of so many leisurely and meditative persons, returns again and again to the mind. How is it that these who burst once out of the East with so much noise and terror, who battered their way through the walls of this city and carried the green standard of the Prophet to the gates of Vienna, sit here now rolling

The plane-tree of Chengel-kyöi

cigarettes and sipping little cups of coffee? Some conclude that their course is run, while others upbraid them for wasting so their time. For my part, I like to think that such extremes may argue a complexity of character for whose unfolding it would be wise to wait. I also like to think that there may be some people in the world for whom time is more than money. At any rate, it pleases me that all the people in the world are not the same. It pleases me that some are content to sit in coffee-houses, to enjoy simple pleasures, to watch common spectacles, to find that in life which every one may possess — light, growing things, the movement of water, and an outlook on the ways of men.

II

MOSQUE YARDS

I OFTEN wonder what a Turk, a Turk of the people, would make of a Western church. In an old cathedral close, perhaps, he might feel to a degree at home. The architecture of the building would set it apart from those about it, the canons' houses and other subsidiary structures would not seem unnatural to him, and, though the arrangement of the interior would be foreign, he would probably understand in what manner of place he was — and his religion would permit him to worship there in his own way. But a modern city church, and particularly an American city church, would offer almost nothing familiar to him. It would, very likely, be less monumental in appearance than neighbouring buildings. There would be little or no open space about it. And strangest of all would be the entire absence of life about the place for six days out of seven. The most active institutional church can never give the sense a mosque does of being a living organism, an acknowledged focus of life. The larger mosques are open every day and all day, from sunrise to sunset, while even the smallest is accessible for the five daily hours of prayer. And, what is more, people go to them. Nor do they go to them as New Yorkers sometimes step into a down-town church at noontime, feeling either exceptionally pious or a little uneasy lest some one catch them in the act. It is as much a matter of course as any other habit of life, and as little one to be self-conscious about. By which I do not mean to imply that there are neither dissenters nor sceptics in Islam. I merely mean that Islam seems to be a far more vital and central force with the mass of those who profess it than Protestant Christianity.

However, I did not set out to compare religions. All I wish is to point out the importance of mosques and their precincts in the picture of Constantinople. The yards of the imperial mosques take the place, in Stamboul, of squares and parks. Even many a smaller mosque enjoys an amplitude of perspective that might be envied by cathedrals like Chartres, or Cologne, or Milan. These roomy enclosures are surrounded by the windowed walls which I have already celebrated. Within them cypresses are wont to cluster, and plane-trees willingly cast their giant shadow. Gravestones also congregate there. And there a centre of life is which can never lack interest for the race of men that likes Stamboul. Scribes sit under the trees ready to write letters for soldiers, women, and others of the less literate sort. Seal cutters ply their cognate trade, and cut your name on a bit of brass almost as quickly as you can write it. Barbers, distinguishable by a brass plate with a nick in it for your chin, are ready to exercise another art upon your person. Pedlers come and go, selling beads, perfumes, fezzes, and sweets which they carry on their heads in big wooden trays, and drinks which may tempt you less than their brass receptacles. A more stable commerce is visible in some mosque yards, or on the day of the week when a peripatetic market elects to pitch its tents there; and coffee-houses, of course, abound. Not that there are coffee-houses in every mosque yard. I know one small mosque yard, that of Mahmoud Pasha — off the busy street of that name leading to the Bazaars — which is entirely given up to coffee-houses. And a perfect mosque yard it is, grove-like with trees and looked upon by a great portico of the time of the Conqueror. There is something both grave and human about mosque yards and coffee-houses both that excellently suits them to each other. The

The yard of Hekim-zadeh Ali Pasha

combination is one that I, at any rate, am incapable of resisting. I dare not guess how many days of my life I have I cannot say wasted in the coffee-houses of Mahmoud Pasha, and Yeni Jami, and Baïezid, and Shah-zadeh, and Fatih. The company has an ecclesiastical tinge. Turbans bob much together and the neighbouring fountains of ablution play a part in the scene. And if the company does not disperse altogether it thins very much when the voice of the *müezin*, the chanter, sounds from his high white tower. "God is most great!" he chants to the four quarters of the earth. "I bear witness that there is not a god save God! I bear witness that Mohammed is the Prophet of God! Hasten to the worship of God! Hasten to permanent blessedness! God is most great!"

In the mosque the atmosphere is very much that of the mosque yard. There may be more reverence, perhaps, but people evidently feel very much at home. Men meet there out of prayer time, and women too, for what looks like, though it may not always be, a *sacra conversazione* of the painters. Students con over their Koran, rocking to and fro on a cushion in front of a little inlaid table. Solitary devotees prostrate themselves in a corner, untroubled by children playing among the pillars or a turbaned professor lecturing, cross-legged, to a cross-legged class in theology. The galleries of some mosques are safety-deposit vaults for their parishioners, and when the parish burns down the parishioners deposit themselves there too. After the greater conflagration of the Balkan War thousands of homeless refugees from Thrace and Macedonia camped out for months in the mosques of Stamboul. Even the pigeons that haunt so many mosque yards know that the doors are always open, and are scarcely to be persuaded from taking up their permanent abode on tiled cornices or among the marble stalactites of capitals.

One thing that makes a mosque look more hospitable than a church is its arrangement. There are no seats or aisles to cut up the floor. Matting is spread there, over which are laid in winter the carpets of the country; and before you step on to this clean covering you put off your shoes from off your feet — unless you shuffle about in the big slippers that are kept in some mosques for for-

From an etching by Ernest D. Roth

"The Little Mosque"

eign visitors. The general impression is that of a private interior magnified and dignified. The central object of this open space is the *mihrab*, a niche pointing toward Mecca. It is usually set in an apse which is raised a step above the level of the nave. In it is a prayer-rug for the *imam*, and on each side, in a brass or silver standard, an immense candle, which is lighted only on the seven holy nights of the year and during Ramazan. At the right of the *mihrab*, as you face it, stands the *mimber*, a sort of pulpit, at the top of a stairway and covered by a pointed canopy, which is used only for the noon prayer of Friday or on other special occasions. To the left, and nearer the door, is a smaller pulpit called the *kürsi*. This is a big cushioned armchair or throne, reached by a short ladder, where the *imam* sits to speak on ordinary occasions. There will also be one or more galleries for singers, and in larger mosques, usually at the *mihrab* end of the left-hand gallery, an imperial tribune enclosed by grille work and containing its own sacred niche. The chandeliers are a noticeable feature of every mosque, hanging very low and containing not candles but glass cups of oil with a floating wick. I am afraid, however, that this soft light will be presently turned into electricity. From the chandeliers often hang ostrich eggs — emblems of eternity — and other homely ornaments.

The place of the mosque in the Turkish community is symbolised, like that of the mediæval cathedral, by its architectural pre-eminence. Mark, however, that Stamboul has half a dozen cathedrals instead of one. It would be hard to overestimate how much of the character of Stamboul depends on the domes and minarets that so inimitably accident the heights between the Golden Horn and the Marmora. And on closer acquaintance the mosques are found to contain almost all that Stamboul has of architectural pretension. They form an achievement, to my mind, much greater than the world at large seems to realise. The easy current dictum that they are

Entrance to the forecourt of Sultan Baïezid II

merely more or less successful imitations of St. Sophia takes no account of the evolution — particularly of the central dome — which may be traced through the mosques of Konia, Broussa, and Adrianople, and which reaches its legitimate climax in Stamboul. The likelier fact is that the mosque of Stamboul, inspired by the same remote Asiatic impulse as the Byzantine church, absorbed what was proper to it in Byzantine art, refining away the heaviness or overfloridness of the East, until in the hands of a master like Sinan it attained a supreme elegance without losing any of its dignity. Yet it would be a

Detail of the Süleïmanieh

mistake to look for all Turkish architecture in Sinan. The mosques of Atik Ali Pasha and of Sultan Baïezid II are there to prove of what mingled simplicity and nobility was capable an obscure architect of an earlier century. His name is supposed to have been Haïreddin, and he, first among the Turks, used the monolithic shaft and the stalactite capital. How perfect they are, though, in the arcades of Baïezid! Nothing could be better in its way than the forecourt of that mosque, and its inlaid minarets are unique of their kind. Nor did architecture die with Sinan. Yeni Jami, looking at Galata along the outer bridge, is witness thereof. The pile of the Süleïmanieh, whose four minarets catch your eye from so many points of the compass, is perhaps more masculine. But the silhouette of Yeni Jami, that mosque of princesses, has an inimitable grace. The way in which each structural necessity adds to the general effect, the climactic building up of buttress and cupola, the curve of the dome, the proportion of the minarets, could hardly be more perfect. Although brought up in the vociferous tradition of Ruskin, I am so far unfaithful to the creed of my youth as to find pleasure, too, in rococo mosques like Zeïneb Sultan, Nouri Osmanieh, and Laleli Jami. And the present generation, under men like Vedad Bey and the architects of the *Evkaf*, are reviving their art in a new and interesting direction.

To give any comprehensive account of the mosques of Stamboul would be to write a history of Ottoman architecture, and for that I lack both space and competence. I may, however, as an irresponsible lounger in mosque yards, touch on one or two characteristic aspects of mosques and their decoration which strike a foreigner's eye. The frescoing or stencilling of domes and other curved interior surfaces, for instance, is an art that has very little been noticed — even by the Turks, judging from the sad estate to which the art has fallen. Some people might object to calling it an art at all. Let such a one be given a series of domes and vaults to ornament by this simple means, however, and he will find how difficult it is to produce an effect both decorative and dignified. The restorers of the nineteenth century spoiled

Yeni Jami

many a fine interior by their atrocious baroque draperies or colour-blind colour schemes. If I were a true believer I could never pray in mosques like Ahmed I or Yeni Jami, because the decorator evidently noticed that the prevailing tone of the tiles was blue and dipped his brush accordingly — into a blue of a different key. Yet there are domes which prove how fine an art the Turks once made of this half-mechanical decoration. One of the best in Stamboul is in the tomb of the princes, behind the Shah-zadeh mosque. The stencilling is a charming arabesque design in black, dark red, pale blue, and orange, perhaps happily toned by time, which a recent restoration was wise enough to spare. The tomb of Roxelana and the great tomb beside Yeni Jami also contain a little interesting stencilling. But the most complete example of good work of this kind is outside Stamboul, in the Yeni Valideh mosque of Scutari. The means used are of the simplest, the colours being merely black and dull red, with a little dull yellow; but the lines are so fine and so sapiently spaced on their broad background of white that the effect is very much that of a Persian shawl. A study of that ceiling should be made compulsory for every decorator of a mosque — and might yield suggestions not a few to his Western cousin.

The windows of mosques are another detail that always interests me. They are rarely very large, but there are a great many of them and they give no dim religious light, making up a great part as they do of the human sunniness of the interior. A first tier of square windows stand almost at the level of the floor, and are provided with folding shutters which are carved with many little panels or with a Moorish pattern of interlaced stars. Higher up the windows are arched and are made more interesting by the broad plaster mullions of which I have already spoken. These make against the light a grille of round, oval, or drop-shaped openings which are wonderfully decorative in themselves. The same principle is refined and complicated into a result more decorative still when the plaster setting forms a complete design of arabesques, flowers, or writing, sometimes framing symmetrically spaced circles or quadrangles, sometimes composing an all-over pattern, and filled in with minute panes of coloured glass. Huysmans compared the windows of Chartres to Persian rugs, because the smallness of the figures and their height above the floor make them merely conventional arrangements of colour. Here, however, we have the real principle of the Oriental rug. Turkish windows contain no figures at all, nor any of that unhappy attempt at realism that mars so much modern glass. The secret of the effect lies in the smallness of the panes used and the visibility of the plaster design in which they are set. And what an effect of jewelry may be produced in this way is to be seen in the Süleïmanieh, and Yeni Jami — where two slim cypresses make delicious panels of green light above the *mihrab* — besides other mosques and tombs of the sixteenth and seventeenth centuries.

Mosques are even more notable than private houses for the inscriptions on their walls. Every visitor to St. Sophia remembers the great green medallions bearing the names of the chief personages of Islam in letters of gold. In purely Turkish mosques similar medallions may be seen, or large inscriptions stencilled like panels on the white walls, or small texts hanging near the floor. But there is a more architectural use of writing, above doors and windows or in the form of a frieze. When designed by a master like Hassan Chelibi of Kara Hissar, the great calligrapher of Süleïman's time, and executed in simple dark blue and white in one of the imperial tile factories, this art became a means of decoration which we can only envy the Turks. Such inscriptions are always from the Koran, of course, and they are often happily chosen for the place they occupy. Around the great dome of the Süleïmanieh, and lighted by its circle of windows, runs this verse: "God is the light of the heavens and of the earth. His light is like a window in the wall, wherein a lamp burns, covered with glass. The glass shines like a star. The lamp is kindled from the oil of a blessed tree: not of the east, not of the west, it lights whom he wills."

It is not only for inscriptions, however, that tiles are used in mosques. Stamboul, indeed, is a museum of tiles that has never been adequately explored. Nor, in general, is very much known about Turkish ceramics. I suppose nothing definite will be known till the Turks themselves, or some one who can read their language, takes the trouble to look up the records of mosques and other public buildings. The splendid tiles of Süleïman's period have sometimes been attributed a Persian and sometimes a Rhodian origin — for they have many similarities with the famous Rhodian plates. The Turks themselves generally suppose that their tiles came from Kütahya, where a factory still produces work of an inferior kind. The truth lies between these various theories. That any number of the tiles of Constantinople came from Persia is impossible. So many of them could not have been safely brought so far overland, and it is inconceivable that they would have fitted into their places as they do, or that any number of buildings would have been erected to fit their tiles. The Rhodian theory is equally improbable, partly for similar reasons though chiefly because the legend of Rhodes is all but exploded.

The Musée de Cluny is almost the last believer in the idea that its unrivalled collection of Rhodian plates ever came from Rhodes. Many of them probably came from different parts of Asia Minor. That tiles were produced in Asia Minor long before the capture of Constantinople we know from the monuments of Broussa, Konia, and other places. They were quite a different kind of tile, to be sure, of only one colour or containing a simple arabesque design, which was varied by a sort of tile mosaic. Many of them, too, were six-sided. The only examples of these older tiles in Constantinople are to be seen at the *Chinili Kyöshk* of the imperial museum — the Tile Pavilion — and the tomb of Mahmoud Pasha. It is a notorious fact, however, that the sultans who fought against the Persians brought back craftsmen of all kinds from that country and settled them in different parts of the empire. Selim I, for instance, when he captured Tabriz, imported the best tile makers of that city, as well as from Ardebil and Kashan — whence one of the words for tiles, *kyashi* — and settled them in Isnik. This is the city which under an older name had already produced the historian Dion Cassius and the Nicene Creed. Other factories are known to have existed in Kastambol, Konia, Nicomedia, and Constantinople itself. One is supposed to have been in Eyoub, though no trace of it remains to-day unless in the potteries of Chömlekjiler. Another, I have been told, flourished at Balat. I know not whether it may have been the same which Sultan Ahmed III transferred in 1724 from Nicæa to the ruined Byzantine palace of Tekfour Seraï. A colony of glass-blowers there are the last remnant to-day of the tile makers of two hundred years ago.

The art itself declined and gradually died out as the

sultans stopped making conquests and building mosques. For the imperial mosques are monuments of victory, built and endowed out of the spoils of war. After the martial period of the empire came to an end with Süleïman I only one mosque of importance, that of Ahmed I, was built by a reigning sultan in his own name. But the tiles of the imperial factories, after many fires and much thieving, still make up what is most brilliant and most durable in the colour of Stamboul. The best tiles are Nicene of the sixteenth century, that extraordinary *cinque-cento*, when so many of the best things of the world were produced. They are distinguished by the transparent white glaze of their background, on which are drawn tulips, carnations, wild hyacinths, and a certain long bent serrated leaf common to the Rhodian plate. The chief colours are a dark and a turquoise blue and a tomato red, green and yellow occurring more rarely. And they are never quite smooth, the red in particular usually being in slight relief. This gives them a variety which is absent from many modern tiles.

The feeling for variety, in fact, was one great secret of Turkish tile making and tile setting. Sinan, for instance, used tiles very sparingly in his larger buildings. He was great enough to depend very little on ornament for his effect, and he knew that tiles would look like paper or linoleum — if such things existed in his day! — on a monumental surface. But he had a perfect tact of using this tapestry wherever he wanted a touch of colour or distinction — over a window, along a cornice, around a *mihrab*. His masterpiece in this decoration is the mosque of Rüstem Pasha, son-in-law and Grand Vizier to Süleïman the Magnificent. This mosque, lifted on retaining walls above the noise of its busy quarter, has a portico which must have been magnificently tiled — judging from the panel at the left of the main door — and the whole interior is tiled to the spring of the dome. The mosque is small enough for the effect of the tiles to tell — and to be almost ruined by the fearful modern frescoes of the vaulting. The guides of Pera have a favourite legend to the effect that Rüstem Pasha brought back these tiles from his wars in Persia and built a mosque for them to save giving them up to his imperial master. But no one need be an expert to see the impossibility of any such story. The tiles must have been designed for the walls which they incrust, and by a supreme master of decoration. I should not be surprised to learn that Sinan himself drew them all. There is a tall narrow panel on either side of the mosque, between two windows, which seems to me one of the most perfect ways imaginable of filling such a space. So are the spandrels of the arches supporting the gallery, and the niche of the *mihrab*, and the back of the *mimber*. All through the mosque, however, the way in which the artist has varied his designs and colours, while never losing his unity of effect, is a piece of genius. Narrow spaces and points of special interest are treated each in its own way; but unbroken surfaces of wall are never allowed to become monotonous by covering them with only one form of tile. They are

Tile panel in Rüstem Pasha

broken up by narrower border tiles into panels, each of which is treated differently though harmonising with its neighbour and balancing the corresponding space on the opposite side of the mosque. Even within one of these

The *mihrab* of Rüstem Pasha

spaces monotony is avoided by the fact that the tiles are almost never of a repeating pattern. Two or four tiles are required to make up the scheme. And then the pattern does not always fit the tiles, so that the interstices come in different places in different parts of the design, and you feel that the tiles could only have been made for that one space. In the case of special panels, of course, many tiles are required to make up

In Rüstem Pasha

the pattern. The splendid flowered panel in the portico contains forty-five tiles, exclusive of the border, and every one of them different. Such work was not commercial tile making. It was an art.

Two mosques of a later period in Stamboul are completely tiled, that of Sultan Ahmed I and the one begun by his wife — Yeni Jami. They prove the wisdom of Sinan in not attempting to tile a large interior. Still, the gallery of Sultan Ahmed also proves that the architect was not altogether ignorant of what he was about. He put his best tiles there, where they can only be seen

Tiles in the gallery of Sultan Ahmed

at close range. And his best is very good. I have counted twenty-nine varieties of tiles there, or rather of designs, divided, like those of Rüstem Pasha, into framed panels. The tiles facing the *mihrab*, where the gallery widens over the main doorway, are so good that I sometimes ask myself if the architect did not borrow from an earlier building. Two series of eleven panels, one above the other, make a tall wainscot whose only fault is that too much richness is crowded into too narrow a space. The lower series is the finer. Five panels to the right balance five panels to the left of a spindle-shaped Persian design. Its two neighbours are conventionalised cypress trees, than which nothing more decorative was ever invented. Then come two magnificent panels of larger spindles against a thicket of peach-blossoms or Judas blossoms, red with small blue centres, followed by two more cypresses. Five panels of the upper series, one of them forming the axis, are latticed again with blossoming sprays. In this case there is no spindle to hide the greater part of the flowers, which are blue with small red centres. The tiles are very nearly if not quite as good as those of the preceding century, and they make a wall more splendid than exists outside the old Seraglio.

Yeni Jami is better suited for tiling, being comparatively a smaller mosque. Its proportions are also much better and the frescoing is not so bad as that of Sultan Ahmed. The tiles themselves are not so interesting. But attached to the mosque, and giving entrance to the imperial tribune, is a suite of rooms which are also tiled. This imperial apartment is carried across the street on a great pointed arch, and is reached from outside by a covered inclined way which enabled the Sultan to ride directly up to the level of his gallery. At the same level is also a little garden, held up by a massive retaining wall, and a balcony with a rail of perforated marble once gave a magnificent view over the harbour. The view has since been cut off by shops, and the apartment itself has fallen into a sad state of neglect or has been subjected to unfortunate restorations. A later and more intelligent restoration has brought to light, under a vandal coat of brown paint, the old gilding of the woodwork. But the tiles of the walls remain — except where they have been replaced by horrible panels of some composition imitating Florentine mosaic. Among them are charming cypresses and peach-trees. There are also remains of lovely old windows, to say nothing of tall hooded fireplaces and doors incrusted with tortoise-shell and mother-of-pearl. The tiles are palpably of a poorer period than those I have described. But there is a great attractiveness about this quaint apartment, that only adds to the general distinction of Yeni Jami.

The original founder of the mosque, as I have said, was the favourite wife of Ahmed I. This princess is one of the most famous women in Turkish chronicles. Whether she was a Greek or a Turk, history does not confirm, though the custom of the sultans to marry none but slaves would point to the former origin. Her name in the Seraglio was Mahpeïker — Moon Face. She is oftenest remembered, however, by the name Kyössem, Leader of a Flock, from the fact that she was the first of a troop of slaves presented to the young sultan. During his reign she gained an increasing voice in the affairs of the empire, and during those of her sons Mourad IV and Ibrahim her word was law. The position of empress mother is an exceptional one in Turkey, as in China, the occupant of it being the first lady in the palace and the land. She is known as the *valideh soultan*, or princess mother — for the word sultan properly has no sex. Our word sultana does not exist in Turkish, being a Greek or Italian invention. The reigning sultan prefixes the title to his own name, while other persons of his blood put it after theirs. When the grandson of Kyössem, the boy Mehmed IV, came to the throne, the great *valideh* continued, against all precedent, to inhabit the Seraglio and to exercise her old influence. But at last the jealousy of Mehmed's mother, defrauded of her natural rank, kindled a palace intrigue that caused the older *valideh*, at the age of eighty, to be strangled one night in the Seraglio. Her mosque, still unfinished, suffered by a fire which ravaged the quarter; and it was finally completed by her young rival, a Russian named Tar'han, or Hadijeh. After the latter the mosque is called to-day the *yeni valideh soultan jamisi*, the mosque of the new empress mother. In common parlance, however, it goes by the name of *yeni jami*, the new mosque — though it has had time to become fairly venerable. And she who became the new *valideh* in 1649 now occupies the place of honour under the dome of the tomb beside the mosque, while the murdered Kyössem rests near her husband in their little marble house on the Hippodrome.

The tombs that accompany mosques are only less interesting than the mosques themselves, both for their architectural character and for their historical associations. When space permits they lie in an inner enclosure of the mosque yard, technically called the garden, behind the mosque. Long before Constantinople became their capital the sultans had perfected a type of mausoleum, or *türbeh*. This is a domed structure, usually octagonal in shape, cheerfully lighted by two or three tiers of windows. Every tomb has its own guardian, called the *türbedar*, and some are attached to a school or other philanthropic institution. These mausoleums are often extremely elaborate in decoration, but they all retain a certain primitive simplicity with regard to their central feature. There is no sarcophagus of marble or porphyry. The occupant of the *türbeh* is buried in the floor, and over his grave stands a plain wooden catafalque covered with green cloth. Like a Turkish coffin, it is ridged and inclined from the head, where a wooden standard supports the turban of the deceased. A woman's catafalque has no standard, a scarf being thrown across the head. Embroideries, of gold on velvet, or of quotations from the Koran in a zigzag pattern, may cover the green cloth. Such embroideries are often a piece of a last year's hanging from the Kaaba at Mecca or from the Prophet's tomb at Medina. But nothing is imposing about the

The tomb of Sultan Ahmed I

catafalque unless its size, which indicates the importance of the person commemorated. The largest one I remember is that of Sultan Mehmed II, the Conqueror. And the rail around the catafalque is all that suggests permanence, and that is generally of wood inlaid with mother-of-pearl. The simple epitaph is written on a placard which hangs casually from the rail, or perhaps from an immense candle to be lighted on holy nights. Near by may be an inlaid folding stand with an illuminated Koran. The floor is matted and covered with rugs like a mosque or a house.

The tombs attached to the imperial mosques are naturally the most important. Not every sultan built his own, however. In the *türbeh* of Ahmed I two other sultans are buried, his sons Osman II — who was the first sultan to be murdered by his own people — and the bloody Mourad IV. Among the innumerable people whom the latter put to death was his brother Prince Baïezid, the hero of Racine's "Bajazet," who lies beside him. In the tomb of Hadijeh at Yeni Jami five sultans rest: her son Mehmed IV, her grandsons Moustafa II and Ahmed III, and her great-grandsons Mahmoud I and Osman III. These and others of the larger tombs are noticeable for the number of little catafalques they contain, marking the graves of little princes who were strangled on the accession of their eldest brother.

The most interesting tombs, from an artistic point of view, are those of the period of Süleïman the Magnificent. How this later Solomon came by his European nickname I can not tell, for the Turks know him as Solomon the Lawgiver. But magnificent without doubt he was, and Stamboul would be another city if all trace of his magnificence were to disappear. His *türbeh*, behind the mosque he built in his own name, is perhaps the most imposing in Constantinople, though neither the largest nor the most splendidly decorated. A covered ambulatory surrounds it, and within are handsome tiles and stained-glass windows. I prefer, however, the tomb of his famous consort. The legend of this lady has enjoyed outside of her own country a success that proves again the capriciousness of fame. For the great Kyössem was a more celebrated princess whose name has been forgotten in Europe. It is perfectly true that Süleïman did put to death his eldest son Moustafa, a prince of the greatest promise, and that Roxelana's son, Selim II, did inherit the throne accordingly — and so cut off the line

In Roxelana's tomb

of great sultans. But it has yet to be proved that Roxelana really was the "fatal woman" of popular history, who instigated her stepson's murder. I suspect the truth of the matter was largely that she had a good press, as they say in French. She happened to fall into the orbit of one of the greatest men of her time, she furnished copy for the despatches of one or two famous ambassadors, and — they gave her a pronounceable name! I have been told that it is a corruption of a Persian name meaning red-cheeked; but I have privately wondered if it had anything to do with the Slavic tribe of Roxolani. Be that as it may, this princess was a Russian slave of so great wit and charm that the Lord of the Two Earths and the Sovereign of All the Seas paid her the unprecedented compliment of making her his legal wife. He even built for her, unlike any other sultan I remember, a tomb to herself. And Sinan subtly put into it a feminine grace that is set off by the neighbouring mausoleum of her husband. In the little vestibule are two panels of rose-red flowers that must have been lovely in their day. In consequence of some accident the tiles have been stupidly patched and mixed up. The interior is sixteen-sided, with alternate windows and pointed marble niehes. The spaces between are delicately tiled, and most so in the spandrels of the niches, where are sprays of rose-coloured flowers like those in the vestibule.

There is another tomb behind another mosque of Süleïman, which is, perhaps, the most perfect monument of its kind in Stamboul. I did not always think so. But the more I look at its fluted dome and at the scheme of its interior tiling, the more I seem to see that here again Sinan, or the great decorator who worked with him, exquisitely found means to express an idea of individuality. This tomb was built, like the mosque to which it belongs, in memory of Süleïman's second and best-beloved son, the young Prince Mehmed. The mosque — so-called of the Shah-zadeh, the Prince — has lost its original decoration, but its graceful lines and its incrusted minarets combine with the smaller buildings and the trees about it to make one of the happiest architectural groups in Stamboul. As for the *türbeh*, it fortunately remains very much as Sinan left it. The design of the tiles is more abstract and masculine than those in Roxelana's *türbeh*, being mainly an intricate weaving of lines and arabesques. But there is about them a refinement, a distinction, which, it is hardly too fantastic to say, insensibly suggest the youth and the royal station of the boy whose burial chamber they beautify. For the colour — rarest of all in Turkish tiles — is a spring green and a golden yellow, set off by a little dark blue. The tomb is also remarkable, as I have already said, for the stencilling of its dome, as well as for the lovely fragments of old stained glass in the upper windows and for a sort of wooden canopy, perforated in the wheel pattern common to the balustrades of the period, covering the prince's catafalque. It is supposed to symbolise the throne which Süleïman hoped his son might inherit. Beside the prince, but not under the canopy, rests his humpbacked younger brother Jihangir. As for the unhappy Prince Moustafa, he was buried in Broussa, in the beautiful garden of the Mouradieh.

The *türbeh* of Prince Mehmed has, in my mind, another pre-eminence which perhaps it does not deserve. As in most other public buildings of Stamboul, an inscription is carved over the door. These inscriptions are generally in poetry and sometimes very long. The uninitiated reader would never guess that the last verse of many of them is also a date, for the Arabic letters, like certain Roman letters, have a numerical value. And the date of many a Turkish monument is hidden in a chronogram, always the last line of the inscription, in which the arithmetical sum of the letters is equivalent to the numeral of the year in which the monument was erected.

I am not learned enough to say when this recondite fashion started, but the chronogram of this tomb is the earliest I happen to know about in Stamboul. It reads: "Grant, Lord, to him who rests here to win the grove of Eden." The arithmetical value of the line is 950, which year of the Hegira is equivalent to 1543 of our era.

There are several other interesting tombs in this enclosure, of which the most important are those of Rüstem Pasha, builder of the tile mosque we have already noticed, and of a certain Ibrahim Pasha, Grand Vizier to Sultan Mourad III. I have a particular fancy for the latter *türbeh*, which seems to me in its neglected way a little masterpiece. Consider me now its door — how admirably drawn it is, provided with what green bronze knockers in the shape of lyres! The tiles of the interior, or the more important of them, are simplified from those of Prince Mehmed, transposed into another key — dark red and less dark blue on white — and set between two encircling inscriptions. There are also certain panels of flowers between high windows. But I think I am most undone by a little dado, one tile high, where two outward curving sprays of wild hyacinth that just do not fit into the breadth of a tile enclose a small cluster of tulips and carnations — inimitably conventionalised and symmetrical. Nothing more simple or more decorative was ever imagined.

Selim II, the unworthy supplanter of him who might have been Mehmed III, lies in a tomb handsomer than he deserves, in the court of a mosque built by a greater than he — St. Sophia. His large *türbeh* lacks the elegant proportion of his brother's, but the tile panels of its porch are very effective. So is the tile tapestry of its inner walls, though a little monotonous — mainly white in effect, dotted with little tulips and other flowers enclosed in small Persian spindles. Four other sultans are buried in the precincts of St. Sophia, the mad Moustafa I and the dethroned Ibrahim lying in dishonourable neglect in the bare, whitewashed chamber that was once the baptistery of the cathedral. And it was through having been the slave of Ibrahim that the *valideh soultan* Hadijeh was able to complete Yeni Jami in her own name and build beside it the great mausoleum in which she lies!

The *türbeh* of Ibrahim Pasha

These *türbehs*, with the fountains of the outer courtyard and the trees that shade them and the minarets that tower above the trees, give an oddly Turkish air to the precincts of St. Sophia. It is to a real mosque, however, that one must go for a typical mosque yard. A part of it that is lacking to St. Sophia, and, indeed, to many mosques, is another inner enclosure called the *haram*, or sanctuary. This forecourt of the mosque is always more architectural than the "garden," being a paved quadrangle surrounded by an arcade. In the centre of the cloister a covered fountain should bubble, sometimes under trees. I have already mentioned one of the best examples of such a court. It belongs to the old mosque of Sultan Baïezid II, more popularly known as the Pigeon Mosque. This is less of a sanctuary than any other forecourt in Stamboul. But the reason is that the mosque lacks an outer yard other than the square of the War Department. And I would be the last to

The court of the Conqueror

find fault with the scribes who sit in the arcades, or to call them Pharisees who sell beads and perfumes there. During the month of Ramazan a busy fair is held there, open only during the afternoon, where the complicated sweetmeats of the season are sold together with other things worthy to be given as presents at *Baïram.* I must say, however, that I have a weakness for the court of another old mosque, that of Sultan Selim I, in a less accessible part of Stamboul. Part of its charm is perhaps due to the fact that it is more remote and therefore more subject to silence. Above the barred windows that look into the outer sunlight are lunettes of

The main entrance to the court of Sokollî Mehmed Pasha

tiles, while around the fountain cypresses and grapevines make an inimitable shade. Nor can I pass by the court of Sokollî Mehmed Pasha, the last and greatest vizier of Süleïman I. This is supposed to be a lesser work of Sinan, but I like it almost better than any other. Within the mosque are treasures of tiles, of stained glass, of painted wood, of perforated marble. Without is one of the noblest porticoes in Stamboul, looking down upon a cloister that is a real cloister. For into its colonnade open cells where live the students of a *medresseh*.

A *medresseh* is a theological school and law school combined, since in Islam the teachings of the Prophet, as embodied in the Koran and the traditions, form not only the rule of life but the law of the land. It is only recently that a difference has been recognised between the *Sheriat* or sacred law and the civil law, but their boundaries are still indistinct, and for many men the same door leads to legal or to spiritual preferment. I have said so much about tombs and tiles and other matters that I have left myself no room to speak of *medressehs* — or schools of other kinds, or libraries, or caravansaries, or baths, or hospitals, or soup-kitchens, or any other of the charitable institutions that cluster around a mosque yard. We are wont to imagine that philanthropy was invented in the West, and that the institutional church is a peculiarly modern development. But before America was discovered institutional mosques flourished in Stamboul and all over Asia Minor, and continue to do so to this day. Almost no mosque, indeed, has not some philanthropy connected with it. They are administered, mosques and dependencies and all, by a separate and very important department of government called the Ministry of the *Evkaf* — of Pious Foundations.

The necessities of space do not always allow these dependencies to gather around their central mosque yard. Or sometimes they are independent foundations and may have a yard of their own of which a small mosque

The interior of Sokollî Mehmed Pasha

is merely one feature. Two very interesting examples are *medressehs* in the vicinity of the mosque of the Conqueror. They both belong to the same period and their

The court of Sokollî Mehmed Pasha

founders were both ministers of Sultan Moustafa II, who was dethroned in 1703. The smaller and more ruinous was built by Feïzoullah Effendi, *Sheï'h ül Islam*, a mighty man of God who did and undid viziers in his day and perished miserably at Adrianople in the upheaval that drove his imperial master from the throne. His *medres-*

seh nearly perished too, in 1912, to make way for a new boulevard. But it was happily saved by the society of the Friends of Stamboul, and in time its little cloister may become less of a jungle. Its chief ornament is the structure to the left of the gateway, where a flight of steps mounts under a wonderful arch or crocket of perforated marble to a pillared porch with a mosque on one side and a library on the other. The mosque is the more dilapidated, but it contains fragments of good tiling and a charming little door. The library has the same little door, shallow-arched and ornamented with fine stalactites of marble. The interior of the library is almost filled by a square cage, which has a corresponding door of its own and a dark inner compartment. On the wired shelves of this structure big books are piled on their sides, and their titles and numbers are written on the edges of the leaves. They are all manuscripts, and some of them are illuminated or beautifully bound. I also saw a finely bound catalogue to which nothing has

Doorway in the *medresseh* of Feïzoullah Effendi

been added for two hundred years. For that matter the library does not look as if any one had consulted it for two hundred years, though the librarian is supposed to be there every day except Tuesday and Friday. He accordingly spends most of his time in his book-shop in the mosque yard of the Conqueror.

Entrance to the *medresseh* of Kyöprülü Hüsseïn Pasha

The other *medresseh*, separated from this one by a straight easterly stretch of the new boulevard, is that of the Grand Vizier Amouja-zadeh Hüsseïn Pasha — the Son of the Uncle. I need hardly point out that Hüsseïn Pasha was not the son of his own uncle, but of that of a famous cousin of his. For he belonged to the great family of the Kyöprülü, who gave Turkey five of her best grand viziers. The head of the house, that iron old man who stopped for a time the decadence of the empire — and put to death thirty-six thousand people in five years — lies in the skeleton *türbeh* of marble and bronze on Divan Yolou, near the Burnt Column. Hüsseïn Pasha's tomb is also open to the street and to the

The *medresseh* of Hassan Pasha
Note the bird-house with minarets

rains of heaven. Its tall stones and taller trees stand behind a cobweb grille to the left of his *sebil,* where an attendant gives cups of cold water to thirsty passers-by. Between the *sebil* and the gate are two grilles of bronze, set in two great windows of delicately chiselled marble, that do much to make this *medresseh* one of the most notable corners of Stamboul. There is a big L-shaped courtyard within, pleasant with trees and a central pagoda of a fountain, looked upon by white cloisters for students, by a library containing no books, by a ruined primary school, and by an octagonal mosque charmingly set in a square ambulatory of pillars.

I should be afraid to guess how many such institutions are in Stamboul or how many thousand students attend them at the expense of their founders. They are a wonderful tribute to the philanthropy of another day — the day of the great schools of Bagdad and Cairo and Cordova, the day of the mediæval cloisters. Stamboul has needed bitter lessons to learn that that day is past. Indeed, a good part of old Stamboul has taken refuge in these courtyards, and would still be true to the old order which made the mosque the centre of the community and supposed all knowledge to be in the Koran. For the race of men that likes Stamboul there is a great charm in these places, with their picturesqueness and their air, part gravity, part melancholy, familiar to the East and particular to all places that have known change and ruin. There is tragedy in them, too, and menace. For they teach too many men too little. But there is also a germ in them of something that might conceivably save Stamboul in spite of herself. "Seek knowledge, even though it be in China," is one of the most famous sayings of the Prophet, and he taught his followers that the greater holy war was against ignorance. Halil Bey and Van Berchem, in their monumental *Corps d'Inscriptions Arabes*, quote an epigraph to the same effect from a thirteenth-century *medresseh* in Sîvas: "The pursuit of knowledge is an obligation imposed on every Moslem. The merit of science is greater than that of devotion." And the *medresseh* of Ali Pasha in Stamboul has this written above the gate: "Whoever taught me a single word, I was his slave." If the spirit that made such utterances could once touch Islam again, would it not be enough?

III

OLD CONSTANTINOPLE

Now you may know that those who had never before seen Constantinople looked upon it very earnestly, for they never thought there could be in all the world so rich a city; and they marked the high walls and strong towers that enclosed it round about, and the rich palaces, and mighty churches — of which there were so many that no one would have believed it who had not seen it with his eyes — and the height and length of that city which above all others was sovereign. And be it known to you, that no man there was of such hardihood but his flesh trembled; and it was no wonder, for never was so great an enterprise undertaken by any people since the creation of the world.—Marzials' G. DE VILLEHARDOUIN: "De la Conqueste de Constantinople."

To many people the colour of Stamboul looks purely Turkish — at first sight. The simplest peasant of Asia Minor could not look at it often, however, without noticing things of an order strange to him — a sculptured capital lying in the street, bits of flowered marble set into a wall, a column as high as a minaret standing by itself, a dome of unfamiliar shape, and mosque walls mysterious with unreadable letters and the sacrilegious picturing of human forms, and ruined masonry or dark subterranean vaultings leading off into myth. For other newcomers it may become a game of the most engrossing kind to track out these old things, and mark how Stamboul has fitted into the ruts of Byzantium, and hunt for some lost piece of antiquity that no one else has found. And there are men for whom Stamboul does not exist. Through it they walk as in some inner city of the mind, seeing only the vanished capital of the Cæsars. Divan Yolou is for them the *Mese* of old. In the Hippodrome they still hear the thunder of Roman chariots. And many a Turkish monument has interest for them only because its marbles are anagrams that spell anew the glory of the ancient world.

Need I say that I am no such man? The essential colour of Constantinople is for me, who am neither Byzantinist nor Orientalist, a composite one, and the richer for being so. I confess I do not like the minarets of St. Sophia, but it is only because they are ugly. I am sorry that the palace of Constantine has so completely disappeared, but I am Philistine enough to suspect that the mosque built on its site may lift quite as imposing a mass against the sky. I like to remember that the most important street of Stamboul was the Triumphal Way of the Byzantine emperors — and earlier still the home-stretch of a famous Roman road, the *Via Egnatia*, which continued from Dyrrhachium on the Adriatic, the Durazzo of Balkan squabbles, the line of the Appian Way; but it seems to me that the sultans added interest to that historic thoroughfare. Nevertheless, I am inconsistent enough to be sorry that Byzantinists are so rare, and to be a little jealous of

the glory that was Greece,
And the grandeur that was Rome.

I do not pretend to set up Constantinople against Rome or Athens. Without them, of course, she would not have been — what she was. But I do maintain that her history was as long, that she played a rôle no less important in her later day, and that without her our modern world could never have been quite what it is. We are unjustly inclined to forget that link in the chain.

Different from Rome and Athens, as they differed from each other, Constantinople fused in her own crucible, with others of Oriental origin, the elements of civilisation which they furnished. Out of these elements she formulated a new religion, created the architecture to embody it, codified a system of law. Having thus collected and enriched the learning of antiquity, she bequeathed it to the adolescent Europe of the Renaissance. We are accustomed to speak of the dark ages that followed the fall of Rome. There was, properly speaking, no darker age than had been. The centre of light had merely moved eastward, and such miserable frontier villages as London, Paris, and Vienna were merely, for the time being, the darker. To them Constantinople was what Paris is to us, the *ville lumière*, and far more. She was the centre of a civilisation whose splendour and refinement were the legend of the West. She contained such treasures of ancient art as are now scattered in a thousand museums. Under her shadow Athens became a sort of present-day Oxford or Venice and Rome not much more than a vociferous Berlin. Entirely new races — Slavs, Huns, Turks — began to be drawn into her orbit, as the Gauls, the Britons, and the Teutons had been drawn by Rome. If the far-away cities of Bagdad and Cordova felt her influence, how much more was it so in countries with which she had more immediate relations? Italy in particular, and Venice above all other Italian towns, owe more to Constantinople than has ever been appraised. Venice would always have been Venice, but a Venice without the St. Mark's we know, without the stolen horses of bronze, without the pillars of the *Piazzetta*, without many of the palaces of the Grand Canal, without the lion, even, which is as Byzantine as Byzantine can be. Several other Italian cities contain notable examples of

Byzantine architecture or decoration, while in half the collections of Europe are ivories, reliquaries, bits of painting and mosaic and goldsmiths' work that came out of Byzantium. That jewel of Paris, the *Sainte-Chapelle*,

Reproduced by permission of C. W. Kraushaar, N. Y.

St. Sophia
From an etching by Frank Brangwyn

is not Byzantine, but it was built to house the church treasures from Constantinople which were a part of the loot of the fourth crusade, and some of them may still be seen in *Notre Dame*. In indirect ways the account is harder to reckon. Some authorities find a Byzantine origin for so remote an architectural language as Romanesque building, while few now deny that the Italian school of painting was derived directly from the mosaics of Constantinople. All admit, at any rate, that the prodigious movement of the Renaissance was fed by the humanists who took refuge in Italy from the invading Turk.

Yet Constantinople has remained, comparatively to her two great rivals, an undiscovered country. The Russians are alone to maintain there such a centre of research as the schools of Rome and Athens, and excavaters take it for granted that Stamboul hides nothing worth their trouble. They would have more reason if the emperors had not collected so many of the masterpieces of antiquity. For about Athens will always linger some glamour of the Periclean age, and its sculpture, like its literature, remains the high-water mark of a certain artistic achievement. The case of Rome, however, is more complicated. Rome never created an art so original as Byzantine architecture or Byzantine mosaic; and Justinian it was, not Cæsar or Augustus, who carried Roman law to such a point that no principle has been added to it since. I think the old *odium theologicum* must have something to do with the fact that the age of Justinian and one or two great periods that followed it enjoy so little general renown. The split between the churches originally destroyed the tradition of renown; and because we are of the West, because we are descended from the crusaders, because we derive our religious traditions from Rome, we still entertain some vague ancestral prejudice against Orthodoxy and its capital. The present masters of Constantinople have, of course, greatly encouraged this prejudice by taking no interest themselves in the history of the city or allowing others to do so. Then other details of accessibility enter into the matter, and of language, and a thousand subtleties of association. Rome, for instance, has long been a province of European literature. Keats and Shelley and Browning, to mention only later English poets, and I know not how many others, besides generations of novelists and playwrights and historians and travellers and painters and sculptors, have made a whole public that knows or cares very little about the Cæsars feel at home in Rome; whereas Gibbon and Byron and Lady Mary Montagu are the sole greater English names that attach themselves to the Bosphorus. It waters, to be sure, a much larger corner of French literature. And the immense learning of Gibbon has perhaps done more than any amount of ignorance and prejudice to weight the scale against Constantinople.

The Rome of literature is not an Augustan Rome. It is the Rome of the popes, the Rome of the Renaissance, the Rome of galleries and haunted palaces and enchanted villas that had no being till Constantinople was at an end. Or it is a simpler Rome still, of the liquid light, of shops and theatres and hotels and a friendly court. Against these Romes I am the last to set up a cry. I merely point out that for most eyes they fill up the picture of the Eternal City; whereas Constantinople can be looked at through no such magnifying-glass. Sacked of her wealth, home of the arts no more, guarded by jealous keepers, and lacking most that is dear to the modern wanderer's heart, how should she compete with Rome? Only in one respect can she hold her own unchallenged against that potent rival, for by no stretch of the imagination can Rome, crouching on her seven ant-hills beside her muddy river, be given the palm of place over Constantinople. And the *campagna* of Rome, that stretches so vast and melancholy on many an eloquent page, is but a dooryard to the *campagna* of Constantinople, which also has imperial aqueducts, and which regards older than Albân hills and the shining spaces of the Marmora dotted by high islands, and far away behind them, like Alps seen across a Venetian lagoon, the blue range, capped three parts of the year with snow, of the Bithynian Olympus.

I follow, however, but an unprofitable trail. Rome is Rome and Constantinople is Constantinople. And a day will no doubt come for the latter when some other impressionist will sigh for the unexploited days of yore. One of the charms of Constantinople, indeed, is that mystery still has room there and one may always hope for treasure-trove. The sacks of 1204 and 1453 undoubtedly made away with the better part of the statuary and other precious things of which Constantinople was so unparalleled a museum, but some buried Greek marble may yet come to light. The soil of Stamboul is virgin so far as excavation is concerned, and you have no more than to scratch it to pick up something — if only a coin or a bit of broken pottery. Until very recently, digging for foundations was the sole thing of the sort permitted. Some most interesting discoveries have been made in this casual way. Quite a museum, for example, could have been formed of the different objects found in the grounds where the American missionaries have their headquarters. While digging, in 1872, for the foundations of the main building, an ancient burial-ground was unearthed. The bones, with lamps and other small objects, were protected by great tiles set triangularly together, and inside each skull was a Roman coin of early imperial times, which once paid, I suppose, a passage over Styx. Near by were ruins of masonry which indicated by their shape a church. Under a later building coins and tiles of the period of Constans were found. A beautiful Corinthian column also came to light, and a life-sized marble statue. When ground was broken for the third building, on the site of a Turkish *konak*, an old man came to the American in charge and asked for a private interview. He then introduced himself as an Armenian whose ancestors had been courtiers of the last emperor Constantine. From them, he said, a tradition had been handed down in his family about the ground where the Turkish house had stood. "When you dig into the ground," he said, "you will come to an iron door. When you open the door you will see stone steps. When you go down the steps you will come into a sort of room. Then you will find a passage leading underground in the direction of St. Sophia — and in it gold, jewels, statues, all manner of things that the emperor and his friends put there for safety during the last siege. I only ask you to give me half!" The missionary thought the Armenian mad and treated him accordingly. But the old man spent all his time watching the work. And one day the diggers uncovered a metal door lying horizontally in the earth. With some difficulty they succeeded in jacking the door off the masonry in which the hinges were embedded, and underneath steps appeared, going down into a black void. At that the missionary began to be interested. When the workmen were out of the way he went down with the Armenian to explore. They descended into the subterranean vault they expected. It was held up by marble pillars with crosses on the capitals. But when they came to look for the passage they discovered that one end of the vault, the end toward St. Sophia, had been cut off by a wall of more recent date. That wall, as it happens, belongs to the great building known as the Valideh Han, erected by the famous *validch soultan* Kyössem. After her death were found, among other property of hers stored there, twenty chests of ducats. And when I read about them I could not help wondering whether any of those ducats came from the passage which the sultana's workmen must accidentally have struck into in the seventeenth century.

Constantinople is full of stories and legends of the same sort, in most of which figures a secret passage leading underground to St. Sophia. I have poked my own nose into two or three such tunnels, which no Turk ever constructed, and can vouch for their existence. In reality, however, there is nothing very mysterious about them. The soil of Stamboul is honeycombed with cisterns of all sizes, from the enormous ones picturesquely called by the Turks the Sunken Palace and the Thousand and One Columns to the small one of the Bible House and Valideh Han. Others, like the cistern beside the mosque of Sultan Selim I, were always uncovered. These are usually called *choukour bostan*, hollow garden, from the fact that vegetable gardens are wont to flourish in the accumulated silt of their centuries. Brick conduits connect many of the reservoirs with a water-system which Hadrian is known to have installed or enlarged while Rome was still the capital of the empire. And it was only natural for such conduits to lead toward St. Sophia, the civic centre of the town. We also know that Constantine constructed deep sewers, on the lines of the *cloaca* of Rome. But as no one has ever been able to study these systems thoroughly, there remains something half mythic about them.

Another casual but more dramatic way in which old Constantinople proves her temper of eternity is by means of the fires that periodically ravage Stamboul. There is no more striking suggestion of Stambouls within Stamboul than to look at the ashes of some familiar, of some regretted quarter, and discover there a solid piece of antiquity about which houses have been built and burned who knows how many times. In my own day the Column of Marcian has reappeared on its hilltop overlooking the Marmora, having long been lost in the

The Myrelaion

yard of a Turkish house. And I have seen the obscure mosque of Boudroun Jami gallantly reassert itself above the ruin of its quarter as the charming little tenth-century church of the Myrelaion — the convent of Myrrh and Oil. The fires which an archæologist might best have been suspected of setting were those of 1912 and 1913, which swept the slope between the Hippodrome and the Marmora. This was the site of the Sacred Palace of the later Roman emperors. No complete account of it remains, but from the reports of ambassadors and other visitors of note, from references of historians, and from the Book of Ceremonies of the emperor Constantine Porphyrogenitus, scholars have been able to reconstitute that city of palaces, churches, terraces, and gardens that overlapped on one side a corner of the present Seraglio grounds and reached on the other nearly to the church of SS. Sergius and Bacchus. Constantine the Great was the founder of this imperial residence. His Palace of Daphne, so called from a statue of the nymph he brought from Rome, stood on the site of the mosque of Sultan Ahmed I, and other structures bordered the Hippodrome, opening by a monumental gateway into the Augustæum, now the square of St. Sophia. To Constantine also was attributed the magnificent hall of the Magnaura, which Ebersolt places a little south and west of the present Ministry of Justice. Here was the throne of Solomon, imitated from the one described in the Book of Kings, whose fame has come down in the memoirs of more than one amazed ambassador. It was guarded by golden lions which, during audiences of state, rose to their feet, beat their tails on the floor, and roared, while golden birds in a tree behind the throne began to chirp and flutter among the golden boughs. Still another construction attributed to Constantine was the Porphyra, the little porphyry palace near the sea where the imperial children were born.

I cannot attempt even to catalogue the other splendours of this unparalleled enclosure or the names of those who continued, during six hundred years, to add palace to palace, one richer than another in jewelled furniture, in the new jewelry of mosaic, in the spoils of ancient art. Nicephorus Phocas was the last emperor to do so, when he enlarged and fortified the waterside Palace of Bucoleon. By the eleventh century the emperors had begun to prefer the Palace of Blacherne. But Boniface, Marquis of Montferrat, found the great ladies of the court assembled in the Bucoleon when the crusaders occupied the city in 1204, and after the restoration of 1261 Michael Palæologus lived there until Blacherne could be put in order. From that time on the Great Palace fell rapidly into decay. When the Florentine Buondelmonte visited it early in the fifteenth century it was already a ruin. Its condition in 1453 suggested to the Turkish conqueror the Persian distich which has been so often requoted: "The spider has woven his web in the palace of kings, and the owl hath sung her watch-song on the towers of Afrasiab." By the sixteenth century little was left of it but a few columns and the ruins of the Bucoleon. The colossal group of a lion and a bull, which gave the smaller palace its name, still stood on the old quay of the imperial galleys in 1532, when it was turned around by an earthquake. Is it impossible that that marble might yet be recovered from the sand of the shore? The westernmost of the palaces composing the Bucoleon, the one associated with the name of the Persian prince Hormisdas, who came as an exile to the court of Constantine the Great, was pulled down as late as 1871, when the Roumelian railway was built. Two lions from a balcony of its sea façade now flank the east staircase of the Imperial Museum. The ruins of the eastern palace, the so-called House of Justinian, where the great emperor may very well have lived before he came to the throne, were barely saved by the Friends of Stamboul when the railway was double-tracked in 1912. To-day this pile of ancient brickwork, rising from the edge of the Marmora, is almost the last vestige of the palace whose legendary splendour filled so many mediæval pages. On the slope behind it the fires to which I have referred laid bare several Byzantine terraces, the entrances to a number of vaulted substructures, and a tower which had been incorporated into the surrounding houses. Might it be,

The House of Justinian

perhaps, the tower of the Great Admiral Apocaucus, which he built as a prison for John Cantacuzene but in which he himself was murdered in 1345? I am not the one to say. But that Palatine Hill, so long the centre of the world, where so much has been enacted that is most coloured and passionate of life, and which now looks so quietly at its quiet sea — and there is a blue keeps no trace of all the keels that have scarred it from the time of the Argonauts! — that Palatine Hill has an immense attraction for me. And I marvel that no one has yet taken advantage of its present accessibility to learn precisely what, after so many fires and earthquakes and other spoilers, may be left of its old arrangement.

A Palatine Hill which might reveal more dominates the opposite end of the city. This ridge above the Golden Horn is the site of the palace whose name of Blacherne — or Vlaherni as I should be tempted to write it if I were not afraid of my friends the Byzantinists — seems to have been derived from that of some barbarian settler. Was he haply a Wallachian? He settled, at all events, on this hilltop in pre-Constantinian days, and outside the line of the Constantinian, or even of the Theodosian, walls. It was only in the seventh century that the emperor Heraclius threw a wall outside the quarter. Which emperor first built a palace there is not known, but Anastasius I enlarged one as early as the fifth century. In 457 the pious Pulcheria, the virgin empress of Marcian, founded the celebrated shrine of the Madonna of Blacherne. Restored and enlarged in different reigns, it was the object of several of those annual imperial pilgrimages which played so large a part in the life of the ancient city. There was even a day in the year when the emperors bathed in the Holy Well of the church. This *ayazma* may still be seen in the waterside quarter of Balat. The name Balat is a Turkish corruption of the Greek word for palace, and Aïvan Seraï, as the adjoining quarter is called, means the Palace of the Balcony. These names are another reminder of the palace that figures so often in the chronicles of the crusades. Of the palace itself more remains than of the Great Palace, though it still waits for a Labarte or an Ebersolt. Bits of masonry erop out of the ground or stand visibly among the houses all the way up the hill.

Indeed, I suspect that a good deal of the hill itself is artificial. Such, at least, is the case of the high terrace bordering the city wall where the mosque of Aïvas Effendi faces two ivy-mantled towers. An innocent-looking hole in the courtyard of the mosque winds down into a black subterranean maze of passages, stairways, cells, and tiers of arches climbing above bottomless pits. So much earth and rubbish have sifted into this extraordinary labyrinth that its true extent can only be guessed at until it is systematically excavated. In the meantime, archæology has been very busy discussing which of the two contiguous towers that form a part of it was the tower of Anemas, and whether either of them was the tower of the emperor Isaac Angelus. The Anemas in question was a Byzantinised Arab, descendant of the Emir who surrendered Crete to Nicephorus Phocas, and he had the honour of being the first of many prisoners of state to be shut up in his tower. Whichever it may have been, however, the most unarchæological visitor is capable of enjoying a dip into that romantic darkness and the view, from the terrace, of a cypressed country beside the Golden Horn.

On top of the hill stands the well-preserved ruin known in Turkish as Tekfour Seraï, the Palace of the Crown-Wearer. As to its real name, there has been the most fanciful variety of opinions. The palace is now generally supposed, however, to have been built in the tenth century by Constantine Porphyrogenitus. It seems to have been separate from the Palace of Blacherne, though on the analogy of the Great Palace it may have belonged to the same group. Architects as well as archæologists take a particular interest in Tekfour Seraï, because it is the only authentic piece of domestic building left of Byzantine Constantinople. The main façade is divided into three tiers of arched windows and ornamented by a mosaic of dark and light stone that recalls the brickwork of later Byzantine churches. What the general effect does not recall is the Venetian version of Byzantine civil architecture. We should not take that version too literally, of course, any more than the Venetian Gothic; but St. Mark's is so true a transcription of a Byzantine church — without the crockets — that one has the more faith in the palaces. The difference may be chiefly one of periods. It is noticeable that the spacing of the arches of Tekfour Seraï is not like that of the *Fondaco dei Turchi*, to whose designed irregularity Ruskin drew attention. Neither has the checker-work of the façade anything in common with the plaques of porphyry and serpentine reflected in the Grand Canal. It suggests, rather, the checker-work of the Ducal Palace. The first tier of arches, too, looks like the same kind of ground arcade. Is it possible that any influence interacted between the two palaces? If so the presumption would be that it worked in Venice, under a Gothic cloak; for the Ducal Palace, or the lagoon front of it, belongs to the century after the Latin occupation of Constantinople. In the light of my question this latter detail is interesting, since the features I have noted decorate only the sea façade of Tekfour Seraï. The question lies so near the fantastic, however, and so far from any track of sober archæology where I have happened to browse, that I merely ask it and hurry on, leaving for some happy expert, with means to excavate and knowledge to compare, to state the true affiliations of the Palace of the Porphyrogenitus.

The richest remains of old Constantinople are its churches. Little as they are generally known, almost every one knows something about the greatest of them. There seems to me a peculiar fitness in the name of Justinian's cathedral, which is not exactly rendered by its current vocable. It was not dedicated to any saint, but to the Divine Wisdom; and the Turks still call it *Aya Sofya.* The cross no longer surmounts that old cathedral, it is true, nor are Christian forms of worship

The Palace of the Porphyrogenitus

permitted within its walls. In the divine wisdom, however, there is room for more than one form of worship. And St. Sophia, whose marbles, borrowed from half the temples of antiquity, have beautified the rites not only of Mohammed and of Christ, but of Apollo, of Pallas, of Asiatic Cybele, of Egyptian Isis and Osiris and how many older divinities of the pagan world, seems to me more than any other temple to express what is universal in religion, stripped of all pettinesses of creed. I shall make no attempt to analyse the elements of so supreme an expression. One is silenced, too, in the face of so many human associations. A thousand years before St. Peter's that great dome swung in the Byzantine air, and under it one is bewildered by a cloud of ghosts. Yet impressions detach themselves — of space, of light, of an immense distinction. All the little Turkish rearrangements are swallowed up in it, as must have been the glitter of the Greek ritual. Decoration has no part in the nobility of that effect. There is nothing to hide. Each of those leaping arches and soaring domes does something — and in a way! But there is also a perfection of detail, rich, coloured, as if suffused by a glamour of dusky gold that is between the white morning clarity of paganism and the Gothic twilight.

The churches of Constantinople neither begin nor end with St. Sophia, however. The oldest of them is St. John the Baptist of the Studion, so called from the Roman senator Studius who about 463 founded a monastery near the Golden Gate. The monks by whom this monastery was first peopled belonged to the order known as the Sleepless Ones, because by a system of relays they kept up an unending series of offices. Nevertheless, they found time to gain renown as copyists and illuminators of manuscripts, and some of the hymns they wrote are still sung. The monks took the unpopular side against the iconoclastic emperors, but after the triumph of the iconodules, in the ninth century, the Studion became the most important monastery in the city. Its abbot took precedence of all other abbots. The emperors visited it annually in state. Two of them even exchanged their crowns for its habit. In 1054 several meetings took place there between Constantine X and the legates who had come from Rome to settle the differences between the Pope and the Patriarch. Cardinal Humbert finally settled those differences by laying on the altar of St. Sophia a bull of excommunication against the Patriarch Cerularius and all his followers. That was the first definite schism between the churches. When Michael Palæologus drove the Latin emperors from Constantinople in 1261, he made the first part of his triumphal entry on foot from the Golden Gate to the Studion. In front of him went in a chariot the famous icon of the *ὁδηγητρία*, the Shower of the Way, which he left in the church. This sacred painting, ascribed to the prolific brush of St. Luke, was acquired with other relics in Jerusalem by Eudoxia, empress of Theodosius II. She gave it to her sister-in-law Pulcheria, who built a special church for it on Seraglio Point. The relic gradually took the place of the Palladium which Constantine brought from Rome. It was prayed to in battles, shown from the walls in sieges, carried in triumphs, and annually borne in procession to the Great Palace for the ceremonies of Easter. The Studion possessed other precious relics of its own, such as the head of John the Baptist and the Sacred Lance. Several persons of importance were buried in the precincts of the monastery. Among them was a Turkish prince, son of Baïezid the Thunderbolt, who died there of the plague in 1417. Brought up as a hostage at the court of Manuel Palæologus, he became a Christian, but for fear of incurring his father's displeasure the monks would not baptise him till his last illness. It was under Baïezid II that the monastery passed into Turkish hands. By way of compensation the Sultan sent to the Pope of the day, who happened to be Alexander Borgia, the Sacred Lance and other relics.

An order of dervishes followed the monks of the Studion, and the church of St. John is now called Emir Ahor or Imrahor Jamisi, the mosque of the Chief of the Stables.

Interior of the Studion

Of the monastery very little remains save a fine cistern and a few fragments of wall. Little more will soon be left of the church unless something be done to save it. A heavy fall of snow crushed in the roof a few years ago, and the powers that be have not yet found means or inclination to preserve that monument of a past in which they had no part. The church is interesting not only because it is the oldest in Constantinople and associated with so much history, but because it is the one pure basilica extant in the city. The best-preserved parts of it are the walls of the narthex, where are still visible the remnants of colonnades with a fine entablature of an early transition period from Corinthian to Byzantine. After the disuse of the basilica as a mosque, the Russian Archæological Institute obtained permission to investigate it and made some interesting discoveries. The north wall of the mosque yard was scraped of its plaster and was found to contain ancient bricks disposed in the form of a cross, proving that the Turkish court takes the place of an early Christian atrium. In the south aisle of the interior three graves were found corresponding perfectly to the description of the last resting-place of the great abbot Theodore of the ninth century. An underground passage was also opened, leading from the bema to the adjoining cistern, and the foundations contained evidence of a more ancient substructure. But the most interesting discovery was that of a beautiful marble pavement beneath the Turkish floor, in which figures of men and animals were framed in marble between squares, disks, and geometrical curves of porphyry and serpentine. Unfortunately, some disagreement arose between the Russians and the Ministry of Pious Foundations, and the work was stopped. Nothing was done, however, to protect the ruined basilica, and the last time I saw it the pavement was lost in weeds.

There are some twenty-five other buildings in Stamboul that were originally Byzantine churches. That is, of course, but a small proportion of the multitude that astonished Villehardouin and his men. Covering as they do a period of ten centuries, however, they exhibit most interestingly the gradual development of ecclesiastical architecture from the Roman basilica to the high-domed trefoil church of the fourteenth century. This development is not always easy to follow, as in some cases the churches have been much altered to suit Turkish needs. The orientation of a mosque, for instance, differs from that of a church, since the *mihrab* must face Mecca, and actual changes of structure have occasionally resulted. Then, of course, all interior decoration too visibly representing Christian symbols or the human form has been destroyed or covered up. And a good deal of exterior brickwork has disappeared under plaster and whitewash. Consequently the prowler in Stamboul is on the lookout, if he have the least tinge of archæology in him, for anything that may hint at a pre-Turkish origin. Not that very much can remain above ground to discover. After so much careful searching it will only be a small built-in structure or fragment that will come to light. But several of the attributions of churches are disputed. Their true names were lost with their original worshippers, and it is a comparatively short time since Christians have been free to circulate at will in the Turkish quarters of Stamboul. And there is reason to hope that under many a piece of baroque stencilling an old mosaic waits to be laid bare.

The art of mosaic existed, of course, long before Constantine. But glass mosaics containing a film of gold were the invention of the later empire, and the Byzantine architects made vast use of them. What a museum of this splendid art Constantinople must once have been we can only guess. Ravenna, however, early became important for the study of mosaics, for in the capital of Justinian many of his masterpieces were destroyed during the iconoclastic controversy. And to-day Salonica, Venice, Sicily, and a few widely scattered monasteries contain the chief remaining specimens. In Constantinople, where palaces, churches, public monuments and private houses without number were tapestried with mosaic, there are in 1914 only four buildings where anything is visible of this lost art. The attendants of St. Sophia used to make quite an income by selling mosaics which they picked out of the walls of the galleries. This infamous commerce has now been checked, but there is no telling what ravages were committed while it flourished. The earthquake of 1894 was also disastrous for the decoration of the mosque, correspondingly enlarging the area of plaster in the nave. The vaulting of the aisles and galleries, however, the soffits of the arcades, and the inner narthex still contain a greater extent of mosaic, and presumably older, than exists elsewhere in the city. The church of St. Irene, long a Turkish armoury and now a military museum, also contains, in the narthex, a little mosaic which may be of Justinian's time. That of the apse belongs to the restoration of the church during the iconoclastic period. And in a chapel of the eighth-century church of the All-blessed Virgin, now Fetieh Jami, where the figures of Christ and twelve prophets still look down from a golden dome, we have work of a much later period — probably the fourteenth century. But a far finer example of the work of that period is to be seen in Kahrieh Jami, once Our Saviour in the Fields.

Kahrieh Jami, popularly known as the mosaic mosque, is in every way one of the most interesting monuments of Constantinople. Like Imrahor Jamisi it was originally the church of a monastery, and its history goes back as far. Like the Studion, also, it suffered from the quarrels of iconoclasm, it gave hospitality at a historic moment — namely during the last siege — to the miraculous icon of the Shower of the Way, and it fell into Turkish hands during the reign of Baïezid II. Kahrieh Jami means the Mosque of Woe, from the scenes that

Kahrieh Jami

were enacted there when the Turks stormed the walls. The church seems always to have had a particular connection with Syria. The abbot Theodore, an uncle of Justinian's empress, came to it from Antioch in 530. Again in the ninth century, when the iconoclasts were finally beaten, the celebrated Syrian monk Michael was made abbot, while pilgrims from Syria always made the monastery their headquarters. The church we know was not the church built outside the walls of Constantine as early, it may be, as the fourth century. The original church was successively rebuilt in the sixth century — by Justinian — in the seventh, in the ninth, and in the eleventh or at the beginning of the twelfth. To this latter restoration by Mary Ducas, a princess with Bulgarian blood in her veins, the church owes its present lines and perhaps a part of its interior decoration.

Photograph by Sébah and Joaillier, Constantinople

Mosaic from Kahrieh Jami: Theodore Metochites offering his church to Christ

The last of the Byzantine restorers was a personage who recalls, as he anticipated, the humanists of the Renaissance. His name was Theodore Metochites, and you may see him in a great striped turban kneeling over the royal door of the inner narthex, offering a model of his church to the seated Christ. He was what we call nowadays, though his history has been repeated in every time and country, a self-made man; and like more than one of those who have risen from nothing to the height of power, he outlived his fortune. Born of poor parents in Nicæa, the city of the creed, and early left an orphan, he went as a young man to Constantinople, where he succeeded by his handsome presence and his talent as an orator in attracting the attention of the emperor Andronicus II. He was, however, more than an orator. He aspired to be a poet as well, and some of his not too intelligible verses have been translated into German. In history he took a particular interest. He became the chief astronomer of his time. His favourite pupil in the latter science was Nicephorus Gregoras, a monk of Our Saviour in the Fields, who, three hundred years before Gregory XIII, proposed to rectify the Julian calendar. If Greek priests realised this fact, and how nearly alike were the names of the two churchmen, they might be more willing to adopt a system which was christened after a Pope. It was characteristic of the time that Metochites took as much interest in astrology as he did in astronomy. Philology was another subject that engrossed him. He made six hundred years ago an attempt which is being made in Athens to-day to restore the Romaic Greek language to its Attic purity, for he was a devoted student of Aristotle and particularly of Plato. With all these scholarly tastes, however, he was a man of affairs. By his success as an ambassador and in other public posts, he rose from one responsibility to another till he became Grand Logothetes — or as we might say, prime minister. He was far-sighted enough to see, a hundred and fifty years before the final catastrophe, the imminence of the Turkish peril. Among his writings, too, are some curiously modern reflections on absolute monarchy. Nevertheless he became involved, through his fidelity to his imperial master, in the long quarrel between Andronicus II and his grandson Andronicus III. When the latter usurped the throne in 1328 Metochites was stripped of his honours and his wealth, his palace — near that of Blacherne — was razed to the ground, and he was sent into exile. Allowed to return after two years, he retired to his own monastery, where he lived only two years more.

If this great man was unhappy in his death, he was happier than perhaps he knew in the monument that has kept alive the memory of his humanism and of his loyalty. The grace of its proportions, the beauty of its marbles, the delicacy of its sculpture, everything about it sets the church apart as a little masterpiece. Kahrieh Jami is also notable for the faded frescoes in its side chapel, where a portrait of Andronicus II looks ghostlike out of a niche, for in no other Constantinople church does there remain any visible trace of painting — or any such tomb as the one, in the same chapel, of the Grand Constable Michael Tornikes, with a long Greek epitaph. What completes, however, this picture of the last days of Byzantium, what gives Kahrieh Jami its unique interest, are its mosaics. In the nave they are still hidden, waiting as if for the day of release from a strange enchantment. But in the narthexes Mohammedan sensibilities have for once spared two long series of scenes from the life of Christ and the legend of Mary. And they make one ask oneself again why so noble an art is practically lost. For richness of effect no other form of surface ornament can equal it. The modern art of painting is, of course, far more expressive; for that very reason it is less suited to mural decoration. Mosaic can carry farther, and for great spaces or distances it is equally expressive — witness the tragic Christ of Cefalù. Moreover, it has decorative effects of its own which painting never can rival, while its greater brilliancy is better

Photograph by Sébah and Joaillier, Constantinople

Mosaic from Kahrieh Jami: the Massacre of the Innocents

Photograph by Alinari Brothers, Florence. Reproduced by permission

Giotto's fresco of the Massacre of the Innocents, in the Arena chapel, Padua

suited to most architectural settings. And it is infinitely more durable. Of the great frescoes of the Renaissance some are already gone, while others crack and darken year by year. The art of Michelangelo and Leonardo will one day be as mythic as that of Zeuxis and Apelles, except for the shadow of it saved by our modern processes of reproduction. But the mosaics of Venice, Ravenna, and Sicily, of Salonica and Constantinople, will last as long as the buildings that contain them.

In this very matter of the relation between fresco and mosaic, Kahrieh Jami happens to play a particular part. The mosaics are disposed with such a mastery of composition, there is so wide a range of colour in them, in life and naturalness and sometimes in choice of subject they differ so greatly from better-known mosaics of an earlier period, that some critics have seen in them a fine Italian hand — and one no less fine than that of Giotto, who painted the Arena chapel in Padua about the time Metochites restored this church. Not that any one has gone so far as to ascribe the Byzantine series to Giotto himself, but that the qualities I have mentioned, together with certain similarities of detail, have been ascribed to the revolutionary influence of the Italian series. It is not yet unanimously decided whether the mosaics all belong to the same period. Perhaps we must wait for the evidence of those still hidden in the nave to know whether any of them belong to the time of Mary Ducas. The Russian archæologist Schmitt, who has written the completest monograph on the subject — and who picked enough plaster away in the nave to assure himself that mosaics were still there — assigns the work to the period of Metochites, but surmises it to have been inspired by some Syrian original of the ninth century. Diehl, the eminent French Byzantinist, sees rather in Kahrieh Jami a last revival of Byzantine art, contemporaneous with but not derived from the early Tuscan school of painting. When these savants expressed their opinions neither of them was aware of an odd little fact quite lately established not by a Byzantinist but by a layman who was looking at some photographs of the mosaics. In the photograph of the central bay of the outer narthex he discovered, above a two-handled jar which a servant carries on his shoulder to the marriage at Cana, a date in Arabic numerals — but real Arabic numerals, not the ones we have made out of them. This date is 6811, which in the Byzantine system of chronography is equivalent to 1303. The find was interesting in itself as being the earliest use yet recorded — if I am not mistaken — of Arabic numerals on a public monument. It has a further interest in pointing to the Syrian affiliations of the monastery and in lending colour, however slight, to Schmitt's theory with regard to the Syrian origin of certain of the mosaics. But it tends more definitely to prove that the mosaics were executed before Giotto's frescoes in Padua, which could hardly have been begun and much less completed by 1303.

Photograph by Sébah and Joaillier, Constantinople

Mosaic from Kahrieh Jami: the Marriage at Cana

I do not know whether any one, in discussing this

matter, has drawn attention to so small a detail as a certain checkered border of disconcerting similarity in the two series. Therefore I, who am nothing of an expert in these questions, will pass it by. But I cannot pass Kahrieh Jami by without pointing out, from the depth of my inexpertness, how unlikely it was that Theodore Metochites, the lover of all things Greek, should send, at the end of the thirteenth century, for one of those hated Latins who had just been driven out of Constantinople, to decorate the church they had left a ruin. Even if it should be proved that the designer of these mosaics was an Italian, however, or that he had watched Giotto in the house of the Scrovegni, it would not alter the fact that the trend of influence was all the other way. Constantinople had for the young Italian cities, down to 1453, an immense artistic prestige. Indeed, the church of the Salute, recalling as it does the lines of a mosque, seems to suggest that in Venice, at least, this influence did not cease with the coming of the Turks. Greek masters of mosaic were invited time and again to decorate Italian interiors. The primitive Italian painters drew Byzantine madonnas on gold backgrounds exactly like mosaicists working in a new — and possibly a cheaper — medium. Giotto himself, like his master Cimabue, made pictures with little cubes of coloured glass. I will not say that the Italians, in turn, never influenced the Greeks; the very name of Constantinople is proof to the contrary. Least of all will I say that Italy had only one source of inspiration. But I will say that there is room to revise our ideas of the Renaissance. Most that has been written about the Renaissance has been written without any first-hand knowledge of Byzantine art, and in the romantic view that the Renaissance was a miraculous reflowering of the classic spirit after a sleep of centuries. Need it dim the glamour of the Renaissance to look upon it as something less of an immaculate conception? If the Renaissance was a reflowering, it was of a plant that had silently grown in another soil. And Kahrieh Jami is the last flower of that plant in its own Byzantine ground.

From Kahrieh Jami to the walls is but a step — in more ways than one. They are the part of old Constantinople that is most visible. They still form an almost complete circuit, of some thirteen miles, around Stamboul. Where the circuit is most broken is along the Golden Horn, though even there large sections of the wall remain. On the land side only one breach has been made, for the railway that leads to Bulgaria and the west. Whether other breaches will follow remains to be seen. For the walls lie under sentence of death. In 1909 a bill passed Parliament and was signed by the Sultan, providing that the walls be pulled down and their materials sold for the public profit. In spite of the disdain under which Constantinople generally lies, I am happy to say that so loud a protest immediately rose to heaven as to dissuade the astonished Young Turks from carrying out their law. I can quite understand that that old rampart of Christendom represents to them merely so much brick and stone in a very bad state of preservation, which they began to demolish five hundred years ago and since have left to encumber the earth. Moreover, they have been to Vienna, they have been to Paris, they have been to all sorts of places. They have seen fine boulevards laid out on the site of ancient fortifications, and they ask themselves: If the Europeans do it, why do they make such a fuss when we propose to? I would rather like to tell them, for Turkey is not the only place where Young Turks grow. However, as none of them will ever read this obscure page I will content myself with saying that I shall never object to the sea-walls being pulled down — provided the railway be made to subside into a tunnel, and the gateways along the Golden Horn be preserved like those of Florence to ornament the city. As for the land walls, they are too great an asset ever to be disposed of except under direst stress of over-population, which now seems remote enough. Only in that case, dear Young Turks, you will also have to cut down your cemetery cypresses outside the walls. And then will double stars be scratched out of many travellers' handbooks!

Constantinople has long been famous for her walls. About the rocky headland of Seraglio Point, which was the acropolis of the first settlers from Megara, may still lie some blocks of the fortifications built by Pausanias after the battle of Platæa, when he drove the Persians out of Byzantium and made it one of the strongest cities of the ancient world. This wall lasted until it was destroyed in 196 by the emperor Septimius Severus, in revenge upon the Byzantines for having taken the part of his rival Pescennius Niger. He also changed the name of the city to Antonina and made it subject to Perinthos, now a sleepy hamlet of the Marmora called Eregli. But he later refortified the town, on the advice of his son Caracalla. The Byzantium thus enlarged extended into the Golden Horn not quite so far as Yeni Jami, and into the Marmora no farther than the lighthouse of Seraglio Point. When in 328 Constantine the Great decided to turn Byzantium into New Rome, he carried the walls to the vicinity of the Oun Kapan-Azap Kapou bridge on one side, and on the other to the gate of Daoud Pasha, in the Psamatia quarter. He set the forum bearing his name, marked to-day by the so-called Burnt Column, at the place where the city gate of Septimius Severus opened on to the *Via Egnatia.* His own city gate opened on to that road at the point now called Issa Kapoussou — the Gate of Jesus. The charming little mosque of Ramazan Effendi stands on the street which follows the line of the wall for a short distance to the north. Of the wall itself nothing that can be identified as such remains visible. It was the emperor Theodosius II, he who first brought to Constantinople those much-travelled bronze horses long since naturalised in Venice, who gave the walls their present extension. The inner of the two lines of land walls he built in 413, the outer wall and the moat being added while Attila was ravaging the Balkan peninsula in 447. Two inscriptions, one in Latin and one in Greek, still record this achievement over the gate now called after the *Yeni Mevlevi Haneh.* Later emperors did no more than repair the work of Theodosius, except at that northwestern corner of the city where the growing importance of the Blacherne quarter necessitated fresh enlargements or defences. Since the Turkish conquest more or less extensive repairs have been carried out by Mehmed II, Mourad IV (1635), and Ahmed III (1721).

An infinite variety of interest attaches to these walls — from the gates that pierce them, the towers that flank them at intervals of some sixty feet, the devices, monograms, and inscriptions of every period they contain, the associations they have had so much time to accumulate. Two points, however, have a special interest for expert and layman alike. I have already spoken of Tekfour Seraï, where the Theodosian wall merges into later additions, and of the imperial quarter of Blacherne. I have yet to speak, even more cursorily, of the Golden Gate. This great triple portal and the marble towers flanking it existed before the walls themselves, having been built as a triumphal arch over the Egnatian Way by Theodosius the Great, after his defeat of Maximus in 388. The statue of the emperor and the other sculptures

The Golden Gate

that adorned it once are gone, but you can still see over the central arch the rivet holes of the original inscription:

HAEC LOCA THEVDOSIVS DECORAT POST FATA TYRANNI
AVREA SÆCLO GERIT QVI PORTAM CONSTRVIT AVRO

When the younger Theodosius extended the walls he made the Golden Gate a part of them, but kept it as the state entrance to the city. Distinguished guests were met there — ambassadors, visiting princes, at least one Pope. Holy processions burned their incense under that archway. Through it passed emperors in splendour when they came to the purple, or when they returned victorious from war. No gateway in Europe can have seen so much of the pomp and glory of the world. Now the arches are blind, save for one small postern in the centre, and that was nearly choked by an earthquake in 1912. One Roman eagle still looks down from a high marble cornice upon the moat, empty of all but garden green, and upon a colony of Turkish gravestones that stand among cypresses where the *Via Egnatia* started away for the Adriatic.

On the other side lies a silent enclosure whose own day has come and gone since the last emperor passed through the Golden Gate. This is the fortress of the Seven Towers — three of which were built by the Turkish conqueror and connected by curtains with the city wall. In the towers are passages and cells as black as the subterranean maze of Blacherne, and they were used for the same purpose. Many are the stories of captivity in this high-walled place that have been told and remain to be told. One of them is briefly legible, in Latin, in a stone of the southeast tower, where it was cut by a Venetian in the seventeenth century. It used even to be the fashion to clap an ambassador into prison there when war broke out between his country and the Porte. Turkish state prisoners, of course, perished there without number. And one sultan, Osman II, when he was no more than eighteen, was barbarously put to death there in 1622. And all that blood and bitterness, which was so desperately the whole of reality for so many breathing men, is now but a pleasant quickening of romance for the visitor who follows a lantern through the darkness of the towers or who explores the battlements of the wall, grassy and anemone-grown in the spring, from which a magnificent view stretches of the sea and the city and the long line of ruined turrets marching up the hill.

If every ended drama of human greatness must come at last to a view, the road around the land walls of Constantinople can do more for the man who walks it than any such road I know. Other cities have walls, it is true. Other walls have moats. Some of their moats contain water, too, while this moat contains only

Outside the land walls

water-wheels and vegetable-gardens. And how much more greenly do the vegetables grow, I wonder, because of all the dead men that have fallen under the ramparts? Other ramparts wear as picturesque a verdure, and blossoming fruit-trees have the same trick of setting them off in the spring. And cypresses are no monopoly of Constantinople. But no such army of cypresses faces other walls, from such a camp of strange grey stones. Nor in any Eternal City does water play so magical a part of background. The landscape is most dramatically accidented where you look past the high terraces of Blacherne toward the landlocked brightness of the Golden Horn. A view is also to be admired down the valley of the Lycus, of the whole city stretching to the sea. But the noblest perspective is the simpler one where the road, avenue-like between the moat and the cypresses, dips and rises and dips again toward the Golden Gate

A last marble tower stands superbly out of the blue

and the Marmora, till a last marble tower stands superbly out of the blue. The contrast of sea and cypresses and tawny stones, always perfect, here takes an insensible colour, I suppose, from the thought of the sentinels who called from tower to tower in old Byzantine nights; and of all the horsemen and banners that have ridden against those walls; and of what they did for the other end of Europe — the walls — till civilisation was safely planted there; and of something yet more intangible, that is deepest and strangest in human fate.

IV

THE GOLDEN HORN

WHY the Golden Horn should be called the Golden Horn is a question that has agitated many serious pens. A less serious pen is therefore free to declare itself for an explanation that does not explain. The Greeks always seem to have been fond of the word gold. In their language as in ours it has a pleasant sound, and it has pleasant implications — the philosophers to the contrary. At any rate, the Greeks of Constantinople made much use of it. The state entrance to the city was through the Golden Gate. One of the most famous parts of the Great Palace was the Golden Hall. The suburb of Scutari was anciently known as the City of Gold. There were in different parts of the town a Golden Milestone, a Golden Arch, a Golden Roof, and a Golden Stream, while the Greek church abounds in golden springs and golden caves. I have even known a Greek serving-maid to address her mistress in moments of expansion as "my golden one"! The Golden Horn, then, was probably named so for even less reason than the orange valley behind Palermo — because some one a long time ago liked the sound of the words.

I always wish I might have seen the Golden Horn before it was bridged. It must have made, opening out of the lake-like basin where the Bosphorus and the Marmora come together, one of the most satisfactory pieces of geography in nature. However, if the bridges cut up that long curving perspective they add something of their own to it, and whoever stands upon them must acknowledge that the Golden Horn is still a satisfactory piece of geography. Consider, for instance, its colour, which may not be quite so blue as Naples but which is far from the muddiness of New York. Consider also the shores that overlook it — how excellently their height is proportioned to its breadth, how superlatively the southern one, in particular, is set off by the pinnacles of Seraglio Point and the mosques that ride the higher crests. Yet do not fail to consider that more intimate element of its character, its busy water life. I say so with rather a pointed air, as if, having already found something to write about one bank of the Golden Horn, I intended to go on and give a compendious account of the Golden Horn itself, to the last fish that swims in it. Alas, no! I have admired the Golden Horn from every conceivable point of view, I have navigated it in every conceivable sense, I have idled much about its banks and bridges, I have even ventured to swim in its somewhat doubtful waters — only to learn how lamentable is my ignorance in their regard. My one consolation is that I never encountered any other man who knew very much about the Golden Horn — save casual watermen and sea-captains who have much better things to do than to write books, or read them.

All harbours bring the ends of the earth together, and the part of the Golden Horn outside the bridges looks a little like them all. Flags of every country fly there, beside stone quays or moored to red buoys in the open. Trim liners and workaday tramps bring in a little atmosphere from the Black Sea, the Mediterranean, the far-off Atlantic. Tugs puff busily about. Cranes take

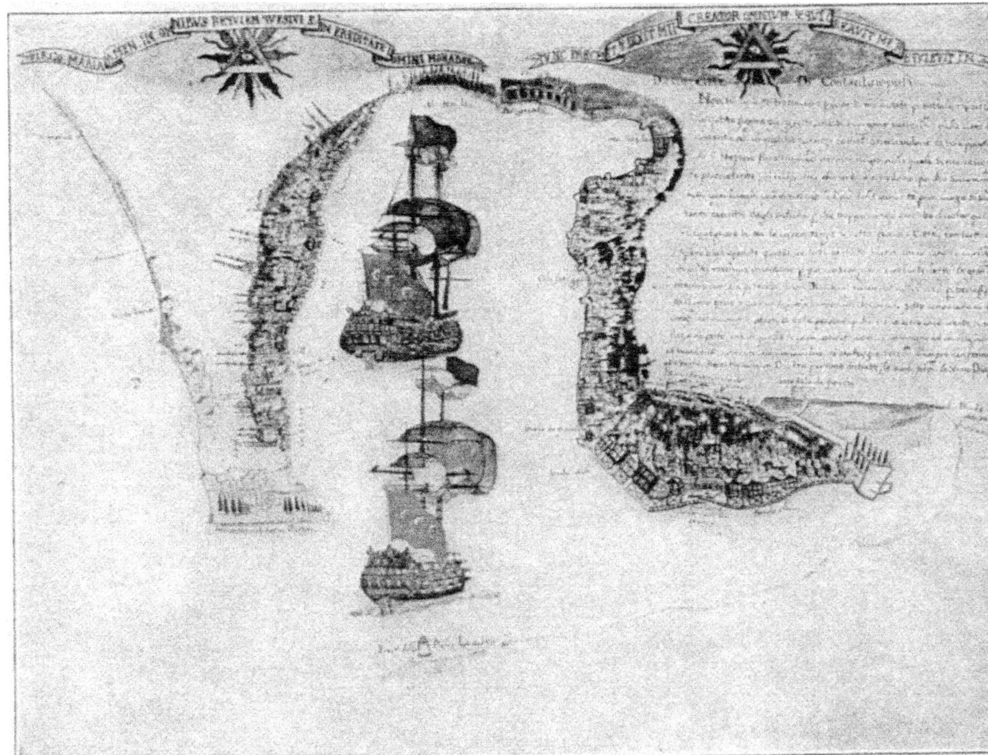

From the *Specchio Marittimo* of Bartolommeo Prato

The Golden Horn

up the white man's burden as naturally as in any other port. Every harbour brings the ends of the earth together in its own way, however, and so does this. If you happen to tie up at a buoy instead of alongside, you will soon make the acquaintance of a gentleman in a rowboat very much like other rowboats, fringed with bumpers. This gentleman will probably be a Greek, though he may be anything, and he will demand all the gold of Ophir to set you ashore, getting not a little of it in the end. If you prefer to stay on board you will very likely make the acquaintance of another gentleman in a trimmer boat, painted blue and green, pointed at both ends and provided at each with an upstanding post which is convenient for tow-lines. This is a bumboat, and the Maltese in command will furnish you almost anything in the way of supplies — for a consideration. Should you have a cargo to land, you must deal with a yet more redoubtable race of beings. These men are Laz, a race of daredevils from the region of Trebizond, which was the ancient Colchis. You may know them by their tight black clothes, by the sharpness of their shoes, ending in a leather thong, and by the pointed hood of two long flaps which they wear knotted about their heads like a turban. Some of them are Mohammedans and some of them are Christians, but all of them speak a mysterious language of their own. Two sorts of boats are peculiar to these brothers of Medea: the *mahona*, a single-masted scow with a raking stem, and a smaller snub-nosed *salapouri*. I do not include the mad little open *taka*, broad of beam, high of board, and gay with painted stars, in which they are not afraid to run down the coast from their own country. Woe be you if you happen to displease a *mahonaji*, for he belongs to a guild that holds the commerce of the port in no gentle hand. He will neither discharge your goods nor let any one else, if so it seem good to him, and not even the government can make him change his mind.

The lightermen are by no means the only guild in the Golden Horn, though I suppose they are doomed to

Lighters

follow the way of the others. These old organisations still persist among the different kinds of watermen. Each guild has its own station, like the *traghetti* of Venice, each has a headquarters, or *lonja* — which is a corruption of the Italian *loggia* — and each a series of officers headed by a *kehaya*. This dignitary takes no actual part, as a usual thing, in the work of the guild, but earns the lion's share of the profits, and in return therefor protects the guild in high quarters. Under the old régime the *kebayas* of the principal guilds were members of the palace camarilla. In older times still the guilds were required to contribute heavily to the expenses of war in recognition of their privileges, and even now the lightermen and the

Sandals

custom-house porters are obliged to give the War Department so many men on so many days a week.

The outer bridge draws a sharp boundary-line between the cosmopolitan part of the harbour and the part where local colour is the rule. For any one who takes an interest in boats and those who have to do with them, the bit of water between Yeni Jami and the Arsenal is one of the happiest hunting-grounds in the world. This is the true home of the water guilds. The lightermen's headquarters are here, and their four anchored flotillas are a distinct note of the scene. Here also are the headquarters of many lesser watermen such as row you across the Horn for a piastre — or even less if you do not insist on a boat to yourself. The smartest ones have their station just inside the bridge. Most of their boats are trim skiffs, gay with carving and gilding, and fitted out with velvet cushions and summer awnings. This skiff, called a *sandal,* has almost ousted the true boat of the Golden Horn, which is the legendary caïque. I am sorry to say it, because I do not like to see the Turks change their own customs for European ones, but truth compels me to add that I have lolled too much in gondolas to be an unbridled admirer of the caïque. A gondola is infinitely more roomy and comfortable, and it has the great advantage of not forcing you to sit nose to nose with a perspiring boatman. The caïque is swifter and easier in its gait, however, and, when long enough for two or three pairs of oars, not even a gondola is more graceful. Caïques still remain at the ferries higher up the Golden Horn—and grubby enough most of them are, for they have fallen greatly in the world since bridges were built and steamers began to ply.

If I were really to open the chapter of caïques I would never come to the end. The word is a generic one, and applies to an infinity of boats, from the stubby little single-oared *piadeh kaïk* of the Golden Horn ferries to the big *pazar kaïk.* You may admire this boat, and the carving that decorates it, and its magnificent incurving beak, and the tassel that should dangle therefrom, at the wharves of Yemish, off the Dried Fruit Bazaar. They all come, early in the morning, from different villages on the Bosphorus, rowed by men who stand to the heavy-handled oars and drop with them to their backs. There are also caïques with sails, undecked boats built on the lines of a fishing caïque, that bring fruit and vegetables from the villages of the Marmora. They are prettier to look at than to navigate, for they have no keel and their mainsail is a balloon, to be pulled from one side to the

Caïques

other of a fearsome stick, boom and gaff in one, that spears the heavens. The human part of the caïque has its picturesque points as well. The sail caïques are navigated more often than not by Greeks. As with fishing caïques, it depends on the village they come from. The men of the bazaar caïques are all Turks, and none of them ever saw a boat till he took ship for Constantinople. What is odder yet, the same is true of most of the ordinary boatmen of the inner Horn. Manv of them are Laz;

many others are Turkish peasants from the hinterland of the Black Sea. Those from one village or district enter one guild, serving a long apprenticeship before they can be masters of their own craft.

Another boundless chapter is that of the larger vessels that frequent the inner Horn. You get an inkling

Sailing caïques

of how boundless it is when you stand on the bridge in front of Yeni Jami and look at the shipping that crowds along the shores. A perfect museum of navigation is there. Modern steamers lie beside the caravels of Columbus — as a matter of fact, the Greeks still call them *karavia* — and motor-boats make way for vessels whose build and rig can have changed very little since the days of the Argo. One notable armada is anchored off Odoun Kapan, the wood market, under the mosque of Süleïman, and the most notable part of it, for me, is always made up of certain ships called *gagalî* because their bows have the curve of a parrot's beak. They have two eyes, like the *bragozzi* of the Adriatic, and their tremendously tilted bowsprit starts from a little one side of the bow.

Galleons that might have sailed out of the Middle Ages anchor there now

But what is most decorative about them is the stern, a high triangle adorned with much painting and carving and an open balustrade along the top, from either end of which a beam juts out horizontally over the sea in the line of the hull.

One or two minor fleets, made up of small Greek *alamánas* or Turkish *chektîrmehs*, are usually tied up off other Stamboul markets. But the most imposing one of all hides the Galata shore. It begins, distinguishably enough, just beyond the landing-stage of the skiffs I have mentioned, with a squadron of lighters and the raft that makes a bobbing street between certain tubby-looking sailing vessels. *Bombarda* is the name of their class, or *vouvartha*, if you prefer, and they bring oil and wine from as far away as the Greek islands. Beyond them rises so intricate a maze of rigging as would have baffled even an old German engraver. I wonder a man can ever find his own ship there, so closely does one elbow another, nor in any single row, all the way to Azap Kapou. This is where the Genoese had shipyards of old, and galleons that might have sailed out of the Middle Ages anchor there now for repairs, with craft that look a little more like Western seas. I despair of ever really knowing anything about them — of ever being able to tell at first shot a *maouna* of the Black Sea from a *maouna* of the White Sea, or a *saïka* from either, or to discover that Flying Dutchman of a craft of whose existence I have been credibly informed, namely, the Ship of the Prophet Noah.

The Black and the White Sea play a great part in these matters, the White Sea meaning the Marmora and the Mediterranean. In the days when guilds were more important than they are now the Captains of the White Sea were the navy, while the Captains of the Black Sea were the merchant marine, and that must have something to do with the fact that the watermen of the Golden Horn still come from the littoral of the Black Sea. The Prophet Noah also, whom I have just mentioned, is likewise involved in matters maritime, as being the father of ship-builders. The archangel Gabriel, according to Mohammedan tradition, taught him how to model the keel of the ark from the breast-

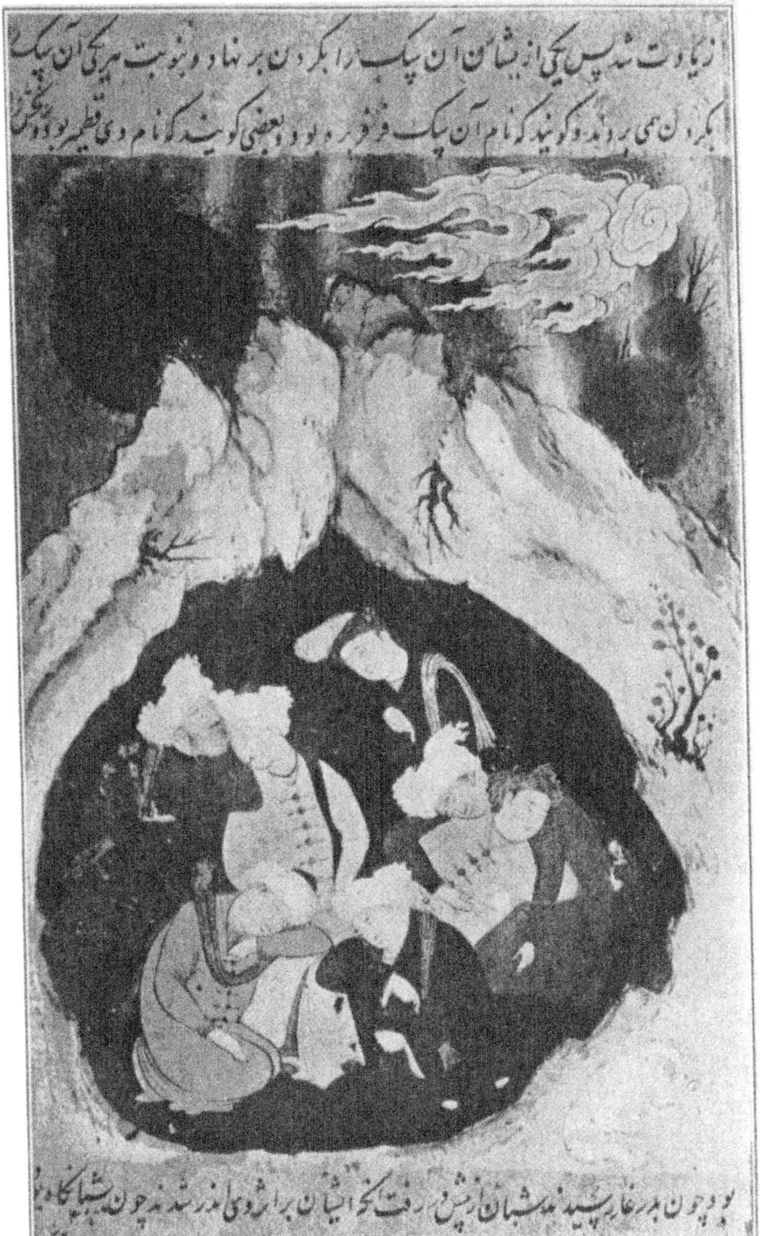

By courtesy of the Bibliothèque Nationale, Paris

The Seven Sleepers of Ephesus

From a Persian miniature

bone of a goose, and wrote talismanic invocations on different parts of the ship — as "O Steadfast One" on the planks, and "O Allotter of the True Path" upon the rudder. The patrons of Turkish seamen are, if you please, the Seven Sleepers of Ephesus! Mohammed seems to have entertained a sympathy for these mythic beings, whose adventures are told in the eighteenth chapter of the Koran. The name of their dog, somewhat variously known as Kitmir or Al Rakim, used to be written on the outside of letters in order to ensure their safe passage across the sea, and this happy animal is one of the few to whom paradise is specifically promised. Von Hammer accounts for the association of so curious a company with seamen on the ground that a verse of the Koran mentions their entering a ship. But astrologically, I believe, they are related to the constellation of the Great Bear; whence it is clear enough why they should be concerned with navigation. It is further to be noted of the seamen of the Golden Horn that whether they belong to the Black Sea or the White, and whether they sacrifice to the Seven Sleepers or to St. Nicholas, the jargon of their trade is almost purely Italian. Even the boatmen in the harbour shout *sía* when they want each other to back water, not suspecting that the gondoliers in Venice do exactly the same — though the gondoliers may not spell it quite as I do. The names of a few kinds of ships and of a few parts of them have been slightly Turkified or Grecicised, as the case may be, but an Italian sailor would be lost only on a steamer. There a Turkish captain uses English words as glibly as you or I. On a motor-boat, however, he would pass to French.

It is rather surprising that the Greeks, who were always a seafaring people, should have taken over so much of the ship language of their Latin conquerors.

The case of the Turks is less surprising, for they are tent men born. Nor have their coreligionaries in general ever been great adventurers upon the deep. The Caliph Omar even went so far as to forbid them sea voyages. Nevertheless, the science of navigation owes much to the Arabs, and we get from them our words arsenal and admiral — meaning "house of construction" and "prince of the sea" — while some of the greatest exploits of the Turks were connected with the sea. The deep valley of Kassîm Pasha, inside the Azap Kapou bridge, is supposed to have been the final scene of one of the most celebrated of those exploits, the one successfully carried out by Sultan Mehmed II during his siege of the city, when he hauled a squadron of eighty galleys out of the Bosphorus, dragged them over the hills in a night, and relaunched them inside the chain that locked the Golden Horn. That chain may be seen to-day in the military museum of St. Irene. Kassîm Pasha does not seem to me altogether to fit the contemporary descriptions, although it would offer the easiest route. There is no doubt, however, about the famous arsenal that sits solidly at the mouth of the valley to this day. How many days it will continue to sit there is another matter, for its long water-front may become more valuable for commercial purposes than for those of a modern shipyard. It was founded by Sultan Selim I in 1515, was enlarged by his son Süleïman the Magnificent, and reached the climax of its importance under his grandson Selim II. Those were the great days when the Captains of the White Sea were the terror of the Mediterranean, and when a disaster like the battle of Lepanto, in which the Turks lost two hundred and twenty-four ships and thirty thousand men, could not shake the empire. The Grand Vizier Sokollî Mehmed Pasha said to the Venetian Balio, apropos of that battle and of the conquest of Cyprus by the Turks which preceded it: "There is a great difference between your loss and ours. In taking a kingdom from you it is an arm of yours that we have cut off, while you, in beating our fleet, have merely shaved our beard." Nor was this a piece of rodomontade. The winter after Lepanto, 1571–2, one hundred and fifty-eight galleys of different sizes were laid down in the Arsenal. And when that famous Prince of the Sea Kîlîj Ali Pasha expressed a doubt as to whether he could find the rigging and anchors he needed, the Grand Vizier said to him: "Lord Admiral, the wealth and power of the empire are such that if it were necessary we would make anchors of silver, cables of silk, and sails of satin."

A few relics of this fallen greatness are to be seen in the museum of the Arsenal, some distance up the Horn from the Admiralty proper. Some wonderful figureheads of galleys are there, flags and pennants of different sorts, a chart of the time of the Conqueror painted on parchment, a few interesting models, and one or two of the big ship lanterns that were the sign of the dignity of an admiral, corresponding to the horsetails of the *vezirs*. A pasha of three lanterns, however, was a much more important personage than a pasha of three tails. Most picturesque of all are a number of great gilded caïques, with swooping bows and high sterns, in which the sultans used to go abroad. The largest of them is said to have been a Venetian galley. It has twenty-two rowlocks on either side, and each oar was rowed by three or four men. As a matter of fact, the long horizontal overhang of the bow does look rather like some of the models in the Arsenal at Venice, while two lions guard the stern. But the lions have no wings, they were always a favourite ornament of Turkish as of Byzantine galleys, and the lines of the hull are precisely those of any caïque. As to the imperial cabin at the stern there is no doubt. It is a triple cupola rather, supported by columns, and all inlaid with tortoise-shell and mother-of-pearl and lumps of garnet glass. Reclining under this wonderful canopy Sultan Mehmed IV used to go about the Bosphorus, while over a hundred men in front of him rose and fell with their oars. What a splash they must have made!

The Arsenal has given a certain colour to the whole suburb of Kassim Pasha. It is chiefly inhabited by naval officers, who under Abd ül Hamid II outnumbered their men! There is a quarter of it called *Kalliounjou Koullouk*, which means the Guardhouse of the Galleon Men. There are also a number of fountains in Kassim Pasha carved with three ship lanterns to show who built them. And not the least famous of the Princes of the Sea lies there himself beside the mosque he raised out of the spoils of his piracies. This Pialeh Pasha was by birth a Croat and the son of a shoemaker. Captured as a boy by the Janissaries, he grew up to command the fleets of his captors, to conquer Chio and sixty-six other islands, and to marry the daughter of Sultan Selim II. But he failed to take Malta from the Knights of St. John, and it was the bitterness of his life. His mosque is almost unknown, so far does it lie in the back of Kassîm Pasha. They say that Pialeh dug a canal to its doors. They also say that he wanted to make it like a ship. The mosque, at all events, is different from all other mosques I know. The nave is shallower than it is wide, its six equal domes being held up by two central pillars like masts, while the single minaret rises out of the wall opposite the *mihrab*. The *mihrab* itself, contained in no apse, is perhaps the finest tiled *mihrab* I know. Some of the tiles have been stolen, however, and the mosque in general has a pillaged appearance. I thought from the bareness of the entrance wall that a large part of the magnificent frieze of blue and white tiles, an inscription by the famous Hassan Chelibi, must have been stolen

The *mihrab* of Pialeh Pasha

too, until the *imam* told me that the frieze originally 11
stopped there, as no true believer may turn his back on any part of the Koran. The outside of the mosque is also unusual, with its deep porch, two-storied at either end. It is the largest mosque on the left bank of the Golden Horn, and even without its historical and architectural interest it would be worth a visit for the charm

of its plane-shaded yard and the cypress grove behind the mosque where Pialeh lies in a neglected *türbeh*.

I perceive that I am now embarked on a chapter more boundless than any. Yet how can one speak of the Golden Horn and be silent with regard to its shores? I have already written three chapters about one of them, to be sure, and I propose to write a fourth about the other. But the quiet inner reaches of the Golden Horn contain much less in the way of water life, and depend much more upon the colour of their banks. This colour must have been vivider before steam lengthened the radius of the dweller in Stamboul and when the Golden Horn was still a favourite resort of the court. Nevertheless there is a great deal of character in the quiet, in the not too prosperous and evidently superseded settlements that follow the outer bustle of the harbour. One of the most characteristic of them is the Greek quarter of Phanar — or Fener, as the Turks call it. In both languages the name means lantern or lighthouse. It originally pertained to a gate of the city wall, being derived from a beacon anciently marking a spit of land in front of the gate. There stood more anciently an inner fortified enclosure in this vicinity called the Petrion. A convent of that name once existed, I know not whether founded by a certain Petrus, a noble of the time of Justinian, who lived or owned property in this neighbourhood. It was here that the Venetians were able to effect their entrance into the city in 1203 and 1204, by throwing bridges from their galleys to the battlements of the wall. No galley would be able to come so close to the wall to-day. But the wall is still there, or large parts of it. And behind it, occupying perhaps the site of the old Petrion, the Greek Patriarchs of Constantinople have had their headquarters for the past three hundred years.

You would never guess, to look at the rambling wooden *konak* or the simple church beside it, that you were looking at the Vatican of the Greek world. Neither would you suspect that the long alley skirting the water, hemmed in between dark old stone houses with heavily

Old houses of Phanar

barred windows and upper stories jutting out toward each other on massive stone brackets, was once the Corso of Constantinople. That was when the great Greek families that furnished princes to Moldavia and Wallachia and dragomans to the European embassies and to the Porte maintained the splendour of a court around the Patriarchate. The ambassadors of the tributary principalities lived there, too, and a house is still pointed out as the Venetian embassy. A very different air blows in the Phanar to-day. Many of the Phanariotes emigrated to Greece or otherwise disappeared at the time of the Greek revolution, while those of their descendants who still remain in Constantinople prefer the heights of Pera. None but the poorest, together with Armenians and Jews not a few, now live in those old stone houses. They are worth looking at, however — and I hope prefectures bursting with modernity and the zeal of street-widening will remember it. None of them, I believe, dates from before the fifteenth century, but after the Palace of the Porphyrogenitus they are all that is left to give an idea what a Byzantine house may have looked like. They also suggest how the old wooden house of Stamboul may have come by its curving bracket. If none of them are very decorative on the outside, we must remember that the house of a mediæval Greek in Stamboul was very literally his castle. Some of the houses originally contained no stairs at all, unless secret ones. Beside the stone house stood a wooden one which contained the stairs, and each floor of the two houses communicated by a narrow passage and two or three heavy iron doors. In case of fire or massacre the inmates betook themselves to the top floor of their stone house and barricaded their iron doors until the coast was clear. Occasionally it was so clear that no wooden house and no stairs were left them. But you would never suspect from outside what pillars and arches, what monumental fireplaces, what plaster mouldings, what marquetry of mother-of-pearl, what details of painting and gilding and carving those top floors hide. And under many of them gardens still run green to the water's edge.

Of a very different character is the hollow of converging valleys outside the city wall where lies, at the end of the Golden Horn proper, the suburb of Eyoub Soultan. Eyoub Soultan, *anglice* Prince Job, takes its name from a friend and standard-bearer of the Prophet who took part in the third Arab siege of Constantinople in 668 and fell outside the walls. Of this good man and

The outer court of Eyoub

his last resting-place so many legendary things are related that I don't know where my chapter would end if I repeated only the few of them I have heard. I can only say that when Sultan Mehmed II was making his own siege, eight hundred years later, he opportunely discovered the burial-place of the saintly warrior. This discovery having stimulated the flagging ardour of the besiegers, with what results we know, the Conqueror built a splendid mausoleum above the grave of the Prophet's friend and beside it the first of the imperial mosques. To this, the holiest shrine of Islam in Constantinople, the sultans come for that ceremony which takes for them the place of a coronation—to be girded with the sword of Osman. So holy a shrine is it that until the re-establishment of the constitution in 1908 no Christian had ever entered that mosque except in disguise, or so much as its outer court. Even now it is not easy for a Christian to see the inside of the *türbeh*. I have not, at all events. But I count myself happy to have seen its outer wall of blue and green tiles, shaded by broad eaves and pierced in the centre by an intricate grille of brass which shines where the fingers of the faithful pass over the letters of the creed. And I must confess that I lay up no grudge against the *imams* for keeping me out. I cannot say it is for the same reason that another man of God, with whom I sometimes sit in front of another tomb in Stamboul, once gave me for never having been himself in the tomb of Eyoub: that he did not feel himself worthy. It is, rather, an inconsistent feeling that I am not sorry if some things and some places still be held sacred in the world. On one side of the tomb, opening out of the same tiled wall, is a *sebil* where an attendant waits to give cups of cold water to the thirsty. On the other side a window opens through a grille of small green bronze hexagons into a patch of garden where a few rose-bushes stand among graves. And in the centre of the quadrangle stand two enormous plane-trees, or what is left of them, planted there by the Conqueror five hundred years ago. The mosque itself is not very interesting, having been restored too many times. It contains one much-prized relic, however, consisting of a print of

Eyoub

the Prophet's foot in stone. Beside the mosque and the forecourt is a second court, larger and irregular in shape, also shaded by plane-trees, where, furthermore, are a fountain of ablution and painted gravestones in railings and a colony of pigeons that are pampered like those of St. Mark's.

The quarter that has grown up around this mosque is one of the most picturesque in Constantinople. No very notable houses are there, but they all have the grave dignity which the Turks contrive to put into everything they do, and the streets take a tone from the great number of pious institutions that line them, interspersed with cypresses and tombs. The quarter is indeed, more than any other, the Pantheon of Stamboul, so many important personages have chosen to be buried near the friend of the Prophet. The pious Mehmed V, however, is the first sultan who has chosen to lie to the last day in the company of all those good and famous men. Several of the most notable mausoleums, though the most neglected, are of the period of Süleïman I, and built by Sinan. In one of them, separated from a little library by a porch of precious tiles, lies the Bosnian slave, nicknamed from his birthplace Sokollî Mehmed, whose destiny it was to become the Treasurer of Süleïman, successor to the terrible admiral Barbarossa, and Grand Vizier of the empire. When his imperial master died on the battle-field of Szigeth, in Hungary, Mehmed Pasha succeeded in hiding the fact until Selim II could reach Constantinople. The young sultan was the worst who had yet ascended the throne, but he stood in such awe of his father's great minister that Sokollî ruled the empire throughout Selim's reign and part of that of Mourad III. Three hundred years before De Lesseps he conceived the idea of the Suez Canal, and might have carried it out had he lived. He was murdered in 1579 — at the instigation, it was whispered, of the jealous and cruel Lala Moustafa Pasha. The latter also has a place in this Turkish Pantheon. He was the barbarian who flayed alive Marcantonio Bragadin, the heroic defender of Famagusta, and stuffed his skin with straw. Having been paraded before the troops in Cyprus and hung up in the Arsenal at Kassîm Pasha for the edification of the galley-slaves, this bloody trophy was at last presented to the Venetians, who gave it honourable burial in their own Pantheon of SS. Giovanni e Paolo. Lala Moustafa was himself of Christian origin, being of the same Serb race as Sokollî Mehmed Pasha, the admiral Pialeh Pasha, and still another son-in-law of the imperial house who lies in Eyoub, Ferhad Pasha, a vizier of Mourad III and Mehmed IV. Although not born in the faith, Ferhad Pasha was renowned for the beauty of his calligraphy. Among this group of mausoleums is that of one real Turk, the celebrated Sheï'h ül Islam Ebou Sououd Effendi, who drew up and interpreted the laws of Süleïman.

The *türbehs* cluster so thickly between the mosque and the water that one avenue is lined by nothing else, and from it little paved alleys wander away between crowded gravestones and arching trees. Few of the trees are cypresses here. The cypresses inhabit a hill beyond this silent quarter, and through them climbs the most picturesque street in Eyoub. Toward the top it forks. Whichever way you take, you will do well, particularly in the spring, when the left-hand lane brings you into sight of a blossoming valley of fruit-trees. But you will do better after all to take the right-hand turn and climb a little farther, the cypresses and gravestones thinning as you climb, till you come to a coffee-house that did not need Pierre Loti to make it famous. Any man who gazes from a height upon leagues of space and many habitations of his fellow men is forced into philosophy. Here, however, you sip in with your coffee strange things indeed as you look down from your high cemetery edge, past cypresses and turbaned stones and

The cemetery of Eyoub

the minarets of the mosque and the procession of siege-battered towers scaling the slope beyond, upon the whole picture of the Golden Horn framed between its two beetling cities. The outer bridge, to be sure, is cut off by the curve of Galata; but the heights of Scutari, or sometimes those of the Bithynian Olympus, are visible to remind you what a meeting-place of nations is here.

On this hilltop stood in old times the castle of Cosmidion, where Godfrey of Bouillon and Bohemund stopped with their men on the way to the first crusade. The castle took its name from the adjoining church of SS. Cosmas and Damian, built by Theodosius the Younger and rebuilt with magnificence by Justinian. In times still older this was the hill called Semistra — or so I shall choose to believe until some one proves me wrong. Walking along its bare crest, where you sometimes meet camels marching strangely in from the villages of Thrace, you overlook that last reach of the Golden Horn which used to be called Argyrolimnai, the Silver Pools. Two small streams come together here, the Cydaris and the Barbyses as they once were called, and they played a particular part in the mythology of Byzantium. Io, fleeing from the jealousy of Hera, gave birth to her daughter Keroessa at the foot of the hill where the two streams meet. The child was nursed by Semistra, who gave her name to the hill in question, and in whose honour an altar anciently stood at the meeting-place of the rivers. Keroessa became in turn the mother of Byzas, founder of Byzantium. The father of Byzas was no less a personage than Poseidon, god of the sea, and the son married Phidalia, daughter of the river Barbyses. How it happened that Byzas also came from so far away as Megara I do not pretend to know; but in the name Keroessa, which seems to be connected with the metamorphosis of Io, we have the mythic origin of the name of the Golden Horn.

The two rivers are now called Ali Bey Souyou and Kiat Haneh Souyou, and a power-house has taken the place of the altar of Semistra. The upper branches of both valleys are bridged by a number of aqueducts, of all periods from Justinian to Süleïman, and emperors and sultans alike loved to take refuge in this pleasant wilderness. How it may have been with the Greeks I do not know, but for the Turks spring has always been the season of the rivers. The northern extremity of Eyoub, bordering the Silver Pools, is still called *Behariéh*, from a spring palace of Sultan Mahmoud I that exists no more. It is with the name of his uncle Ahmed III, however, that the two valleys are chiefly associated. The last words of Nero might more justly have been uttered by this humane and splendour-loving prince — *qualis artifex pereo!* He delighted above all things in flowers, water, and illuminations — though I cannot conceal that he also cherished an extreme admiration for breathing beauty. He was one of the greatest builders who have reigned in Constantinople, and he had the good fortune to discover a grand vizier of like tastes with himself. It happened that an intelligent young envoy of theirs, known by the curious name of Twenty-eight Mehmed, from the number of his years when he signed the Peace of Passarowitz went, in 1720, on a special embassy to Paris. He brought back such accounts of the court of Louis XV, such pictures and presents also, as to change the whole course of Ottoman architecture. So vivid a description in particular did the ambassador give of the new palace of Versailles and of its older rival at Marly-le-Roi, that Ahmed III resolved to imitate them. He had already built a seat on the banks of the Ali Bey Souyou, whose magnificent planes and cypresses may still be admired there. He then turned his attention to the Kiat Haneh valley, where he played strange tricks with the river, laid out gardens, built a palace, and commanded his courtiers to follow his example — *à la* Louis XIV and the Signs of the Zodiac. There grew up as by magic a continuous line of villas and gardens from the village of Kiat

Haneh to that of Sütlüjeh, opposite Eyoub. And the fête which the sultan gave when he inaugurated this new pleasure-ground was the most splendid of the many that marked his long reign. It befell him, however, in 1730, to be dethroned. Whereupon a fanatical mob asked permission of his successor to burn the palaces of Kiat Haneh. Mahmoud I replied that he could not allow the palaces to be burned, lest other nations draw unfavourable conclusions with regard to the inner harmony of the empire, but that the palaces might be destroyed! They accordingly were — one hundred and seventy-three of them. Of so much magnificence not one stone now remains upon another, and he who rows past the Silver Pools to-day is almost asphyxiated by the fumes of the brick-kilns that have replaced the pleasances of old.

As for the river itself, it comes nearer deserving the name which Europeans have given it, of the Sweet Waters of Europe. Why they did so I do not know, unless they thought the real name too prosaic. Kiat Haneh means Paper House, from a mill originally built there by Süleïman I. The valley it waters has remained an open meadow of occasional trees — perhaps in accordance with the old Turkish usage, whereby any place where the sultan pitches his tent belongs thereafter to his people to the end of time. I presume the meadow of Kiat Haneh is destined ultimately to become a city park. In the meantime a palace of Abd ül Aziz, looking rather like a frosted cake, stands in the walled park of Ahmed III. The huge rooms are empty of furniture, and no one is there to watch the river splash down its marble cascades except two sour custodians and the gentle old *imam* of the adjoining mosque. But for a few weeks in spring, beginning with the open-air festival of Hîdîr Eless, the lower part of the valley is a favourite place of resort. Sunday and Friday are the popular days. Then arbours of saplings thatched with dried boughs follow the curve of the river; then picnic parties spread rugs or matting on the grass, partaking of strange meats while masters of pipe and drum enchant their ears; then groups of

Kiat Haneh

Turkish ladies, in gay silks, dot the sward like tulips; then itinerant venders of fruit, of sweets, of nuts, of ice-cream, do hawk about their wares; then fortune-tellers, mountebanks, bear tamers, dancers, Punch and Judy shows may be seen; and boats pass and repass on the river like carriages on the Corso. Most of them are *sandals* of the smarter kind. But once in a while the most elegant craft in the world skims into sight — a three-oared caïque, with a piece of embroidered velvet, whose corner tassels trail in the water, thrown over the little deck behind the seat. The *kaïkjis* are handsome fellows, in fuller white cotton knickerbockers than you can imagine, in white stockings, in shirts of crinkly Broussa gauze and short sleeveless jackets embroidered with gold.

Most of the ladies are in the modern Turkish costume, with a kind of silk mantilla of the same material as the dress falling from the head to the waist. The effect is very Spanish and graceful — more so than when the ladies wear a white scarf over their hair and a long garment as shapeless as a waterproof. In these degenerate days veils are more often absent than not. I must warn you, however, that the Sweet Waters of Europe are not the Sweet Waters of Asia. I remember noticing one day on the river a gaudy little skiff rowed by two young and gaily costumed boatmen. In the stern sat an extremely fat Turkish lady, steering. She was dressed decorously in black, and the black veil thrown back from her face allowed every one to remark that she was neither in her first youth nor particularly handsome. Yet boatmen snickered as she passed, and rowdies called after her in slang which it seemed to me should not be used to a lady. I said as much to my *kaïkji*, who told me that the lady was a famous *demi-mondaine*, named Madam Falcon, and that for the rest I must never expect such good manners at Kiat Haneh as at Gyök Sou. I must confess that I looked at Madam Falcon with some interest the next time we passed; for the Turkish half-world is of all half-worlds the most invisible, and so far as I knew I had never seen a member of it before. Madam Falcon paid no attention to the curiosity she aroused. Sitting there impassively in her black dress, with her smooth yellow skin, she made one think of a graven image, of some Indian Bouddha in old ivory. So venerable a person she seemed, so benevolent, so decorous and dead to the world, that she only made her half-world more remote and invisible than ever. But she was a sign — in spite of the smart brougham driving slowly along the shore with a Palace eunuch sitting on the box — that the great days of Kiat Haneh are gone. Nevertheless it has, during its brief time of early green, a colour of its own. And the serpentine river, winding between tufts of trees and under Japanesey wooden bridges, is always a pleasant piece of line and light in a spring sun. But beware of the coffee-house men on the shore! For their season is short, and if they catch you they will skin you alive.

V

THE MAGNIFICENT COMMUNITY

Galata, que mes yeux désiraient dès longtemps. . .
— ANDRÉ CHÉNIER.

In Pera sono tre malanni:
Peste, fuoco, dragomanni.
— LOCAL PROVERB.

IT is not the fashion to speak well of Pera and Galata. A good Turk will sigh of another that he has gone to Pera, by way of saying that he has gone to the dogs. A foreign resident will scarcely admit that so much as the view is good. Even a Perote born pretends not to love his Grande Rue if he happens to have read Loti or Claude Farrère. And tourists are supposed to have done the left bank of the Golden Horn when they have watched the Sultan drive to mosque and have giggled at the whirling dervishes. A few of the more thoroughgoing will, perhaps, take the trouble to climb Galata Tower or to row up the Sweet Waters of Europe. For my part, however, who belong to none of these categories, I am perverse enough to find Pera and Galata a highly superior place of habitation. I consider that their greatest fault is to lie under the shadow of Stamboul — though that gives them one inestimable advantage which Stamboul herself lacks, namely the view of the dark old city crowned by her imperial mosques. Pera — and I now mean the whole promontory between the Golden Horn and the Bosphorus — Pera occupies a really magnificent site, it has a history of its own, it contains monuments that would make the fortune of any other town, and it fairly drips with that modern pigment known as local colour. Who knows, it may even be destined to inherit the renown of the older city. Stamboul tends to diminish, whereas Pera grows and has unlimited room for growing. The left bank is already the seat of the Sultan and of the bulk of the commerce and finance of the capital. Moreover, the battles of the revolution fought there in 1909 give the place a peculiar interest in the eyes of the Young Turks. On that soil, less encumbered than Stamboul with the débris of history, they may find conditions more favourable for the city of their future.

If the story of Pera cannot compare with that of the grey mother city, it nevertheless can boast associations of which communities more self-important might be proud. Jason stopped there on his way to get the Golden Fleece, and after him Beshiktash was known in antiquity as Iasonion. In the valley behind that picturesque suburb there later existed a famous laurel grove, sacred of course to Apollo, who, with Poseidon, was patron of Byzantium. The sun-god was also worshipped at a sacred fount which still exists in Galata, within the enclosure of the Latin church of St. George. Legend makes this spring the scene of the martyrdom of St. Irene, daughter of a Roman ruler, who was put to death for refusing to sacrifice to Apollo and who became herself the patron saint of the new Christian city of Constantinople. Christianity is said to have been brought there by no less a person than the apostle Andrew. He is also reputed to have died in Galata, though another tradition makes Patras the scene of his death; but in any case he was buried in Constantine's Church of the Holy Apostles. The church of St. Irene where he preached, somewhere in the vicinity of Top Haneh, was restored with magnificence by Justinian. An earlier emperor, Leo the Great, had already built in the neighbourhood of Beshiktash the celebrated church of St. Mamas, together with a palace that was long a favourite resort of the imperial family. In the light of recent history it is interesting to recall that Krum, King of Bulgaria, sacked and burned the suburb of St. Mamas, with the rest of Thrace, in 811.

Among the antiquities of the town, its names have been the subject of much research and confusion. Pera is a Romaic word meaning opposite or beyond, and first applied indiscriminately with Galata to the rural suburb on the north shore of the Golden Horn. This hill was also called Sykai, from the fig-trees that abounded there; and when the mortar-loving Justinian beautified and walled the suburb, he renamed it after himself. With regard to the word Galata there has been infinite dispute. I myself thought I had solved the question when I went to Genoa and saw steep little alleys, for all the world like those I knew in Genoese Galata, which were named *Calata* — a descent to the sea — and of which the local dialect made the *c* a *g*. But the accent was different, and I lived to learn that the name, as that of a castle on the water's edge, has been found in Byzantine MSS. dating from two hundred years earlier than the time Genoa founded her colony there. Villehardouin also speaks of the tower of "Galathas," which the crusaders stormed as a preliminary to their capture of Constantinople. It apparently stood in the vicinity of the custom-house, and to it was attached the chain that padlocked the Golden Horn. I would like to believe that the name came from Brennus and his Gauls, or Galatians, who passed this way with fire and sword in the third century B. C. There is more certainty, however, with regard to its own derivatives. The Italian word *galetta* is one of them, more or less familiar in English and very common in its French form of *galette.* Another French word, *galetas*, is also derived from Galata, meaning a high garret and hence a poor tenement. Belonging at first to the castle alone, the name seems to have spread to the whole surrounding settlement. It now applies to the lower part of the hill, formerly enclosed by the Genoese wall, while Pera is the newer town on top of the hill, "beyond" the old.

The history of the town we know began in the Latin colonies that originally fringed the opposite shore of the Golden Horn. Constantinople has always been a cosmopolitan city. The emperors themselves were of many races and the empire they governed was as full of unassimilated elements as it is to-day. Then even from so far away as England and Denmark men came to trade in the great city that was named from a citizen of York. It was natural that Italians should come in the greatest number, though they felt less and less at home as the emperors became more and more Greek. The people of Amalfi and Ancona, the Florentines, the Genoese, the Lombards, the Pisans, and the Venetians, all had important colonies in Constantinople. And by the twelfth century four of them at least had their own settlements between Seraglio Point and the Azap Kapou Bridge. The easternmost were the Genoese, whose quarter was near the present railway station; next came the Pisans, then the men of Amalfi — not far from Yeni Jami — and last the Venetians.

The Venetian colony was long the most important.

Basil II, the Slayer of the Bulgarians, as early as 991 granted to Venice definite commercial privileges, which were greatly extended a hundred years later by Alexius II in gratitude for the help the Republic had given him against Robert Guiscard and the Normans. The colony occupied an important strip of water-front, from the western side of the outer bridge to the anchorage of the wood galleons under the Süleïmanieh. During the Latin occupation the Venetians naturally extended their borders, since the Republic had taken so important a part in the Fourth Crusade; and the Doge now added to his other titles that of Lord of a Quarter and a Half of the Roman Empire. But in spite of the Greek restoration of 1261 and the consequent rise of Genoese influence, the Venetians still maintained their foothold. They continued to keep their strip of the Golden Horn and to form an *imperium in imperio* after the manner of foreign colonies in Constantinople to-day. The origin, indeed, of the capitulations which embarrass the Turks so much is perhaps the *Capitulare Baiulis Constantinopolitani* which governed the Balio. This functionary, sent every two years from Venice, was both the viceroy of his colony and minister resident to the emperor. As such he had places of honour in St. Sophia and the Hippodrome, and the Byzantine government allowed him certain supplies. The office continued, in fact, down to the end of the Republic, though under the Turks the Balio was less viceroy than ambassador. No trace seems to remain, however, of that long occupation. I have often wondered if any of the old stone *hans* in the quarter of the Dried Fruit Bazaar go back so far, or the two marble lions which still spout water into a pool in the court of one of them. I have also asked myself whether the small *medresseh* of Kefenek Sinan, with its odd octagonal tower, ever had anything to do with Venice. But the only indisputable relic of Venice I have come across is the *Varda!* the porters shout when they warn you out of their way. That is the Venetian dialect for *guarda*, or "look out" — as any man can verify in Venice to-day.

Lion fountain in the old Venetian quarter

In the growing rivalry between Venice and Genoa the former enjoyed a constant advantage in Constantinople until 1261. Then the Genoese very nearly succeeded in dislodging the Venetians from Stamboul altogether. They took possession of the Venetian churches and destroyed the palace of the Balio, sending its stones to Genoa to be built into the cathedral of San Lorenzo. A generation later they provoked a massacre of the Venetians, in which the Balio himself was killed; and the fleets of the two republics more than once came to blows in the Bosphorus. In the meantime Michael Palæologus had given the Genoese, partly as a reward for their services against the Venetians, partly to get rid of allies so formidable, the town of Perinthos, or Eregli, in the Marmora. About 1267, however, the Genoese succeeded in obtaining the far more important site of Galata. The conditions were that they should not fortify it, and that they should respect the emperor as their suzerain. But the enmity of Venice and the decadence of the Greeks brought it about that Galata presently built walls, captured the old castle of the chain, and otherwise conducted herself as an independent city. The existing Galata Tower marks the highest point of the walls, which were twice enlarged, and which in their greatest extent ran down on one side to Azap Kapou and on the other as far as Top Haneh. The colony was governed by a Podestà, sent every year from Genoa, who, like the Venetian Balio, was also accredited as minister to the emperor.

Galata existed as a flourishing Genoese city for nearly two hundred years. The coming of the Turks in 1453 put an end to the conditions which had made her independence possible. Although cut off from Genoa, however, she did not immediately cease to be an Italian city. Indeed, the Conqueror might have been expected to deal more hardly with the Latin suburb than he did; for while the Galatiotes had entered into amicable relations with the invaders and had in the end voluntarily surrendered, they had also been the backbone of the Greek defence. But in accepting the keys of Galata Sultan Mehmed II assured the colonists the enjoyment of their goods and their faith, merely enjoining them to build no more churches, to forego the use of bells, and to throw down their land fortifications. This last condition seems never to have been carried out.

Genoese archway at Azap Kapou

Under the new régime Galata proceeded to reorganise herself as the *Magnifica Communità di Pera*. The head of this Magnificent Community was a *magnifico*, prior of the Brotherhood of St. Anne, who was aided by a subprior and twelve councillors. Their deliberations chiefly concerned the churches, since in civil affairs they were naturally subject to the Porte. The Rue Voïvoda, the Wall Street of Galata, perpetuates the title of the Turkish functionary who was the superior temporal power of the Magnificent Community. The churches diminished in number, however, as the Latin population dwindled, and by 1682 their administration had passed into the hands of religious orders, or of the Patriarchal Vicar. This dignitary represented that member of the papal court whose title of Patriarch of Constantinople was the last shadow of the Latin occupation. The Patriarchal Vicar has now been succeeded by an Apostolic Delegate. On the other hand, the ambassadors of the Catholic powers, and particularly of France, gradually assumed protection of the Latin colony — which was no longer distinctively Genoese or Venetian. The Magnificent Community, accordingly, ceased to have corporate existence. But the Latin "nation" still forms one of the constituent elements of the Ottoman empire. And while the population of Galata is now more Greek, even more Turkish and Hebrew, than European, it is only within a generation or two that French has begun to supersede Italian as the *lingua franca* of the town, and it still retains an indefinable Italian air.

Of that old Italian town modern Galata contains little enough, except for the fanatic in things of other times. The Tower, of course, the whilom *Torre del Cristo*, is the most visible memorial of the Genoese period. The top, however, has been repeatedly remodelled. This great round keep was built in 1348, during the first enlargement of the walls, which originally extended no farther than the Rue Voïvoda. The Genoese took advantage of the absence of the emperor John Cantacuzene to carry out this contravention of his authority, and they further secured themselves against reprisals by burning his fleet. He built another one in order to punish his so-called vassals, but they defeated it and trailed the emperor's flag in disgrace through the Golden Horn. Galata Tower has now degenerated to the peaceful uses of fire watchers and of those who love a view, the small square at its base being also visited once a year by a Birnam Wood of Christmas-trees. Of the fortifications that originally extended from it there remains here only a reminiscence in the name of the Rue Hendek — Moat Street. The greater part of the walls was torn down in 1864, the inscriptions and coats of arms they contained being ultimately removed to the imperial museum. Further down the hill remnants of masonry still exist, and a few turrets. The garden of the monastery of S. Pierre is bounded by a fragment of the turreted city wall of 1348, while in the wall of S. Benoît is another turret, probably of the wall of 1352. One or two others are to be seen along the water-front at Yagh Kapan. The most picturesque fragment of all, and perhaps the oldest, is behind the bath of Azap Kapou, where a little Turkish street called Akar Cheshmeh — the Fountain Drips — passes through an archway in a high wall. Above the arch is a tablet containing the arms of Genoa — the cross of St. George — between the escutcheons of the two noble houses of Doria and De Merude*; and an olive-tree waves banner-like from the top of the wall.

Galata has always been famous for its fires, to say nothing of its earthquakes. These, and changes of population, with the street-widening and rebuilding of our

* For this information I am indebted to F. W. Hasluck, Esq., of the British School at Athens.

day, have left us very little idea of the architecture of the Genoese colony. In the steep alleys on either side of the Rue Voïvoda are a number of stone buildings, with corbelled upper stories and heavily grated windows, which are popularly called Genoese. They bear too close a resemblance to Turkish structures of the fifteenth and sixteenth centuries, and to the old houses of the Phanar, to be so named without more study than any one has taken the trouble to give them. But they are certainly mediæval and they suggest how Galata may once have looked. The façade of one of them, in the Rue Perchembé Bazaar, is decorated with a Byzantine marble panel. This was the fashionable quarter of Genoese Galata. The palace of the Podestà was there, at the northeast corner of the place where Perchembé Bazaar crosses Voïvoda. Indeed, this Ducal Palace, much transformed, still survives as an office building and rejoices in the name of Bereket Han — the House of Plenty.

Such slender honours of antiquity as Galata may boast cluster chiefly about certain churches and missions. The story of these is a picturesque chapter in the history of the mediæval orders. The Franciscans were the first to come to Constantinople, opening a mission on Seraglio Point in 1219, during the lifetime of St. Francis, and establishing themselves in Galata as early as 1227. No trace of them now remains in either place, each of the various branches into which the order divided having eventually removed to Pera. The church of San Francesco d'Assisi, belonging to the Conventuals, was the cathedral of the colony, and one worthy of Genoa the Superb. Partially destroyed by fire in 1696, it was seized by the mother of Sultans Moustafa II and Ahmed III, who built on its site — below the Imperial Ottoman Bank — the existing Yeni Valideh mosque. The church of

Sant' Antonio, on the Grande Rue de Pera, is the direct descendant of the cathedral of San Francesco and the missionaries of 1219.

The Dominicans were also settled at an early date on both sides of the Golden Horn. Arab Jami, the mosque whose campanile-like minaret is so conspicuous from the water, was formerly their church of San Paolo. Tradition ascribes its foundation to St. Hyacinth, the great Dominican missionary of the Levant. The fathers were dispossessed about 1535 in favour of the Moorish refugees from Spain, who also invaded the surrounding quarter. The quarter is still Mohammedan, though the Albanian costume now gives it most colour. Refugees of a less turbulent character had come from Spain a few years earlier and found hospitality at different points along the Golden Horn. These were the Jews driven out by Ferdinand and Isabella in 1492. There was already a considerable colony of Jews in Constantinople. Many of them had been Venetian subjects and lived on the edge of the Venetian settlement, at the point where the mosque of Yeni Jami now stands. When the great sultana Kyössem acquired that property she exempted forty of the residents from taxation for life and engaged herself to pay the Karaïte community an annual ground rent of thirty-two piastres. This was a considerable sum in 1640, but it now amounts to little more than a dollar a year! The sultana furthermore granted the Jews new lands at the place called Hass-kyöi — which might roughly be translated as Village of the Privy Purse — and a large Jewish colony still lives there, most of whose members speak a corrupt Spanish.

As for the Dominican fathers, they took refuge in what is now the Mission of S. Pierre. The building had originally been a convent of nuns of St. Catherine and gardens were added to it by a generous Venetian, in whose memory a mass is still performed once a year. This monastery has been burned and remodelled so many times that little can be left of its original appearance. Among its other claims to interest, however, is a Byzantine icon kept in the church, said to be none other than that celebrated icon of the Shower of the Way which I have already mentioned. The latter end of this venerable work of art is involved in as great mystery as its origin. According to the Greeks it was found in Kahrieh Jami by the Turks in 1453 and cut to pieces. Whether they admit the icon of Kahrieh Jami to have been the identical icon which the emperor Baldwin presented to St. Sophia in 1204, and which the Venetian Balio took away by force and put into the church of Pantocrator, now Zeïrek Kilisseh Jami, I cannot say. The Latins, however, claim that the Venetians never lost it, and that consequently it was never cut to pieces by the Turks, but that it ultimately came into possession of the Dominican fathers. Where doctors of divinity disagree so radically, let me not presume to utter an opinion!

In the court of the church and on the façade of the monastery toward the Rue Tchinar — the Street of the Plane-Tree — are stone escutcheons bearing the lilies of France and the arms of a Comte de St. Priest. He was a French ambassador at the time of our Revolutionary War. The building being under French protection and on the central street of old, of oldest Galata — the one which climbs past the palace of the Podestà from the water's edge to the Tower — was occupied at different times by the notables of the French colony. Among these, about the middle of the eighteenth century, was a merchant named Louis Chénier. Settling as a young man in Galata, he had become deputy of the nation — an office peculiar to the colony from the time of Colbert — right-hand-man to the ambassador, and husband, like many a European before and after him, of a Levantine lady. Her family, that is, were of European — in this case of Spanish — origin, but by long residence in the Levant and by intermarriage with Greeks had lost their own language. The seventh child of this couple was André Chénier, the poet of the French Revolution. His birthplace is marked by a marble tablet. The poet never saw the Street of the Plane-Tree, however, after he was three years old. He grew up in Paris, where, as every one knows, he was almost the last victim of the Terror.

The largest mission left in Galata is S. Benoît, whose walls now overshadow the least monastic quarter of the town. Its history is even more varied than that of S. Pierre, having been occupied and reoccupied at different times by the Benedictines, the Observants, the Capuchins, and the Jesuits. The last were the longest tenants, carrying on a devoted work for nearly two hundred years. After the secularisation of their order in 1773 they were succeeded by the Lazarists, who have not fallen behind in the high traditions of the mission. The place has a distinctly mediæval air, with its high walls, its Gothic gateway, and its machicolated campanile. Nothing is left, alas, of the mosaics which used to decorate the church. After so many fires I fear there is no chance of their being discovered under modern plaster. But the pillars of the porch are doubtless those which a diplomatic father obtained by gift from the Sheï'h ül Islam in 1686. And there are a number of interesting tablets about the building. One of them records not too truthfully the rebuilding of the church by Louis XIV. The most notable, perhaps, is the tombstone of Rakoczy, Prince of Transylvania and pretender to the throne of Hungary, who lived twenty years in exile at Rodosto, on the Sea of Marmora. When he died there in 1738 his friends asked permission to bury him in Galata, but were refused. They accordingly pretended to inter him at Rodosto. As a matter of fact, his coffin was sent in one of the many boxes containing his effects to S. Benoît. There the royal exile was secretly buried in the church, his grave long remaining unmarked. Another grave, all mark of which seems to have disappeared, is that of Jan Van Mour, a Fleming whom Louis XV made "peintre ordinaire du roy en Levant." He had the good fortune to live in Constantinople during the brilliant reign of Ahmed III, and he was the painter who started in France the eighteenth-century fashion of *turquerie.* The Museum of Amsterdam contains a large collection of Turkish documents from his brush, while there are others in France and in the castle of Biby in Sweden.

The stones of Galata have more to tell than those who ungratefully tread them are wont to imagine. But they are by no means Christian stones alone. Although the Latins naturally diminished in number after the Turkish conquest, the city quickly outgrew its walls. While part of this growth was due to the influx of Venetians, and later of Greeks, from the opposite side of the Horn, a good deal of it came about through Turkish colonisation. This was chiefly without the walls. You can almost trace the line of them to-day by the boundary between populations. The Turkish settlements gathered around mosques, palaces, and military establishments built by different sultans in the country about Galata, mainly on the water-front. One of the oldest of these settlements grew up in the deep ravine just west of the Galata wall. It is now engaged in readjusting its relations to the rest of the world, but it still remains like a piece of Stamboul, and it is the home of many dervishes. It took its name from a vizier of Süleïman the Magnificent, the conqueror of Nauplia and twice governor of Egypt. He was known as Handsome Kassîm, but he ended his days in bad odour. His quarter is supposed to take after him in the latter rather than in the former particular by those who do not appreciate what Kassîm Pasha adds to the resources of Pera. No one, however, should be incapable of appreciating what the cypresses of Kassîm Pasha do for the windows of Pera. They are all that is left of the great grove of the *Petits Champs des Morts,* the old burial-ground of Galata. As the city grew, the cemeteries, both Christian and Mohammedan, were removed to the *Grands Champs des Morts* at the Taxim. They, too, have now been overtaken by the streets and turned in great part to other uses. But a field of the dead was there again when the Young Turks took Pera from Abd ül Hamid in 1909.

I have already mentioned the mosque of Pialeh Pasha and the naval station which are among the greater lions of the left bank. A detail of history connected with this famous shipyard is that we perhaps get our word arsenal from it, through the Italian *darsena.* The accepted derivation is from the Arabic *dar es sanaat,* house of construction, from an ancient shipyard in Egypt captured by the founder of this Arsenal. But as likely an origin is the Turkish word — from the Persian, I believe — *terssaneh,* the house of slaves. At all events, this is where the great bagnio of the galley-slaves used to be. These were Christians captured in war: and of course the Christian powers repaid the compliment by capturing all the Turks they could for their own galleys. At all times during the fifteenth, sixteenth, and seventeenth centuries there were from three to four thousand slaves in the Arsenal, while several thousand more were chained to the oars of the imperial galleys. No less than fifteen thousand were said to have been freed at the battle of Lepanto. As the Turks became less warlike the number naturally declined, and came to an end with the abolition of slavery in 1846. One of the principal activities of the Catholic missions was among the inmates of this and other bagnios. The fathers were allowed access to the Arsenal and even maintained chapels there, confessing the slaves, arranging when they could for their ransom, and heroically caring for them through epidemics. St. Joseph of Leonissa, one of the pioneer Capuchins, caught the plague himself from the slaves but recovered to labour again in the bagnio — so zealously that he even aspired to reach the ear of the Sultan. He was accordingly arrested and condemned to death. The sentence was already supposed to have been executed when he was miraculously rescued by an angel and borne away to his native Italy, living there to a ripe old age. If the angel might have been discovered to bear some resemblance to the Venetian Balio, his intervention doubtless seemed no less angelic to the good missionary.

Another Turkish settlement grew up on the east side of Galata wall at Top Haneh, Cannon House. The place has been the seat of artillery works from the beginning of the Turkish era, for it must be remembered that Mehmed II, in the siege of Constantinople, was the first general to prove the practicability of cannon, and that during the whole of their martial period the Turks had no superiors in this branch of warfare. The conqueror turned a church and its adjoining cloisters into a foundery, and his son Baïezid II built barracks there for the artillerymen, while Süleïman I and Ahmed III restored and added to these constructions. There was also another shipyard at Top Haneh, and another Prince of the Sea is buried there near the mosque he built.

The mosque of Don Quixote and the fountain of Sultan Mahmoud I

I know not how it is that this mosque has so miraculously escaped notoriety. The exterior, to be sure, is less imposing than the neighbouring Nousretieh Jami, but there is a perfect little stone courtyard, with such doorways as only Sinan knew how to draw, while the interior is as happy in proportion as it is in detail.

The *mihrab* is unusual in being brightly lighted, and the windows, set among tiles, contain exquisite fragments of old stained glass. There are also tiled inscriptions, by Hassan Chelibi of Kara Hissar, above the other windows. The *mimber*, too, is a masterpiece of its kind, with its delicately perforated marbles. Then the gallery contains a finely designed arcade and an interesting marble rail and small rose windows — apparently of brickwork — above the spandrels of the arches. A characteristic touch is the big ship's lantern that swings in front of the *mihrab*. This beautiful mosque was built by an Italian. Born in Calabria and captured by Algerian pirates, he turned Turk after fourteen years in the galleys, and changed his name of Ochiali to Oulouj Ali — Big Ali. The ex-galley-slave then became a commander of galleys. At the battle of Lepanto he saved a shred of Turkish honour by capturing the flag-ship of the Knights of Malta, turning the squadron of Doria, and bringing forty galleys safely back to Constantinople. For this exploit he was made high admiral of the fleet and his name was turned into Sword Ali — Kîlîj Ali. An interesting side-light is thrown on this picturesque character from so unexpected a source as the novel of "Don Quixote." In chapter XXXII of the first part of that book, "in which the captive relates his life and adventures," Cervantes tells, with very little deviation from the fact, how he himself lost his left hand in the battle of Lepanto, how four years later he was captured by pirates and taken to Algiers, and how he lived there five years as the slave of a cruel Albanian master. Trying then to escape, he was caught and brought for trial before a personage whom he calls Uchali, but who was none other than our friend Kîlîj Ali. The upshot of the matter was that the builder of our beautiful

Interior of the mosque of Don Quixote

mosque bought the author of our immortal novel, whom he treated with great kindness, and presently accepted for him, in 1581, the very moderate ransom of five hundred crowns. So might a half-forgotten building in Top Haneh be brought back to light as the mosque of Don Quixote!

The greatest of the Princes of the Sea lies farther up the Bosphorus, at Beshiktash. The name is a corruption of *besh tash*, five stones, from the row of pillars on the shore to which he used to moor his galleys. Known to Europe by the nickname Barbarossa, from his great red beard, his true name was Haïreddin. Beginning life as a Greek pirate of Mitylene, he entered the service of the Sultan of Tunis, captured Algiers on his own account, and had the diplomacy to offer his prize to Selim I. Under Süleïman the Magnificent he became the terror of the Mediterranean and his master's chief instrument in a lifelong rivalry with Charles V. He died in 1546, full of years and honours, leaving a fortune of sixty thousand ducats and three thousand slaves. He wished to be buried by the sea, at the spot where he moored so often in his lifetime; but shanties and boat yards now shut him off from the water. Nothing could be quainter or quieter than the little railed garden near the steamer landing, where a vine-covered pergola leads to the *türbeh* of that turbulent man of blood. His green admiral's flag

Drawn by Kenan Bey

The admiral's flag of Haïreddin Barbarossa

hangs over his catafalque, marked in white with inscriptions, with an open hand, and with the double-bladed sword that was the emblem of his dignity, while his admiral's lanterns hang in niches on either side of the simple mausoleum.

The harbour of Jason and Barbarossa — and very likely the one that gave access to the Byzantine suburb of St. Mamas — is also the place where Sultan Mehmed II started his ships on their overland voyage. At least I can never see the valley of Dolma Ba'hcheh — the Filled-in Garden — into which the sea formerly entered, without convincing myself that it must have been the channel of that celebrated cruise and not the steeper hill of Top Haneh. However that may be, the descendants of Mehmed II have long shown a partiality for the neighbourhood. Ahmed I built a summer palace there as long ago as the beginning of the seventeenth century. Mehmed IV, Ahmed III, and Mahmoud I constructed others, while for the last hundred years the sultans have lived there altogether. The existing palace of Dolma Ba'hcheh, which occupies most of the old harbour, dates only from 1853. The villas of Yîldîz are more recent still. The neighbourhood of majesty has done less for the imperial suburb than might elsewhere be the case. No one seems to find anything incongruous in the fact that one of the Sultan's nearest neighbours is a gas house. The ceremony of *selamlik*, salutation, when the Sultan drives in state to mosque on Friday noon, is the weekly spectacle of Beshiktash — though less dazzling than it used to be. After his prayer the Sultan gives audience to ambassadors and visitors of mark. I know not whether this custom goes back to the time of Albert de Wyss, ambassador of the Holy Roman Empire, who used to turn out his embassy when Selim II rode by to mosque, or to that of the later Byzantine emperors, who received every Sunday the heads of the Latin communities.

The waterside settlements outside the walls of Galata were and are prevailingly Turkish. The Christian expansion followed the crest of the hill, founding the modern Pera. But there is a leaven of Islam even in Pera. Baïezid II built a mosque in the quarter of Asmali Mesjid — Vine Chapel — and a palace at Galata Seraï. This palace finally became a school for the imperial pages, recruited from among the Christian boys captured by the Janissaries, and existed intermittently as such until it was turned into the Imperial Lyceum. Galata Seraï means Galata Palace, which is interesting as showing the old application of the name. The word Pera the Turks have never adopted. They call the place Bey O'lou — the Son of the Bey. There is dispute as to the identity of this Bey. Some say he was David Comnenus, last emperor of Trebizond, or Demetrius Palæologus, despot of Epirus — the youngest son of the latter of whom, at any rate, turned Turk and was given lands in the vicinity of the Russian embassy. Others identify the Son of the Bey with Alvise Gritti, natural son of a Doge of Venice, who became Dragoman of the Porte during the reign of Süleïman the Magnificent, and exercised much influence in the foreign relations of that monarch. Süleïman himself built in Pera, or on that steep eastward slope of it which is called Fîndîklî — the Place of Filberts. The view from the terrace of the mosque he erected there in memory of his son Jihangir is one of the finest in Constantinople. It was his father Selim I who established the Mevlevi, popularly called the Whirling Dervishes, in Pera. There they remain to this day, though they have sold the greater part of the vast estates they once owned, a little island of peace and mysticism in the unbelieving town that has engulfed them. It is the classic amusement of tourists on Friday afternoons to visit their *tekkeh;* and a classic contrast do the noise and smiles of the superior children of the West make with the plaintive piping, the silent turning, the symbolism and ecstasy of that ritual octagon. Among the roses and ivy of the courtyard is buried a child of the West who also makes a contrast of a kind. He was a Frenchman, the Comte de Bonneval, who, after serving in the French and Austrian armies and quarrelling with the redoubtable Prince Eugene, came to Constantinople, became general of bombardiers, governor of Karamania, and pasha of three tails. He negotiated the first treaty of alliance made by Turkey with a Western country, namely, with Sweden, in 1740.

There are many other Turkish buildings in Pera, but the suburb is essentially Christian and was built up by the Galatiotes. It began to exist as a distinct community during the seventeenth century — about the time, that is, when the Dutch were starting the city of New York. The French and Venetian embassies and the Franciscan missions clustered around them were the nucleus of the settlement on a hillside then known as The Vineyards. We have already seen how the Conventuals moved to Pera after the loss of San Francesco. Their grounds for two hundred years adjoined those of the French embassy, but have gradually been absorbed by the latter until the fathers lately built on another site. The first Latin church in Pera, however, was S. Louis, of the Capuchins, who have been chaplains for the French embassy since 1628. Ste. Marie Draperis is also older in Pera than Sant' Antonio. The church is so called from a philanthropic lady who gave land in

Galata to the Observants in 1584. It passed to the Riformati because of the scandal which arose through two of the brothers turning Turk, and in 1678 moved to The Vineyards for the same reason as the Conventuals. It is now under Austrian protection and serves as chapel for the embassy of that Power, though the fathers are still Italians. The Observants, also known as Padri di Terra Santa, preceded them by a few years in Pera, where they acted as chaplains for the Venetian Balio. Their hospice, marked by the cross of Jerusalem is between Ste. Marie and the Austrian embassy.

The first European ambassadors were not many in number nor did they regularly follow each other, and they were usually quartered in a *han* detailed for that use in Stamboul, facing the Burnt Column. The Venetian Balio, I believe, always had a residence of his own. The French, however, set up a country-seat at The Vineyards as early as the time of Henri IV. And during the reign of Sultan Ibrahim, who in his rage at the Venetians over the Cretan War threatened to kill every Christian in the empire, beginning with the Balio, the ambassadors moved to the other side for good. The Venetians occupied the site since pre-empted by the Austrians. The Austrian embassy was originally on the other side of the Grande Rue, beside the now disused church of the Trinitarians, while the Russian embassy was the present Russian consulate. The existing Russian embassy was the Polish embassy. The Dutch and the Swedes acquired pleasant properties on the same slope. All these big gateways and gardens opening off the Grande Rue give colour to another theory for the Turkish name of Pera — that it was originally Bey Yolou, or the Street of Grandees.

The British embassy is by no means so young a member of this venerable diplomatic colony as our own, but its early traditions are of a special order. They are bound up with the history of the Levant Company. This was one of those great foreign trading associations of which the East India Company and the South Sea Company are, perhaps, more familiar examples. Hakluyt tells us that at least as early as 1511 British vessels were trading in the Levant, and that this trade became more active about 1575. In 1579 it was in some sort regularised by letters which were exchanged between Sultan Mourad III and Queen Elizabeth—"most wise governor of the causes and affairs of the people and family of Nazareth, cloud of most pleasant rain, and sweetest fountain of nobleness and virtue," as her imperial correspondent addressed her. At a later date high-sounding epistles also passed between the Virgin Queen and her majesty Safieh — otherwise the Pure — favourite wife of the Grand Turk, who wrote: "I send your majesty so honourable and sweet a salutation of peace that all the flock of nightingales with their melody cannot attain to the like, much less this simple letter of mine." The latter lady adds a touch of her own to her time, having been in reality a Venetian, of the house of Baffo. While on her way from Venice to Corfu, where her father was governor, she was kidnapped by Turkish corsairs and sent as a present to the young prince Mourad. So great became her influence over him that when he succeeded to the throne she had to be reckoned with in the politics of the Porte. Another royal correspondent of the Baffa, as the Balio called his countrywoman in his reports to the Council of Ten, was Catherine de' Medici. In the meantime Queen Elizabeth had already issued, in 1581, letters patent to certain London merchants to trade in the Levant. In 1582 the first ambassador, Master

William Harbone, or Hareborne, who was also chief factor of the Levant Company, betook himself and his credentials from London to Constantinople in the good ship *Susan*. The charter of "the Right Worshipful the Levant Company" was revised from time to time, but it was not definitely surrendered until 1825. And until 1821 the ambassador to the "Grand Signior," as well as the consuls in the Levant, were nominated and paid by the company. It was under these not always satisfactory conditions that Mr. Wortley Montagu brought his lively Lady Mary to the court of Ahmed III in 1717. Lord Elgin, of the marbles, was the first ambassador appointed by the government. I have not succeeded in gaining very much light as to the quarters provided by the Levant Company for its distinguished employees. In the Rue de Pologne there is a funny little stone house, now fallen, I believe, to the light uses of a dancing-school, which was once the British consulate. The present embassy is a Victorian structure and known to be in a different place from the one where Lady Mary wrote her letters.

The town that grew up around these embassies is one of the most extraordinary towns in creation. First composed of a few Galatiotes who followed their several protectors into the wilderness, it has continued ever since to receive accretions from the various nationalities of Europe and Asia until it has become a perfect babel, faintly Italian in appearance but actually no more Italian than Turkish, no more Turkish than Greek, no more Greek than anything else you please. Half a dozen larger worlds and nobody knows how many lesser ones live there, inextricably intermingled, yet somehow remaining miraculously distinct. There is, to be sure, a considerable body of Levantines—of those, namely, who have mixed—but even they are a peculiar people. The fact gives Pera society, so far as it exists, a bewildering hydra-headedness. The court is not the centre of things in the sense that European courts are. The Palace ladies do not receive, and it is an unheard-of thing for the Sultan to go to a private house, while in other ways there are profound causes of separation between the ruling race and the non-Moslem elements of the empire. By the very constitution of the country the Armenians, the Greeks, the Hebrews, and other fractions of the population form communities apart. Even the surprisingly large European colony has historic reasons for tending to divide into so many "nations." These have little in common with the foreign colonies of Berlin, Paris, or Rome. Not students and people of leisure but merchants and missionaries make up the better part of the family that each embassy presides over in a sense unknown in Western cities. The days are gone by when the protection of the embassies had the literal meaning that once attached to many a garden wall. But the ambassadors cling to the privileges and exemptions granted them by early treaties, and through the quarter that grew up around their gates the Sultan himself passes almost as a stranger.

This diversity of traditions and interests has, of course, influenced the development of Pera. Not the least remarkable feature of this remarkable town is its lack of almost every modern convenience. I must admit, of course, that a generation before New York thought of a subway Pera had one — a mile long. And it is now installing those electric facilities which Abd ül Hamid always objected to, on the ground that a dynamo must have something to do with dynamite. But it will be long before Pera, which with its neighbours sprawls over as much ground as New York, will really take in the conception of rapid transit, or even the more primitive one of home comfort. I hardly need, therefore, go into the account of the more complicated paraphernalia of modern life. There are no public pleasure or sporting grounds other than two dusty little municipal gardens, laid out in old cemeteries, which you pay to enter. Pictures, libraries, collections ancient or modern, there are none. I had almost said there is neither music nor drama. There are, to be sure, a few modest places of assembly where excellent companies from Athens may be heard, where a visitor from the Comédie Française occasionally gives half a dozen performances, and where the failures of European music-halls oftenest air their doubtful charms. On these boards I have beheld a peripatetic Aïda welcome Rhadames and a conquering host of five Greek supers; but Brünnhilde and the Rhine maidens have yet to know the Bosphorus. Not so, however, a translated "Tante de Charles." When the "Merry Widow" first tried to make her début, she met with an unexpected rebuff. Every inhabitant of Pera who respects himself has a big Croat or Montenegrin, who are the same rose under different names, to decorate his front door with a display of hanging sleeves and gold embroidery. It having been whispered among these magnificent creatures that the "Lustige Witwe" was a slander on the principality — as it was then — of Nicholas I, they assembled in force in the gallery of the theatre and proceeded to bombard the stage with chairs and other detachable objects until the company withdrew the piece.

Consisting of an accretion of villages, containing the conveniences of a village, Pera keeps, in strange contradiction to her urban dimensions, the air of a village, the separation of a village from the larger world, the love of a village for gossip and the credulity of a village in rumour. This is partly due, of course, to the ingrained belief of the Turks that it is not well for people to know exactly what is going on. The papers of Pera have always lived under a strict censorship, and consequently there is nothing too fantastic for Pera to repeat or believe. Hence it is that Pera is sniffed at by those who should know her best, while the tarriers for a night console themselves with imagining that there is nothing to see. I have never been able to understand why it should be thought necessary nowadays for one town to be exactly like another. I, therefore, applaud Pera for having the originality to be herself. And within her walls I have learned that one may be happy even without steam-heat and telephones. In despite, moreover, of the general contempt for her want of intellectual resources, I submit that merely to live in Pera is as good as a university. No one can hope to entertain relations with the good people of that municipality without speaking at least one language beside his own. It is by no means uncommon for a Perote to have five or six at his tongue's end. Turkish and French are the official languages, but Greek is more common in Pera and Galata proper, while you must have acquaintance with two or three alphabets more if you wish to read the signs in the streets or the daily papers. And then there remain an indeterminate number of dialects used by large bodies of citizens.

A town so varied in its discourse is not less liberal in other particulars. Pera observes three holy days a week: Friday for the Turks, Saturday for the Jews, Sunday for the Christians. How many holidays she keeps I would be afraid to guess. She recognises four separate calendars. Two of them, the Julian and the

Gregorian, followed by Eastern and Western Christians respectively, are practically identical save that they are thirteen days apart. There are, however, three Christmases in Pera, because the Armenians celebrate Epiphany (Old Style); and sometimes only one Easter. As for the Jews, they adhere to their ancient lunar calendar, which is supposed to start from the creation of the world. The Turks also follow a lunar calendar, not quite the same, which makes their anniversaries fall eleven days earlier every year. Their era begins with the Hegira. But in 1789 Selim III also adopted for financial purposes an adaptation of the Julian calendar, beginning on the first of March and not retroactive in calculating earlier dates. Thus the Christian year 1914 is 5674 for the Jews, and 1332 or 1330 for the Turks. There are also two ways of counting the hours of Pera, the most popular one considering twelve o'clock to fall at sunset. These independences cause less confusion than might be supposed. They interfere very little, unless with the happiness of employers. But where the liberty of Pera runs to licence is in the matter of post-offices. Of these there are no less than seven, for in addition to the Turks the six powers of Europe each maintain their own. They do not deliver letters, however, and to be certain of getting all your mail — there is not too much certainty even then — you must go or send every day to every one of those six post-offices.

For those branches of learning of which Pera is so superior a mistress, an inimitable hall of learning is her much-scoffed Grande Rue — "narrow as the comprehension of its inhabitants and long as the tapeworm of their intrigues," as the learned Von Hammer not too good-humouredly wrote. I am able to point out that it has broadened considerably since his day, though I must add that it is longer than ever! It begins under another name in Galata, in a long flight of steps from which you see a blue slice of the harbour neatly surmounted by the four minarets of St. Sophia. It mounts through a commerce of stalls and small shops, gaining

Grande Rue de Pera

in decorum as it rises in altitude, till it reaches the height which was the heart of old Pera. Here was the *Stavrothromo* of the Perotes, where the Rue Koumbaradji — Bombardier — climbs laboriously out of Top Haneh and tumbles down from the other side of the Grande Rue into Kassîm Pasha. The Grande Rue now attains its climax of importance much farther on, between Galata Seraï and Taxim, whence, keeping ever to the crest of the hill, it passes out into the country like another

Broadway between apartment-houses and vacant lots. Other Grandes Rues may be statelier, or more bizarre and sketchable. This Grande Rue must have been more sketchable in the time of Von Hammer, who found nothing picturesque in the balconies almost meeting across the

The Little Field of the Dead

street, in the semi-oriental costumes of the Perotes and the high clogs in which they clattered about the town. But even now the Grande Rue is by no means barren of possibilities — where a motor-car will turn out for an ox-cart or a sedan-chair, and where pedestrians are stopped by an Anatolian peasant carrying a piano on his back, by a flock of sheep pattering between two gaunt Albanians, or by a troop of firemen hooting half-naked through the street with a gaudy little hand-pump on their shoulders. There are any number of other types that only need the seeing eye and the revealing pencil which Pera has too long lacked. And few Grandes Rues can be full of contrasts more profound than meet you here where East and West, the modern and the mediæval, come so strangely together.

There are other streets in Pera, and streets that are visibly as well as philosophically picturesque. There is, for instance, that noisome shelf which ought to be the pride of the town, overhanging the Little Field of the Dead, where cypresses make a tragic foreground to the vista of the Golden Horn and far-away Stamboul, and where crows wheel in such gusty black clouds against red sunsets. There are also the heights of Fîndîklî, from which you catch glimpses, down streets as steep as Capri and Turkish as Eyoub, of the kingdoms of the earth and the glory of them. But for the sketchable, for the pre-eminently etchable, Galata is the place — humble, despised, dirty, abandoned Galata, with its outlying suburbs. If the Grande Rue de Pera is Broadway, the main street of Galata is the Bowery. It runs along the curve of the shore from Azap Kapou, at the Arsenal wall, to the outer bridge and the Bosphorus. And nobody knows it, but some very notable architecture adorns this neglected highway. Besides the old Genoese Arab Jami and the mosque of Don Quixote, there is at Azap Kapou another masterpiece of Sinan, a lovely little mosque founded by the great Grand Vizier Sokollî Mehmed Pasha. At Fîndîklî, too, there is an obscure waterside mosque whose aspect from the Bosphorus is admirable, set as it is among boats and trees, with a valley cleaving the hill behind it. And even the tall Nousretieh at Top Haneh, built by Sultan Mahmoud II, has its points. These points, particularly as exemplified in the twin minarets, are an inimitable slimness and elegance. And I don't care if the great door opening on to the parade-ground, and the court at the north, are rococo; they are charming. There are also two or three of the handsomest fountains in all Constantinople on this long

The fountain of Azap Kapou

street — notably the big marble one at the corner of this very parade-ground, by Mahmoud I, and the one of his mother at Azap Kapou. The same princess left near Galata Tower, in that old Grande Rue of the Genoese where the Podestà lived and André Chénier was born, a wall fountain whose lamentable state of ruin is a reproach to the city that can boast such a treasure. The entire left bank, in fact, is particularly rich in these interesting monuments. This is the only part of the city for which the sultans installed an entirely new water-system.

I could easily pass all bounds in enumerating the glories of Galata, which Murray's guide-book dismisses with little more than a remark about the most depraved population in Europe. Of depravity I am not connoisseur enough to pass judgment on this dictum. I can only say that if the Galatiotes are the worst people in Europe, the world is not in so parlous a state as some persons have imagined. I presume it must be to the regions called Kemer Altî — Under the Arch — lying between Step Street and the pious walls of S. Benoît, that the critic refers. Here the primrose path of Galata winds among dark and dismal alleys, Neapolitan save for the fezzes, the odour of mastic, and the jingling *lanterna*, the beloved hand piano of Galata. Yet even here simplicity would be a truer word than depravity. Among primrose paths this is at once the least disguised and the least seductive which I have happened to tread. There is so little mystery about it, its fantastic inhabitants make so little attempt to conceal their numerous disadvantages, that no Ulysses should be compelled to stop his ears against such sirens.

But Galata is by no means all primrose path. Other, more laborious paths abound there, of drudgery manifold but chiefly of those who go down to the sea in ships. The tangle of narrow streets between the "Bowery" and the harbour is given up almost entirely to sailors and watermen — their lodging, their outfitting, and their amusement. The thickest of these streets in local colour are in the purlieus of Pershembeh Bazaar. Pershembeh Bazaar means Thursday Market, and Thursday is a day to come here. Then awnings shade the little streets around Arab

Fountain near Galata Tower

Jami, and venders of dreadful Manchester prints, of astonishing footwear, of sweets, of perfumes, of variegated girdles, leave no more than a narrow lane for passers-by, and there is infinite bargaining from sunrise to sunset. The next morning there will be not a sign of

The Kabatash breakwater

all this commerce. It has gone elsewhere: to be precise, to Kassîm Pasha. On Tuesdays you will find these peripatetic merchants near Top Haneh.

If the Thursday Market goes, the rest of Galata remains, and the best of it: the alleys of jutting upper stories that know so well the value of a grape-vine, the quaint shops and coffee-houses, the cavernous bakeries, the place of broken lights where the oar makers ply the local variation of their trade, the narrow courtyard where the sailmakers sit, the wharves and landings of the Golden Horn, the quays of Top Haneh, the breakwater of Kabatash — which is at its best in a south wind — and all that enticing region called Kalafat Yeri, the Place of Pitch, where from time immemorial men have built boats and caulked them, and fitted them out with gear. In front of this shore, off the old Galata which the Genoese originally walled in, lies the noble mass of shipping of which I have already spoken. That is the supreme resource of Galata, and one which is hidden under no bushel, waiting patiently to make the fortune of the man who will etch it. Where were Mr. Murray's eyes when he came to Galata? Her vices would hardly have attracted his attention if he had taken in the virtue of her contribution to the pictorial.

VI

THE CITY OF GOLD

UNDER this designation, gentle reader or severe, you probably never would recognise the straggling settlement of wooden houses, set off by a few minarets and shut in from the southeast by a great black curtain of cypresses, that comes down to the Asiatic shore opposite the mouth of the Golden Horn. That is because you have forgotten its old Greek name, and mix it up in your mind with a certain notorious town in Albania. Moreover, your guide-book assures you that a day, or even half a day, will suffice to absorb its interest. Believe no such nonsense, however. I have reason to know what I am talking about, for I have spent ten of the best years of my life in Scutari, if not eleven, and have not yet seen all its sights. By what series of accidents a New English infant, whose fathers dwelt somewhere about the Five Towns long before Mr. Arnold Bennett or even Mr. Josiah Wedgwood thought of making them famous, came to see the light in this Ultima Thule of Asia, I hesitate to explain. I tried to do so once before an election board in that sympathetic district of New York known as Hell's Kitchen, and was very nearly disfranchised for my pains. Only the notorious example of the mayor, who also happened to be born on the wrong side of the Atlantic and who nevertheless had reached his high office without any intermediate naturalisation, preserved to me the sacred right of the ballot. But the fact gives me the right to speak of guide-books as cavalierly as I please.

Yet it also singularly complicates, I find, my intention of doing something to draw my native town from the obscurity into which it has too long relapsed. In considering its various claims to interest, for instance, my first impulse is to count among them a certain lordly member of the race of stone-pines. I used to look up at it with a kind of awe, so high did its head tower above my own and so strangely did it parley with the moving air. Our heads are not much nearer together now; but unaccountable changes have taken place in the thatch of mine, while the pine has lost none of the thickness and colour that delighted me long ago. I suppose, however, that other pines are equally miraculous, and that the pre-eminence of this one in my eyes is derived from the simple fact that I happened to be born in sight of it. I will therefore struggle as valiantly as I may against the enormous temptation to do a little Kenneth Grahame over again, with Oriental variations. For the rest, there must have been less difference between a Minor Asiatic infancy and a New English one than might be imagined. It was conducted, for the most part, in the same tongue. It was enlivened by the same games and playthings. It was embittered by the same books and pianos. Its society was much more limited, however, and it was passed, for the most part, behind high garden walls, to adventure beyond which, without governess or guardian of some sort, was anathema.

I could easily lose myself in reminiscences of one or two Scutari gardens. In fact, I can only save myself — and the reader — from such a fate by making up my mind to write a separate chapter about gardens in general. As for the houses that went with the gardens, they were very much like the old houses of Stamboul. They were all halls and windows, and they had enormously high ceilings, so that in winter they were about as cosy as the street. I remember one of them with pleasure by reason of the frescoes that adorned it, with beautiful deer in them and birds as big as the deer stalking horizontally up the trunks of trees. Another was a vast tumbledown wooden palace of which we humbly camped out in one corner. It had originally belonged to an Armenian grandee who rejoiced in the name of the Son of the Man Who Was Cooked. The Son of the Man Who Was Cooked had the honour to be a friend of the Sultan of his day, who not seldom visited him. His majesty used to come at all hours, it is said, and sometimes in disguise. This was partly because the Son of the Man Who Was Cooked loved to go loaded with jewels, as the legend went, and the Sultan hoped by finding him in that case to have the better ground for raising loans. But it is also whispered that other reasons entered into the matter, and that on the men's side of the house a secret stair was built, enabling majesty to circulate in the house without attracting too much attention. Certain it is that such a stair, black and breakneck, existed, for my room was at the top of it —

Fresco in an old house in Scutari

and as I lay in bed in winter I could look out through the cracks in the wall and see the snow in the garden. But I never wondered then, as I have wondered since, whether the legend that Abd ül Hamid was half an Armenian had any connection with our house. Another of its attractions was that it boasted in the cellar a bottomless pit — or so the servants used to assure us.

These were they who lent, perhaps, the most local colour to that Minor Asiatic youth. They were daughters of Armenia, for the most part. And I sometimes think that if William Watson had enjoyed my opportunities he never would have written "The Purple East." Surely he never squirmed under an Armenian kiss, which in my day partook both of sniffing and of biting and which left the victim's cheek offensively red and moist. Yet how can I remember with anything but gratitude the kindly neighbours to whom foreign children, coming and going between the houses that in those distant days made a small Anglo-American colony in upper Scutari, were always a source of interest? For some mysterious reason that is buried in the heart of exiled Anglo-Saxondom, we really knew wonderfully little about our neighbours. We never played with their children or entered other than strangers the world outside our garden wall. Nor was it because our neighbours were unwilling to meet us half-way. They paid us the compliment of naming a certain place of amusement which existed in our vicinity the American Theatre, hoping thereby to gain our patronage. But I fear this hope met with no response. At any rate, I never came nearer the unknown delights of the American Theatre than the top of our garden wall, from which I remember once listening entranced to such strains of music as never issued from our serious piano. I recognised them years afterward, with a jump, in an opera of Suppé. I have also lived to learn that Scutari, or the part of it where we lived, is a sort of Armenian Parnassus, perhaps even an Armenian Montmartre, given over entirely to the muses. Emancipated Armenian ladies, they tell me, do such unheard-of things as to walk, on their own two feet, vast distances over the hills of Asia with emancipated Armenian gentlemen in long locks and flowing neckties; and imperishable Armenian odes have celebrated the beauties of Baghlar Bashi and Selamsîz.

Nevertheless, we did not suffer the consequences of our aloofness. Between our garden and another one, to which we were in time allowed to go alone, there existed, unbeknownst to our elders, certain post stations, as it were, where a wayfarer might stop for rest and refreshment. Out of one barred window a lady always passed me a glass of water. She rather reminded me of some docile overgrown animal in a cage. Indeed I am not sure she could have got out if she tried — which apparently she never did — for she was of immeasurable proportions. I thought of her when I later came to read of a certain Palace lady pet-named Little Elephant, who built a mosque in Scutari. I know not whether this was the same whom a Sultan, having sent messengers to the four quarters of the empire in search of the fattest beauty imaginable, found in my native town, almost under his palace windows, and led away in triumph. As George Ade has told us, slim princesses used not to be the fashion in Turkey. From another window, higher above the street, attentions of another sort used to be showered on us by an old gentleman who never seemed to dress. He was always sitting there in a loose white gown, as if he had just got up or were just going to bed, and he would toss us down pinks or chrysanthemums, according to the season. But the person most popular with us was a little old woman who lived in a house so old and so little that I blush when I remember how greedy I used to be at her expense. She used to reach out between the bars of her window spoonfuls of the most heavenly preserve I have ever tasted, thick and white and faintly flavoured with lemon. So distinguished a sweetmeat could only possess so distinguished a name as bergamot.

Returning to Scutari long afterward, it came upon me with a certain surprise that no one offered me sweets or flowers, or even a glass of water. My case was oddly put to me by a man like one of Shakespeare's fools, who perhaps should not have been at large but who asked himself aloud when he met me at a mosque gate: "I wonder what he is looking for — his country?" If Scutari tempts me to do Kenneth Grahame over again, it also tempts me to do Dr. Hale over again, to whose famous hero I could give other points than that of the election board in Hell's Kitchen. The enduring taunt of my school-days was that I never could be President, and it was a bitter blow to me when I learned that my name could never be carved in the Hall of Fame above the Hudson. Yet when I went back to Scutari, as a man will go back to the home of his youth, the inhabitants were so far from recognising me as one of themselves that the thought occurred to me how amusingly like life it would be if I, who am not notable for the orthodoxy of my opinions, were massacred for a Christian in the town where I was born! Nevertheless I have discovered with a good deal of surprise, in the room of the vanished Scutari I used to know, a Scutari that I never saw or heard of when I was young — I speak, of course, to the race of men that likes Stamboul — a place of boundless resources, of priceless possibilities — a true City of Gold.

The favourite story is that Chrysopolis was so called because of the Persian satraps who once lived there and heaped up the gold of tribute. Others have it, and I like their theory better, that the city took its name from Chryses, son of Chryseis and Agamemnon, who, fleeing after the fall of Troy from Ægisthus and Clytemnestra, met there his end. A few poetic-minded individuals have found an origin for the word in the appearance the town presents from Constantinople at sunset with all its panes on fire. I don't know that the idea is more far-fetched than any other. An equal variety of opinion prevails with regard to the modern name. Certain authorities claim that it is a corruption of Üsküdar, used by the Turks, which is from a Persian word meaning a post messenger. For myself, I am feebly impressed by all these Persians, who seem to me dragged in by the ears. A Turkish savant told me once that he believed Üsküdar to be a corruption of an old Armenian name, Oskitar or Voskitar, which is merely a translation of Chrysopolis. When Mehmed II captured Constantinople he brought a great many Armenians into it, to repopulate the city and to offset the Greeks; and the richest of them, who came from Broussa, he settled in Scutari, which has always retained a certain Armenian tinge. I learn that in ancient Armenian some such word could have been made out of Chrysopolis. But the name Scutari is much older than the Turkish conquest. Villehardouin and at least one Byzantine historian speak of the palace of Scutari, on the promontory that juts out toward Seraglio Point. Also, I seem to remember reading in Gibbon of a corps of *scutarii* who had their barracks on that side of the strait. I have never been able to lay my hand on those *scutarii* again, and so cannot found very much of an argument upon them. Any Latin lexicon, however, will give you the word *scutarius*, a shield-bearer, and tell you that a corps of them existed under the later empire. Wherefore I formally reject and contemn Murray, Von Hammer and Company, with their Persian postboys, and take my stand on those Roman shields. In all probability the name spread, as in the case of Galata, from a barracks or a palace to the entire locality, and Üsküdar must be a Turkish attempt to pronounce the Greek Σκουτάριον.

Of that oldest Scutari I did not set out to write an account, but it is convenient that the visitor should be aware of how ancient and honourable a town he is treading the streets. I find it a little difficult to write coherently, however, for two ancient and honourable towns are there. The second one, lying next to the south and facing the Marmora instead of the Bosphorus, is the more ancient, and I suppose in the eyes of the world the more honourable. Chalcedon was its name — derived, by one report, from the Homeric soothsayer Chalkas — and it is represented to-day by the suburbs of Haïdar Pasha, Kadi Kyöi, and Moda. The history of these adjoining quarters is so intertwined that it is sometimes hard to distinguish between Chalcedon and Chrysopolis. Chalcedon, like Byzantium, was founded by colonists from Megara, but a few years earlier. Its greater accessibility and hospitality to ships and the flatness of its site gave it advantages which Chrysopolis did not possess. Chrysopolis, on the other hand, nearer Byzantium and commanding the mouth of the Bosphorus, occupied the more strategic position with regard to the traffic of the strait. Both cities suffered greatly during the Persian wars, and were for a time ruled by the satraps of Darius. The Athenians seized them early in the history of their league, in order to levy tolls on passing ships. So early arose the vexed question of the straits. Philip of Macedon included the two cities in his siege of Byzantium, but was driven away by the Athenians. Xenophon stopped a week in Chrysopolis on his way back from Persia. Hannibal ended his troubled days in a suburb of Chalcedon. Nicomedes III of Bithynia left that town in his will to the Romans, who fought over it with Mithridates of Pontus. The Goths ravaged it on the occasion of their first raid into Asia Minor. The fate of the Roman world was settled on the heights of Chrysopolis in 324, when that other man without a country, Constantine of York, vanquished his last rival, Licinius, and took him prisoner. The experiences and associations of that victory must have had much to do with the transfer of the capital from the Tiber to the Bosphorus. From that time onward the two Asiatic cities lost something in importance but gained in peace — though Persians, Saracens, and Turks later troubled them again. The fourth Ecumenical Council sat in Chalcedon in 451, in that church of St. Euphemia which had been a temple of Venus. The famous oracle of Apollo Constantine destroyed, using its marbles for his own constructions on the opposite side of the strait. From Chrysopolis he also took a celebrated statue of Alexander the Great. His example was followed by the emperor Valens, who utilised the walls of Chalcedon as a quarry for the aqueduct that still strides across a valley of Stamboul. And even Süleïman the Magnificent was able to find materials for his greatest mosque in the ruins of the church of St. Euphemia and of the palace of Belisarius.

To-day a few sculptured capitals remain above ground

in Scutari, and every now and then some one in Kadi Kyöi digs up in his garden a terra-cotta figurine. Otherwise there is nothing left to remind you of the antique cities that sat in front of Byzantium. They have disappeared as completely as the quaint little Scutari of my youth. But two settlements still remain there, and still different, although so long united under one destiny. When projected trolley-cars and motor roads come into being, as they are destined shortly to do, I fancy that this separation will become less and less marked. For the time being, however, Scutari and Kadi Kyöi might be on opposite sides of the Bosphorus. Kadi Kyöi, with its warmer winds, its smoother lands, its better harbours, its trim yachts, its affluent-looking villas, its international *Bagdadbahn*, has acquired a good deal of the outward appearance of Europe. Whereas Scutari remains Asiatic and old-fashioned. It is very much what it was before Bagdad railways, when the caravans of the East marched through its narrow streets, when the Janissaries pounded their kettledrums in the square of Doghanjiler — the Falconers. And it contains almost all that is to be seen in the two towns of interest to the comer from afar.

The great sight of Scutari, after all, is Scutari itself — which very few people ever seem to have noticed. In front of it opens, somewhat north of west, a nick in the shore known as the Great Harbour. As a matter of fact it is very little of a harbour, whose inner waters are barely safe from the swirl of the Bosphorus as it begins to squeeze past Seraglio Point. The front door of Scutari is here, however, and one altogether worthy of the City of Gold. Seen from the water it is admirably bordered with boats and boat-houses, being no less admirably overlooked by minarets and hanging gardens and climbing roofs and the dark overtopping wall of the great cemetery, while nearer acquaintance proves it to be amply provided with local colour in the way of plane-trees, fountains, and coffee-houses galore. The heart of

The Street of the Falconers

the town lies in an irregular amphitheatre which twists back from the Great Harbour. Into the floor of the amphitheatre project half a dozen buttresses of an upper gallery, and through the long narrow corridors between them streets climb, sometimes by steps, to the cypresses and their amply sweeping terrace. In this scene, if you like, a lesser Stamboul is set. It has its old houses, its vines, its fountains, its windows of grille work, its mosque yards, its markets, its covered bazaar, even its own edition of the Sacred Caravan and the Persian solemnity of *Mouharrem.* But it has an air of its own, as the storks will tell you who nest near the flower market. It does not imitate, it complements Stamboul. And it contains monuments so remarkable that I am constantly amazed and scandalised to find out how little people know about them.

Four mosques in particular are the pride and jewels of my native town. They were all erected by princesses — the two oldest after the designs of Sinan. The earliest one, dating from 1547, is the first you see when you come to Scutari. It stands, like the mosque of Rüstem Pasha, on a terrace above the hum of the landing stage. As a matter of fact it was built by the wife of Rüstem Pasha, who was also the daughter of Süleïman the Magnificent and Roxelana. Mihrîmah, this lady was called, which means Moon and Sun. Her mosque is named after her, though it is also called the Great Mosque and the Mosque of the Pitcher — for what reason I have yet to penetrate. It is a little stiff and severe, to my way of thinking. The minarets have not the spring that Sinan afterward learned to evoke, and the interior is rather bare. Perhaps it has been pillaged. But the courtyard, looking out through trees to the Bosphorus, is a delightful spot, and it contains one of the most admirable mosque fountains I know. There are also other fountains in the court, and an old sun-dial, too overgrown by leaves to do its work, and a *mouvakît haneh.* When I was speaking of mosque yards in general I did not mention this institution. It may seem to us that people who count twelve o'clock at sunset cannot pay much attention to the science of time keeping. But the exact hours of prayer, like the exact direction of Mecca, are very important matters for Mohammedans. The Arabs, I believe, were the first inventors of clocks. At all events, the first clock seen in Europe was a present to Charlemagne from Haroun al Rashid. A clock is an essential part of the furniture of every mosque. Haroun al Rashid is a long time dead,

Fountain in the mosque yard of Mihrîmah

however, and most of the clocks seen to-day were made in England. Mosques of any size, nevertheless, have their own corps of timekeepers, who do their work in a pavilion called the *mouvakît haneh* — the house of time — and incidentally repair the watches of the neighbourhood. Some of them also take solar observations with instruments that were made for a museum.

Next in chronological order is the mosque of the *Valideh Atik* — which might be translated as the Old or, more politely, as the Wise Mother. It is more popularly known as Top Tashi, or Cannon Stone. In a steep street near the mosque lies a big stone cannon-ball from which the quarter may take its name. However, the Wise Mother was a certain Nour Banou, Lady of Light, who lies buried beside her husband, Sultan Selim II, in the courtyard of St. Sophia. Her mosque stands on the second story of Scutari, and its two minarets and contrasting cypresses, with their encompassing arcade and massive-walled dependencies, make the most imposing architectural group in the town. The mosque has recently undergone a thorough restoration, which is rarely a very happy proceeding. Luckily the restorers left the painted wooden ceilings that decorate the under-side of the gallery — or so much of them as had not been painted out before. There is also an elaborately perforated marble *mimber*, whose two flags would seem to indicate that a church once stood here. But what is best is the tiled recess of the *mihrab*. The tile makers of Nicæa had evidently not begun to lose their cunning in the day of the Lady of Light — unless she borrowed from some other place. In any case, the two panels at right angles to the *mihrab* are so high an ornament of my native town that Scutari deserves to be celebrated for them alone. They seem to me to rank among the finest tiles in Constantinople, though Murray passes them by without a word. In Turkish eyes this mosque has a further interest as being one of the spots known to have been visited by Hîdîr or Hîzîr, lord of the Fountain of Life. In the porch of the mosque hangs an illuminated manuscript commemorating this illustrious visit, and near it are three holes by which Hîzîr is supposed to have moved the mosque in token of his presence.

Tiles in the mosque of the Valideh Atik

The third princess to build in Scutari was one whose acquaintance we have already made, the great *valideh* Kyössem. Her mosque also stands on the upper terrace, at the head of the long corridor known as Chaoush

Deresi. The Turks call it Chinili Jami, which really means the China Mosque. It is a tiled mosque, much smaller than Rüstem Pasha, faced on the inside and

Chinili Jami

along the porch with blue and white tiles of not so good a period. Between 1582, when the Lady of Light tiled her *mihrab*, and 1643 something had evidently happened in Nicæa. As a matter of fact, I believe the tiles came from Kütahya. Nevertheless the mosque is charming, there is the quaintest pagoda-like fountain in one corner of the court, and the main gate of the yard composes with the fountain and the mosque and the cypresses around it in the happiest possible way.

The fountains of the Valideh Jedid

The latest of our four mosques was erected by the sultana who, being by birth a Greek, took away San Francesco in Galata from the Conventuals. At least that lady was the builder if she was the mother of Ahmed III as well as of Moustafa II. She atoned, however, for that eminently feminine piece of high-handedness by her mosque in Scutari. It is popularly called the Valideh Jedid, the mosque of the New Mother, and it belongs to that early period of Turkish rococo which Ahmed III borrowed from Louis XV. For the mosque of a new mother, the style is admirably adapted. It is to be seen at its most characteristic in the fountain of marble embroideries which stands outside the north gate of the mosque yard. A second fountain stands beside the first, of the sort where cups of water are filled for passers-by. Then comes the tomb of the foundress, who lies like the Kyöprülüs under a skeleton dome of bronze. And you should see the roses that make a little garden around her in May. They are an allusion, I suppose, to her graceful Turkish name, which may be less gracefully rendered as Rose Attar of Spring. The mosque yard has no great interest — except on Fridays, when a fair is established along its outer edge. But I must draw attention to the bird-house, like a cross-section of a little mosque with two minarets, on the façade of the forecourt, and to the small marble beehive that balances it. This forecourt is the only one of its kind in Scutari. As for the mosque itself, you may find the windows too coquettish even for a New Mother. For myself I rather like their flower-pots and flowers, though they clearly belong to a day other than that of the old window jewellery of Sinan's time. The green tiles about the *mihrab* also betray a symptom of decadence in that they are of a repeating pattern. But the chief point of the mosque is one to which I drew attention a good many pages back, namely its stencilling. Being a native of Scutari, I can without presumption recommend to all Ministers of Pious Foundations that they preserve that old painting as long as the last flake of it hangs to the ceiling, and that before the last flake falls they learn the secret of its effect. So may they in days to come restore to Rüstem Pasha and Sultan Ahmed and Yeni Jami a part of their lost dignity.

Interior of the Valideh Jedid

In the gallery at the left is the imperial tribune

You are not to suppose that Scutari has no other mosques than these. Ayazma Jami and the Selimieh are two other imperial monuments whose delightful yards make up for their baroque interiors. And the small Ahmedieh is an older structure which you must not

The Ahmedieh

attribute to any Sultan Ahmed. Oldest of all is Roum Mehmed Pasha, once a Greek church. If I pass it by, however, I simply cannot pass by a mosque which stands in its own *medresseh* court on the south side of Scutari harbour. I would rather study theology there than anywhere else in the world. At least, I do not believe any other theological school has so perfect a little cloister lying so close to the sea. And while other cloisters were designed by Sinan, I know of no other that was founded by a poet. The name of this poet was Shemsi Pasha, and he was a soldier and a courtier as well. But it was the poetry in him, together with his quick wit and gay humour, that first drew him into the notice of Süleïman the Magnificent. Unlike many men of his circle, he was a real Turk, being descended from a Seljukian family that reigned at one time on the shores of the Black Sea. He became a greater favourite of Selim II than he had been of Süleïman. Selim made him master of ceremonies to receive the ambassadors who came to Adrianople to congratulate the new Sultan on his accession. Among these was a Persian, whom his European colleagues greatly astonished by taking off their hats as he rode in with his magnificent suite. The Persian asked Shemsi Pasha what the extraordinary gesture might signify, and Shemsi Pasha told him it was a Christian way of showing that they were ready to drop their heads at the feet of the Sultan. Under Mourad III Shemsi Pasha reached an even higher pitch of fortune, and it was then that he built his *medresseh*. He jokingly began to call himself the Falcon of Petitions, for it was his business to receive petitions that people brought to the Sultan — and the presents that accompanied them. One day he came away from the Sultan in high good humour, saying: "At last I have avenged the dynasty of my fathers, for if the house of Osman caused our ruin I have prepared that of the house of Osman." Asked what he meant, he explained that he had just induced the Sultan — for forty thousand ducats — to sell his favour. "From to-day the Sultan himself will give the example of corruption, and corruption will dissolve the empire."

Were I a little more didactically inclined, this speech should inspire the severest reflections on the man who made it and on the ironical truth of his lightly uttered prophecy. As it is, I am more inclined to reflect on the irony of the fact that ill-gotten gains may do more good or create something nearer the immortal than the

Shemsi Pasha

savings of honest toil. At any rate, the *medresseh* of Shemsi Pasha is such a place as only a poet or a great architect could imagine; and many homeless people found refuge there during the late Balkan War. The cloister is very small and irregular. There are cells and a covered arcade on two sides. The third, I think, from three or four quaint little windows of perforated marble that remain in a corner of the wall, must once have been more open to the Bosphorus than it is now. On the fourth side, and taking up a good deal of the court, are the mosque and the tomb of the founder. The mosque must have been a little jewel in its day. It is half a ruin now. The minaret is gone and so is all but the pillars of the portico that looked into the court. Within, however, are intricately panelled shutters, and a little gallery painted on the under-side, and a carved *mimber* of woodwork like that in the tombs of Roxelana and her sons. The refugees of 1912, poor wretches, saw no reason why they should not drive as many nails as they needed into that precious wood. The greatest ornament of the mosque is a magnificent bronze grille in the archway that opens into the adjoining tomb. This grille is rather like one they show you at Ravenna, in a crypt window of Sant' Apollinare in Classe, except that it has an arrow in each of the arched openings; and the surmounting lunette is a more complicated design. Did Shemsi Pasha, who seems to have had rather a genius for picking things up, get hold of a real Byzantine grille and make this perfect use of it? The tomb itself is in a piteous state of neglect. Nothing is left to show which of the three bare and broken wooden catafalques marked the grave of the dead poet. Windows in the outer wall look through a little marble portico upon a ruined quay. And, tempered so, the splash and flicker of the Bosphorus come into the mosque.

One of the sights of Scutari which always interests me is to be seen behind Shemsi Pasha, where a bluff first begins to lift itself above the sea. Here on any summer day you will notice what you may think to be lines of clothes drying in the wind. The clothes are really those soft figured handkerchiefs which are so greatly used in the East. Bare-legged men dip them in the sea to set the colours; and from them you may follow a gory trail of dye till you come to a house with thick wooden bars tilted strangely out under the eaves like gigantic clothes-horses. This is the *bassma haneh* — the printing-house. It has belonged to the same family for two hundred years, and during that time it can hardly have changed

The bassma haneh

its methods of wood-block printing. Every bit of the work is done by hand. Every stitch of it is lugged down to the salt water for the colours to be made fast, and lugged back. And the factory, like other old-fashioned institutions in Constantinople, is open only from the day of Hîd'r Eless, in May, to that of Kassîm, in November. Once, as I rather intrusively poked my way about it, I came upon a man, whether old or young I could not say, who sat on the floor blocking out the first pattern on long white strips of cloth that were ultimately, as he told me, to make turbans for the people of Kürdistan. The room was almost dark, and it contained hardly anything beside the mattress where the man slept at night and a sizzling caldron beside him. The mixture in the caldron, into which he kept dipping his block, was a dye of death: so he told me, literally in those words, adding that it had already cut ten years off his life. But his employers never could afford to put some sort of a chimney over the caldron — and they assured him that employment like his was to be found in no other country. Was it true? he asked me. I thought to myself that the idyllic old days of hand labour, after which so many of us sigh, may not always have been so idyllic after all.

If you go to the *bassma haneh* by following the shore from the Great Harbour, it is very likely that you will never get there, by reason of the bluff to which I have just alluded. No road runs along the edge of that bluff to Haïdar Pasha and Moda, as perhaps in some far distant day of civic improvement may be the case; but here and there the houses are set a little back, and so many streets come vertically down toward the water that there are plenty of places to take in what the bluff has to offer. And then you will see why so many sultans and emperors built palaces there of old. I may, however, draw your attention for a moment to the island lighthouse falsely known as Leander's Tower. In an old Italian map it is put down as *Torre della Bella Leandra*, and I have wondered if there, haply, was a clew to the name or whether it is simply a sailor's jumble of the legend of the Dardanelles. In Turkish it is called *Kîz Koulesi* — the Maiden's Tower — and it has a legend of its own. This relates to a Greek emperor who, being told that his daughter would one day be stung by a serpent, built a little castle for her on that sea-protected rock. But it happened to her to be seen by an Arab gallant, who expressed his admiration by bringing her flowers in disguise. Among them a viper chanced to creep one day, before the gallant left the mainland, and

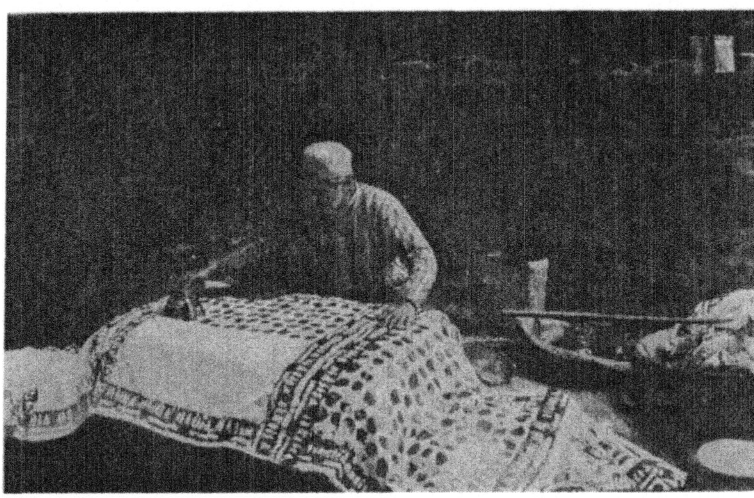

Hand wood-block printing

the princess's prophecy was fulfilled. The gallant immediately sucked the poison out of her wound, however, and ran away with the princess. He was the celebrated hero Sid el Battal, forerunner of the Spanish Cid, who commanded the fifth Arab siege of Constantinople in 739 and who now lies buried in a town named after him in Asia Minor. The existing Maiden's Tower was built in 1763 by Sultan Moustafa III. But a Byzantine one existed before it, of the emperor Manuel Comnenus, from which a chain used to be stretched in time of war across to Seraglio Point. And many centuries earlier the rock bore the statue of a heifer in memory of Damalis, wife of that Athenian Chares who drove away Philip of Macedon. After her the bluff itself used to be called Damalis — which again may be connected with the intricate myth of Io and the Bosphorus.

Every one knows the old story of the Delphian Oracle, who told the colonists of Byzantium to settle opposite the City of the Blind. The City of the Blind turned out to be the place whose inhabitants had passed by the site of Seraglio Point. The reproach cannot be fastened on the City of Gold, because Chalcedon really incurred it. But I have already associated the two towns, and I am willing to do so again. For to live in Scutari is to prove either that the oracle was blind or that Byzas made a mistake. No other conclusion is possible for him who loiters on the bluffs opposite Seraglio Point. One of the best places to see Stamboul is there, where you look at it against the light. And it is something to see in the early morning, with mists melting out of the Golden Horn and making a fairyland of all those domes and pinnacles. As for the sunsets of Scutari, with Stamboul pricking up black against them, they are so notable among exhibitions of their kind that I cannot imagine why they were not long ago put down among sunsets of San Marco and moonlights of the Parthenon and I know not how many other favourite wonders of the world.

I never heard, however, of guides recommending so simple an excursion. What they will sometimes grudgingly recommend is to climb the hill of Chamlîja. Chamlîja — the Place of Pines — is a hill of two peaks, one a little higher than the other, on the descending terraces of which amphitheatrically sprawls the City of Gold. Chamlîja is the highest hill on the Bosphorus, and therefore is it dear to the Turks, who are like the Canaanites of old in that they love groves and high places. The groves, it is true, are now rather thinly represented by the stone-pines that give the height its name; but Turkish princes, like their Byzantine predecessors, have villas among them, while the hill is a favourite resort of their

The Bosphorus from the heights of Scutari

subjects. The widest prospect, of course, is to be had from the top of Big Chamlîja. But a more picturesque one is visible from the south side of Little Chamlîja, taking in a vivid geography of cypress forest and broken Marmora coast, and Princes' Isles seen for once swimming each in its own blue, and far-away Bithynian mountains; while to the explorer of a certain northern spur, running straight to Beïlerbeï Palace, is vouchsafed one of the most romantic of all visions of the Bosphorus. Chamlîja has an especial charm for the people of the country because of its water. No European can quite understand what that means to a Turk. Being forbidden to indulge in fermented liquors, he is a connoisseur of water — not mineral water, but plain H_2O — as other men are of wine. He calls for the product of his favourite spring as might a Westerner for a special vintage, and he can tell when an inferior brand is palmed off on him. A dervish named Hafid Effendi once published a monograph on the waters of Constantinople in which he described the sixteen best springs, which he himself had tested. I will not enumerate all the conditions which he laid down for perfect water. One of them is that it must be "light"; another is that it should flow from south to north or from west to east. A certain spring of Chamlîja meets these requirements better than any other in Constantinople. A sultan, therefore, did not think it beneath him to house this famous water of my native town, and gourmets pay a price to put it on their tables.

A second pretext do guides and guide-books, out of the capriciousness of their hearts, allow outsiders for visiting Scutari, and that is to see the great cemetery. For that matter, few people with eyes of their own and a whim to follow them could look up from the water at that wood of cypresses, curving so wide and sombre above the town, without desiring to know more of it. I have wondered if Arnold Böcklin ever saw it, for in certain lights, and from the right point of the Bosphorus, Scutari looks strangely like a greater Island of Death. In spite of its vast population of old grey stones, however, there is to me nothing so melancholy there as in our trim Western places of burial, shut away from the world and visited only with whispers. There is, of course, a gravity, the inseparable Turkish gravity, but withal a quiet colour of the human. For the Turks have a different attitude toward death from ours. I do not mean that they lack feeling, but they seem to take more literally than we their religious teaching on the subject. They have no conventional mourning, and the living and the dead seem much nearer to each other. Nor is it merely that tombs and patches of cemetery ornament the busiest street. "Visit graves," says a tradition of the Prophet: "Of a truth they shall make you think of futurity." And "Whoso visiteth every Friday the graves of his two parents, or one of the two, he shall be written a pious son, even though he had been disobedient to them in the world." And people do visit graves. The cult of the *türbeh* is a thing by itself, while every cemetery is a place of resort. The cypresses of Scutari are, therefore, the less funereal because the highways of common life run between them. I speak literally, for the main thoroughfares between Scutari and Kadi Kyöi pass through the cemetery. Under the trees the stonecutters fashion the quaint marble of the graves. Fountains are scattered here and there for the convenience of passers-by. People sit familiarly among the stones or in the coffee-houses that do not fail to keep them company. I remember an old man who used to keep one of the coffee-houses, and how he said to me, like a Book of Proverbs: "Death in youth and poverty in age are hard, but both are of God." He was born in Bulgaria, he told me, when it was still a part of Turkey, but he wished to die in Asia, and so he had already taken up his abode among the cypresses of Scutari. A more tragic anticipation of that last journey has been made by a colony of lepers. I went to visit them once, when I thought less of my skin than I do now. They live in a stone quadrangle set back from the Haïdar Pasha road, with windows opening only into their own court. In front of the gate is a stone post where people leave them food. When they offered me some of it, out of the hospitality of their hearts, I must confess I drew the line. They kept house in families, each in its own little apartment, and the rooms were clean and comfortable in the simple Turkish way. But the faces and hands of some of the inmates were not good to see. It made one's heart sick for the children who are born and innocently grow up in that place of death.

The stones of Scutari are a study which I have often wished I had the knowledge to take up. Every grave has a headstone and a footstone, taller and narrower than our old-fashioned tombstones. You can tell at a glance whether a man or a woman is buried beneath the marble slab that generally joins the two stones. In old times every man wore a special turban, according to his rank and profession, and when he died that turban was carved at the top of his headstone. The custom is still continued, although the fez has now so largely taken the place of the turban. Women's stones are finished with a carving of flowers. Floral reliefs are common on all monuments, which may also be painted and gilded. And in the flat slab will be a little hollow to catch the rain — for thirsty spirits and the birds. The epitaphs that are the chief decoration are not very different from epitaphs all over the world, though perhaps a little more flowery than is now the fashion in the West. The simpler ones give only the name and estate of the deceased, with a request for a prayer or a *fatiha* — the opening invocation of the Koran — and some such verse as "He is the Everlasting," "Every soul shall taste death," or "We are God's and we return to God." This sentiment is also characteristic: "Think of the dead. Lift up your hands in prayer, that men may some time visit your grave and pray." The epitaph is often rhymed, though it may be of a touching simplicity — like "O my daughter! O! She flew to Paradise and left to her mother only the sorrow of parting," or "To the memory

Gravestones

of the spirit of the blessed Fatma, mother of Ömer Agha, whose children find no way out of their grief." Others are more complicated and Oriental, ending, like the inscriptions on public buildings, in a chronogram. Von Hammer quotes one, not in this cemetery, which is peculiarly effective in Turkish:

The joy of the life of Feïzi, inspector of markets,
Has vanished into the other world. O how to help it!

For he has lost his rose-bud of a daughter,
Whose like will bloom no more. O how to help it!
The wind of death blew out in the lantern
The light of the feast of life. O how to help it!
In bitterness his eye swells with tears
That are like the tide of the sea. O how to help it!
In bitterness was written the verse of the number of the year:
Hüsseïna has gone away! O how to help it!

Behind the house of the lepers a trail branches away into the most lonely part of this strange forest, ultimately leading down a hill, too rough for any but the most adventurous carriage, to a quaint little stone arch mysteriously called Bloody Bridge that spans a thread of water beside a giant plane-tree. On this southward-looking slope the cypresses attain a symmetry, a slenderness, a height, a thickness of texture and richness of colour unmatched in Stamboul. They grow in squares, many of them, or in magic circles. The stones under them are older than the others, and more like things of nature in the flowered grass. On certain happy afternoons, when the sun brings a fairy depth and softness of green out of the cypresses, when their shadows fall lance-like across bare or mossy aisles, and the note of a solitary bird echoes between them, it is hard not to imagine oneself in an enchanted wood.

In the eyes of most comers from afar the dervishes, those who are ignorantly called the howling dervishes, stand for Scutari and all its works. And the fact always irritates me because it indicates so perfect a blindness to the treasures of the City of Gold — and something else that no sightseer ever pardons in another. The tourists are not in the least interested in dervishes in general. The subject of mysticism and its Oriental ramifications is not one they would willingly go into. They do not dream that Scutari is full of other kinds of dervishes. They have never heard of the *Halveti*, as it were the descendants of the Sleepless Ones of the Studion,

Scutari Cemetery

who consider it a lack of respect to the Creator to sleep lying down, or even to cross their legs, and who repeat every night in the year the *temjid*, the prayer for pity of insomnia, which is heard elsewhere only in Ramazan. No one has ever taken a tourist to see so much as the beautiful ironwork of the tomb of the holy Aziz Mahmoud Hüdaï, who lived eighteen years in a cell of the ancient mosque of Roum Mehmed Pasha. They do not even know that *Roufaï* is the true name of the dervishes they go to stare at, and that there is more than one *tekkeh* of them in Scutari. The traditional "howling" is all that concerns them. And if I were the sheikh of that *tekkeh* I would shut its doors to all tourists — or at least to more than one or two of them at a time. They make more noise than the dervishes.

Having relieved my mind on this subject, in my quality of a native of Scutari, I am able to continue in my other quality of peripatetic impressionist. And incidentally I may record my observation that tourists have, after all, rather a knack for choosing sights that are interesting to see. I am a great admirer of the oblong wooden hall of the *Roufaï*, coloured a dull green, with its weapons and inscriptions and brass candlesticks at the end of the *mihrab*, and its recess of tombs, and its latticed gallery. The floor under the gallery is railed off and set apart for the spectators, who also overflow into the central quadrangle in case of need — if they be of the faith. The ceremony itself has been described so often that there is no need for me to describe it again, though I would like to do so with a little more tolerance for unfamiliar religious observances than some books show. I have never read, however, of such a ritual as I once happened to see on the Mohammedan Ascension Day. Part of the service was a sermon from the black-bearded *sheï'h* upon the miraculous event of the day. At the end of the usual rite all the dervishes and many of the spectators formed a great ring in the centre of the hall, holding hands, and circled in a time of eight beats, calling "*Allah! Allah! Al-lah!*" The rhythm grew faster and faster, and the calling louder and hoarser, until two or three visiting dervishes of another familiar sect slipped into the middle of the ring and began to whirl in their own silent way, while an old man with a rose tucked under his black turban sang with a wildness of yearning that only Oriental music can convey. Then the ring broke and they all marched in a long line into the recess of the tombs, where each man prostrated himself before the first of the turbaned catafalques.

Whether that was the end I have no means of knowing, for I was asked to leave. That is always the case, I notice, when I want to stay after the rest of the sightseers have got tired and gone away. It rather annoys me that I should be classed with unbelievers, and made to sit with them on a bench behind the railing instead of squatting on a sheepskin mat like the other people of Scutari. Yet if it were not so it would never have befallen me to come into contact with so eminent a personality of my day as Mme. Bernhardt — or at least with her parasol. The actress has often been to Constantinople, and she must have seen the howling dervishes many times. Who knows what so great an expert in expression may have caught from the ritual frenzy of the *Roufaï?* It so happened that one of those times was also the occasion of my first visit. I went early, in order to secure a good place. Mme. Bernhardt did not. She has no doubt learned by long and flattering experience that however late she arrives she is sure of a good place. Nor can I suppose she always manages it in the way she did then. She arrived late, I say, and by the time she arrived there was no room left in the front row of benches. I regret to confess that I did not at once hop out of my seat and put her into it. The performance had already begun, tourists were all the time coming in, and while I caught some buzz about the Divine Sarah, I was just then paying more attention to the men of God in front of me. Presently, however, I felt a fearful poke in my back. I knew that poke. It was the eternal feminine. It was beauty. It was genius. It was the Divine Sarah, desiring impressions and not to be debarred from them by a small tourist *quelconque* — and divinely unconscious that she might be imparting them, yet not unaware that many a man would jump into the Seine or the Bosphorus at a poke from her. What would you? I was young, the parasol was hard, and the Divine Sarah was the Divine Sarah. I accordingly slipped out of my place, I hope not without a gracious smile. And what I saw of the dervishes that day was through the foliage of a very complicated hat. I must say that I resented it a little. But I consoled myself by murmuring behind Sarah's back — and the poet's —

"*To poke is human, to forgive divine.*"

VII

THE GARDENS OF THE BOSPHORUS

Giardini chiusi, appena intraveduti,
o contemplati a lungo pe' cancelli
che mai nessuna mano al viandante
smarrito aprì come in un sogno! Muti
giardini, cimiteri senza avelli,
ove erra forse qualche spirto amante
dietro l'ombre de' suoi beni perduti!

—GABRIELE D'ANNUNZIO: "Poema Paradisiaco."

IN the matter of gardens the Turk has never acquired the reputation of his Moorish and Persian cousins. Perhaps it is that he belongs to a younger race and has had more conflicting traditions out of which to evolve a style. For no man likes a garden better than he. He never could put up with a thing like the city back yard or the suburban lawn of the New World. He is given to sitting much out-of-doors, he does not like to be stared at while he is doing it, and he has a great love of flowers. This is one of his most sympathetic traits, and one which was illustrated for me in an unexpected quarter during the late Balkan War when I saw soldiers in a temporary camp laying out patches of turf and pansies around their tents. The fashion of the buttonhole is not yet perfectly acclimated in Constantinople, but nothing is commoner than to observe a grave personage marching along with one rose or one pink in his hand — of which flowers the Turks are inordinately fond. Less grave personages do not scorn to wear a flower over one ear, with its stem stuck under their fez. And I always remember a fireman I once beheld who was not too busy squirting water at a burning house to stop every now and then and smell the rose he held between his teeth.

I cannot claim to know very much about the gardens of Stamboul, though no one can walk there without continually noticing evidences of them — through gateways, over the tops of walls, wherever there is a patch of earth big enough for something green to take root. Any one, however, may know something about the gardens of the Bosphorus. The nature of the ground on which they are laid out, sloping sharply back from the water to an average height of four or five hundred feet and broken by valleys penetrating more gradually into the rolling table-lands of Thrace and Asia Minor, makes it possible to visit many of them without going into them. And the fact has had much to do with their character. Gardens already existed on the banks of the Bosphorus, of course, when the Turk arrived there, and he must have taken them very much as he found them. Plane-trees still grow which, without any doubt, were planted by Byzantine gardeners; and so, perhaps, were certain great stone-pines. I have also wondered if the Turks did not find, when they came, the black and white pebbles, generally arranged in un-Oriental-looking designs, that pave so many garden paths. I am more inclined to believe that these originated in the same order of things as the finer mosaic of church walls than that they were imported from Italy. Perhaps the Italians imported them from Constantinople.

It would be interesting to know whether the Byzantine influence played any part in the gardens of the Renaissance, as it did in so many other arts. However, there is no doubt that the Italian influence came back to Constantinople after the Turkish period. It began to come most definitely, if by a roundabout road, when Sultan Ahmed III imitated the gardens of Versailles. It came again from the same quarter when the successor of Ahmed III sent the son of Twenty-eight Mehmed on another mission to Paris. And it came more definitely still, by a still more roundabout road, when a Russian ambassador brought to Constantinople, at the end of the eighteenth century, a painter named Melling. Like Van Mour, Melling has left most interesting records of the Bosphorus of his day. In the course of time it befell him to be recommended as landscape-gardener to a member of the imperial family, the celebrated Hadijeh *Soultan*. Through the good graces of this enlightened princess he later became architect to her brother, Sultan Selim III, the Reformer. I do not know whether it was the painter, in turn, who obtained for the Sultan the brother of the gardener of Schönbrunn. But altogether Melling must have done a good deal more for the gardens of the Bosphorus than to paint them.

At the same time, no one has done more for them than the Bosphorus itself. A terrace ten feet long may be as enviable as an estate reaching from the water's edge to the top of the hill, since it is the blue panorama of the strait, with its busy boats and its background of climbing green, that is the chief ornament of the garden. The Turks lean, accordingly, to the landscape school. Their gardens have, really, very little of an Italian air. The smallest patch of ground in Italy is more architectural than the largest Turkish estate. However much stone and mortar the Turks put together in retaining and enclosing walls, the result has little architectural effect. They do not trim terraces with marble balustrades, while the lack of garden sculpture is with them a matter into which religion enters. Nor do they often plant trees like the Italians — to balance each other, to frame a perspective, to make a background. Still less, I imagine, do they consciously make colour schemes of flowers. And Lady Mary Montagu noted a long time ago the absence of the trim parterres to which she was

In a Turkish garden

accustomed. It is perfectly in keeping with Oriental ideas of design, of course, for a Turkish garden not to have too much symmetry. Yet it does have more symmetry than an out-and-out landscaper would countenance, and definitely artificial features. I always wonder whether the natural look of so many paths and stone stairs and terraces is merely a result of time or whether it is an accidental effect of the kind striven for by a school of our own gardeners.

If Turkish gardens tend to look a little wild, it is partly because they contain so many trees. In Constantinople, at least, there is so little rain in summer that it would be almost impossible to keep the gardens green without them — to say nothing of the shade and privacy they afford. The old gardeners evidently studied the decorative effect of different kinds of trees. Those who have never visited Constantinople sometimes imagine the Bosphorus to be overhung by palms — I suppose because it washes the coast of Asia and flows into the Mediterranean. They are accordingly sadly disillusioned when they come to it at the end of a winter in other parts of the Mediterranean and encounter a snow-storm. As a matter of fact, the Bosphorus, which lies in about the same latitude as Long Island Sound, has been solidly frozen over two or three times in history. The last time was in February, 1621. That winter, if I remember correctly, was also severe for certain adventurers lately come from England to Massachusetts Bay. But if palms are as great a rarity in Constantinople as in New York or Connecticut, the trees that do grow there belong to a climate more like northern Italy. Among the most striking of them, and happily one of the commonest, is the stone-pine. These are often magnificent, marching in a row along the edge of a terrace or the top of a hill with full consciousness of their decorative value. The cypress, even more common, seems to me never to have been made the most of. Perhaps the Turks, and the Greeks before them, associated it too much with death to play with it as did the Italians of the Renaissance. The Constantinople variety, it is true, inclines to raggedness rather than to slenderness or height. Other evergreens, including the beautiful cedar of Lebanon, have been domesticated in smaller numbers. Being unscientifically minded, I can say that the magnolia might properly be classed among them, the *Magnolia grandiflora* of our Southern States, since it keeps its glossy leaves all winter long. One of the less tenacious brotherhood, the plane-tree, is easily king of the Bosphorus, reaching a girth and height that almost fit it for the company of the great trees of California. It always seems to me the most treey of trees, so regularly irregular are the branches and so beautiful a pattern do they make when the leaves are off. Limes, walnuts, chestnuts, horse-chestnuts, Lombardy poplars, acacias of various sorts, mulberries, the Japanese medlar, the dainty pomegranate, the classic bay, are also characteristic. The pale branches of the fig are always decorative, and when the leaves first begin to sprout they look in the sun like green tulips. The olive and the glorious oleander will only thrive in sheltered corners, while oranges and lemons grow in pots. In the hillside parks that are the pride of the larger estates, nightingale-haunted in the spring, pleasantly green in rainless summers, and warmly tawny in the autumn, deciduous trees predominate

A Byzantine well-head

altogether. Among them is one of heart-shaped leaves and dark capricious branches with whose Latin name I am unacquainted but which is one of the greatest ornaments of the Bosphorus. The Turks call it *ergovan*, and its blossoming is the signal for them to move to their country houses. In English, I believe, we call it the Judas, after some legend that makes it the tree on which the traitorous apostle hanged himself. He would apparently have been of high descent, for the flowers, which took thereafter the stain of his blood, have a decided violet tinge. They fledge the branches so thickly before the leaves are out that they paint whole hillsides of April with their magenta.

A garden wall fountain

In addition to the woodiness of the Bosphorus gardens, Lady Mary Montagu remarked another element of their character which, I am afraid, has become less frequent since her day. However, if garden sculpture of one kind is rare, garden marbles of another kind do very definitely exist. Here, too, I fancy the Turk found something when he came. There is a smiling lion to be found in certain gardens who, unless I am greatly mistaken, has Byzantine blood in his veins — if that may be said of a water spouter. He is cousin german to the lion of St. Mark, who only improved on him by growing wings. There are also well-heads which are commonly supposed to have been turned to that use by the Turks out of Byzantine capitals. But I do not see why some of them may not be original well-heads. One sees exactly the same sort of thing in Italy, except that the style of ornament is different in the two countries. The purely Turkish garden marbles are of the same general order, having to do with water. And, although there was less need of them when nature had already been so generous, they are what the Turk brought most of himself to the gardens of the Bosphorus. The Turkish well-heads are not particularly interesting, being at their best not much more than a marble barrel. Much more interesting are the marble basins and the upright tablets behind them which mark the head of a water-pipe. These tablets are sometimes charmingly decorated with arabesques and low reliefs of flowers. But the real fountains are the most characteristic, and it seems to me that they offer the most in the way of suggestion to the Western gardener. I think no one has ever understood like the Oriental the poetry of water. Western architects and gardeners have, of course, made great use of decorative water; but we never seem to be happy unless we have a mountain of marble and a torrent of water to work with. Whereas the architects of the East have always known in this matter how to get the greatest effect out of the least material. There are charms in a shallow pool or a minute trickle of water which are of an entirely different order from those of an artificial lake or cascade.

Almost every Turkish garden contains visible water of some sort, which at its simplest is nothing but a shallow marble pool. In thé centre of the pool is sometimes a fountain which I always think of with regret when there is pointed out for my admiration a too fat marble infant struggling with a too large marble fish, or a dwarf holding an umbrella over its head. This fountain consists of nothing but a series of jets, generally on

A jetting fountain in the garden of Halil Edhem Bey

varying levels, set in a circle of those marble stalactites — here should one call them stalagmites? — which are so familiar in Oriental architecture. Nothing could be simpler, apparently, but nothing could combine more perfectly all the essentials of a jetting fountain. There is another fountain which deals even more delicately with the sound of water. This is a dripping fountain, set always against a wall or a bank. It is a tall marble tablet, decorated, perhaps, with low reliefs of fruit and flowers, on the face of which a series of tiny basins are carved. I have seen one where water started at the top from the eyes of two doves and trickled into the first little basin, from which it overflowed into two below, then back into one, and so on till it came into three widening semicircular pools at the bottom. *Selsebil* is the name of this fountain in Turkish, which is the name of a fountain in Paradise; and a fountain of Paradise it may be indeed with all its little streams atinkle. A more delightful ornament for a garden does not exist, being equally adapted for the end of a vista or for a narrow space; and it requires the smallest supply of water.

A *selsebil* at Kandilli

The Turkish architects have not scorned more imposing effects when they had the means, as did Ahmed III at Kiat Haneh. The marble cascades into which he turned the Barbyses are called *chaghleyan* — something which resounds. I have seen a smaller *chaghleyan* in a garden on the Asiatic shore of the Bosphorus. This is a series of descending pools, one emptying into another till the water finally runs into a large round marble basin. The water starts, between two curved flights of stone steps, from three marble shells in the retaining wall of a terrace; and from the terrace an arbour looks down the perspective of mirroring pools to an alley that leads from the last basin away between arching trees. This beautiful old garden belongs to the Turkish painter Ressam Halil Pasha, who studied in Paris at a time when the plastic arts were still anathema among the Turks. In his studio are figure studies, made during his student days, which even now he could scarcely exhibit in Constantinople; and it would be thought a scandalous thing if he tried to get Turkish models to sit for such pictures. When he heard where I came from he asked if there were in America a painter called Mr. Cox, who had studied with him under Gérôme.

A *selsebil* of Halil Edhem Bey

There is rivalry between the gardens of the upper, the middle, and the lower Bosphorus with regard to their advantages of position. The upper Bosphorus is the most desirable from the European point of view.

This preference is fairly well established, for Lady Mary Montagu wrote letters from Belgrade Forest two hundred years ago, and about the same time a summer colony composed of Europeans and of the great Phanariote families began to gather at Büyük Dereh and Therapia. In much earlier times, however, the Byzantine emperors built villas at Therapia, and the very name of the place indicates the antiquity of its repute as a place of resort. The name has come down in the story of Jason and the Argo, who sailed between these shores in the dawn of legend. When those early voyagers returned from Colchis with Medea, that formidable passenger threw out poison on the Thracian shore; whence the name Pharmakia, changed by the euphemism of the Greeks to Therapia, or Healing. There are reasons, to be sure, why it is better to look at Therapia than to be in it. The view it commands is the bleakest on the Bosphorus, and the prevailing north wind of midsummer, the *meltem*, which keeps the strait much cooler than you would imagine from its latitude, sometimes gets on one's nerves. Nevertheless Therapia is a centre for an extraordinary variety of pleasant excursions, there are delicious gardens in the clefts of its hills, and from May till October the embassies impart to it such gaiety as the somewhat meagre social resources of Constantinople afford. I shall be surprised if the proximity of Belgrade Forest and the magnificent beach of Kilios on the Black Sea, to say nothing of the various other resources of the Bosphorus and the Marmora, do not some day make Therapia much more famous as a summer resort.

Constantinople is, I believe, the sole diplomatic post to which summer residences are attached. Each envoy also has a launch for keeping in touch with the Sublime Porte, fifteen miles away. The local legend is that the birds which are so characteristic a feature of the Bosphorus — halcyons are they ?— for ever skimming up and down just above the surface of the water, are the souls of the Phanariote dragomans who used to go back and forth so often between Therapia and Stam-

In the garden of Ressam Halil Pasha

boul. A despatch-boat, as well, is at the disposal of each ambassador except the Persian. These dignities came about very naturally by reason of the epidemics and disorders which used to break out in the city, the distance of Constantinople from other European resorts, and the generosity of the sultans. The English, French, and German governments all own beautiful estates at Therapia, presented to them by different sultans, while the Russians are magnificently established at the neighbouring village of Büyük Dereh. Their great hillside park is a perfect wood, so dense in summer that the water is scarcely visible from it. The Italians also make *villeggiatura* at Therapia, the Austrians and Persians being installed farther down the Bosphorus. Our ambassador is the sole envoy of his rank obliged to hunt up hired quarters, though even some of the small legations occupy their own summer homes. Should Congress ever persuade itself that diplomatic dignity is a thing worthy to be upheld, or should some sultan present us with one of the old estates still available, I hope we shall build an embassy, like the one the French occupied so long, in keeping with its surroundings and not such a monstrosity as other Powers have put up. The charming old French embassy, which originally belonged to the famous Ypsilanti family, was one of the sights of the Bosphorus until it burned up in 1913. The grounds are not so large as some of the other embassy gardens, but none of the others seem to me so happily placed or so sapiently laid out. A bridge led from the house to the first terrace, whose trees and flowers irregularly follow the curve of the hillside. A formal avenue and steep wood paths mount to the grassy upper terrace, commanding between noble pines and beeches the mouth of the Black Sea.

There are Turks, of course, in the upper Bosphorus, as there are Christians in the middle Bosphorus. One of the most conspicuous of all the Bosphorus gardens is at Beïkos, on the Asiatic shore — which, for the rest, is much more Turkish than the European. Beïkos is also connected with the Argonauts, being the place where they met with so unkind a welcome from Amycus, king of the Bebryces. He or some other mythic personage

The garden of the Russian embassy at Büyük Dereh

is supposed to have been buried on the hilltop behind Beïkos. This height, popularly known as Giant's Mountain, is the only one on the Bosphorus from which you can see both the Black Sea and the Marmora — as Byron recorded in a notorious stanza. A giant grave

The upper terrace of the French embassy garden at Therapia

is still to be seen there, some twenty feet long, which the Turks honour as that of rather an unexpected personage. A little mosque adjoins the grave — built, I believe, by the ambassador Twenty-eight Mehmed — and in the mosque is this interesting inscription: "Here lies his excellency Joshua, the son of Nun, who although not numbered among the apostles may well be called a true prophet sent of God. He was despatched by Moses (on whom be peace) to fight the people of Rome. While the battle was yet unfinished the sun set. Joshua caused the sun to rise again and the Romans could not escape. This miracle convinced them; and when Joshua invited them, after the battle, to accept the true faith, they believed and accepted it. If any man doubts, let him look into the sacred writings at the Holy Places of the Christians and he will be satisfied." The garden I have wandered so far away from rises on a pyramid of terraces at the mouth of a smiling valley which bears the grim name of *Hounkyar Iskelesi* — the Landing-Place of the Manslayer. A white palace crowns the pyramid, facing the long river-like vista of the Bosphorus. The palace was built by the great Mehmed Ali, of Egypt, to whom the sultan of the day paid the honour of coming to see his new pleasure-house and of expressing his admiration of it. The viceroy accordingly assured his majesty, as Oriental etiquette demands, that the palace and everything in it was his. Whereupon his majesty, to the no small chagrin of the viceroy, graciously signified his acceptance of the gift.

Beïkos and the shores of its great bay were a favourite resort of sultans long before the day of Mehmed Ali. In general, however, the Turks have always preferred the narrow middle stretch of the Bosphorus; and for most reasons I am with them. The summer *meltem* — which some derive from the Italian *maltempo* — often intensely irritating near the mouth of the Black Sea, is here somewhat tempered by the windings of the strait. Then here the coasts of the two continents approach each other most closely, are most gracefully modelled and greenly wooded. The Asiatic shore in particular, which opposite Therapia is forbidding enough, is here a land of enchantment, with its gardens, its groves, its happy valleys, its tempting points and bays, its sky-line of cypresses and stone-pines, its weathered wooden villages, its ruined water-side castle of Anadolou Hissar, its far-famed Sweet Waters — and most so if seen from Europe in a light of sunset or early morning. If Mehmed Ali lost his palace at Beïkos — and on Arnaout-kyöi Point there are the ruins of another one which he was stopped from building — several of the most enviable estates along this part of the Bosphorus belong to his descendants. The beautiful wooded cape of Chiboukiou, on the Asiatic side, is crowned by the mauresque château of the present Khedive. Directly opposite, on the southern point of Stenia Bay, is the immense old tumble-down wooden palace of his grandfather Ismaïl, the spendthrift Khedive of the Suez Canal, who died there in exile. The garden behind it is the largest and, historically, one of the most interesting on the Bosphorus. The name of the bay is derived, according to one story, from that of the Temple of Sosthenia, or Safety, built by the Argonauts after their escape from King Amycus. A temple of Hecate was also known there in more authentic times, and a church dedicated to the Archangel Michael by Constantine the Great. On a stormy night of 1352, the admirals Nicolò Pisani of Venice and Paganino Doria of Genoa unwittingly took shelter in the bay within bow-shot of each other, during an interval of a long sea-fight which raged between them the whole length of the Bosphorus. Emirgyan, the name of the village in which the khedivial estate is situated, was that of a Persian general who surrendered Erivan to Sultan Mourad IV in 1635, and who ended his days in pleasant captivity on this wooded shore. His beautiful Persian palace of Feridoun was the wonder of its day. His conqueror used often to visit him there, for Emirgyan was a man of wit and an accomplished musician. Not only did he first introduce into Turkey a sort of Persian bassoon and the four-stringed Persian *chartar* from which we get our guitar, but he marked a new epoch in Turkish music. There were also other reasons why Mourad used to visit the palace of Feridoun, where, "in the design of refreshing his vital spirits and of summoning the warmth which awakens joy, it pleased" the Sultan "to give rein to the light courser of the beverage of the sunrise" — as a discreet historian put that violent young man's propensity to strong waters. It was after a debauch here that he died, at the age of twenty-eight, having beheaded a hundred thousand of his people and having entertained a strange ambition to be the last of his line. He gave orders on his death-bed that the head of his brother Ibrahim, the last surviving male of his blood, be brought to him. But his courtiers took advantage of his condition to dissemble their disobedience, and the imperial family to-day springs from that brother. As for the luckless Emirgyan, he saved his head from the elder brother, only to be deprived of it by the younger.

At Roumeli Hissar, still farther to the south, is a neglected garden which belonged to Halim Pasha, brother of the prodigal Ismaïl. In it are two unpretentious houses which look as if they were built of brown stucco. There is sentiment in that stucco, however, for it is really mud brought from the banks of the Nile. According to the law of Islam Halim would have been Khedive in turn if Ismaïl had not bound the Turkish government, by a substantial *quid pro quo*, to make the viceroyalty hereditary to the eldest son in his own family. And Halim Pasha's family later suffered the misfortune to be nearly ruined by an English speculator.

But there is one spot in their park which must have gone far to make up for their disinheritance. It is the brow of a bluff which seems to drop sheer into the Bosphorus. There an artful group of cypresses and one gnarled olive frame the blue below; and there on sunny afternoons, there most notably on starry evenings, when shore lights curve fantastically through the underlying darkness and all land and water sounds have some summer magic in them, an Antony might dream away content the loss of Egypt.

Halim Pasha owned another splendid garden on Bebek Bay. Next to his faded pink wooden *yalì* in the dignified old Turkish style, and likewise linked by bridges across the public road to a park that climbs the hill behind, is the trim *art-nouveau* villa of the actual Khedive's mother. This majestic old lady is one of the most familiar figures on the Bosphorus. Her annual approach and departure on her son's big turbine yacht *Mahroussah* are the signals for spring and autumn to open their campaigns, while her skimming mahogany steam-launch is an integral part of summer. She is, moreover, a person whom the poor of her neighbourhood have cause to bless. During the lenten month of Ramazan she provides *iftar*, the sunset breakfast of the day, for any who choose to come to her door. So many choose to come that during that month her grocery bills must be quite appalling. And on occasions of public rejoicing she literally keeps open house — or open garden. She admits any and all within her gates, offers them coffee, ices, and cigarettes, and entertains them with music.

The custom, for the rest, is common among the Turks at all times of festivity. I remember going one night to another garden in Bebek, not by invitation but because any one was free to go in order to celebrate the accession day of his majesty Abd ül Hamid II. The garden belonged to a younger brother of that personage, popularly known as Cowherd Solomon Esquire. For Turkish princes have no title other than that of their humblest subject. A band was playing in the garden, which is on the very top of Bebek hill, and the Greeks of the village were dancing among the flower-beds, while a row of little princes and princesses in big gilt armchairs looked solemnly on. Beyond them a clump of huge umbrella-pines lifted themselves darkly against the fairy scene of the illuminated Bosphorus. Every other villa was outlined in light, the water burned with reflections of architectural designs or of Arabic texts of fire, and the far-away hill of Chamlîja was one twinkling field of the cloth of gold. Süleïman Effendi was reported to be not too strong in the head but to make up for it by possessing the Evil Eye and the greatest understanding of cows of any man in Constantinople. Of these he kept a large herd, selling their milk like any commoner; and when he wished to add to their number no man dared refuse to sell to him. If he did the cow in question was sure to die within the month by reason of the Evil Eye of the imperial milkman. Abd ül Hamid caused this eccentric old gentleman much unhappiness, tormenting him greatly with spies. Süleïman Effendi lived long enough to see the last of the spies, however, if not of Abd ül Hamid. And he must have been not altogether destitute of human qualities, for his wife died of grief the day after his death.

The picturesque bay of Bebek and the opposite headland of Kandilli are so involved with historic memories that I am more and more tempted to stray out of my gardens. Kandilli, in particular, is full of plane-trees and terraces and rows of stone-pines to prove that older generations were not blind to its enchantments. Among other sultans, Mehmed IV spent much of his time there. His favourite wife was the lady of taste and determination who built the mosque of the New Mother in Scutari.

The Villa of the Sun, Kandilli

Discovering once that her lord spent more of his hours than she found proper in the society of a Circassian dancing-girl, she caused a man slave of her own to be educated in the terpsichorean art and presented him to the Sultan. She then asked one night, as they sat at the edge of the water at Kandilli, that the two dancers perform together for her amusement. The slaves accordingly danced on the terrace before their imperial masters, nearer and nearer the water, till the man, by a seemingly careless thrust of his foot, tripped his companion into the Bosphorus. She was immediately carried away into the dark by the current, here extremely swift; and the Sultana doubtless slept the more sweetly, knowing there was one less dancer in the world.

I do not know whether the imperial villa near the boat landing that was torn down in 1913 was the scene of this little drama. *Yalî* is the true name of such a country house, if it is built, as it should be, on the edge of the water, with gateways letting a little of the Bosphorus into the lower hall and making there a boat-house and *porte cochère* in one. In every country place of any size there is a *kyöshk* as well, otherwise a kiosk, built somewhere in the garden and constituting one of its more formal ornaments. I once had the honour of being received in a kiosk belonging to a member of the imperial family, which was larger than the *yalî* to which it belonged. It was, alas, no such place as I have read of in Lady Mary Montagu, who describes a room built by the sultan of her day for his daughter, "wainscotted with mother of pearl fastened with emeralds like nails." She also speaks of wainscotting of "cedar set off with silver nails" and "walls all crusted with Japan China," "the whole adorned with a profusion of marble, gilding, and the most exquisite painting of fruit and flowers." These splendours were no invention of Lady Mary, for many other visitors testify to them, as well as Melling, Van Mour, and all their school of painters of the Bosphorus. Those villas never were of an enduring architecture, and the spell of Europe — more potent than ever for us was that of the gorgeous East — has been more fatal to them than time and fire. Still, the most modern *yalî*, if designed by an architect of the country, almost always has some saving touch of its own. And in the middle Bosphorus there are quite a number of houses which preserve the graceful old architecture.

The number of those which preserve even a remnant of the old interior decoration is much more limited. One of them is a kiosk at Emirgyan belonging to the *Sherifs* of Mecca. And it is quaint to see what an air, both whimsical and distinguished, that faded eighteenth-century decoration gains from the ugly modern furniture set about a fountain in the cross-shaped saloon of those descendants of the Prophet. The most complete example of the work of the same period is the house on Arnaoutkyöi Point belonging to an Armenian family, unmistakable by its projecting upper stories and the agreeable irregularity of its silhouette. Passers along the quay may catch a glimpse of a high rococo ceiling in rose and gold. But a glimpse of a more perfect ceiling is to be caught by any one who rows up the Asiatic shore from Anadolou Hissar — if he be not too contemptuous of certain crazy wooden piles which his caïque will pass.

This ceiling, and the whole room to which it belongs, is the most precious thing of its kind in all Constantinople, if not in all the world. The design of the room is that of the earlier Broussa mosques, a T-shaped arrangement with the top of the T in the garden and three square bays, slightly raised above a central square, leaning out on piles above the water. At the intersection of the two axes stands a fountain, with a cluster of marble stalactites rising from a filigree marble pedestal, in the centre of a shallow square tank of marble. On the garden side, where the door is, there are no windows, but a series of cupboards and niches of some light wood once delicately inlaid with wavy stems and pointed leaves. On the water side an unbroken succession of windows, not very tall and set at the level of the divan, look north and west and south, and bring the Bosphorus like a great sparkling frieze into the pavilion. They also make the water light, by reflection, the upper part of the room. At the height of the window tops a shelf, slightly carved and gilded, runs entirely

An eighteenth-century villa at Arnaout-kyöi

around the walls. Above that rises a frieze of painted panels in which tall sprays of lilies and other flowers stand in blue and white jars, each in a pointed arch and each framed by garlands of tiny conventionalised flowers. And above all hangs a golden ceiling, domed over the fountain, over each bay hollowed into an oblong recess, lovely with latticework and stalactites and carved bosses and Moorish traceries of interlaced stars, and strange border loops of a blue that echoes the jars below or the sea outside, and touches of a deep green, and exquisite little flowers, all shimmering in a light of restless water.

The golden room of Kyöprülü Hüsseïn Pasha

The creator of this masterpiece was that great friend of the arts Kyöprülü Hüsseïn Pasha, to whose *medresseh* in Stamboul I have already referred. His *yalî* has disappeared and his legendary pleasure-grounds are now a wilderness, albeit superlatively pleasant still either to look into or to look out of. In them is one of the sixteen famous springs of Hafid Effendi. Historic garden-parties were given in this garden, and ambassadors whom sultans delighted to honour were taken to sit in the golden room. It used to be a detached kiosk in Hüsseïn Pasha's garden. In modern times a house has been added to it, and a retired provincial governor has inherited the fallen splendour of the Kyöprülüs. Some day, I suppose, it will all go up in smoke or tumble into the Bosphorus. In the meantime the fountain is still, the precious marquetry has been picked out of the doors, the woodwork cracks and sags, the blue jars and the flowers become more and more ghostly, the gold of the ceiling grows dimmer every day. But even so, the golden room has a charm that it can never have had when the afternoon sun first shimmered into it.

The gardens of the lower Bosphorus are in many ways less picturesque than those nearer the Black Sea. The hills on which they lie are in general lower, farther apart, and more thickly covered with houses. With their milder air, however, their more Mediterranean light, and their glimpse into the Sea of Marmora, they enjoy another, a supreme, advantage. The upper Bosphorus — well, in other places you may see sharply rising slopes terraced or wooded. Beside the Nordfjord, the coast of Dalmatia, or Lake Como, where would the Bosphorus be? But nowhere else may you behold the silhouette of Stamboul. And that, pricking the sky above its busy harbour, just not closing the wide perspective that shines away to the south, is the unparalleled ornament of the gardens of the lower Bosphorus. The garden that Melling laid out for the princess Hadijeh was in this part of the strait, at the point of Defterdar

Bournou, above Orta-kyöi. Abd ül Hamid, who to his other crimes added a culpable crudity of taste, pulled down the princess's charming old house in order to build two hideous new ones for two daughters of his own. Most of the finest sites in the neighbourhood, or on the opposite shore, belong or have belonged to different members of the imperial family. Abd ül Hamid himself was brought back from Salonica at the outbreak of the Balkan War and shut up in the Asiatic garden of Beïlerbeï. In this old pleasance of the sultans Abd ül Aziz built a palace for the empress Eugénie when she went to the East to open the Suez Canal. It must have been strange to Abd ül Hamid to look out from its windows at the opposite park where he reigned for thirty-three years. The city of palaces which grew up around him there was never known otherwise than as Yîldîz Kiosk — the Pavilion of the Star — from a *kyöshk* his father built. Another pavilion in that park, also visible from Beïlerbeï, is the Malta Kiosk, where Abd ül Hamid's older brother Mourad passed the first months of his long captivity, and where Midhat Pasha, father of the Turkish constitution, was iniquitously tried for the murder of Abd ül Aziz. In the pleasant lower hall of this little palace, almost filled by a marble basin of goldfish, it is not easy to reconstitute that drama so fateful for Turkey — which did not end when Abd ül Hamid received from Arabia, in a box labelled "Old Japanese Ivory," the head of the murdered patriot.

The park of Yîldîz originally belonged to the palace whose name of Chira'an — The Torches — has been corrupted by Europeans into Cheragan. Only a ruin stands there now, on which Abd ül Aziz once squandered half the revenues of the empire. He stumbled on the threshold the first time he went into his new house, and never would live in it; but after his dethronement he either committed suicide or was murdered there. His successor, Mourad V, dethroned in turn after a reign of three months, lived in his unhappy uncle's palace for nearly thirty years. Abd ül Hamid is said to have kept his brother so rigorously that the ladies of the family were at one time compelled to dress in the curtains of the palace. The so-called mad Sultan, deprived of books and even of writing materials, taught his children to read and write by means of charcoal on the parquet floor. The imperial prisoner occupied the central rooms of the palace, the doors leading from which were nailed up. When architects were called after his death to put the palace in order they found a foot of water standing on the marble floor of the state entrance, at the north end; and street dogs, jumping in and out of the broken windows, lived in the magnificent throne-room above. Upon his own dethronement, Abd ül Hamid begged to be allowed to retire to this splendid residence. It was presented, instead, to the nation by Sultan Mehmed V for a parliament house. But after two months of occupancy as such it was destroyed by fire. It was only the last of many palaces, one of which was built by Selim III and in which Melling, again, had a hand. The name Chira'an goes back, I believe, to the time of Ahmed III, whose Grand Vizier and son-in-law, Ibrahim Pasha, had a palace there. This minister, by some reports a renegade Armenian, is famous in Turkish annals for his liberal administration, for his many public buildings, and for his introduction of printing into the Ottoman Empire. Among his other talents was one for humouring the tastes of his splendour-loving master. Ibrahim Pasha gave the Sultan one night at Chira'an a garden-party, at which countless tortoises, with lights fastened to their shells, made a moving illumination among the trees. Whence the name of The Torches.

Ahmed III gave many similar entertainments in his own gardens on Seraglio Point, sometimes fêtes of lights, sometimes fêtes of flowers. Of the latter he had such an admiration that he created at his court a Master of Flowers, whose credentials, ornamented by gilt roses, ended thus: "We command that all gardeners recognise for their chief the bearer of this diploma; that they be in his presence all eye like the narcissus, all ear like the rose; that they have not ten tongues like the lily; that they transform not the pointed pistil of the tongue into the thorn of the pomegranate, dyeing it in the blood of inconvenient words. Let them be modest, and let them keep, like the rosebud, their lips closed. Let them not speak before their time, like the blue hyacinth, which scatters its perfume before men ask for it. Finally, let them humbly incline themselves before him like the violet, and let them not show themselves recalcitrant." The tulip does not seem to be mentioned in this document, but the culture of tulips under Ahmed III and his congenial Grand Vizier became as extravagant a rage as ever it did in Holland. Indeed, tulips were first introduced into the Low Countries from Constantinople, by the Fleming Ogier de Busbecq, ambassador of the Holy Roman Empire to Süleïman the Magnificent. Under the Latinised form of his name he has left a quaint memoir of his two embassies. The word tulip is a corruption of the Turkish word *dülbend* — turban — which was a favourite nickname of the flower among the Turks. Ahmed III always celebrated tulip time, inviting the grandees of the empire to come and admire his tulip beds. He devised a way of illuminating them at night with the small glass cup lamps used in mosques.

Mahmoud I was of a taste to continue this pretty custom. He also laid out special tulip and hyacinth gardens behind the summer palace he built at the water's edge. Alleys of cypress-trees were there, and a great pool of marble, and about it the slaves of the harem would sing and dance in the fairy light of the illuminated flowers.

Nothing is left now of this garden, or the palace to which it belonged, or the Gate of the Cannon, after which they were named. A disastrous fire and the building of the Bulgarian railway long made a waste of the tip of Seraglio Point, until in 1913 it was turned into a public park. Seraglio Point is an Italian misnomer for the Turkish *Seraï Bournou* — Palace Point. But a palace and gardens remain, not far away, and to them has been transferred the title of Top Kapou — Cannon Gate. Although this is now the oldest palace in Constantinople, the name of *Eski Seraï* — the Old Palace — belongs to the site of that older one which the Conqueror built on the hill of the War Department. He was the first, however, to set apart Seraglio Point as a pleasure-ground for his family, and he built the *Chinili-Kyöshk,* now of the Imperial Museum. His son and grandson built other pavilions of their own, but it was not until the reign of his great-grandson Süleïman I that the court was definitely transferred to the Seraglio. As in the Palace of Celestial Purity in the Forbidden City, no woman had up to that time been permitted to sleep there. And it is perhaps significant that the decadence of the empire began very soon after the transfer of the harem to the new palace. From that time on the Old Palace, whose grounds Süleïman greatly curtailed to make room for his two principal mosques, was reserved for the families of deceased sultans, while the new palace was continually enlarged and beautified. Something legendary attaches to it in the eyes of the common people, who are pleasantly inclined to confuse King Solomon, the friend of the Queen of Sheba, and a great personage in Mohammedan folk-lore, with their own Sultan Süleïman. A soldier from Asia Minor related to me once how Sultan Solomon sent out four birds to the four quarters of heaven to discover the most perfect site for a palace, and how they came back with the news that no place was to be found in the world so airy or so beautiful as Seraglio Point. He accordingly built the palace of Top Kapou. And beneath it he hollowed out a space reaching far under the sea in which he planted a forest of marble pillars. I cannot vouch for the last part of the story, but I am inclined to agree with the Sultan's birds. Certainly the garden of the Seraglio has its superb situation between the Golden Horn and the Marmora, its crescent panorama of cities, seas, and islands, and its mementoes of the past, to put it alone among the gardens of the world. Acropolis of ancient Byzantium, pleasance of Roman, Greek, and Ottoman emperors for sixteen hundred years, it is more haunted by associations than any other garden in Europe. One could make a library alone of the precious things its triple walls enclose: the column of Claudius Gothicus, the oldest Roman monument in the city; the church of St. Irene, originally built by Constantine, whose mosaics look down as Justinian and Leo left them on the keys of conquered cities, the battle-flags of a hundred fields, the arms and trophies of the martial period of the Turks; the sarcophagus of Alexander, which is but one of the glories of the museum; the imperial library, where the MS. of Critobulus was discovered; the imperial treasury, with its jewels, coins, rare stuffs, gemmed furniture, the gifts and spoil of kings, in vaults too dim and crowded for their splendour to be seen; the sacred relics of the Prophet which Selim I captured with Egypt and which constitute the credentials of the sultans to the caliphate of Islam. The structure in which these are preserved, its broad eaves and crusting of flowered tiles reflected in a pool bordered by lanterns to be lit on holy nights, is one of the things that make that garden incomparable. Then there are quaint turrets and doorways; there are kiosks; there are terraces; there are white cloisters a little grassy and neglected; there are black cypresses and monstrous plane-trees into which the sun looks with such an air of antique familiarity.

Of all this every one has written who has ever been to Constantinople. But not many have written of a part of the garden which until the fall of Abd ül Hamid almost no outsider had visited. A few wrote then of the strange scene which took place there when the slaves of the deposed Sultan were set at liberty, and any Circassian who believed himself to have a relative in the imperial harem was invited to come and take her away. The dramatic contrasts and disappointments one could imagine made a true term to all the passionate associations of that place. No one lives there now. When a few more years have passed and no breathing person has any vital memory connected with it, the harem of the old Seraglio will be, like how many other places devised by a man to house his own life, a resort for sightseers at so much a head, a mere piece of the taste of a time. As it is, the Gate of Felicity does not open too easily, and one can still feel the irony of its name.

The entrance to the harem is under the pointed tower which catches the eye from afar. You go first into the court of the black eunuchs, narrow, high-walled on one side, overlooked on the other by a tiled porch and by a series of cells which never can have been light enough for the tiles that line them to be visible. A great hooded fireplace terminates the dark passage into which they open. Up-stairs are roomier and lighter quarters, also tiled, for

Photograph by Abdullah Frères, Constantinople

In the harem of the Seraglio

the superior dignitaries of this African colony. A few vestiges of their power remain in the vestibule at the farther end of the court, in the shape of various instruments of torture. In a dark angle of this place, which communicates with the Court of the Pages and the Sultan's quarters, a lantern hanging behind a rail marks where the old *valideh* Kyössem was strangled with a curtain cord. Tiles of the same period as her mosque face one of the side walls with an elegant row of cypress-trees. Beyond them opens another court. More tiles are there, and a lane of turf, where only the Sultan might ride, leads between the flagstones to a marble block. The interior of the harem is a labyrinth so complicated that I would have to visit it many more times to bring away any clear idea of its arrangement. There is very little of what we would call splendour in those endless rooms that sultan after sultan added to without order or plan. They contain, as true Turkish rooms should, almost no furniture. What furniture they do contain is late Empire, rather the worse for wear. Ugly European carpets cover a few floors. Stuffy European hangings drape a few windows. Gilded canopies cover a daiş or two where a *valideh soultan* held her court — and almost the whole of a dark cupboard where a sultana did not disdain to sleep. There are ceilings more or less elaborately carved and gilded. There are big niches for braziers. There are doors inlaid with tortoise-shell and ivory and mother-of-pearl. There are wall fountains, some of them lovely with sculptured reliefs and painting. There are baths, also containing fountains, and screens of filigree marble, and marble tanks. There are, above all, tiles and tiles and tiles. They line almost all the rooms, and many of them are very bad. The new fashion in taste which Ahmed III imported from France became more and more popular until it nearly swallowed up the whole palace. Who knows what priceless walls were rifled in order to make room for cheap Dutch tiles and frescoes of imaginary perspectives! Porcelain and marble have been visibly painted over in some places, and panels that end up-stairs or in another room prove how ruthlessly partitions were put up. Yet there is a seducing quaintness about the Turkish rococo at its best. And there are enough good tiles left in the palace to make up for all the rest. I remember some simple ones in a passage, representing nothing but the tents of a camp, and several showing the holy places of Mecca. These, I believe, were of the time of Mehmed III. Oth-

Photograph by Abdullah Frères, Constantinople

The "Cage" of the Seraglio

ers are absolutely the most superb things of their kind in Constantinople. A room of Mourad III, the gallery so called of Sultan Selim, and a magnificent hall which Süleïman himself might have built, if he did not, give an idea of what a magic place that old labyrinth may originally have been. Two rooms of Ahmed I are also charming, one a small dining-room delicately painted with fruit and flowers, the other a library, with inlaid cupboards for books and a quantity of cool green tiles.

Interesting in another way is the *Kafess*, the Cage, where the young princes lived until it was time for them to ascend the throne — or to be strangled. Sultan Ibrahim was there when courtiers came to do homage to him, with the news that his terrible brother Mourad IV was dead; but he would not believe it until his mother, the great Kyössem, ordered Mourad's body to be shown him. The broad eaves and exterior tiles of the Cage overhang a court of two levels, through the middle of whose stone pavement a fantastic little river is cut for running water. The one open side, guarded by a balustrade of perforated marble, overlooks a sunken garden and a bit of the Golden Horn. And I remember another court, higher in the air, where an upper story leaned out on brackets, as if for a better view of the Bosphorus, and where cherry-trees stood in blossom around a central pool.

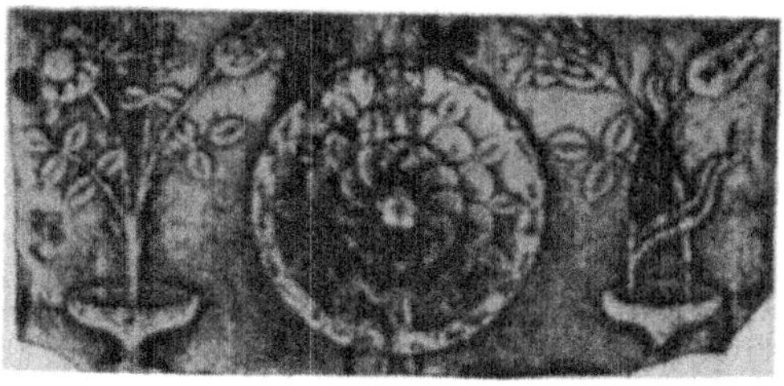

VIII

THE MOON OF RAMAZAN

In the name of the most merciful God: Verily we sent down the Koran in the night of Al Kad'r. And what shall make thee understand how excellent the night of Al Kad'r is? The night of Al Kad'r is better than a thousand months. Therein do the angels descend, and the spirit of Gabriel also, by the permission of their Lord, with his decrees concerning every matter. It is peace until the rising of the morn. — Sale's KORAN.

WHILE Ramazan is the sole month of the Mohammedan calendar generally known to the infidel world, the infidel world has never been very sure whether to spell its last syllable with a *d* or with a *z*. Let the infidel world accordingly know that either is right in its own domain. The Arabs say Ramadan, the Persians and the Turks say Ramazan. And they all observe throughout the month a species of fast that has no precise counterpart in the West. So long as the sun is in the sky, food or drink of any kind may not pass the true believer's lips. He is not even allowed the sweet solace of a cigarette. But from the firing of the sunset gun until it is light enough to distinguish a white hair from a black he may feast to surfeiting.

Nothing is more characteristic of late afternoons in Ramazan than the preparations for the evening meal which preoccupy all Moslems, particularly those who work with their hands. As the sun nears the horizon, fires are lighted, tables are spread, bread is broken, water is poured out, cigarettes are rolled, and hands are lifted half-way to the mouth, in expectation of the signal that gives liberty to eat. This breaking of the daytime fast is called *iftar*, which means feast or rejoicing, and is an institution in itself. The true *iftar* begins with *hors-d'œuvres* of various sorts — olives, cheese, and preserves, with sweet *simits*, which are rings of hard pastry, and round flaps of hot unleavened bread, called *pideh*. Then should come a vegetable soup, and eggs cooked with cheese or *pastîrma* — the sausage of the country — and I know not how many other dainties peculiar to the season, served in bewildering variety and washed down, it may be, with water from the sacred well Zemzem in Mecca. Any Turkish dinner is colossal, but *iftar* in a great house is well nigh fatal to a foreigner. Foreigners have the better opportunity to become acquainted with them because Ramazan is the proverbial time for dinner-parties. The rich keep open house throughout the month, while the poorest make it a point to entertain their particular friends at *iftar*. The last meal of the night also has a name of its own, *sohour*, which is derived from the word for dawn. Watchmen patrol the streets with drums to wake people up in time for it, while another cannon announces when the fast begins again.

In a primitive community like that of the Prophet's Arabia and in a climate where people anyway sleep during much of the day, Ramazan might be comparatively easy to keep. Under modern conditions, and especially in a town containing so large an alien population as Constantinople, it is not surprising that the fast is somewhat intermittently observed. The more Europeanised Turks make no pretence of fasting, to the no small scandal of their servants. Others strengthen their resolution by an occasional bite in private or a secret cigarette. Every now and then some such person is arrested and fined, for church and state are still officially one in Turkey, and the *Sheriat* is a system of Blue Laws that would leave very little room for individual judgment if it succeeded in altogether having its way. Those who are most conscientious are those upon whom the fast falls most heavily — peasants and workmen who cannot turn day and night about. So complete a derangement of all the habits of life naturally has its effect. No one who employs Turks or does business with them can get anything done, and tempers habitually mild grow strained as the month proceeds. Thus in one way or another does Ramazan continue to colour the whole life of the cosmopolitan city.

Stamboul, always solemn under her centuries and proud even in decay, is never prouder or more solemn than when illuminated for the holy month of Islam. It is one of the sights of the world to see the dark city under the moon of Ramazan, constellated with circlets of light that bead the galleries of numberless minarets. The imperial mosques that cut out so superb a silhouette above the climbing roofs have two, four, or six minarets to illuminate, some of them with three galleries apiece. And they use a yet more magical device. Lines are slung between minaret and minaret, and from them are suspended small glass mosque lamps in some decorative order. During the first half of the month they spell, as if in sparks of gold, a simple phrase like "O Allah!" or "O Mohammed!" After the fifteenth they often trace in the dark sky the outline of a flower or a ship. There is something starlike about these graceful illuminations, but they are called *mahieh* — moonlight.

Théophile Gautier called Ramazan a Lent lined with a Carnival. The phrase is a happy one if it does not lead the reader into attributing a Latin vivacity to Turkish merrymakings. The streets of Stamboul, ordinarily so deserted at night, are full of life during the nights of Ramazan. But their gaiety is little enough like the uproar of a European Carnival. Even in the busiest centres of amusement, where a carriage or even a man often finds difficulty in passing, there is none of the wild hilarity whereby an Occidental must express his sense of the joy of life. The people stroll quietly up and down or sit quietly in the coffee-houses, making their *kef* in a way that reveals Turkish character on its most sympathetic side. They are practically all men. Early in the evening veiled women in their loose street costume may sometimes be seen, accompanied by a servant with a lantern. But as the hours wear on they disappear, leaving only fezzes and turbans in the streets. Even the Christian women, who also inhabit their quarters of Stamboul, observe the custom. It is the rarest thing in the world for an Armenian or a Greek of the poorer classes to take his wife out with him at night.

The coffee-houses are, perhaps, the most characteristic feature of Stamboul streets during the nights of Ramazan. In the daytime they are closed, or the purely Turkish ones are, as there is then no scope for their activities. They are open all night long, however. And few be they that do not attempt to add in some way to their customary attractions. This is often accomplished in a simple manner with the aid of an instrument that we do not associate with the East — I mean the gramophone, which enjoys an enormous popularity in Constantinople. There, however, it has been taught to utter sounds which might prevent many from recognising an old friend. I confess that I prefer myself the living executant to his mechanical echo. One never has to go far during Ramazan to find him. Itinerant gipsies, masters of pipe and tom-tom, are then much in evidence in the humbler coffee-houses. There they go, two and two, a man and a boy, in the wide black trousers, the dark-red girdle, and the almost black fez which they affect. In larger coffee-houses there will be a whole orchestra, so called, of the fine lute, if one may so translate its Turkish title — a company of singers who also play on instruments of strange names and curves that suit the music they make. One such instrument, the *out*, is ancestor to the European lute. There are those, indeed, who find no music in the broken rhythms, the mounting minor, of a harmony which the Russian composers have only recently begun to make comprehensible to Western ears. For myself, I know too little of music to tell what relation it may bear to the antique modes. But I can listen, as long as musicians will perform, to those infinite repetitions, that insistent sounding of the minor key. It pleases me to hear in them a music come from far away — from unknown river gorges, from camp-fires glimmering on great plains. There are flashes, too, of light, of song, the playing of shepherds' pipes, the swoop of horsemen, and sudden outcries of savagery. But the note to which it all comes back is the monotone of a primitive life, like the day-long beat of camel bells. And more than all, it is the mood of Asia, elsewhere so rarely understood, which is neither lightness nor despair.

Dancing is not uncommon in the coffee-houses of the people during Ramazan. Sometimes it is performed by the gipsy girls, dressed in vivid cotton prints and jingling with sequins, who alone of their sex are immodest enough to enter a coffee-house. Dancing boys are oftener the performers — gipsies, Greeks, or Turks — who perpetuate a custom older than the satyr dances of India or the Phrygian dances of Cybele. *Alimeh,* whence the French *almée,* and *köchek* are the technical names of these not too respectable entertainers. Sometimes the habitués of the coffee-house indulge in the dancing themselves, if they are not pure Turks, forming a ring and keeping time to the sound of pipe and drum. Of recent years, however, all this sort of thing has grown rare. What has become rarer still is a form of amusement provided by the itinerant story-teller, the *mettagh,* who still carries on in the East the tradition of the troubadours. The stories he tells are more or less on the order of the Arabian Nights, and not very suitable for mixed companies — which for the rest are never found in coffee-shops. These men are often wonderfully clever at character monologue or dialogue. They collect their pay at a crucial moment of the action, refusing to continue until the audience has testified to the sincerity of its interest by some substantial token.

A more elaborate form of entertainment is provided by coffee-houses fortunate enough to possess a garden or some large back room. This is the marionette theatre, and it is to be seen at no other time of the year. The Turkish marionettes, known by the name of their star performer, Kara-gyöz, are a national institution. In fact, their repertory includes almost all there is of a national theatre. In common with other Asiatic marionettes, they do not appear in person. The proscenium arch of their miniature stage is filled with a sheet of lighted paper. The tiny actors, cleverly jointed together of transparent materials, move between the light and the paper, so that their coloured shadows are all that the public sees. It is enough, however, to offer an amusement worth seeing. The theatre of Kara-gyöz would make an interesting study in itself, reflecting as it does the manners of the country. Sometimes, indeed, it has reflected them so faithfully as to require the intervention of the censor. But Kara-gyöz himself, otherwise Black-eye, is always amusing, whatever may be his lapses from propriety. This truculent individual must

A Kara-gyöz poster

be a relative of Punch, although he is said to be a caricature of a veritable person, one of Saladin's viziers. He is a humpback with a black beard and a raucous voice, to whom no enterprise is too difficult or too absurd. He is accompanied by a right-hand man who points his repartee and is alternately his dupe and his deceiver. The adventures of this amorous pair and those of the crack-voiced ladies, the brilliantly costumed gentlemen, the wonderful dogs, cats, mice, and other creatures that go to make up the company, create a scene that a spectator of simple tastes willingly revisits. Among the elements of his pleasure must be counted the ill-lighted barrack or tent in which the representation takes place, the gaily dressed children composing the better part of the audience — here, for once, ladies are allowed! — the loquacious venders of sweets and drinks, and the music of pipe and drum to the accompaniment of which the little coloured shadows play on their lighted paper.

The shadow shows are by no means the only species of the dramatic art to tempt the audiences of Ramazan. There are full-grown theatres that take themselves, the drama — everything except the lives of their patrons — more seriously. They are perfect fire-traps wherein the play's the thing, innocent as they in great part are of those devices of upholstery which are the chief pride of the modern stage. The pit is aligned with rush-bottomed stools and chairs, above which rise, in the European fashion, tiers of not too Sybaritic boxes. A particularity of them is that, like the cafés and the streets, they contain no ladies. While there are Turkish theatres which ladies attend in the daytime, it is contrary to custom for ladies to take part in public entertainments at night. Consequently the European ladies who sometimes penetrate Stamboul during the nights of Ramazan make themselves more conspicuous than is likely to be pleasant and the objects of comment which it is well that they do not understand. Women do appear on the stage, but they are never Turks. They are usually Armenians, occasionally Syrians or Greeks, whose murder of the language is condoned by the exigencies of the case.

The performances last the better part of the night.

They begin at three o'clock Turkish, or three hours after sunset at any season of the year, and close in time for the last meal of the night. There is a curtain-raiser, which is not seldom drawn from the manners of the people. The piece of resistance, however, is a comedy or melodrama adapted from the European stage. The first is more likely to be interesting to an outsider, for the Turks are capital comedians. But the more serious pieces are characteristic, too, in their mixture of East and West. Madam Contess, as she is flatly pronounced, will be attended by servants in fez and *shalvars*, and two gentlemen in top hats will salute each other with earth-sweeping salaams.

Between the two plays intervene a couple of hours or so of singing and dancing that are to many the meat in the sandwich. These entertainments are also highly characteristic of the city that straddles two continents. The costume of the performers is supposably European, although no Western *almée* would consent to be encumbered with the skirts and sleeves of her Armenian sister, or let her locks hang so ingenuously down her back. She would also be more scrupulous with regard to her colour schemes. Whatever the tint of their costume, the *ballerine* of Stamboul cherish an ineradicable partiality for pink stockings. As feminine charm increases, to the eye of an Oriental admirer, in direct proportion to the avoirdupois of the charmer, the effect is sometimes startling.

The entertainment offered by these ladies is more of the East than of the West. It is a combination of song and dance, accompanied by strings and the clapping of the castanet. The music is even more monotonous, in the literal sense of the word, than that of the fine lute. To the tyro one song sounds exactly like another, each beginning on the same high note and each *glissando* to the same low one. And you are inclined to protest that a lady suffering from so cruel a cold should never be permitted to leave her room, much less appear in pink stockings at midnight on a ramshackle wooden stage. But there is a melancholy passion in those endless love-songs that haunts the memory — at least of most of those present, who listen in the silence of perfect appreciation. The dancing into which each song dies away has been a little more tampered with by the West. While the basis of it is the Arab *danse du ventre,* it is a *danse du ventre* chastened by the cult of the toe. What there may be of grossness about it is pleasantly tempered for an occasional spectator by the personal equation. I remember watching, once, an *almée* who must have been in her prime before many of her public were in their cradles. But they had grown up in her tradition, and cries of "One more!" greeted each effort of her poor old cracked voice. There was nothing pitiable about it. The audience had a frank affection for her, independent of her overripe enchantments, and she danced terrible dances for them, eyes half shut, with a grandmotherly indulgence that entirely took away from the nature of what she was doing.

So popular is this form of entertainment that it is thrown in as a sop to sweeten most of the variety performances with which Ramazan abounds. The street of Stamboul where the theatres cluster is a perfect Bowery of cinematographs, music-halls, shooting-galleries, acrobatic exhibitions, and side-shows of a country circus. But it is a Bowery with the reputation of Broadway, and a picturesqueness that neither can boast. Part of the picturesqueness it had when I first knew it has gone — in the shape of the quaint arcades that lined one stretch of it. But the succession of bright little coffee-houses remains, and the white mosque, ethereal at night among its dark trees, that Süleïman the Magnificent built in memory of his dead son. Crowds and carriages abound in Ṣhah-zadeh-Bashi until two o'clock

Wrestlers

in the morning, itinerant peddlers of good things to eat and drink call their wares, tom-toms beat, and pipes cry their wild invitation to various smoky interiors.

One interior to which they invite is the open space, enclosed by green tent-cloth and not too brilliantly lighted, where may be seen the great Turkish sport of wrestling. Spectators of distinction are accommodated with chairs under an awning; the others squat on their heels around the ring. The wrestlers, sometimes several pairs at a time, appear barefooted, in leather breeches reaching just below the knee. Their first act, if you please, is to anoint themselves from head to foot with oil. That done, each couple stand side by side, join right hands, and bend with the right foot forward, while an old man recites over them some incomprehensible rubric, giving their names and recommending them to the suffrage of the public. They then prance forward to the tent of honour, alternately clapping their hands and their leather legs. There they kneel on one knee and salaam three times. Finally, after more prancing and slapping, during the course of which they hastily shake hands once as they run past each other, they are ready to begin. They do so by facing each other at arm's length, putting their hands on each other's shoulders and bending forward till their heads touch. They make no attempt at clinching. That is apparently the one hold forbidden. The game is to throw their opponent by pushing his head down till they can get him around the body or by catching at his legs. Slippery as the wrestlers are with oil, it is no easy matter. Time after time one will seem to have his man, only to let him wriggle away. Then they go at each other again with a defiant "Ho-ho!" The trick is generally done in the end by getting hold of the breeches. When, at last, one of the two is thrown, the oily opponents tenderly embrace and then make a round of the ring collecting tips. Celebrated wrestlers, however, collect their money first. The scene is picturesque enough under the moon of Ramazan, with the nude figures glistening in the lamplight, the dimmer ring of faces encircling them, and the troubled music of pipe and drum mounting into the night.

I must beware of giving the impression that Ramazan is merely a holiday season. It is a holy month, and during its term religious zeal rises higher than at any other time. It is enjoined upon the faithful to read the Koran through during Ramazan, and to perform other meritorious deeds. The last prayer of the day, which occurs two hours after sunset, takes on a special significance. Ordinarily known as *yassî*, it is then called *teravi* — repose — and in place of the usual five prostrations twenty-two are performed. The ungodly say that this is to aid the digestion of those who have just eaten a heavy *iftar*. Preaching also takes place every night in the mosques, and many of the services are attended by women. This custom was utilised during the Ramazan of 1326, otherwise 1908, for enlightening the provinces on the subject of the constitution, as it was in the capital for various attempts to subvert the same.

Two dates in the month have a particular importance. On the earlier of these, the fifteenth, takes place the ceremony of kissing the Prophet's mantle. It used to be one of the most picturesque spectacles of the city. It still must be for those fortunate enough to enter the Chamber of the Noble Robe in the Seraglio. I have never done so, nor has any other Christian unless in disguise. This is the place where the relics of the Prophet are kept — his cloak, his banner, his sword, his bow, his staff, one of his teeth, and several hairs of his beard. One of the last has occasionally been given away as a mark of the highest possible honour. The swords and other relics of the first three caliphs and of the companions of the Prophet are also preserved there, together with a silver key of the Kaaba. The most important are the Sacred Standard, which used to lead the Sultan's armies to war, and the Sacred Mantle. This was given by Mohammed to a poet of his day, who composed the celebrated ode in honour of the Prophet entitled *Al*

Borda — The Mantle. When, reciting it for the first time, he came to the verse, "For the Prophet is a sword, drawn from the scabbard of God," Mohammed threw his own cloak over his shoulders. The poet religiously preserved the gift and handed it down to his descendants, who performed miracles with the water into which they dipped it.

To house these treasures Sultan Selim I, who captured them among the spoils of Cairo, built a pavilion in the grounds of the Seraglio, which was restored and enlarged at immense cost by Mahmoud I. Those who have seen it say that the Chamber of the Noble Robe is a great domed room lined with magnificent tiles, and that the sacred relics; under a sort of silver baldacchino, are kept behind a wrought-silver screen in a chest of beaten gold. The ceremony of opening them is performed by the Sultan in person, who is supposed to oversee the necessary preparations on the fourteenth, and who, on the morning of the fifteenth, goes in state to the Seraglio accompanied by the members of his family and the grandees of the empire. The mantle is said to be wrapped in forty silk covers. Whether all of them or any of them are removed for the ceremony I cannot say. At all events, those who attend it are given the privilege of kissing the relic, in order of rank. Each time the spot is wiped with a silk handkerchief inscribed with verses from the Koran, which is then presented to the person whose kiss it removed. At the end of the ceremony the part of the mantle or of its cover which received the homage of those present is washed in a silver basin, and the water is preserved in ornamental bottles for the Sultan and a few other privileged persons. A drop of this water is considered highly efficacious against all manner of ills, or is a much-prized addition to the drinking water of *iftar*. The ceremony is repeated for the benefit of the ladies of the palace and other great ladies. And a sort of replica of it takes place in the mosque of Hekim-zadeh Ali Pasha, in the back of Stamboul, where a second mantle of the Prophet is preserved.

Mohammedan doctors have greatly disagreed as to the most important date of Ramazan. The Turks, at all events, now celebrate it on the twenty-seventh. They then commemorate the night when the Koran was sent down from the highest heaven to the lowest and when Gabriel began to make revelation of it to the Prophet. Mohammedans also believe that on that night are issued the divine decrees for the following year. They call it the Night of Power, after the ninety-seventh chapter of the Koran, and keep it as one of the seven holy nights of the year. Consequently, there is little to be seen in the pleasure resorts of Stamboul on the Night of Power — which, as foreigners are inclined to forget, is the eve of the anniversary. Most people spend the evening in the mosques. A special service takes the place of the usual prayer, and after it the larger congregations break up into a series of groups around *mollahs*, who expound the events of the sacred day.

On that one night of the year the Sultan goes to prayer outside of his palace. The state with which he does so is a sight to be seen, being a survival of a curious corollary of the tradition of the day. An old custom made it obligatory upon the Sultan to take a new wife on the Night of Power, in the hope that, as the divine gift of the Koran had come down on that night to Mohammed, so to his Caliph would heaven send an heir. Despite the solemnity of the occasion, therefore, the imperial progress to the mosque partakes of the nature of a gala procession. This was particularly so in the time of Abd ül Hamid, who devoutly maintained the customs of his fathers. I happened to see the last of the processions with which he went out on the Night of Power. The short avenue leading from Yîldîz Palace to the Hamidieh mosque was lined with arches and loops of light, the mosque itself was outlined with little oil-lamps, and the dip beyond was illuminated by Arabic texts and architectural designs. The effect was fairylike against the dark background of the harbour and the city, twinkling with the dim gold of far-away masts and minarets. While the crowd was smaller than at the ordinary Friday *selamlîk*, the police precautions were even stricter. But Turkish police have their own way of enforcing regulations. I remember a young man in a fez who approached the mosque too closely. A gorgeous officer went up to him: "My bey, stand a little down the hill, I pray you." The young man made an inaudible reply, evidently an objection. The gorgeous officer: "My brother, I do not reprimand you. I pray you to stand a little down the hill. It is the order. What can I do, my child?" The young man stood a little down the hill. Presently other young men came, to the sound of music, their bayonets glittering in the lamplight. Some of them were on horseback, and they carried long lances with red pennons. They lined the avenue. They blocked up the cross streets. They surrounded the mosque. Before the last of them were in place the Palace ladies, spectators of all pageants in which their lord takes part, drove down and waited in their carriages in the mosque yard. For some of them too, possibly, this was an anniversary. Finally, the voice of the *müezin* sounded from the ghostly minaret. In his shrill sweet minor he began to chant the *ezan* — the call to prayer. Then bands broke into the Hamidieh march, fireworks filled the sky with coloured stars and comets' tails, and the imperial cortège poured from the palace gate — a mob

Drawn by E. M. Ashe

The imperial cortège poured from the palace gate

of uniforms and caparisons and big white wedding lanterns, scintillating about a victoria drawn by two superb white horses. The man on the box, magnificent in scarlet and gold, was a more striking figure than the pale, bent, hook-nosed, grey-bearded man in a military overcoat behind him, who saluted in response to the soldiers' "*Padisha'm chok yasha!*" The procession wheeled into the mosque yard, and majesty entered the mosque. For an hour fireworks exploded, horses pranced, and the crowd circulated very much at its will, while a high sweet chanting sounded at intervals from within. Then majesty reappeared, mob and wedding lanterns and all, the soldiers shouted again, and the tall white archway once more received the Caliph of Islam.

What takes place within the mosque, and, I suppose, within all mosques on the Night of Power, Christians are generally allowed to watch from the gallery of St. Sophia. The sight is most impressive when the spectators are most limited in number — as was the case the first time I went, ostensibly as a secretary of embassy. But I must add that I was considerably impressed by the fact that another spectator was pointed out to me as Sir Arthur Conan Doyle! Of course the place itself contributes chiefly to the effect. Its hugeness, its openness, its perfect proportion, its reaching of pillar into arch, of arch into vault, of vault into dome, make an interior that predisposes to solemnity. The gold mosaic that was once its splendour is now largely hidden under the colour wash of the modern restorer, but the Night of Power brings out another gold. The cornices of the three galleries, the arches of the first, the vast space of the nave, are illuminated by thousands of wicks whose soft clear burning in glass cups of oil is reflected by the precious marbles of the walls. You look down from the gallery through a haze of light diffused by the chandeliers swinging below. These, irregularly hung about three central chandeliers, are scalloped like flowers of six petals. They symbolise the macrocosm, I believe, but they might be great water-lilies, floating in their medium of dusky gold. Under them the nave is striated by lines of worshippers, their darkness varied by the white of turban or robe, men all, all shoeless, standing one close to the next with hands folded and heads down. There is not an exception to the universal attitude of devotion — save among the chattering spectators. The *imam*, from his high hooded pulpit with the sword and the banners of conquest, recites the prayers of the evening. Choirs, sitting cross-legged on raised platforms, chant responses from the Koran in a soaring minor that sounds like the very cry of the spirit. Every now and then a passionate "*Allah!*" breaks out or a deep "*amin*" reverberates from the standing thousands. The long lines bow, hands on knees, and straighten again. Once more they bow, drop to their knees, bend forward and touch their foreheads to the ground, with a long low thunder that rolls up into the dome. The Temple of the Divine Wisdom can rarely have witnessed a more moving spectacle of reverence and faith.

IX

MOHAMMEDAN HOLIDAYS

In nothing is the natural soberness of the Turk more manifest than in his holidays. He keeps fewer of them than his Christian compatriot, and most of them he celebrates in such a way that an outsider would scarcely suspect the fact. This is partly, perhaps, a matter of temperament, and partly because Islam has not yet passed a certain stage of evolution. A holiday, that is, is still a holy day. Secular and patriotic festivals are everywhere of comparatively recent origin. In Turkey, where church and state are one to a degree now unknown in Western countries, there was no real national holiday until 1909. Then the first anniversary of the re-establishment of the constitution was celebrated on the 23d of July (July 10, old style). A highly picturesque celebration it was, too, in Constantinople at least, with its magnificent array of rugs and mediæval tents on the Hill of Liberty, its review of troops by the Sultan, its procession of the guilds of the city, and its evening illuminations.

Illuminations, however, were not invented by the constitution. Long before a 23d or a 4th of July were, the splendour-loving Sultan Ahmed III discovered how unparalleled a theatre for such displays were the steep shores of the Golden Horn and the Bosphorus. The accession day of the reigning sovereign made an annual occasion for great families to set their houses and gardens on fire with an infinity of little oil-lamps and, in all literalness, to keep open house. This was the one purely secular holiday of the year — unless I except the day of Hîd'r Eless. I have already pronounced the name of this mysterious divinity, who is also called Hîzîr, and whom Mohammedan legend associates with the Fountain of Life and with the change of the seasons. He is a distant relative of the prophet Elijah, of the god Apollo, and I suspect of personages still more antique. His day coincides with that of the Greek St. George, namely, April 23d, old style, or May 6th according to our mode of reckoning. I must add that he is frowned upon in orthodox circles, and feasted only in Constantinople or other localities subject to Greek influence. Nevertheless, many men who scorn the authenticity of his claims to reverence scorn not to go forth into the fields on his day, where they roast a lamb on a spit, eat *pilaf*, and otherwise rejoice over the return of the sun. And you should follow them to Kiat Haneh, if you wish to see a sight — so great and so characteristic is the press of those who celebrate the day. Perhaps they do so the more willingly because their coreligionaries the Persians keep in that way, a few weeks earlier, their own feast of *No-rouz*. *No-rouz*, New Day, is the most sensible New Year's I know, falling as it does at the vernal equinox. The Turks also observe *No-rouz*, to the degree of sending each other pots of sweetmeat and poetical wishes that life may be as free from bitterness.

Having made these exceptions to the rule that holidays are holy days in Turkey, I now perceive I must make one more. It is almost as trifling as the last, however, for New Year's is scarcely a holiday at all with the Turks. It is not a day of feasting, of visit-paying, or of present-giving. Persons of sufficiently exalted rank go to the palace to felicitate the Sultan or to inscribe their names in his register, and each receives a new gold piece — of no great denomination in these economical days. Ordinary mortals content themselves with exchanging good wishes and small change — lucky pennies, as it were. A penny is the luckier if it is obtained on some pretext, without mentioning the day. About this day is none of the monotonous invariability which distinguishes our own calendar. It is, indeed, the first day of the first month, Mouharrem, but of the old lunar year of Arabia. It therefore falls eleven days earlier every year, making the backward round of the seasons in a cycle of thirty-three years. A further element of latitude enters into its determination, and that of other strictly Mohammedan holidays, by the fact that the month is not supposed to begin until the new moon has been discovered by the naked eye. In the good old times this verification of the calendar gave rise to most refreshing divergences of opinion. New Year's might be celebrated in different towns on a number of different days, according to the cloudiness of the sky; or, in case of a conflict of authorities, two days might even be celebrated in the same town. But the advent of the telegraph and a growing laxity in interpretations have brought it about that some one in the empire is pretty sure to see the new moon at the right hour. The day of the ascertaining of the new moon has a name of its own, *arifeh*. And mark that a Mohammedan, like a Hebrew day, begins and ends at sunset. The celebration of the eve of a holiday in Western countries is doubtless due to the old prevalence of the same usage.

The true holidays of Islam are connected with the life and teachings of its founder. These are seven in number. They commemorate the birth of the Prophet

(12th of the third moon, Rebi ül Evvel); his conception (6th of the seventh moon, Rejeb); his ascension — accomplished, be it remembered, during his lifetime — (27th Rejeb); the revelation and completion of his mission (15th of the eighth moon, Shaban, and 27th of the ninth, Ramazan); the close of the fast of Ramazan (1st Shevval); and the sacrifice of Abraham (10th of the last moon, Zilhijeh). This is not the place to discourse of comparative religions, but it is interesting to note in passing the relation between these observances and those of the two other great religions which had their origin so near Arabia. This relation is further indicated by the lenten month of Ramazan and by the paschal week of *Kourban Baïram*. It is characteristic, however, of the puritanism of Islam and of the Prophet's desire to put from him every pretence of divinity that his own anniversaries are celebrated the most simply. They have never been an occasion, like the great Christian festivals, for general feasting. On Mohammed's birthday, to be sure — known as *Mevloud*, from a celebrated panegyric of the Prophet read in the mosques on that day — the hours of prayer are announced by cannon, and sweets are distributed, particularly to the poor and to orphan children. On that day, also, the Sultan goes in state to mosque. But otherwise the outsider knows of these anniversaries only by the illumination of the galleries of minarets. Whence the seven holy nights have come to be called the Nights of Lamps.

Equally characteristic, in a different way, are the two general holidays of the Mohammedan calendar. They are both known as *Baïram* — feast — and the outsider has no difficulty in being aware of them. Indeed, it would be rather difficult to remain unaware of so much cannon firing and flag flying. The month of

Ramazan has certain festal features, but they are largely discounted by the total fast which every good Moslem observes during the daylight hours. The close of Ramazan is marked by three days of unlimited festivity. This, the lesser *Baïram*, is called *Sheker*, or sometimes *Mendil Baïram* — Sugar or Handkerchief Feast. Then people exchange sweets and handkerchiefs, if nothing else. It is, however, the time to tip servants and dependants, to make presents, to discharge debts, and in general to fulfil the law of the Prophet by dispensing *zekyaat*, the surplus of one's goods. I was once presented with an interesting little leaflet, printed in silver, which was less a discreet advertisement than a tract as to the true Moslem's duty in this regard. It represented half a fruit of the tree *touba*, under which in paradise all true believers will gather on the resurrection day, and the seeds of this fruit were circles in which were printed the exact quantity of certain comestibles to be given away at *Baïram*. Preparations for this generosity may be seen during the afternoons of Ramazan, when the bazaars and the fashionable street of Shah-zadeh-Bashi are crowded with shoppers. The courtyard of the mosque of Baïezid is also turned into a fair during Ramazan. There the *beau monde* of Stamboul resorts, that is to say the masculine part of it, two or three hours before sunset. Sweetmeats are by no means all that you may buy. Eatables of all sorts, perfumes, tobacco, cigarette-holders, and beads of amber and other materials are also sold, besides silks and rugs. In Abd ül Hamid's time there was always a booth for the sale of porcelain from his little factory at Yîldîz. And every year the ancient pottery works of Kütahya send up a consignment of their decorative blue ware.

Both *Baïrams* are an occasion for paying visits.

Everybody calls on everybody else, so that it is a wonder if anybody is found at home. In the case of the Sultan, however, there is no uncertainty. On the first morning of each *Baïram* he holds a great levee, which is attended by every one of a certain rank. The ceremony has taken place every year since the time of Baïezid the Thunderbolt, who held his court in Broussa in the fourteenth century. Foreigners take no part in this *mouayedeb* (exchange of feast-day wishes), or *baise-main*, as they prefer to call it, but the diplomatic corps and other notables of the European colony are invited to watch it from the gallery of the throne-room. Or sometimes a humbler individual may be introduced in the suite of

Baïram sweets

his embassy, as was the fortune of the present scribe on the occasion of the first *baise-main* of Sultan Mehmed V.

It rather reminded me of youthful operatic days to march through the endless corridors and to climb the immeasurable stairs of Dolma Ba'hcheh Palace and to look down at last from the high east gallery of the throne-room. The top galleries of my youthful days, however, did not contain gilt chairs upholstered in blue and white satin or buffets set out with gold plate and presided over by lackeys in red and gold. The lackeys, though, did look a little like the stage. While a Turk makes a magnificent soldier or horseman, he never attains, impassive though he be, the sublime superiority of a European footman. Is it that his livery is unnatural, or is the human in him too strong to be quite purged away? The operatic impression was further carried out by a crystal chandelier, swinging from the dome exactly where it would cut off somebody's view, and by the rococo arches surrounding the central square of the throne-room. This huge space was empty save for a crystal candelabrum standing at each corner and a covered throne in the middle of the west side. The throne was a small red-and-gold sofa, as we presently saw when an old gentleman removed the cover. He also looked carefully under the throne, as might a queen apprehensive of burglars or mice; but I suppose it was to make sure no bomb was there.

In the meantime the courtiers began to assemble: the cabinet at the left of the throne, the army and navy — in much gold lace — at right angles to the cabinet, the church under the east gallery. On the south side of the hall, facing the military, stood for the first time the new parliament. The senators, who have all been official personages in their day, wore their various uniforms of state. The deputies looked very European in evening dress and white gloves, but capped, of course, with the fez of rigour. Last to come in, taking their stand at the right of the throne, were the imperial princes. They had been waiting with the Sultan in an adjoining room, where they had paid homage to him in private. Then, preceded by the grand master of ceremonies, the Sultan himself entered. Every one made a *temenna* to the ground, that graceful triple sweep of the hand which is the Turkish form of salutation, while a choir hidden under one of the galleries chanted: "Thou wilt live long with thy glory, O Sultan, if God wills. Great art thou, but forget not that One is greater." For those who had made obeisance the year before and many other years to Abd ül Hamid II there must have been something strangely moving in the spectacle of the kindly faced old man, after all not very majestic in person, who walked a little as if his shoes were too tight, yet who took his place at the head of that great company with the natural dignity of his house and race. He wore a stubby new beard, acquired since his accession; for it is not meet that the Commander of the Faithful should go shorn.

The ceremony was opened by a little old man in green, the *Nakib ül Eshraf*, whose business it is to keep the pedigrees of the descendants of the Prophet. He appeared from behind one of the crystal candelabra, bowed low in front of majesty, made a deep *temenna*, stepped backward, and offered a prayer. The Sultan and all the other Moslems present listened to it with their hands held up in front of them, palms inward. Then the first chamberlain of the court, holding a red velvet scarf fringed with gold, took his place at the left of the throne, the band in the north gallery — and a very good one — began to play, and the *baise-main* commenced. It was not a literal *baise-main*. I suppose the Sultan could hardly be expected to hold out his hand long enough for several hundred people to kiss. It was a *baise-écharpe* rather, as the Grand Vizier was the first to prove. He made the *temenna* — or salaamed, as we put it in English — stepped in front of the Sultan and salaamed a second time, kissed the chamberlain's scarf and touched it to his forehead, salaamed a third time, and backed to his place. Hilmi Pasha was followed by his colleagues in order. When the last of them had paid homage, the chamberlain passed behind the throne to the right, and it was the turn of parliament. The senators, for most of whom the *baise-main* was no novelty, followed the example of the cabinet. But when it came to the deputies, they emphasised a new order of things by merely saluting, without kissing the scarf. To their speaker, the ex-exile Ahmed Riza Bey, the Sultan paid the honour of offering his hand. Ahmed Riza Bey started to kiss it, but the Sultan prevented him, at the same time drawing him forward past the throne and giving him a place at the left beyond the Grand Vizier.

The most picturesque part of the ceremony was when the *ülema*, the dignitaries of the cult, in their gold-collared robes and white turbans ornamented by a band of gold, paid homage. They did not come singly, as had their predecessors, but in a long flowing line of colour. At their head marched the *Sheï'h ül Islam*, the highest religious official in the empire, who is also a minister of state. He wears white, like the Pope. He was followed by the *Sherif* Ali Haïdar Bey, Minister of Pious Foundations. This handsome green-robed Arab is one of the greatest aristocrats in Islam, being an authentic descendant of the

Prophet. And he has, if you please, an English wife. After him came a brilliant company of lesser green robes, followed by a succession of fawn-coloured and purple ones. Four dark blues and one sombre greybeard in black made a period to the procession. The long double line had, to the detached gallery-god view, the appearance of a particularly effective ballet as it advanced parallel to the diplomatic gallery, turned half-way across the hall at right angles, moved forward to the throne, and backed out as it came. And the band did not a little to forward the detachment of the gallery-god view by irreverently playing a potpourri from "Carmen" as the fathers of the cult made obeisance before the throne. The *ülema* were followed by the heads of the non-Moslem religions of the empire. This also was an innovation, and the Greek Patriarch made a brief address in honour of it. Last of all the army, the navy, and the civil dignitaries took their turn. This time the band played the march from "Tannhäuser"; and with real courtiers paying homage to a real ruler in a real throne-room, to that music, illusion became fantastic. When the last member of the official hierarchy had made his last *temenna* the Sultan withdrew, followed by the court, while the visitors in the gallery were invited to refresh themselves at the buffet. Then the chiefs of missions and their wives — but not humble individuals in their suites — were invited, by way of further innovation, to have audience of his majesty.

The unofficial side of *Baïram* is quite as full of colour in its more scattered way. Then every man who can afford it, or whose master can, puts on a new suit of clothes. He at least dons something new, if only a gay handkerchief about his fez or neck. It is interesting to stand at some busy corner in a Turkish quarter and watch the crowd in its party-coloured holiday finery. Friends meeting each other stop, seize a hand between their two, and solemnly rub cheeks. Inferiors try to kiss the hand of superiors, who try in turn to snatch the hand away, their success depending on the degree of their superiority. And everybody wishes everybody else a blessed *Baïram.* The *bekjis* — watchmen who have beaten drums during the nights of Ramazan in order to get people up in time for their last meal — march about collecting tips. They announce themselves by their drums, to which they often add a pipe or a small violin, and they carry a pole that is gaudy with the handkerchiefs people give them. The sound of music, however, often means that dancing is on. There is sure to be something of the sort wherever Kürds or Laz gather together. Your true Turk is too dignified for such frivolities. And be it well understood that the only women who dance in the open at *Baïram* are gipsies, hussies who love to deck themselves out in yellow and who blush not to reveal their faces or their ankles. I regret that I am too little of an expert in matters terpsichorean to enter into the fine points of these performances. I can no more than sketch out an impression of a big green tent in some vacant lot, of the high lights of brass that go with tea and coffee drinking in its shadow, and of fiercely moustachioed persons in tall felt caps, in hooded or haply goatskin jackets, and in wide trousers, if they be Kürds, or of slighter Laz with tight black legs that bulge out at the top and hoods picturesquely knotted about their heads, who join hands and begin very slowly a swaying step that grows wilder and wilder with the throbbing of a demon drum.

It is the children, however, to whom *Baïram* chiefly belongs. In their honour all the open spaces of the Mohammedan quarters are utilised for fairs and playgrounds. The principal resort of the kind is the yard surrounding the mosque of the Conqueror — or it used to be before gardens were planted there. I discovered it quite by accident one day when I went to Stamboul to see how *Baïram* was being celebrated and saw a quantity of carts, dressed out with flags and greens, full of children. I followed the carts until I came upon the most festive confusion of voices, of tents, of music, of horses,

The open spaces of the Mohammedan quarters are utilised for fairs

of donkeys, of itinerant venders, of fezzed papas, of *charshafed* mammas, of small girls in wonderful silks and satins, and small boys as often as not in the uniform of generals. Amidst them I remarked with particular pleasure a decorative Arab in white, who strode about with a collection of divinatory green birds. A countryman of his had a funny little peep-show, inlaid with mother-of-pearl, into which I was dying to look but considered myself too dignified to do so. Neither did I go into the tent which bore this ingratiating sign: "Ici on expose animaux vivans et la demoiselle laquelle à la poitrine une cavité." In other tents the physical man was more particularly catered to. Indeed, stuffing seems to be the great affair of *Baïram*. I must not omit, however, the numerous contrivances for inducing motion more or less violent. Merry-go-rounds propelled by hand, swings in the form of boats, milder swings for girls, where one could sit under an awning like a lady and run no risk of being dashed to death, and a selection of miniature vehicles for the very little person, were so many arguments against Mr. Kipling and the East-is-East theory. Another argument was put forward by the discreet gambler, with his quick eye for the police, who in various familiar ways tempted youth to flirt with destiny.

It was with some misgiving that I first entered this assemblage, mine being the only hat and camera visible. But during the several *Baïrams* that I returned there no one ever seemed to resent my presence except one young and zealous police officer who made up his mind that I had no other purpose in visiting the fair of Fatih than to take photographs of ladies. At a tent where wrestling was going on they once demanded a pound of me for admission, supposing that I was a post-card man and would make vast gains out of their entertainment. But at another, where I paid the customary ten cents or less, I was invited into the place of honour; and there, no seats being left, a naval officer insisted on my occupying his — because, as he said, I was an amateur of the great Turkish sport and a guest, *i. e.*, a foreigner. Occidental hospitality does not often take that particular form. Another trait struck my transatlantic eye when I happened once to be at Fatih on the last day of *Baïram*. The barkers had all been shouting: "Come, children! Come! To-morrow is not *Baïram!*" Presently cannon banged to announce *ikindi*, the afternoon hour of prayer, which is both the beginning and the end of *Baïram*. All about me I heard people saying: "*Baïram* is finished." And *Baïram* was finished. It was only the middle of a sunny afternoon, and in any other country the merrymaking would have gone on till night. But the children went away, and men began taking down the swings and tents in the most philosophical manner. In 1911 and 1912 *Baïram* was hardly celebrated at all, as a mark of mourning for the Italian and Balkan wars.

The greater *Baïram*, called *Kourban Baïram*, or the Feast of Sacrifice, is more of a religious observance. It lasts one day longer than the other. It commemorates, as I have said, the sacrifice of Abraham. According to Mohammedan tradition, however, Ishmael and not Isaac was the hero of that occasion. In memory of the miracle of his escape every household that can afford to do so sacrifices at least one ram on the 10th Zilhijeh. Among the rich a ram is provided for each member of the family, and those who have recently died are not forgotten. It is also the custom to make presents of rams, as between friends, engaged couples, and masters and dependants. The Sultan is naturally distinguished among these donors by the scale of his generosity. He gives a sacrificial ram to each of the imperial mosques and theological schools, as well as to those whom he delights to honour. These huge creatures belong to a very aristocratic race. They are bred by a semi-religious, semi-agricultural community called the *Saïeh Ojaghî*, established since the early days of the conquest in the inner valley of the Golden Horn. The members of this community still maintain their mediæval customs and costumes and enjoy certain traditional privileges. In return for these they rear the imperial rams, which they bring in procession to the Palace every year about a week before *Kourban Baïram.* There the rams are bathed, their horns and hoofs are gilded, and they are further adorned by velvet muzzles a-glitter with gold fringe and mirror glass. It is not an uncommon sight, although in the already mythic days of Abd ül Hamid it was far more common, to see an immaculate aide-de-camp driving in an open victoria with one of these gaudy companions.

It naturally requires a great many rams to supply the demand of *Kourban Baïram.* Consequently the open spaces of the Mohammedan quarters are full of baa-ing and bargaining for a week or ten days before the sacrifice. The landing-stages of Scutari and Beshiktash are headquarters of this traffic, Top Haneh, and the vicinity of the mosques of Yeni Jami, St. Sophia, Mohammed II, and Baïezid II. The last is perhaps the largest and most characteristic of these markets. Single rams that have been grown for the occasion stand picketed near the mosque awaiting a well-to-do purchaser. They are sometimes as large and as gaily dressed as the Sultan's rams. They wear a necklace of blue beads to keep off the Evil Eye, and bits of their uncut fleece will be tied up with tinsel or ribbon. I remember one which had a red silk sash on which was printed his name in gold letters — *Arslan,* lion. Such a *kourban* represents a sacrifice of five to fifteen pounds. Most buyers prefer to patronise the shepherds who bring their flocks into the city for the occasion. These shepherds, usually Albanians, make a very picturesque addition to the scene with their huge square-shouldered cloaks of felt, fancifully painted in red and blue. The sheep, too, are daubed with colour, to distinguish one flock from another. They sell for rather less than a pound apiece, growing cheaper as the day of sacrifice approaches. It is amusing to watch and to listen to the bargaining that goes on be-

Sheep-market at Yeni Jami

tween shepherd and householder until their demands come within sight of each other. Most amusing, though, is it to see the ram — which, I suspect, is not seldom a sheep — when the bargain is made, carried away pick-aback by one of the innumerable *hamals* who hang around for such an opportunity. These strange couples are the characteristic harbinger of *Kourban Baïram,* the ram staring over the man's shoulder with vast apparent interest in the sights he sees, his hind quarters making the roundest and most comfortable curve in the small of the *hamal's* back.

The actual sacrifice I have never seen, and I hope I never may. I once witnessed a cinematographic representation of what takes place at the Palace, and that was enough for me. The moving pictures represented his majesty returning from early morning prayer, alighting at the great door of Dolma Ba'hcheh, and greeting the dignitaries there assembled to receive him. He then read a brief prayer, took a knife from a platter handed him by an attendant, and passed it to the actual executioner. In theory, the head of each house is supposed to perform the sacrifice. The flesh must be given away, and the fleece, or its proceeds, is used for some charitable purpose.

X

TWO PROCESSIONS

I HAD been in and out of Constantinople a good many years before I even heard of the Sacred Caravan. The first I heard of it then was on the Bridge one day, when I became aware of a drum beating out a curious slow rhythm: *one*, two, *three*, *four*, five, six; *one*, two, *three*, *four*, five, six. I waited to see what would happen, and presently from the direction of Stamboul straggled a procession that, of course, I had no camera to photograph, against the grey dome and springing minarets of Yeni Jami. It was led by two men with tom-toms beating in unison the rhythm I had heard. I later learned that those tom-toms have a special name, *kyöz*. After the drummers marched a number of boys in pairs, carrying small furled flags of red silk embroidered with gold. Behind the boys strode a serious-looking person who held a small round shield and a drawn sword. He was followed by a man bearing a big green standard, embroidered and fringed with gold, on a white staff tipped by a sort of brass lyre in which were Arabic letters. Next came a palanquin of white wood slung between mules. It had glass windows and wooden shutters, and looked very cosy with its red silk cushions; but nobody was there to enjoy them. In the rear of the palanquin were men carrying staves with bunches of dyed ostrich feathers at their tips, like enormous dusters. And then slouched along a magnificent camel. He wore a green silk saddle-cloth embroidered in white, and above that a tall green silk hoodah with gold embroidery; and ostrich plumes nodded from him in tufts, and at his knees he wore caps of coloured beads. Behind him trotted a lot of mules in pairs, all loaded with small hair trunks. I did not know that the trunks were full of presents for the good people of Mecca and Medina.

So lamentable a state of ignorance would not be possible, I suppose, in Cairo, where the annual departure of the *Mahmal* is one of the stock sights. But if the Constantinople caravan attracts less attention in the larger city, it is the more important of the two. The Sultan Bibars Boundoukdari, founder of the Mameluke dynasty of Egypt in the seventh century, was the first to send every year to Mecca a richly caparisoned camel with a new cover for the Kaaba. In the process of time other gifts were sent by the Sacred Caravan to both the holy cities. The first of the Turkish sultans to imitate this pious custom was Mehmed I, builder of the beautiful Green Mosque in Broussa. His great-great-grandson Selim I conquered Egypt in 1517, and with Egypt the relics of the Prophet and the insignia of the caliphate, which were removed to Constantinople. Having become by virtue of his conquest Protector and Servitor of the Holy Cities, Selim largely increased the generosity of his fathers. His descendants of to-day are unable to display the same munificence, but the annual *sourreh* still forms the strongest material bond between Turkey and Arabia. It consists of money in bags, of robes, of uncut cloth, of shoes, and even of a certain kind of biscuit. The total value of these and other articles, which are all minutely prescribed by tradition and which are the perquisite of particular families or dignitaries, now amounts to some £T. 30,000. As for the covering of the Kaaba, it is still made in Egypt and sent from there. The old coverings afford quite a revenue to the eunuchs in charge of the temple. The smallest shred is a relic of price, while a waistcoat of the precious fabric is supposed to make the wearer invulnerable and is a fit present for princes. The hangings for the Prophet's tomb at Medina, changed less frequently, are woven in Constantinople. The work is a species of rite in itself, being performed in a room of the old palace, near the depository of the relics of the Prophet, by men who must be ceremonially pure, dressed in white.

The arrival of the imperial presents in Mecca is planned to coincide with the ceremonies of the greater pilgrimage. These take place at the Feast of Sacrifice, which with the two days preceding constitutes the holy week of Islam. Pilgrimage is a cardinal duty of every Moslem, expressly enjoined in the twenty-second *Soura* of the Koran. The first *Haj* took place during the lifetime of the Prophet, and every year since then has seen the faithful gather in Mecca from the four quarters of the Mohammedan world. Constantinople is one of their chief rallying places, as being the seat of the Caliph and the natural point of departure for the pilgrims of northern Asia. These holy palmers add a note of their own to the streets of the capital during their seasons of migration, with their quilted coats of many colours, their big turbans, and their Mongol caste of feature. The day for the departure of the Sacred Caravan is the eve of *Berat Gejesi*, or the night when Gabriel revealed his mission to the Prophet. This is nearly four months before the great day of *Kourban Baïram*. In the times when the caravan marched overland from Scutari to Mecca, four months was none too much. But the pilgrimage has been vastly shortened in these days of steam, and will be shorter still when the last links of rail are laid between Constantinople and Mecca. For the time being, however, the Sacred Caravan still makes its official departure on the traditional day, going over to Scutari and waiting there until it is ready to embark for Beyrout. It makes a stop of twenty-five days in Damascus, where the imperial benevolence begins, and thence it proceeds by the new Hejaz railway to Medina. There is also a traditional day for the return of the pilgrims. Part of the ceremony of the Prophet's birthday is the delivery to the Sultan of a letter from the *Sherif* of Mecca, sent back by the leader of the Sacred Caravan in response to the Sultan's own, together with a cluster of dates from the Holy City.

The ceremonial attending the departure of the Sacred Caravan is one of the last bits of Oriental colour left in Constantinople. I have now seen it several times, however, and every year it seems to lose something. My best procession was my first, which also happened to be the last under a Caliph of absolute power to draw upon the public funds. And although I had a camera with me that time, I was not allowed to use it. The convoy I had encountered on the bridge was merely a preliminary of the true pageant, escorting the *sourreh* from the Ministry of Pious Foundations to Yîldîz Palace. There the presents, installed for two days under rich tents, were inspected by Abd ül Hamid and given into the custody of the *Sourreh Emini.* Then after an imposing religious ceremony the Sacred Caravan commenced its march. For a spectator without the palace walls the first intimation of its approach was given by several carriages of Palace ladies, who take an unofficial part in most public spectacles. Religious and military dignitaries also began sauntering down the road, which was bordered by soldiers, with an air of dispersing after some important function. Presently a double line of cavalrymen came into sight, preceding more religious and military dignitaries on horseback. One of them was the *Emir ül Haj*, the official head of the caravan, with much gold embroidery on his

Church fathers in the Sacred Caravan

long coat. His post, still an important one, was far more so in the days when the caravan was less certain to escape attack on the way. Some of the horses, particularly of the *ülema*, were led by grooms; others were followed by orderlies carrying big cloth bundles. The body of the procession was made up of an irregular crowd of priests, officers, eunuchs, Palace servants, and nondescripts of various sorts, chanting at the top of their voices, followed by the big camel I had already seen, and the palanquin. But there were eight other camels this time, of all sizes, down to a fluffy little white one that everybody wanted to pat; and two children were immensely enjoying a ride in the palanquin. Behind that rode an official holding

Housings in the Sacred Caravan

out on a red satin cushion an autograph letter from the Sultan to the *Sherif* of Mecca, confirming him in his office for the coming year. Another bore a huge parcel in his arms, done up in white tissue-paper. This was a robe of honour sent by the Sultan to the *Sherif*. Others still carried silver vessels in which sweet savours burned — "in honour of the angels," as a dervish once expressed it to me. Next marched a second irregular crowd, louder and more amazing than the first. In front of it were two rows of black men in scarlet robes, beating on tom-toms the rhythm I knew, which they alternated with a quicker one. And midway of the crowd a ring of excited persons brandished swords and challenged the enemies

The sacred camel

of the Prophet to mortal combat. They were an unaccustomed reminder, in tolerant Constantinople, of the early days of the faith. And then, tied with very new rope to the backs of some thirty mules walking two and two, each gay with flags and ostrich feathers and led by a solemn artilleryman, were the quaint little hair trunks in which the Commander of the Faithful sent his gifts to the far-away people of the Prophet.

There is another annual procession to be seen in Constantinople which recalls to Western eyes even more strangely than that of the *sourreh* an older day of faith. Turks take no part in it, however, although they also observe the 10th of Mouharrem, on which it falls, as

The palanquin

the anniversary of Joseph's deliverance from prison in Egypt and of Noah's exit from the ark. They make in honour of the occasion and present to their friends a sweet pudding to which they have given the name of the anniversary — *ashoureh*, or tenth day. The basis of it is boiled wheat, to which are added all manner of grains, nuts, and dried fruits; and the legend is that Noah and his people made a similar pudding on Mount Ararat out of what was left in the bins of the ark.

It is for the Persians that the day is peculiarly sacred. They also make a special dish for it, called *zerdeh*, of rice, sugar, and saffron. But that is a mere detail of what is

Tied with very new rope to the backs of some thirty mules . . . were the quaint little hair trunks

for them the holiest season in the year. The Persians and the Turks belong to two different sects that have divided the Mohammedan world since the death of the Prophet. It is not for an unlettered unbeliever lightly to declare that so serious a matter was in the beginning a question of *cherchez la femme*. Still, it is a fact that the enmity of Aïsheh, the youngest wife of Mohammed, toward Ali, the Prophet's cousin and son-in-law, did much to embitter those early differences of opinion. This lady, while on a journey, once caused tongues to wag by disappearing from her litter at a compromising hour and being brought back by a man considerably younger than her distinguished husband. Mohammed was finally forced to silence the voice of scandal by the twenty-fourth *Soura* of the Koran, entitled Light. In the meantime, however, consulting with his four closest friends and followers as to what should be done, he was assured by three of them that there could be no doubt as to the innocence of the Mother of the Moslems. The fourth, Ali, ventured to suggest that the matter would bear investigation. Aïsheh never forgave the doubt of her step son-in-law, and her enmity was a potent factor in keeping Ali from the caliphate. He eventually did succeed, the fourth to do so, twenty-four years after the Prophet's death. But the Sunnites regard him as the least of the first four Caliphs. The Shiïtes, on the other hand, do not recognise the first three Caliphs at all. They even fête the anniversary of the death of the second one, Omar. Ali is for them the vicar of God, and they hold his descendants to the ninth generation in peculiar reverence. The twelfth of these *Imams*, as they are called, the *Mehdi*, is supposed never to have died. It is believed that he will reappear before the last judgment in order, curiously enough, to overthrow antichrist. As for Ali, the hatred of Aïsheh pursued him even after he became Caliph, and stirred up disaffection against him. He was finally stabbed. His two sons, Hassan and Hüsseïn, also met violent deaths, the former being poisoned and the latter falling under thirty-three wounds on the heroic field of Kerbela. These tragic events are what the Shiïtes commemorate on the 10th of Mouharrem.

In Persia the entire month is a time of mourning. During the first ten days public passion-plays represent with bloody realism the lives and deaths of the first *Imams*. In Sunnite Constantinople, where there are some six thousand Persians, the commemoration is naturally less public, although the two sects no longer come to blows over it. Most of the Persian colony are from

A Persian miniature representing the death of Ali

the region of Tabriz, where a Turkish dialect is spoken. Their headquarters are in a number of old stone *hans* near the bazaars and the War Department. Large tents are put up in the courts of these *hans* during Mouharrem, and there every evening *mollahs* recite the story of the tragedy of Kerbela. It took place more than a thousand years ago, and religious feeling has cooled much in those thousand years, but the story still has a strange power to draw tears from the crowding Persians who listen to it. After the third night men with banners and torches give a greater semblance of reality to the recitation. On the tenth night, or on the night of the tenth day, which is the anniversary of the martyrdom of Hüsseïn, the torches and banners march about to the various *hans* where Persians live.

The last time I saw this ceremony it included picturesque features new to me; and, by way of marking a dramatic contrast between century and century, an aeroplane suddenly whirred across the square of sky visible from the Valideh court. But I shall always remember the first of the processions that I saw. It was in the same paved courtyard of Valideh Han, surrounded by half-ruined cloisters. The central mosque, the temporary shed in one corner, the sparse trees, the silently waiting spectators, made so many vague shapes in the February dusk; and snow was falling. A strange clamour of pipes and drums and shouting began to make itself heard in the distance. Suddenly the archway giving entrance to the *han* lighted up with a smoky glare, and the procession surged slowly into the court. It was led by men carrying flaming cressets of iron basketwork and three enigmatic steel emblems on long staves. The central one was a sort of sword-blade above a spindle-shaped fretting of Arabic letters, while the other two were tridents springing from a similar base; and from all three floated streamers of crape. Next came two files of standard-bearers, dressed in black, with black caps on their heads. The flags they bore were black or dark-coloured, triangular in shape, with the names of the *Imams* and other holy inscriptions embroidered on them in silver. On top of some of the staves was an open hand of brass. I was told that it commemorated the mutilation of Hüsseïn. Behind the standard-bearers marched more men in black, chanting in a rhythm of six beats and striking their bare breasts on the fifth. Even a foreigner could distinguish the frequent names of Ali and Hüsseïn. Others held in both hands a chain at the end of which was a bunch of smaller chains. With

Valideh Han

this, first over one shoulder and then over the other, they beat their backs. The thud kept time with the chanting, and vigorously enough to leave visible, sometimes sickening signs, under the torn black of the single garment they wore. Two white horses followed. The first, with rich saddle-cloth and head-stall, carried a little boy on his back. On the saddle of the second, caparisoned in blood-streaked white, were two doves. Then came a band of musicians, singing, playing pipes, beating drums, and clashing cymbals. And last of all, slowly advancing sidewise in two long lines, appeared a gruesome company of men in white, who chanted hoarsely and slashed their shaven heads with bloody swords. The blood-stained figures in white, the black flagellants, the symbolic horses, the mourning banners, the points of steel answering the flare of the torches, made strange matter indeed for the imagination, moving with desperate music through that veil of driving snow.

The procession marched round the courtyard three times and then went into the tent, where a dirge was chanted in honour of the martyrs of Kerbela. At different moments of the ceremony, and particularly at sight of the child and the doves on horseback — symbolic of Hüsseïn's son, who was killed in his arms, and of the souls of the martyrs — many a Persian among the spectators sobbed uncontrolledly. Other spectators smiled at the tears streaming down bearded cheeks and at the frenzy of the flagellants. For myself, I can never help feeling respect for any real emotion, however far I may be from sharing it. People say, indeed, that these processions are not what they used to be and that much of the slashing is feigned. That may well enough be. Still, I found myself compelled to turn aside when the men in white passed in front of me. More than one of them, too, had to be helped staggering away before the procession came to an end. It is not every one who takes part in these ceremonies. The participants are men who fulfil a vow of their own or of their parents, usually in gratitude for some deliverance. Their zeal is so great that it is necessary to draw up a preliminary schedule for the processions, so that no two shall meet and dispute the right of way. Each forms in its own courtyard, but the men in white do not begin their cutting till they are in the street. When the marchers finally return to their own *han* — having, in the meantime, visited the public bath — they spread rugs on the floor of the tent and spend the evening drinking tea and entertaining their friends.

This ceremony is repeated in a milder form in Scutari, on the day after *ashoureh*. Early in the morning the Persians flock to a valley of cypresses called Seïd Ahmed Deresi, which is a corner of the great cemetery reserved for their use. There they rejoice over such as have by their own blood atoned for that of Hüsseïn. I have followed them thither only once, but I am happy to say that no interment took place. Tents were set up on the edge of the cemetery, of a faded green that admirably set off the darker cypresses, and close-packed Persians squatted in them, drinking tea or smoking their terrible *toumbeki*. More Persians, recognisable by their black caps if not by their cast of feature, roamed among the trees. Most of them were of the humbler sort, in skirted coats of dull colours. Here and there was one in a long stiff fuzzy black cloak, with a touch of gold at the throat. Many had beards decoratively reddened with henna, and wore their hair shaved high about the neck and off the middle of the forehead. There was much embracing between hairy monsters who had not met, perhaps, since last Mouharrem; and much patronising was there of ambulatory venders of good things to eat. Finally, at what signal I know not, a company of men in black marched out among the graves, bearing triangular flags of the sort I have already described. At some distance they joined forces with a company of coloured flags, headed by the strange ornaments of steel. Two of the coloured flags should have been in a museum rather than in Scutari cemetery on a wet winter day. They were unusually fine examples of the Persian wood-block printing, and in the centre of each smiled an inimitable lion with a curly tail. These two companies marched chanting together to the end of the cemetery, where they met a third made up of flagellants. But this time there were no men in white and no bloody blades. Then they all proceeded down the long road to the water, the steel emblems and the coloured flags first, the black banners next, and the flagellants last, chanting, beating their breasts, and swinging their heavy chains. Every few steps they stopped and went through their rite with greater zeal. The stops were longest in front of institutions and great houses, where a *mollah* would intone from a parchment manuscript he carried. And in the picturesque little square of Top Tashi, where some fallen Greek pillars lie in front of the madhouse attached to the mosque of the Valideh Atik, a *Roufaï* dervish, whom I remembered to have seen in the *tekkeh* of Karaja Ahmed, sang a long threnody in honour of the martyred Hüsseïn. The procession was followed by hundreds of Persians who joined in the chanting and breast beating. Their number, and the many stops, made an opportunity for street vendors and for beggars. Cripples sat on either side of the narrow street with a handkerchief spread out in front of them on which lay a few suggestive coins. Gaudy gipsy girls were not ashamed to show themselves on so solemn an occasion. I saw two women of a race strange to me, with coppery faces and a perpendicular mark painted in ochre on their foreheads. Strangest of all was a holy man who stood humbly by the wayside.

Yet, after all, he was of one brotherhood with the mourners for Hüsseïn. He did not raise his eyes as the procession passed him, nor did he hold out his hand. What first attracted my attention to the goodness of his face were two small round reddish things between which I saw it. Then I made out the reddish things to be onions, spitted on either end of a steel skewer that pierced both his cheeks.

XI

GREEK FEASTS

One of the most characteristic things about Constantinople is that while it has become Turkish it has not ceased to be Greek. The same is true of Thrace, Macedonia, and the fringe of Asia Minor, which contain large Turkish and other populations, but which still form a part of the Greek world to which they always belonged. The two races have indisputably influenced each other, as their languages and certain of their customs prove. A good deal of Greek blood now flows, too, in Turkish veins. Nevertheless there has been remarkably little assimilation, after five hundred years, of one element by the other. They coexist, each perfectly distinct and each claiming with perfect reason the land as his own.

This is perhaps one cause why religious festivals are so common among the Greeks of Turkey. It is as a religious community that they have remained separate since the conquest. Through their religious observances they live what is left them of a national life and assert their claim to the great tradition of their race. The fact doubtless has something to do with the persistence of observances that elsewhere tend to disappear. At all events, those observances are extremely interesting. They have a local colour, for one thing, of a kind that has become rare in Europe and that scarcely ever existed in America. Then they are reckoned by the Julian calendar, now thirteen days behind our own, and that puts them into a certain perspective. Their true perspective, however, reaches much farther back. Nor is it merely that they compose a body of tradition from which we of the West have diverged or separated. Our religious customs and beliefs did not spring out of our own soil. We transplanted them in full flower from Rome, and she in turn had already borrowed largely from Greece and the East. But in the Levant such beliefs and customs represent a native growth, whose roots run far deeper than Christianity.

In the Eastern as in the Western church the essence of the religious year is that cycle of observances that begin with Advent and culminate at Easter. It is rather curious that Protestantism should have disturbed the symbolism of this drama by transposing its climax. Christmas with the Greeks is not the greater feast. One of their names for it, in fact, is Little Easter. It is preceded, however, by a fast of forty days nearly as strict as Lent. The day itself is purely a religious festival. A midnight mass, or rather an early mass, is celebrated at one or two o'clock on Christmas morning, after which the fast is broken and people make each other good wishes. They do not exchange presents or follow the usage of the Christmas tree, that invention of Northern barbarism, except in places that have been largely influenced by the West.

The real holiday of the season is New Year's Day. This is called *Aï Vassíli*, or St. Basil, whose name-day it is. There is an old ballad relating to this venerable Bishop of Cappadocia — too long, I regret, to translate here — which men and boys go about singing on St. Basil's eve. The musicians are rewarded with money, theoretically for the poor of the community. If it happens to stick in the pockets of the performers, they doubtless regard themselves as representative of the brotherhood for whose benefit they sing. This custom is imitated by small boys who go among the coffee-houses after dark, begging. They make themselves known by lanterns that are oftenest wicker bird-cages lined with coloured paper. I have also seen ships, castles, and aeroplanes of quite elaborate design. These curious lanterns are used as well on Christmas and Epiphany eves of both calendars. The principal feature of St. Basil's eve is the *vassilópita,* a kind of flat round cake or sweet bread something like the Tuscan *schiacciata.* At midnight the head of the house cuts the *pita* into as many pieces as there are members of the family. A true *pita* should contain a coin, and whoever gets it is sure to have luck during the new year. The next day people pay visits, exchange presents, tip servants, and make merry as they will. They also go, at a more convenient hour than on Christmas morning, to church, where the ancient liturgy of St. Basil is read.

Epiphany, or the old English Twelfth-Night, has retained in the East a significance that it has lost in the West. The day is supposed to commemorate the baptism of Christ in the Jordan. Hence it is the day of the blessing of waters, whether of springs, wells, reservoirs, rivers, or the sea. Holy water plays a particular rôle in the Greek Church — although the Roman custom of moistening the fingers with it, before making the sign of the cross on entering a church, is not followed. On the first of every month except January a ceremony called the Little Blessing takes place in the churches, when water is blessed; and this ceremony may be repeated by request in private houses. In January the Little Blessing takes place on Epiphany eve, the fifth. But on Epiphany itself, as early in the morning as local custom may dictate, takes place the Great Blessing. It is performed in the middle of the church, on a dais decorated with garlands of bay, and the important feature of the long ceremony is the dipping of a cross into a silver basin of water. The water is carefully kept in bottles throughout the next year and used as occasion may require. It

Blessing the Bosphorus

is sometimes administered, for instance, to those who are not thought fit to take the full communion. The outdoor ceremony which follows this one is extremely picturesque. In Constantinople it may be seen in any of the numerous Greek waterside communities — by those who care to get up early enough of a January morning. One of the best places is Arnaout-kyöi, a large Greek village on the European shore of the Bosphorus, where the ceremony is obligingly postponed till ten or eleven o'clock. At the conclusion of the service in the church a procession, headed by clergy in gala vestments and accompanied by candles, incense, banners, and lanterns on staves of the sort one sees in Italy, marches to the waterside. There it is added to by shivering mortals in bathing trunks. They behave in a highly unecclesiastical manner in their anxiety to get the most advantageous post on the quay. The banners and lanterns make a screen of colour on either side of the priests, incense rises, choristers chant, a bishop in brocade and cloth of gold, with a domed gilt mitre, holds up a small cross; he makes the holy sign with it, and tosses it into the Bosphorus. There is a terrific splash as the rivals for its recovery dive after it. In days gone by there used to be fights no less terrific in the water over the precious object. The last time I saw the ceremony, however, there was nothing of the kind. The cross was even made of wood, so that there was no trouble in finding it. The first man who reached it piously put it to his lips and allowed the fellow nearest him to do the same. Then the half dozen of them paddled back to shore and hurried off to get warm. The finder of the cross is a lucky man in this world and the world to come. He goes from house to house with the holy emblem he has rescued from the deep, and people give him tips. In this way he collects enough to restore his circulation and to pass a convivial Epiphany. The cross is his to keep, but he must provide a new one for the coming year.

The blessing of the waters is firmly believed by many good people to have one effect not claimed by mother church. It is supposed, that is, to exorcise for another year certain redoubtable beings known as *kallikántzari*. The name, according to one of the latest authorities on the subject,[1] means the good centaurs. Goodness, however, is not their distinguishing trait. They are quarrelsome, mischievous, and destructive monsters, half man, half beast, who haunt the twelve nights of the Christmas season. One of the most efficacious means of scaring them off is by firebrands, and I have wondered if the coloured lanterns to which I have alluded might owe their origin to the same idea. Many pious sailors will not venture to sea during the twelve days, for fear of these creatures. The unfurling of the sails is one of the ceremonies of Epiphany in some seaside communities. Similarly, no one — of a certain class — would dream of marrying during the twelve days, while a child so unfortunate as to be born then is regarded as likely to become a *kallikántzaros* himself. Here a teaching of the church perhaps mingles with the popular belief. But that belief is far older than the church, going back to Dionysus and the fauns, satyrs, and sileni who accompanied him. In many parts of the Greek world it is still the custom for men and boys to masquerade in furs during the twelve days. If no trace of the custom seems to survive in Constantinople it may be because the early fathers of the church thundered there against this continuance of the antique Dionysiac revels, which became the Brumalia and Saturnalia of the Romans.

I should not say that no trace survives, because Carnival is, of course, a lineal descendant of those ancient winter celebrations. As it exists in Constantinople, however, Carnival is for the most part but a pale copy of an Italian original, imported perhaps by the Venetians and Genoese. It affords none the less pleasure to those who participate in it, and curiosity of various colours to the members of the ruling race. I remember one night in

[1] J. C. Lawson: "Modern Greek Folklore and Ancient Greek Religion."

Pera overhearing two venerable fezzes with regard to a troop of maskers that ran noisily by. "What is this play?" inquired one old gentleman, who evidently had never seen it before and who as evidently looked upon it with disapproval. "Eh," replied the other, the initiated and the more indulgent old gentleman, "they pass the time!" The time they pass is divided differently than with us of the West. The second Sunday before Lent is called *Apokreá* and is the day of farewell to meat. Which for the religious it actually is, although the gaieties of Carnival are then at their height. The ensuing Sunday is called Cheese Sunday, because that amount of indulgence is permitted during the week preceding it. After Cheese Sunday, however, no man should touch cheese, milk, butter, oil, eggs, or even fish — though an exception is made in favour of caviar, out of which a delicious Lenten savoury is made. Lent begins not on the Wednesday but on the Monday, which is called Clean Monday. In fact the first week of Lent is called Clean Week. Houses are then swept and garnished and the fast is stricter than at any time save Holy Week. The very pious eat nothing at all during the first three days of Lent.

Clean Monday, nevertheless, is a great holiday. In Constantinople it is also called Tatavla Day, because every one goes out to Tatavla, a quarter bordering on open country between Shishli and Hasș-kyöi. A somewhat similar custom prevails in Venice, where every one goes on Ash Wednesday to promenade on the ordinarily deserted quay of the Zattere. But no masks are seen on the Zattere on Ash Wednesday, whereas masks are the order of the day at Tatavla on Clean Monday. They are not so much the order of the day, however, as the progress of a traditional camel, each of whose legs is a man. It carries a load of charcoal and garlic, which are powerful talismans against evil, and it is led about by a picturesquely dressed camel driver whose face is daubed with blue. This simple form of masquerading, a common one at Tatavla, descends directly from the pagan

The dancing Epirotes

Dionysia. Another picturesque feature of the day is the dancing by Epirotes — Greeks or Christian Albanians. Masquerading with these exiles consists in twisting a handkerchief about their heads in guise of a fillet and in putting on the black or white *fustanella* — with its accompanying accoutrements — of their native hills. They form rings in the middle of the crowd, which is kept back by one of their number called the Shepherd. Like the Christmas mummers of the Greek islands, he wears skins and has a big bronze sheep or camel bell fastened to some part of him. He also carries a staff to which is attached a bunch of garlic for good luck. He often wears a mask as well, or is otherwise disguised, and his clowneries give great amusement. In the meantime his companions join hands and dance around the ring to the tune of a pipe or a violin. The first two hold the ends of a handkerchief instead of joining hands, which enables the leader to go through more complicated evolutions. Sometimes he is preceded by one or two sword dancers, who know how to make the most of their hanging sleeves and pleated kilts. Some of these romantic young gentlemen are singularly handsome, which does not prepare one to learn that they are butchers' boys.

The Greeks keep no *mi-carême*, as the Latins do. Their longer and severer fast continues unbroken till Easter morning — unless Annunciation Day happens to fall in Lent. Then they are allowed the indulgence of fish. Holy Week is with them Great Week. Services take place in the churches every night except Wednesday, and commemorate the events of Jerusalem in a more dramatic way than even in the Roman Church. The symbolic washing of the disciples' feet, however, which takes place in Jerusalem on Holy Thursday, is not performed in Constantinople except by the Armenians. On Good, or Great, Friday a cenotaph is erected in the nave of each church, on which is laid an embroidery or some other representation of the crucifixion. Sculpture is not permitted in the Greek Church, although on this one occasion a statue has sometimes been seen. The faithful flock during the day to the cenotaph, where they kiss the embroidery and make some small donation. Each one receives from the acolyte in charge a jonquil or a hyacinth. This graceful custom is perhaps a relic of the Eleusinian Mysteries, which Easter superseded and with whose symbolism, celebrating as they did the myth of Demeter and Persephone, it has so much in common. Spring flowers, at all events, play a part at Easter quite different from our merely decorative use of them. Flower stands are almost as common at church doors as candle stands. For people also make the round of the icons in the churches, on Good Friday, lighting votive tapers here and there. The true use of the tapers, however, is after dark. Then a procession figuring the entombment of Christ issues from the church with the image of the cenotaph and makes the circuit of the court or, in purely Greek communities, of the surrounding streets, accompanied by a crowd of lighted candles. The image is finally taken to the holy table, where it remains for forty days.

An even more striking ceremony takes place on Saturday night. About midnight people begin to gather in the churches, which are aromatic with the flowering bay strewn on the floor. Every one carries a candle but none are lighted — not even before the icons. The service begins with antiphonal chanting. The ancient Byzantine music sounds stranger than ever in the dim light, sung by the black-robed priests with black veils over their tall black caps. Finally, the celebrant, in a purple cope of mourning, withdraws behind the *iconostásion*, the screen that in a Greek church divides the holy table from the chancel. As the chant proceeds candles are lighted in certain chandeliers. Then the door of the sanctuary is thrown open, revealing a blaze of light and colour within. The celebrant comes out in magnificent vestments, holding a lighted candle and saying: "Come to the light." Those nearest him reach out their own tapers to take the sacred fire, and from them it is propagated in an incredibly short time through the entire church. In the meantime the priests march in procession out-of-doors, headed by a banner emblematic of the resurrection. And there, surrounded by the flickering lights of the congregation, the celebrant chants the triumphant resurrection hymn. At this point tradition demands that the populace should express their own sentiments by a volley of pistol-shots. But since the reactionary uprising of 1909, when soldiers took advantage of the Greek Easter to make such tragic use of their own arms, an attempt has been made in Constantinople to suppress this detail. I have been told that each shot is aimed at Judas. The unfaithful apostle, at all events, used to be burned in effigy on Good Friday at Therapia. And I have heard of other customs of a similar bearing.

The patriarchal church at Phanar is the most interesting place to see the ceremonies of Easter morning. They are not for every one to see, by reason of the smallness of the church. One must have a friend at court in order to obtain a ticket of admission. Even then one may miss, as I once did through ignorance, and perhaps through a lack of that persistence which should be the portion of the true tourist, certain characteristic scenes of the day. Thus I failed to witness the robing of the Patriarch by the prelates of his court. Neither did I get a photograph of them all marching in procession to the church, though I had moved heaven and earth — *i. e.*, a bishop and an ambassador — for permission to do so. Nevertheless, I had an excellent view of the ceremony of the second resurrection, as the Easter morning vespers are called. The procession entered the church led by small boys in white and gold who carried a tall cross, two gilt *exeptérigha* on staves, symbolic of the six-winged cherubim, and lighted candles. After them came choristers singing. The men wore a species of fez entirely covered by its spread-out tassel. One carried an immense yellow candle in front of the officiating clergy, who marched two and two in rich brocaded chasubles. Their long beards gave them a dignity which is sometimes lacking to their Western brothers, while the tall black *kalymáfhion*, brimmed slightly at the top with a true Greek sense of outline, is certainly a more imposing head-dress than the biretta. The Patriarch came next, preceded and followed by a pair of acolytes carrying two and three lighted candles tied together with white rosettes. These candles symbolise the two natures of Christ and the Trinity; with them His Holiness is supposed to dispense his blessing. He wore magnificent vestments of white satin embroidered with blue and green and gold. A large diamond cross and other glittering objects hung about his neck. In his hand he carried a crosier of silver and gold and on his head he wore a domed crown-like mitre. It was surmounted by a cross of gold, around it were ornaments of enamel and seed pearls, and in the gold circlet of its base were set immense sapphires and other precious stones. The Patriarch was followed by members of the Russian embassy, of the Greek, Montenegrin, Roumanian, and Servian legations, and by the lay dignitaries of his own entourage, whose uniforms and decorations added what they could to the splendour of the occasion. These personages took their places in the body of the nave — standing, as is always the custom in the Greek Church — while the clergy went behind the screen of the sanctuary. The Patriarch, after swinging a silver censer through the church, took his place at the right of the chancel on a high canopied throne of carved wood inlaid with ivory. He made a wonderful picture there with his fine profile and long white beard and gorgeous vestments. On a lower and smaller throne at his right sat the Grand Logothete. The Grand Logothete happens at present to be a preternaturally small man, and time has greatly diminished his dignities. The glitter of his decorations, however, and the antiquity of his office make him what compensation they can. His office is an inheritance of Byzantine times, when he was a minister of state. Now he is the official representative of the Patriarch at the Sublime Porte and accompanies him to the Palace when His Holiness has audience of the Sultan.

No rite, I suppose, surpasses that of the Greek Church in splendour. The carved and gilded iconostasis, the icons set about with gold, the multitude of candles, precious lamps, and chandeliers, the rich vestments, the clouds of incense, make an overpowering appeal to the senses. To the Western eye, however, there is too much gilt and blaze for perfect taste, there are too many objects in proportion to the space they fill. And certainly to the Western ear the Byzantine chant, however interesting on account of its descent from the antique Greek modes, lacks the charm of the Gregorian or of the beautiful Russian choral. At a point of the service the Gospels were read by different voices in a number of different languages. I recognised Latin and Slavic among them. Finally, the Patriarch withdrew in the same state as he entered. On his way to his own apartments he paused on an open gallery and made an address to the crowd in the court that had been unable to get into the church. Then he held in the great saloon of his palace a levee of those who had been in the church, and each of them was presented with gaily decorated Easter eggs and with a cake called, curiously enough, by the

Persian name of *chörek* — except that the Greeks mispronounce it *tsouréki*. These dainties are the universal evidence of the Greek Easter — these and the salutation "Christ is risen," to which answer is made by lips the least sanctimonious: "In truth he is risen." Holy Thursday is the traditional day for dyeing eggs. On Holy Saturday the Patriarch sends an ornamental basket of eggs and *chörek* to the Sultan. *Chörek* is like the Easter cake of northern Italy. It is a sort of big brioche made in three strands braided together.

Easter Monday is in some ways a greater feast than Easter itself. In Constantinople the Christian population is so large that when the Greeks and Armenians stop work their fellow citizens find it easy to follow suit. The Phanar is a favourite place of resort throughout the Easter holidays, an open space between the patriarchate and the Golden Horn being turned into a large and lively fair. The traditional place for the celebration of the day, however, is in the open spaces of the Taxim, on the heights of Pera. The old travellers all have a chapter about the festivities which used to take place there, and remnants of them may still be seen. The Armenians gather chiefly in a disused cemetery of their cult, where the tomb of a certain St. Kevork is honoured at this season and where peasants from Asia Minor may sometimes be seen dancing among the graves. A larger and noisier congregation assembles at the upper edge of the parade-ground across the street. Not a little colour is given to it by Greeks from the region of Trebizond, who sometimes are not Greeks at all, but Laz, and who often wear the hood of that mysterious people knotted around their heads. They have a strange dance which they continue hour after hour to the tune of a little violin hanging from the player's hand. They hold each other's fingers in the air, and as they dance they keep up a quivering in their thighs, which they vary by crouching to their heels and throwing out first one leg and then the other with a shout. An even more positive touch of colour is given to the scene by the Kürds. They set up a tent in front of which a space is partially enclosed by screens of the same material. I remember seeing one such canvas that was lined with a vivid yellow pattern on a red ground. There swarthy Kürds in gaily embroidered jackets or waistcoats gather to smoke, to drink tea, and to dance in their own more sedate way, while gipsies pipe unto them and pound a big drum. I once asked one of the dancers how it was that he, being no Christian, made merry at Easter time. "Eh," he answered, "there is no work. Also, since the constitution we are all one, and if one nation rejoices, the others rejoice with it. Now all that remains," he went on, "is that there should be no rich and no poor, and that we should all have money together." Interesting as I found this socialistic opinion in the mouth of a Kürdish *hamal*, I could not help remembering how it had been put into execution in 1896, when the Kürds massacred the Armenian *hamals* and wrested from the survivors the profitable guild of the street porters. It was then that the Easter glory departed from the Taxim. But the place had already been overtaken by the growing city, while increasing facilities of communication now daily lengthen the radius of the holiday maker.

One assembly of Easter week which still is to be seen in something of its pristine glory is the fair of Balîklî. This takes place on the Friday and lasts through Sunday. The scene of it is the monastery of Balîklî, outside the land walls of Stamboul. It is rather curious that the Turkish name of so ancient a place should have superseded even among the Greeks its original appellation.

The Byzantine emperors had a villa there and several of them built churches in the vicinity. The name Balîklî, however, which might be translated as the Fishy Place, comes from the legend every one knows of the Greek monk who was frying fish when news was brought him that the Turks had taken the city. He refused to believe it, saying he would do so if his fish jumped out of the frying-pan — not into the fire, but into the spring beside him. Which they promptly did. Since when the life-giving spring, as it is called, has been populated by fish that look as if they were half fried. The thing on Balîklî day is to make a pilgrimage to the pool of these miraculous fish, to drink of the water in which they swim, to wash one's hands and face and hair in it, and to take some of it away in a bottle. The spring is at one end of a dark chapel, half underground, into which the crowd squeezes in batches. After receiving the benefits of the holy water you kiss the icons in the chapel. A priest in an embroidered stole, who holds a small cross in his hand, will then make the holy sign with it upon your person and offer you the cross and his hand as well to kiss, in return for which you drop a coin into the slot of a big box beside him. Candles are also to be had for burning at the various icons. The greater number of these, however, are in the monastery church hard by. And so many candles burn before them that attendants go about every few minutes, blow out the candles, and throw them into a box, to make room for new candles. There are also priests to whom you tell your name, which they add to a long list, and in return for the coin you leave behind you they pray for blessing upon the name. All this is interesting to watch, by reason of the great variety of the pilgrims and the unconscious lingering of paganism in their faith. And, while there is a hard commercial side to it all, you must remember that a hospital and other charitable institutions largely profit thereby.

There are also interesting things to watch outside the monastery gate. Temporary coffee-houses and eating places are established there in abundance, and the hum of festivity that arises from them may be heard afar among the cypresses of the surrounding Turkish cemetery. I must add that spirituous liquors are dispensed with some freedom; for the Greek does not share the hesitation of his Turkish brother in such matters, and he considers it well-nigh a Christian duty to imbibe at Easter. To imbibe too much at that season, as at New Year's and one or two other great feasts, is by no means held to impair a man's reputation for sobriety. It is surprising, however, how soberly the pleasures of the day are in general taken. As you sit at a table, absorbing your own modest refreshment, you are even struck by a certain stolidity in those about you. Perhaps it is partly due to the fact that the crowd is not purely Greek. Armenians are there, Bulgarians, Albanians, Turks too. Then many of the pilgrims are peasants, come in ox-carts from outlying villages and dazzled a little by this urban press. They listen in pure delight to the music that pours from a hundred instruments. The crowning glory of such an occasion is to have a musician sit at the table with you, preferably a hand-organ man or a gipsy with his pipe. Gipsy women go about telling fortunes. "You are going to have great calamities," utters one darkly when you refuse to hear your fate. "Is that the way to get a piastre out of me?" you ask. "But afterward you will become very rich," she condescends to add. Other gipsies carry miniature marionette shows on their backs in glass cases. Wandering musicians tempt you to employ their arts. Vendors of unimaginable sweets pick their way among the tables. Beggars exhibit horrible deformities and make artful speeches. "May you enjoy your youth!" is one. "May *you* know no bitternesses!" exclaims another with meaning emphasis. "May God forgive your dead," utters a third. "The world I hear, but the world I do not see," cries a blind man melodramatically: "Little eyes I have none." Diminutives are much in favour among this gentry. And every two minutes some one comes with a platter or with a brass casket sealed with a big red seal and says, "Your assistance," adding, "for the church," or "for the school," or "for the hospital," if you seem to fail to take in what is expected of you. Your assistance need not be very heavy, however, and you feel that you owe something in return for the pleasures of the occasion.

Beyond the circle of eating places stretches an open field which is the scene of the more active enjoyment of the day. There the boat-swings beloved of Constantinople children are installed, together with merry-go-rounds, weights which one sends to the top of a pole by means of a hammer blow, and many another world-old device for parting the holiday maker and his money. One novel variant is an inclined wire, down which boys slide hanging from a pulley. Dancing is the favourite recreation of the men. When they happen to be Bulgars of Macedonia they join hands and circle about one of their number who plays the bagpipe. Every few steps the leader stops and, steadied by the man who holds the other end of his handkerchief, indulges in posturings expressive of supreme enjoyment. The *pas'baliático* of the Greeks is less curious but more graceful. After watching the other dances, picturesque as they are, one seems to come back with it to the old Greek sense of measure. And it is danced with a lightsomeness which is less evident with other races. The men put their hands on each other's shoulders and circle in a sort of barn-dance step to the strains of a *lanterna*. Of which more anon.

The feast of Our Lady of the Fishes is one of the greatest popular festivals in Constantinople. By no

Bulgarians dancing

means, however, is it the only one of its kind. The cult of holy wells forms a chapter by itself in the observances of the Greek Church. This cult has an exceptional interest for those who have been touched by the classic influence, as offering one of the most visible points at which Christianity turned to its own use the customs of paganism. An *ἁγίασμα*, an *áyazma* as the Greeks colloquially call it, is nothing more or less than the sacred fount of antiquity. Did not Horace celebrate such a one in his ode to the *Fons Bandusiæ?* As a matter of fact, a belief in naiads still persists among Greek peasants. And you can pay a lady no greater compliment than to tell her that she looks, or even that she cooks, like a nereid.

Greeks dancing to the strains of a *lanterna*

For under that comprehensive style the nymphs are now known. But as guardians of sacred founts they, like some of the greater divinities, have been baptised with Christian names. There is an infinity of such springs in and about Constantinople. Comparatively few of them are so well housed as the *áyazma* of Balîklî. Some of them are scarcely to be recognised from any profane rill in the open country, while others are in Turkish hands and accessible only on the day of the saint to which they are dedicated. On that day, and in the case of an *áyazma* of some repute on the days before and after — unless the nearest Sunday determine otherwise — is celebrated the *paniyíri* of the patron of the spring. *Paniyíri*, or *panayíri* as perhaps it is more commonly known, has the same origin as our word panegyric. For the reading of the saint's panegyric is one of the religious exercises of the day. Which, like the early Christian agape and the contemporary Italian *festa*, is another survival of an older faith. During the Byzantine period the annual pilgrimage in state of an emperor to one of the shrines of the city was a πανήγυρις. But religious exercises are not the essential part of a *panayíri* to most of those who take part in one. Nor need a *panayíri* necessarily take place at a holy well. The number of them that do take place is quite fabulous. Still, as the joy of life was discovered in Greece, who shall blame the Greeks of to-day for finding so many occasions to manifest it? And it is natural that these occasions should oftenest arise during the clement half of the year, when the greater feasts of the church are done.

One of the earliest "panegyrics" of the season is that of *Aï Saránda*, which is held on the 9th/22d of March. *Aï Saránda* means St. Forty to many good people, although others designate thereby the Forty Martyrs of Sebaste — now the Turkish city of Sîvas. There is a spring dedicated to these worthies on the outskirts of Pera, between the place called The Stones and the Palace of Dolma Ba'hcheh. I find it difficult to share the popular belief that the forty martyrs of Sîvas ever had anything to do with this site. It is true that the pious Empress Pulcheria dug them up in the fifth century and transported them with great pomp to the church she built for them on the farther side of the Golden Horn. It is also true that their church was demolished shortly before the Turkish conquest, and its marbles used in fortifying the Golden Gate. But why should a Turkish tomb on the hillside above the *áyazma* be venerated by the Greeks as the last resting-place of "St. Forty"? Has it anything to do with the fact that the forty martyrs are commemorated at the vernal equinox, which happens to be the New Year of the Persians and which the Turks also observe?

Being ignorant of all these matters, my attention was drawn quite by accident to the tomb in question by some women who were tying rags to the grille of a window. The act is common enough in the Levant, among Christians and Mohammedans alike. It signifies a wish on the part of the person who ties the rag, which should be torn from his own clothing. More specifically, it is sometimes supposed to bind to the bar any malady with which he may happen to be afflicted. Near this grille was a doorway through which I saw people coming and going. I therefore decided to investigate. Having paid ten *paras* for that privilege to a little old Turk with a long white beard, I found myself in a typical Turkish *türbeh*. In the centre stood a ridged and turbaned catafalque, while Arabic inscriptions adorned the walls. I asked the *hoja* in attendance who might be buried there. He told me that the Greeks consider the tomb to be that of St. Forty, while the Turks honour there the memory of a certain holy Ahmed. I would willingly have known more about this Dr. Jekyll and Mr. Hyde of a saint; but others pressed behind me, and the *hoja* asked if I were not going to "circulate." He also indicated the left side of the catafalque as the place for me to begin. I accordingly walked somewhat leisurely around the room. When I came back to the *hoja* he surprised me not a little by throwing a huge string of wooden beads over my head, obliging me to step clear of them. He then directed me to circulate twice more, which I did with more intelligence, he muttering some manner of invocation the while. The third time I was considerably delayed by a Greek lady with two little boys who carried toy balloons. The little boys and their balloon strings got tangled in the string of the big wooden beads, and one of the balloons broke away to the ceiling, occasioning fearful sounds of lamentation in the holy place. The *hoja* kept his temper admirably, however. He was not too put out to inform me that I owed him a piastre for the service he had rendered me. I begged his pardon for troubling him to remind me, saying that I was a stranger. He politely answered that one must always learn a first time, adding that a piastre would not make me poor nor him rich. I reserved my opinion on the latter point when I saw how many of them he took in. At the foot of the catafalque a Turkish boy was selling tapers. I bought one, as it were an Athenian sacrificing to the unknown god, lighted it, and stuck it into the basin of sand set for the purpose. That done, I considered myself free to admire the more profane part of the *panaïr* — as the Turks say.

Part of it covered the adjoining slopes, where peaceably inclined spectators, including Turkish women not a few, might also contemplate the blossoming peach-trees that added their colour to the occasion, and the farther panorama of Bosphorus and Marmora. But the crux of the proceedings was in a small hollow below the tomb. I must confess that I shrank from joining the press of the faithful about the grotto of the sacred fount. I contented myself with hovering on their outskirts. A black group of priestly cylinders marked the densest part of the crowd, and near them a sheaf of candles burned strangely in the clear spring sunlight. A big refreshment tent was pitched not too far away to receive the overflow of devotion, reaching out canvas arms to make further space for tables and chairs. The faded green common to Turkish tents was lined with dark red, appliquéd to which were panels of white flower-pots and flowers. I wondered if the tent-man wittingly repeated this note of the day. For flowers were everywhere in evidence. Lilacs, tulips, hyacinths, jonquils, violets, and narcissi were on sale under big green canvas umbrellas at the edge of the hollow, while every other pilgrim who came away from the *áyazma* carried a bottle of holy water in one hand and a spring flower in the other.

Interesting as is the *panayíri* of the forty martyrs, it does not rank with the later and greater spring festival of St. George. This also has Turkish affiliations — at least in Constantinople and Macedonia. Both races count St. George's Day, April 23d/May 6th, the official beginning of summer — of the good time, as modern Greek pleasantly puts it. The Turks, however, dedicate the day to Hîd'r Eless. But it is not too difficult to relate this somewhat vague personage to our more familiar friend Elijah, who in his character of St. Elias shares with St. George the mantle of Apollo. Nor is the heavenly charioteer the only one of the Olympians whose cult survives to-day among their faithful people. The Hebrew prophet would doubtless have been much astonished to learn that he was to be the heir of a Greek god. He owes it partly to the similarity of his name to the Greek word for sun and partly to the chariot of fire that carried him out of the world. As for "the infamous George of Cappadocia," as Gibbon denominates the patron saint of our ancestral island, his part in the heritage of Apollo is due to his dragon, cousin german to the python of the Far Darter. The sanctuaries of these two Christian legatees of Olympus have replaced those of Apollo on all hilltops, while their name-days are those when men feasted of old the return and the midsummer splendour of the sun.

The place among places to celebrate St. George's Day is Prinkipo. That delicious island deserves a book to itself. Indeed, I believe several have been written about it. One of them is by a political luminary of our own firmament who flamed for a moment across the Byzantine horizon and whose counterfeit presentment, in a bronze happily less enduring than might be, hails the motor men of Astor Place, New York. Sunset Cox's work bears the ingratiating title of "The Pleasures of Prinkipo; or, The Diversions of a Diplomat" — if that be the order of the alternatives. The pleasures of Prinkipo are many as its red and white sage roses, but none of them is more characteristic than to climb the Sacred Way through olive and cypress and pine to the little monastery crowning the higher hill of the island, and to take part in the ceremonies of rejoicing over the return of the sun. This is a *panayíri* much frequented by the people of the Marmora, who come in their fishing-boats from distant villages of the Marble Sea. Their costumes become annually more corrupt, I am pained to state; but there are still visible among them ladies in print, sometimes even in rich velvet, trousers of a fulness, wearing no hat but a painted muslin handkerchief over the hair, and adorned with dowries in the form of strung gold coins. They do not all come to make merry. Among them are not a few ill or deformed, who hope a miracle from good St. George. You may see them lying pale and full of faith on the strewn bay of the little church.

They are allowed to pass the night there, in order to absorb the virtue of the holy place. I have even known of a sick child's clothes being left in the church a year in hope of saving its life.

But these are only incidents in the general tide of merrymaking. Eating and drinking, music and dance, go on without interruption for three days and three nights. The music is made in many ways, of which the least popular is certainly not the way of the *lanterna*. The *lanterna* is a kind of hand-organ, a hand-piano rather, of Italian origin but with an accent and an interspersing of bells peculiar to Constantinople. It should attract the eye as well as the ear, usually by means of the portrait of some beauteous being set about with a garland of artificial flowers. And it is engineered by two young gentlemen in fezzes of an extremely dark red, in short black jackets or in bouffant shirt-sleeves of some magnificent print, with a waistcoat more double-breasted than you ever saw and preferably worn unbuttoned; also in red or white girdles, in trousers that flare toward the bottom like a sailor's, and in shoes or slippers that should have no counter. Otherwise the rules demand that the counter be turned under the wearer's heel. Thus accoutred he bears his *lanterna* on his back from patron to patron and from one *panayíri* to another. His companion carries a camp-stool, whereon to rest his instrument while turning the handle hour in and hour out. I happen, myself, to be not a little subject to the spell of music. I have trembled before Fitzner, Kneisel, and Sevčik quartettes and I have touched infinity under the subtlest bows and batons of my time. Yet I must confess that I am able to listen to a *lanterna* without displeasure. On one occasion I listened to many of them, accompanied by pipes, drums, gramophones, and wandering violins, for the whole of a May night on St. George's hilltop in Prinkipo. What is more, I understood in myself how the Dionysiac frenzy was fed by the cymbals of the mænads, and I resented all the inhibitions of a New England origin that kept me from joining the dancers. Some of them were the Laz porters of the island, whose exhausting measure was more appropriate to such an orgy than to Easter Monday. Others were women, for once; but they kept demurely to themselves, apparently untouched by any corybantic fury. The same could not be said of their men, whose dancing was not always decent. They were bareheaded, or wore a handkerchief twisted about their hair like a fillet, and among them wêre faces that might have looked out of an Attic frieze. It gave one the strangest sense of the continuity of things. In the lower darkness a few faint lights were scattered. One wondered how, to them, must seem the glare and clangour of this island hilltop, ordinarily so silent and deserted. The music went up to the quiet stars, the revellers danced unwearying, a half-eaten moon slowly lighted the dark sea, a spring air moved among the pines, and then a greyness came into the east, near the Bithynian Olympus, and at last the god of hilltops rode into a cloud-barred sky.

The second feast of Apollo takes place at midsummer, namely on St. Elias's Day (July 20/August 2). Arnaout-kyöi is where it may be most profitably admired. Arnaout-kyöi — Albanian Village — is the Turkish name of a thriving suburb which the Greeks call Great Current, from the race of the Bosphorus past its long point. It perhaps requires a fanatical eye to discover anything Apollonic in that lively settlement. No one will gainsay, however, that the joy of life is visible and audible enough in Arnaout-kyöi during the first three days of August.

There also is a sacred way, leading out of an odoriferous ravine to a high place and a grove, whither all men gather in the heat of the day to partake of the water of a holy well. But waters less sanctified begin to flow more freely as night draws on, along the cool quay and in the purlieus thereof. Fringes of coloured paper are strung from house to house, flags hang out of windows or across the street, wine-shops are splendid with banners, rugs, and garlands of bay, and you may be sure that the sound of the *lanterna* is not unheard in the land. The perfection of festivity is to attach one of these inspiriting instruments to your person for the night. The thing may be done for a dollar or two. You then take a table at a café and order with your refreshments a candle, which you light and cause to stand with a little of its own grease. In the meantime perhaps you buy as many numbers as your means will allow out of a bag offered you by a young gentleman with a watermelon under his arm, hoping to find among them the mystic number that will make the melon your own. But you never do. When your candle has burned out — or even before, if you be so prodigal — you move on with your *lanterna* to another café. And so wears the short summer night away.

To the sorrow of those who employ Greek labour, but to the joy of him who dabbles in Greek folk-lore, *panayíria* increase in frequency as summer draws to a close. The picturesque village of Kandilli, opposite Arnaout-kyöi — and any church dedicated to the *Metamorphosis* — is the scene of an interesting one on Transfiguration Day (August 6/19). No good Greek eats grapes till after the Transfiguration. At the mass of that morning baskets of grapes are blessed by the priests and afterward passed around the church. I know not whether some remnant of a bacchic rite be in this solemnity. It so happens that the delicious *chaoush* grapes of Constantinople, which have spoiled me for all others that I know, ripen about that time. But as the blessing of the waters drives away the *kallikántzari*, so the blessing of the grapes puts an end to the evil influence of the *thrímes*. The *thrímes* are probably descended from the dryads of old. Only they now haunt the water, instead of the trees, and their influence is baleful during the first days of August. Clothes washed then are sure to rot, while the fate of him so bold as to bathe during those days is to break out into sores.

The next great feast is that of the Assumption, which is preceded by a fortnight's fast. Those who would see its panegyric celebrated with due circumstance should row on the 28th of August to Yeni-kyöi and admire the plane-shaded avenue of that fashionable village, decorated in honour of the occasion and musical with mastic glasses and other instruments of sound. A greater *panayíri*, however, takes place a month later in the pleasant meadows of Gyök Sou, known to Europe as the Sweet Waters of Asia. Two feasts indeed, the Nativity of the Virgin and the Exaltation of the Cross (September 8/21 and 14/27), then combine to make a week of rejoicing. There is nothing to be seen at Gyök Sou that may not be seen at other fêtes of the same kind. I do recollect, though, a dance of Anatolian peasants in a ring, who held each other first by the little finger, then by the hand, then by the elbow, and lastly by the shoulder. And the amphoræ of the local pottery works in which people carry away their holy water give the rites of the *áyazma* a classic air. But this *panayíri* has an ampler setting than the others, in its green river valley dotted with great trees, and it enjoys an added importance because it is to all practical purposes the last of the season. No one can count on being able to make merry out-of-doors on St. Demetrius's Day (October 26/November 8). St. Demetrius is as interesting a personality as St. George. He also is an heir of divinity, for on him, curiously enough, have devolved the responsibilities of the goddess Demeter. He is the patron of husbandmen, who discharge labourers and lease fields on his day. Among working people his is a favourite season for matrimony. I know not how it is that some sailors will not go to sea after *Aï Thimítri*, until the waters have been blessed at Epiphany. Perhaps it is that he marks for Greeks and Turks alike the beginning of winter, being known to the latter as Kassîm. This division of the seasons is clearly connected with the Pelasgian myth of Demeter.

The feast of her successor I have never found particularly interesting, though I must say I have seen it only at Kourou Cheshmeh. Kourou Cheshmeh, or Dry Fountain, as the Turks call it, is where Medea, during her somewhat stormy honeymoon in the Argo, planted a laurel, and where a very different notability of a later day, St. Daniel the Stylite, stood for many years on a pillar. No sign of laurel or pillar are there to-day, or of the famous Byzantine church of the Archangel Michael, which existed somewhere in the vicinity and which Sultan Mehmed II pulled down to build into Cut-Throat Castle. But there is a remnant of antiquity in Kourou Cheshmeh which goes very well with feasts of Demeter. This is an old altar, half buried in the earth near the mosque of the village, festooned about with garlands between battered rams' heads — a curiously vivid symbol of the contrasts and survivals that are so much of the interest of Constantinople.

I never saw any one lay a sacrifice to the Goddess of Plenty on that ancient marble. A real rite of sacrifice may be seen, however, at the last *panayíri* of the year, in the village of San Stefano. The *panayíri*, as you might suppose, is that of St. Stephen. In the Greek calendar St. Stephen's Day falls on the 27th of December (Jan-

The mosque and the Greek altar of Kourou Cheshmeh

uary 9th), instead of the 26th. The most characteristic part of the *panayíri* is a church procession which takes place on the afternoon before the feast, when priests and choir-boys march through the village with banners and incense and a small flock of sheep. The sheep are gaily decorated, like those of *Kourban Baïram*, and they come to the same end. In fact, the Greeks apply to their own sacrifice the Turkish name of *kourban*. The main differerence is that each animal represents some special votive offering. And the offering may take different forms, according to the means of the giver. One rainy winter afternoon I was watching the sheep, daubed with paint and decorated with ribbons and artificial flowers, gather in the yard of the church, when an old crone came into the porch. She had pulled two or three of her many skirts over her head to protect herself from the rain, and when she dropped them into place there appeared in her arms a big rooster. "My *kourban*," she said, showing him to a neighbour who greeted her, and she made no bones about taking him with her into the church. Holding him tightly under one arm she proceeded to buy, at the stall inside the door, three big candles, one of which she lighted at the shrine of St. Stephen, another at that of the Virgin, and a third in front of an icon which I did not recognise. That done, she made the round of all the icons in the church, twice over, kissing each one and piously crossing herself before it. Then she sat down in a stall at the back of the church, her rooster blinking around as if determined to pass his last hour with credit. The old woman encouraged him with pats and with remarks which I was sorry not to catch. In the meantime candles multiplied before the icons, a sharp sweet odour added itself to that of the strewn bay on the floor, a brisk business was done by a choir-boy who sold, wrapped up in gay tissue-paper, dried leaves supposed to be of the plant which sprang from St. Stephen's crown of martyrdom, and a big frosted cake was brought in with ceremony and put between two candles on a table opposite the bishop's throne. At last the Bishop himself arrived, rather wet and out of breath, and was inducted into his vestments beside the stove at the back of the church, not far from where the old woman was sitting with her cock. At that point the latter, unable to contain his emotions any longer, suddenly filled the holy place with a loud and pagan crow.

These *panayíria* are only a few of an inexhaustible list, for every church and spring has its own. I have not even mentioned certain famous ones that are not easily visited. Of this category, though less famous than the fairs of Darîja, Pyrgos, or Silivri, is the feast of the *Panayía Mavromolítissa.* This madonna in the church of Arnaout-kyöi is a black icon reputed to have been found in the fields at the mouth of the Black Sea. Every year on the 5th of September she is carried back in a cortège of fishing-boats — weeping, it is said — by priests and well-wishers who hold a picnic *panayíri* in the vicinity of the Cyanean Rocks. I have not spoken, either, of Ascension Day, which it is proper to celebrate by taking your first sea bath. Or of St. John's Day, known by its bonfires and divinations. The Greeks often burn in the fires of St. John one or two effigies which are said to represent Judas, though Herod and Salome should rather perish on that occasion. Then there is May Day, when young men and maidens get up early in the morning, as they do in Italy, and go out into the fields to sing, to dance, to drink milk, to pick flowers, and to make wreaths which the swain hangs up on the door-post of the lady of his heart. And equally characteristic, in a different way, are the days when men eat and drink in honour of their dead.

No one, I suppose, tries any longer to prove that the modern Greek is one with his classic ancestor. Yet he remains curiously faithful to the customs of ancient Greece. Whereby he affords us an interesting glimpse into the processes of evolution. In him the antique and the modern world come together, and we see for ourselves, more clearly than on the alien soil of the West, how strangely habit is rooted in the heart of man, and how the forms of Christianity are those of the paganism that preceded it.

XII

FOUNTAINS

An anonymous American traveller who visited Turkey something less than a hundred years ago wrote, in comparing the water facilities of New York and Constantinople, that "the emporium of the United States is some centuries behind the metropolis of Turkey." I doubt whether the comparison would still hold, since the building of Croton and other dams. Nevertheless, the fact remains that water — fresh water, at all events — is an element less native to the Anglo-Saxon than to the Turk. We have our proverb about cleanliness and godliness, and we have our morning tubs, and we have our unrivalled systems of plumbing; but we also have our Great Unwashed. In Turkey, however, there is no Great Unwashed — save among those who are not Turks. The reason is that for a follower of the Prophet godliness is next to cleanliness. His religion obliges him to wash his face, hands, and feet before each of his five daily prayers, while innumerable public baths exist for the completer ablutions required of him. Add to that the temperance enjoined upon him, whence is derived his appreciation of good drinking water, and you will begin to understand why there are so many fountains in Stamboul.

The fountains of Constantinople are very little like those of Rome and Paris. There are no figures about them, and not many of them spout or splash. In fact, I recently saw the most famous of them referred to in an architectural handbook as a kiosk, so little resemblance does it bear to the customary fountain. Fountains are, none the less, one of the chief ornaments of Constantinople. If they are intended more strictly for use than Western fountains, they also take the place — and often most happily — of commemorative sculpture in Western countries. And so faithfully have they followed all the vicissitudes of the art of building in Turkey, have they reflected changes of taste and successive foreign influences, that a study of them would yield valuable material toward a history of Ottoman architecture.

I do not propose to make any such study of them now. The variety of these small monuments is so great, however, that I must be academic enough to divide them into four or five categories. Of which the first would include the private fountains alluded to in earlier chapters. Numerous and interesting as private fountains are, a foreigner naturally has little opportunity to become acquainted with them. Their commonest form is that seen in all Turkish houses — of a niche in the wall containing a tap set over a marble basin. This arrangement, of course, amounts to nothing more or less than a wash-stand. But mark that the hole in the bottom of the basin contains no stopper. A Mohammedan would consider that we wash our hands in dirty water, preferring, himself, to use only the stream running from the faucet. Turkish houses — real Turkish houses — are like Japanese ones in that they contain very little furniture or bric-a-brac. The old architects, therefore, made the most of the opportunity afforded by the ritual use of water, and found nothing incongruous in treating a sanitary fixture architecturally, or even in making it an important feature of decoration. This they oftenest accomplished by setting the tap in the lower part of a tall marble tablet, called the *aïna tashi*, or mirror stone, which they shaped to suit the niche in which it stood and ornamented more or less elaborately with carving and sometimes with painting too.

Not many early examples can remain, on account of the unfortunate propensity of Turkish houses to burn up. A number, however, are to be seen in the old palace of Top Kapou. Perfectly simple but characteristic and charming of their kind are the tiny wall fountains of a room in the "Cage," at each end of the window-seat in front of each of the four windows. The same principle is used for more ornamental purposes by putting one basin below another in such a way that the second will catch the overflow of the first. There is a big wall fountain of this sort in the splendid hall of Süleïman the Magnificent. In a private house of much later date I have seen three graduated basins projecting from their niche, rounded and scalloped like shells. There is also a pretty *selsebil* of a new kind in one of the baths of the Seraglio, where the surface of the mirror stone is notched into a series of overlapping scales so as to multiply the ripple of the water. But the prettiest dripping fountain I know is in an old house in Bebek, on the European shore of the Bosphorus. It stands in the entrance hall, at an odd little angle where it will best catch the light, and it combines the miniature basins of an ordinary *selsebil* with a lower

Photograph by Abdullah Frères

Wall fountain in the Seraglio

surface of marble scales. What is least ordinary about it, however, are the spaces of marble lace work bordering the shallow arched niche where the water trickles. There is a free space behind them in order to give the proper

Selsebil in Bebek

relief to the design. And there is an irregularity about the intertwined whorls which a Western artist would have thought beneath him, but which only adds interest to the work.

This original *selsebil* partakes also of the nature of a *fìskieh*, as the Turks onomatopoetically call a spurting fountain. In the stalactites bordering the two shallow basins at the bottom are jets which used to add to the complicated tinkle of the fountain. Spurting fountains seem to be rarer indoors than out, though I have already mentioned the beautiful one in the Kyöprülü kiosk. They are not uncommon in the outer hall of public baths. One that contravenes the canons of orthodox Mohammedan art is to be admired in the handsome bath of St. Sophia—a work of Sinan—where three dolphins, their tails in the air, spout water into a fluted basin. I have wondered if these unorthodox creatures, like the lions of so many gardens, may not perpetuate a Byzantine tradition if not actual Byzantine workmanship. I have already referred to the pigeons on a *selsebil* in Candilli. I have not yet referred to, though I have been considerably intrigued by, a fat goose that is the pride of a street fountain outside the Golden Gate. But on another fountain in Stamboul there is to be seen another unorthodox creature, that is of unimpeachable Mohammedan descent. The fountain is of the bubbling

The goose fountain at Kazlî

kind which sometimes very pleasantly adorns the centre of a room. In this case it was put into a niche in the Tile Pavilion which the Conqueror built in the Seraglio grounds. The fountain, however, would seem to date from Sultan Mourad III, who restored the kiosk in 1590. On either side of the deep rectangular recess are poetical inscriptions of that Sultan, gold on green, with a quaint little climbing border picked out of the marble in gold, and a surmounting shell. That shell, dear to the Renaissance designers and how many before them, is supposed to have made its entrance into Mohammedan architecture from this very inche. At the back of the niche is another shell, and under it the unorthodox creature, a peacock, spreads his fan. It was perhaps to diminish the importance of this unorthodox, of this probably heretical Shiïte peacock, that the artist coloured him more soberly than the flowers that bloom on either side of him, and made him combine with the shell to form the outline of a symbolic egg.

The wall fountain of Chinili-Kyöshk

A few interesting interior fountains are to be seen in

mosques, though Constantinople cannot equal Broussa in this respect. St. Sophia contains two such fountains, put there by Sultan Mourad III, which are big alabaster jars fitted with taps. Two more typical ones are in Sultan Ahmed, their graceful mirror stones set against two of the enormous piers that hold up the dome. The real mosque fountains, however, are those which exist for purposes of ritual ablution outside of the smallest *mesjid.* There you will always see a row of small taps, set near the ground against the wall of the mosque or its yard, with stepping-stones in front of them. They are rarely treated with much elaboration except in later mosques like Nouri Osmanieh, but they agreeably break up a flat wall surface. And at Eyoub they really form one element of the picturesqueness of the outer court, with the bracketed roof that protects them from the weather and their clambering vine.

Most mosques, as well as *medressehs* and other pious institutions, also have a larger and more decorative fountain which usually stands in the middle of the court. The technical name of such a fountain is *shadrîvan*, or *shadîravan*, really meaning "for the peace of souls." The fountain, that is, not only aids the faithful in their religious exercises, but adds so much to the celestial credit of the builder or of the person whom he commemorates. For many *shadrîvans* were built, after the mosque to which they are attached, by another person. Those in the courts of Baïezid and Selim, for instance, are the work of Mourad IV, whose soul needed what peace it could find, while so late a sultan as Mahmoud I built the fanciful *shadrîvan* in the somewhat stern court of the Conqueror as well as that in the court of St. Sophia. The last two are charming examples of the Turkish rococo. The commonest form of *shadrîvan* is a basin or reservoir, encircled about the bottom by taps and protected by a roof from sun and rain. The simplest type is to be seen in the *medresseh* yard of Kyöprülü Hüsseïn Pasha, with a perfectly plain reservoir and a pointed roof held up by wooden pillars. A similar one which lies more on the track of sightseers is in front of the

Shadrîvan of Kyöprülü Hüsseïn Pasha

mosque known as Little St. Sophia, anciently the church of Sts. Sergius and Bacchus. Here the reservoir is an octagon terminating in a cone, while the roof is tiled and ornamented at the apex with a bronze *alem* — a lyre or crescent containing a cobweb of Arabic letters. There are also seats between the posts for the greater convenience of those who use the fountain. Some *shadrîvans* are partially enclosed and made into pavilions, where it is very pleasant to rest. An excellent example exists in the yard of the mosque of Ramazan Effendi, in Issa Kapou. The perforated marble enclosing the upper part of the reservoir of this *shadrîvan* is a thing that is seen in many such fountains. Sometimes a handsome grille work protects the water, as at St. Sophia and Sokollî Mehmed Pasha. The latter fountain is uncommon in that the

Shadrîvan of Ramazan Effendi

large round reservoir is the whole *shadrîvan*, with projecting eaves to shelter the people at the taps. But not all *shadrîvans* are for purposes of ablution. At the Süleïmanieh and at Yeni Jami they are merely covered tanks without taps. The *shadrîvan* of the Valideh Jedid in Scutari is of the same kind, except that the water falls invisibly from the roof of the tank, filling the court with a mysterious sense of sound and coolness.

I do not suppose that street fountains are actually more numerous than private ones, but they naturally seem so to a foreigner wandering through Stamboul. It is not easy to classify them clearly, so many are the forms they take. They affect, however, two principal types, known in Turkish as *cheshmeh* and *sebil*, either of which

Shadrîvan of Sokollî Mehmed Pasha

may be attached to a wall or may exist as an independent structure. The original form is the applied *cheshmeh*, which is merely a wall fountain put outside the house, and enlarged in scale accordingly. These fountains are a very characteristic feature of Constantinople streets. There are literally thousands of them, and they offer so great a variety of interest that it is a wonder no one has taken the trouble to give them the study they deserve. They are a wide-spread example, for one thing, of Turkish philanthropy — and incidentally of a passing conception of public utilities. Every one of those fountains was originally a public benefaction, often made by a Sultan, it is true, and on an imperial scale, but oftener by a private citizen who wished to commemorate some member of his family, to ornament the street in which he lived, or to confer a benefit upon his neighbours. He therefore endowed his fountain, in many instances. Such endowments form an appreciable fraction of the property administered by the Department of Pious Foundations. Sometimes the benefactor stipulated that water-carriers or other persons were or were not to have the right of selling the water of his fountain. The water-carrier, the *saka*, belongs to a race by no means yet extinct in Constantinople, though I doubt if his guilds are quite what they were. There used to be two such guilds, of the horse *sakas* and of the hand *sakas*. The patron of both was the hero who attempted to carry water to Hüsseïn in the battle of Kerbela. The members of both may be recognised by the dripping goatskins in which they carry water from house to house. In these degenerate days, however, a hand *saka* is more likely to carry a couple of kerosene tins slung over his shoulder from either end of a pole. But if he has the right to be paid for carrying water, every man has the right to go himself to the fountain and draw water without money and without price.

Until a few years ago Constantinople possessed no other water-system. Now modern water companies operate in their more invisible ways. But the Ministry of Pious Foundations is still the greatest water company of them all. That it was a fairly adequate one our American traveller of a hundred years ago is witness. Only recently, however, has the department attempted to make some sort of order out of the chaos of systems which it administers — some larger, like the water-supplies of the Sultans, some limited to the capacity of one small spring, and all based on the idea of a charity rather than that of a self-paying utility. Even now I doubt if any exact and complete map exists of the water-supply of Constantinople. The knowledge necessary to make such a map is distributed between an infinity of individuals known as *souyoljìs*, waterway men, who alone can tell, often, just where the pipes lie and how they are fed. And very useful, if occasionally very trying, gentlemen are these to know. This is sometimes amusingly illustrated on the outskirts of the city, where a house or a group of houses may be supplied from some small independent source of water. As time has passed and property has changed hands, the tradition of the waterway has been preserved only in some humble family that has profited by its knowledge, perhaps, to cultivate a tidy vegetable garden. And every now and then the water runs low or stops altogether in the quarter for whose benefit it was originally made to flow, until on payment of a tip to the *souyoljì* it miraculously begins to flow again.

This system is probably the one the Turks found in use when they entered the city. Water still runs in the aqueducts of Valens and Justinian, and until the present generation Stamboul had no other water-supply than that first collected by Hadrian and Constantine. The Sultans restored and improved it, but I have no doubt that the conduits of many a Turkish fountain were laid by a Roman emperor. Of Byzantine fountains remaining to this day, I am not sure that any can positively be identified as such. Many of the fountains of Stamboul, however, must occupy the place of Byzantine fountains, whose materials may have been used in their construction. And it would not have been strange if the new masters of the city adapted to their own use models which they saw about them. The great quadruple fountain of Kîrk Cheshmeh — Forty Fountains — is a case in point. The Turks connect with it the name of Sultan Süleïman I, who is said to have left forty fountains in the city. But its original level was considerably below the existing street, and one of the four niches is ornamented with a Byzantine relief of peacocks, while other Byzantine fragments are built into the structure. The arches of two of the niches, moreover, are round, which was not characteristic of Süleïman's period. So we are not without reasons for thinking that the fountain may have been a Byzantine one restored by Süleïman — who also restored the aqueduct that feeds it. The same is likely of others of his forty fountains. No others of them bear Byzantine sculptures. In fact, the only other street fountain on which I have seen any such decoration — unless the goose of Kazlî be Byzantine — is that of the small Koumrülü Mesjid, between Fatih and the Adrianople Gate. But the large Horhor Cheshmeh near Ak Seraï, and another farther up the hill toward the old Forum Amastrianon, have a distinct Byzantine air. At the same time, their general form is that of the Turkish wall fountain — an arched niche, containing a faucet above a stone or marble trough.

This form, in its simplest state, without any ornament or even a "mirror stone," is found in what may be the oldest Turkish fountain in Constantinople. It lies within the enclosure of the castle of Roumeli Hissar. The niche is deeper than in later fountains, and the bricks used in its construction are the large flat ones which the Turks borrowed from their predecessors. If truth compels me further to record that the arch is not the pointed one preferred by the Turks until the eighteenth century, I am able to add that neither are the arches of the castle itself.

The Byzantine fountain of Kîrk Cheshmeh

I suppose it is natural that few fountains of that early period remain to us. The newcomers probably found the city well enough supplied already, and five hundred years is a long time for such small structures to last in the open. The oldest inscribed wall fountain I know is that of Daoud Pasha, outside the mosque of the same personage, who was Grand Vizier to the Conqueror's son Baïezid II (A. H. 890/A. D. 1485). There is little about the pointed arch or fairly deep niche to attract attention, save the bold inscription above a small mirror stone of palpably later date: "The author of charity deceased, the Grand Vizier Daoud Pasha." This is the earliest form of ornament that appears on Turkish fountains — though I fancy the broad eaves that protect many of them did not wait long to be invented. I have already dwelt on the importance of writing in all Turkish decoration. I therefore need not add that the simplest inscription on a fountain has for the Turks an importance of a kind we do not appreciate. Some fountains are famous merely for the lettering on them — as in its day was that of Feïzoullah Effendi, outside his *medresseh*, whose inscription was designed by the celebrated calligraph Dourmoush-zadeh Ahmed Effendi.

It must not be inferred that the matter of the inscription is comparatively of less importance — though here again the Western critic is not quite competent to judge. The commonest of all inscriptions is a verse from the Koran: "By water all things have life." Other verses, mentioning the four fountains of Paradise and the pool Kevser into which they flow, are also frequent, together with references to the sacred well Zemzem, which Gabriel opened for Hagar in Mecca, to Hîzîr and the Spring of Life, and to the battle of Kerbela, in which Hüsseïn and his companions were cut off from water. Or the central tenet of Islam, "There is no God but God and Mohammed is the Prophet of God," may be carved above the niche — sometimes without any indication of the name or epoch of the founder. The majority, however, are not so modest. They are more likely to give ampler information than he who runs may read. And after the time of Süleïman the Magnificent it became increasingly the fashion for celebrated poets to compose the verses which celebrated calligraphs designed. Thus the historian Chelibi-zadeh records the end of the inscription on a reservoir of Ahmed III: "Seïd Vehbi Effendi, the most distinguished among the word-wizards of the time, strung these pearls on the thread of his verse and joined together the two lines of the following chronographic distich, like two sweet almonds breast to breast: 'With what a wall has Ahmed dammed the waters! For of astonishment stops the flood in the midst of its course.' "

Chronograms are as common on fountains as they are on other monuments. The earliest I have happened to come across is an Arabic one on a fountain near the Studion, which points the reader's attention as follows — "The date fell: We gave thee the fountain of Paradise." The latter phrase is from the Koran. Its numerical value is 970, or 1563 of our era, which is twenty years later than the chronogram on the tomb of the Prince. The ideal chronogram should contain the name of the builder of the fountain and that of the writer of the verse — though I must confess I never found one that attained that height of ingenuity. Most of them mention the founder's name alone, as "Sultan Mourad's fountain is a gift" (994/1586), or "O God, grant Paradise to Moustafa Pasha!" (1095/1684). But the exigencies of arithmetic may relegate the names to the earlier part of the inscription — as on one of two neighbouring fountains in the quarter of Ak Bîyîk (*anglice*, White Whisker): "When the mother of Ali Pasha, Vizier in the reign of Sultan Mahmoud, quenched the thirst of the people with the clear and pure water of her charity, Riza of Beshiktash, the *Nakshibendi*" — an order of dervishes — "uttered the following epigraph: Come and drink water of eternal life from this joyful fountain." The value of the last phrase is 1148, or 1735. Even in so general a sentiment, however, it is not always easy to get the required figure.

Various ingenious devices are resorted to, of which a handsome Renaissance fountain in Kassîm Pasha is an excellent example: "The famous Vizier, the victorious warrior Hassan Pasha, made this fountain as a trophy for Mohammedans. His aims were always philanthropic

The two fountains of Ak Bîyîk

and he provided this fountain with water like Zemzem. This fountain is so well situated and built in so pleasant a place that one would take it as the site where flows the water of eternal life. Those who look upon it drive away all sorrow from their hearts." The numerical value of the last sentence is 2080, a date even farther from the Mohammedan calendar than from ours. But the value of the single word "sorrow" is 1040. Drive it away, or in other words subtract 1040 from 2080, and you get 1040 again, which is evidently the date of the construction (1631). The light values of this inscription are as enigmatic as its numerical values, so that I have never been able to photograph it properly. It also states that the water rights are free, meaning that no one *saka* may sell the water. The builder of this interesting fountain was in his day a saddler, a cook, and a sergeant, which did not prevent him from eventually becoming high admiral of the fleet, inflicting a memorable defeat upon the Russians in the Black Sea, and marrying the sister of Sultan Mourad IV.

The taste for chronograms has continued to this day, but in time the arithmetic of the reader was helped out by an incidental date. The earliest numerals I have found are of the time of Süleïman the Magnificent, on a fountain built by a Jew in the suburb of Hass-kyöi (931/1525). The same fountain is also decorated with the earliest reliefs I have noted, consisting merely of a little tracery on the mirror stone. Altogether this period was an important one for fountains as it was for all Turkish architecture. But while a few of them are admirably proportioned, like the little fountain in Avret Bazaar at the gate of the soup-kitchen of the *Hasseki* — she was Hourrem, the Joyous One, who bore to Süleïman his ill-fated son Moustafa — many of them are disappointingly heavy. It may be that the great Sinan did not consider such small monuments worth his while, or that they have suffered by restoration. At all events, the lesser sultans who followed Süleïman left fountains generally more graceful. Ahmed I is said to have built not less than a hundred of them. In the meantime they gradually developed in detail. The tracery, less floral than geometrical, covered more and more of the marble. Conventionalised cypresses, with tops mysteriously bent, sprang up on either side of the taps. Conventionalised roses, often having a mystic symbolism, became a favourite ornament for the apex of the arch. The occult pentagram or hexagram, symbolic of microcosm and macrocosm and talismanic against evil, were sometimes carved at the corners. And the top, when it was not shaded by broad eaves, was finished in various decorative ways.

The golden age of street fountains was in the first half of the eighteenth century, during the reigns of those notable builders Ahmed III and his nephew Mahmoud I. The change which they introduced into the architecture of their country was in many ways an unhappy one. It led the Turks out of their own order of tradition, which is rarely a safe or useful thing to do, into strange byways of bad taste where they lost themselves for two hundred years. Still, an architecture that tries experiments is an architecture that lives, and at its beginning the Turkish rococo has an inimitable grace and spirit. The fountains of the period are decorated, as no fountains had been decorated before, with floral reliefs a little like those of the Renaissance tombs and with fruits and flowers in various quaint receptacles. The earlier of the garden *selsebils* I have already mentioned is an example, and a more typical one is the wall fountain of the Valideh Jedid in Scutari. The sculptures also began to be touched up with colour and gilding, as in the larger of the two fountains of Ak Bîyîk. So must have been the charming fountain, now most lamentably neglected, on the street that drops from Galata Tower to Pershembeh Bazaar.

Until this time the old pointed arch had been preferred, though, as we have seen, the rounded shell of the Renaissance had already made its appearance. But now round or broken arches began to be the order of the day; and so great richness of detail could only degenerate into the baroque. Yet I have bad taste enough to like, sometimes, even the out-and-out baroque. There is a little

Street fountain at Et Yemez

fountain, for instance, in the Asiatic suburb of Kanlîja, with a florid arch and rather heavy traceries and four very Dutch-looking tiles set into the wall above them, which I think is delightful. Long after photographing it I came across some more of those tiles in the imperial tribune of the mosque built in Scutari by Moustafa III, which gave me a clew to the date of the fountain. And after that I was fortunate enough to make the acquaintance of the gentleman whose summer *yalî* lies across the road from the fountain, and he told me that the fountain was built by the Shei'h ül Islam of Moustafa III. There is, too, a fountain at Emirgyan, in front of the Khedival garden, which, for all its baroque lines, seems to me to terminate a vista very happily. But I do not hesitate to add that few wall fountains built since the middle of the eighteenth century are worth any attention.

We can hardly call it a discovery that the architects made when they first detached a street fountain from the wall and made something more monumental out of it. The thing had already been done indoors and in the courts of mosques. The earliest specimens, however, show their evolution very clearly. They are nothing but wall fountains applied to a cube of masonry. I suppose the religious associations of the *shadrîvan* kept its tradition from being followed, but with experience freedom was gained in the treatment of the detached fountain. Typical of its kind is a fountain in the waterside grove of plane-trees at Chibouklou, to which Ibrahim Pasha, the Grand Vizier of Ahmed III, gave the name of Feïzabad — Place of the Abundant Blessing of God. A great oblong pool reflects the trees, and nearer the Bosphorus is a raised space of the kind the Turks call a turf sofa. On one side of it a concave tablet, carved with a lamp swinging from a chain, indicates the direction of prayer. On the other stands a simple marble fountain, bearing three chronograms of 1133 or 1721. Twenty-eight Mehmed was then in Paris, and the new fashion was not yet launched in fountains. An early and a very happy experiment in that fashion adorns Ahmed's park at Kiat Haneh. But the model and masterpiece of this little golden age is the great fountain at Top Haneh, beside the mosque of Don Quixote. It lacks, alas, the domed roof and broad eaves that Melling represents in one of his pictures. Moreover a trolley post has been planted squarely at its most conspicuous corner, while

Fountain of Ahmed III in the park at Kiat Haneh

ugly iron fences attack two of its sides; and the War Department thinks nothing of making a dumping-ground of the enclosed angle. Yet none of these indignities affect the distinction of the floral reliefs that cover its white marble, or of its frieze of gold inscriptions spaced in a double row of blue cartouches.

A less ornamental but a deservedly famous fountain of the same period is to be seen on the upper Bosphorus, at Beïkos. I suspect, however, that it was once more ornamental than it is. A tall marble pavilion hospitably opens its arches on three sides to the streets of the village. At the bottom of the wall on the fourth side water pours noisily out of fifteen bronze spouts — or I believe they

Detail of the fountain of Mahmoud I at Top Haneh

are thirteen now — into three marble troughs sunk below the level of the street, and runs away through a marble channel in the middle of the pavilion. From this T-shaped lower level steps rise to two marble platforms at the outer corners, where you may sip a coffee while drinking in the freshness and music of the water. This delightful fountain was also built by Mahmoud I. I know not whether the inhabitants of Roumeli Hissar got from Beïkos the idea of a fountain of their own, much

Fountain of Abd ül Hamid II

smaller, which is flat on top and furnished with benches that are very popular on summer evenings. Another, at Beïlerbeï, has a place of prayer on the top, which you reach by a steep little stair of stone. Yet another might be pointed out at Top Haneh, in front of the big mosque, as at least one good deed of the late Sultan Abd ül Hamid II. It would not be fair to compare this structure with its greater neighbour at the other end of the parade-ground. Nevertheless, in spite of its ugly sculpture, it is one of the most successful modern fountains in Constantinople. Suggested, perhaps, by a fountain behind the Arsenal, built by the Admiral Süleïman Pasha in 1750, it is much happier in its lines. And the architect had something like a stroke of genius when he opened a space above the taps and filled it with twisted metal work. The little dome was originally surmounted by an intricately wrought *alem*. But the winter after the donor retired to Salonica this ornament disappeared as well.

No one can explore much of Stamboul without noticing certain large grilled windows with metal cups chained to their sills. These are the windows of *sebils*, which I have referred to as one type of street fountain. If I have not yet mentioned them more fully it is because their chronological place is after the wall fountain. They are also much less numerous, though architecturally rather more important. The word *sebil* means way or path: to build a *sebil* is a step on the way to God. The water comes into a small room or pavilion, and an attendant is supposed to keep cups filled where they will be easily accessible from the street. A simpler form of foundation provides for a man to go about the streets giving water to those who ask for it. Or sometimes dervishes seek this "way" of acquiring merit. They usually wear green turbans, and the inside of the small brass bowl into which they pour water from a skin slung over their shoulders is inscribed with verses from the Koran.

The Seljukian Turks of Asia Minor, I have been told,

were the inventors of this graceful philanthropy, remembering the thirst of the martyr Hüsseïn at Kerbela and the women who brought water to the companions of the Prophet at the battle of Bed'r. The earliest *sebil* I know

Sebil behind the tomb of Sultan Mehmed III

of in Constantinople, however, is the one at the corner of the triangular enclosure where the architect Sinan lies buried, near the great mosque he built for Sultan Süleïman. Small and simple though it is, the lines have the elegance that distinguishes the work of this master. And it proved full of suggestion for succeeding architects.

It showed them, for one thing, how to treat a corner in a new and interesting way. And while the metal work of the windows is the simplest, the designers in iron and bronze found a new field for their craft. One or two architects took a hint from the openwork that lightens the wall beyond the *sebil* and filled their windows with pierced marble, as in the fountain adjoining the tomb of Sultan Mehmed III at St. Sophia. But most architects preferred the lightness and the contrast of metal. Some of their experiments may be rather too complicated and spidery. Nevertheless, the grille work of *sebil* windows would make an interesting study by itself.

In time *sebils* were treated in the same variety of ways as other street fountains. Perhaps the first example of an applied *sebil* is that of the eunuch Hafîz Ahmed Pasha. The fountain forms an angle of his mosque, not far from that of the Conqueror. Ahmed Pasha was twice Grand Vizier under Sultan Mourad IV. Shortly before his death the Conqueror appeared to him in a dream, angrily reproaching him for building a mosque so near his own and threatening to kill him. The old man was greatly troubled by this vision of evil omen; and, sure enough, he was murdered about two months afterward. There is something very attractive in his unpretentious *sebil*, with its tall pointed windows, its little arched door, and its lichened cupola. Another applied corner *sebil*, built by Sultan Ahmed I behind his mosque, is unusual in that it is lined with tiles. Similar tiles are to be seen in the window embrasures of that Sultan's tomb. Their conventionalised peacock eyes, a green-rimmed oval of blue on a white ground, would be too coarse in the open; but seen in shadow through the small hexagons of the grille, they are wonderfully decorative. By an odd chance they were not destroyed by the fire that raged through this quarter in 1912. Among other fountains which came off less happily was one uniting a *sebil* and a *cheshmeh*. This experiment, if I am not mistaken, was first tried in the time of Ahmed III. A beautiful example is to be seen on the busy street of Shah-zadeh, where Ahmed's Grand Vizier, Ibrahim Pasha, is buried within

Sebil of Sultan Ahmed III

his own *medresseh*. Four windows round the corner with a curve of handsome grille work, while the tall arch of the *cheshmeh* decorates the side street with its gilding and delicate reliefs.

The most beautiful example of all, the king, in fact, of Constantinople street fountains, is the one which Ahmed III built outside the great gate of the Seraglio. It stands four-square on a circular marble base, having a curved *sebil* window at each corner and the pointed arch of a *cheshmeh* in the middle of each side. The over-hanging roof is crowned by five fantastic little domes and gilded *alems*. The traceries are not quite so delicate, perhaps, as those of Top Haneh, nor does the whiteness of marble make up any of the effect of this fountain. The brightness of its original polychrome decoration has acquired a soft patina of time. The main effect is given here by the great gold inscriptions on a blue-green ground, framed in plain terra-cotta, and by a frieze of blue and white tiles enclosed between two bands of a delicious dark velvety green. The principal chronogram of the fountain, facing St. Sophia, was written by the Sultan himself. It is said that his first version added up to four less than the required sum, which should have been 1141 (1729). It read: "The date of Sultan Ahmed flows from the tongue of the faucet. Praising God, drink of the fountain and pray for Ahmed Khan." A witty ecclesiastic to whom his majesty confided his dilemma solved the difficulty by suggesting that it was necessary to turn on the water before it would flow. The imperial poet thereupon added the word "open" to his second hemistich and completed the chronogram. The other inscriptions were chosen by competition from among the chief poets of the day. This fountain is unsurpassed for the richness of its detail. Even the under-side of the eaves is decorated with wavy gilt mouldings and painted reliefs of fruit and flowers. But the details take nothing away from the general effect. It is the balance of them, after all, the admirable silhouette, the perfect proportion, that give this monument its singular beauty and dignity.

There is another large detached *sebil* in Galata, near the bridge of Azap Kapou. It was built soon after the fountain of Ahmed III by the mother of Sultan Mahmoud I. Crowded between the surrounding houses, it enjoys no such advantages of perspective as its more famous rivals of St. Sophia and Top Haneh. The greater part of the edifice, indeed, is no more than a blank stone reservoir. But the side facing the main street is treated with a masterly sense of its position. Projecting out from the centre is the circular *sebil* window, filled with a rich bronze grille, while set a little back on either side, and slightly inclined toward either perspective of the street, are two tall *cheshmehs*. The niche of each and the whole face of the structure is incrusted with intricate floral reliefs more delicate even than those of Top Haneh, though not executed in so white a stone. There are also pots and vases of flowers and sheaves of wheat, and above the tap of each niche is a pointed openwork boss of bronze. Here, too, the richness of the ornament combines with the composition and height of the façade and the sweep of the eaves to reach something not far from a grand air.

No other *sebil* of the left bank is executed in so refined a style as this. But many other fountains, in all parts of the city, have a happy knack of filling a space or turning a corner or screening a dark interior with twisted metal work. The difficulty is to choose instances. I might mention the *sebil* of Baïram Pasha at Avret Bazaar; of Mehmed Emin Effendi, half fountain and half tomb, which lends its elegance to the neighbourhood of Dolma Ba'hcheh Palace; of Abd ül Hamid I at Fîndîklî; of Laleli Jami, the Tulip Mosque, which Moustafa III built at Ak Seraï. For the Western architect they are full of unexpected suggestions, if he have the eye to see, while to the mere irresponsible impressionist they make up a great part in the strangeness and charm of the Turkish capital.

XIII

A TURKISH VILLAGE

THERE are larger villages. There are more prosperous villages. There are villages more fashionable. Great ladies lift their eyebrows when we pronounce its name, even ladies not so great, and decide that we will hardly do for their visiting lists. But few villages are so picturesque as ours. And in one respect at least we are surpassed by no village. For we sit on that cleft promontory of the Bosphorus where, during the league-long coquetry of the two continents before their final union, Europe most closely approaches Asia. The mother of nations, as we see her some eight hundred yards away, is a slope sunburnt or green according to the time of year but always discreetly overlooked by farther heights of blue, a slope sharp enough, not too high, admirably broken by valleys and points and one perfect little bay for which I sometimes think I would give all the rest of the Bosphorus, a slope beaded irregularly along the bottom with red-roofed summer *valîs*, variegated with gardens and hamlets and nestling patches of wood, and feathered along the top with cypresses and stone-pines in quite an Italian manner. For my part, I fail to see why any one should ever have desired to leave so delectable a continent, particularly at a period when the hospitality of our village must have been more scant than it is now. But history has recorded many a migration to our side of the strait.

Here Xenophon crossed with the remnant of his ten thousand. Here Darius sat upon a throne of rock and watched Persia swarm after him against the Scythians. Here, too, the great emperor Heraclius, returning to Constantinople after his triumphs in the East, caused a pontoon bridge to be railed high with woven branches in order to screen from his eyes the water he dreaded more than blood. And here Sultan Mehmed II opened the campaign which ended in the fall of the Roman Empire.

The castle he built in 1452, the summer before he took Constantinople, is what gives our village its character and its name. Roumeli Hissar means Roman, Greek, European, or western castle, distinguishing us from the opposite village of Andolou Hissar, where stand the ruins of the earlier fortress of Baïezid the Thunderbolt. To see the two round towers of Roumeli Hissar facing each other across a ravine, the polygonal keep at the water's edge, the crenelated walls and turrets irregularly enclosing the steep triangle between them, you would never guess that they sprang up in about the time of a New York apartment-house. Yet that they did so is better attested than the legend that their arrangement reproduces the Arabic letters of their builder's name. Having demanded permission of the Greek emperor to put up a hunting-lodge on the Bosphorus, the Conqueror proceeded to employ an army of masons, in addition to his own troops, with orders to destroy any buildings they found convenient to use for material. So it is that the shafts and capitals of columns, the pieces of statues, the fragments of decorative brick and marble, that give so interesting a variety of detail to the structure are a last dim suggestion of the ancient aspects of the village. One of its Byzantine names was that of the *Asomaton*, the Bodiless Angels, to whom a monastery in the place was dedicated, while earlier still a temple of Hermes had existed there. In three months the hunting-lodge was ready for occupancy, and the Sultan called it Cut-Throat Castle, a play on the Turkish word which means both throat and strait. It put the Bosphorus at his mercy, as a Venetian galley that went to the bottom under a big

Cut-Throat Castle from the water

stone cannon-ball was the first to testify — though the Genoese commanded the mouth of the Black Sea from another pair of castles. But in spite of their hasty construction the walls have withstood the decay and the earthquakes of nearly five hundred years. Will as much be said of existing New York apartment-houses in the twenty-fifth century?

Powerful as the fortress was in its day, and interesting as it remains as a monument to the energy and resource of its builder, it never played a great part in the martial history of the Turks. The Bosphorus was not then the important highway it is now. After the capture of Constantinople the castle degenerated into a garrison of Janissaries and a state prison of less im-

The castle of Baïezid the Thunderbolt

portance than the Seven Towers. Not a few passages of romance, however, attach to that diminished period. More than one European diplomat spent a season of repose within the walls of Cut-Throat Castle, in days when international law was less finical on such points than it since has grown. And it formed a residence less agreeable than the present country embassies, if we may judge from the account that has come down to us of one such *villeggiatura.* This was written by a young Bohemian attaché who spent two years of the sixteenth century in enforced retirement at Roumeli Hissar. His name, Wenceslas Wratislaw, with those of other prisoners, may still be seen in the stone of a little chamber high in the north tower. In the same tower, commanding a magnificent view, the Conqueror lived while preparing his great siege. Whether this, or the angular tower by the water, or some other donjon of the Bosphorus was the Black Tower which has so unsavoury a name in Turkish annals I have never quite made up my mind.

To-day the castle has outlived even that period of usefulness. The true cutthroats skulk in the bare hills at the mouth of the Black Sea, while the ambassadors — with the single exception, it is true, of our own — pass their summers in pleasant villas presented to them by different Sultans. As for the towers, they survive only to add their picturesqueness to the narrowest part of the Bosphorus, to flaunt ivy and even sizable trees from their battlements, and to afford a habitation to bats and carrion-crows. The last vestige of military uses clinging to them is the pseudo-classic guard-house that crouches under the waterside keep. The walls at least subserve the purpose, however, of sheltering a quarter of our village. One of our thoroughfares enters the double gate by the north tower, descends a breakneck alley of steps lattice-bordered and hung with vine, pauses between a fountain, a ruined mosque, and a monstrous mulberry-tree, and finally emerges upon the quay by a low arch that was once the boat entrance to the sea tower. There is to a prying foreigner some inheritance of other days in the inhabitants of this hanging suburb. They are all of the ruling race and there is about them something intrenched and aloof. The very dogs seem to belong to an older,

The north tower of the castle

a less tolerant, dispensation. The Constantinople street dog, notwithstanding the reputation that literature has attempted to fasten upon him, is in general the mildest of God's creatures. But the dog of Cut-Throat Castle is quite another character. He is a distinct reactionary, lifting up his voice against the first sign of innovation. It may be that generations of surrounding walls have engendered in him the responsibilities of a private dog. At all events he resents intrusion by day, and by night is capable of the most obstinate resistance thereto.

Another memento of that older time is to be seen in the cemetery lying under the castle wall to the south. It is, perhaps, the oldest Mohammedan burying-ground in Constantinople, or at least on the European shore of the Bosphorus. It certainly is the most romantic, with its jutting rocks, its ragged black cypresses, its round tower and crenelated wall, overhanging a blue so fancifully cut by Asiatic hills. It has, too, a spicy odour quite its own, an odour compounded of thyme, of resinous woods, of sea-salt, and I know not what aroma of antiquity. But its most precious characteristic is the grave informality it shares with other Mohammedan cemeteries. There is nothing about it to remind one of conventional mourning — no alignment of tombs, no rectilinear laying out of walks, no trim landscape gardening. It lies unwalled to the world, the gravestones scattered as irregularly on the steep hillside as the cyclamens that blossom there in February. Many of them have the same brightness of colour. The tall narrow slabs are often painted, with the decorative Arabic lettering, or some quaint floral design, picked out in gold. It is another expression of the philosophy of the guard-house soldiers who so often lounge along the water, of the boy who plays his pipe under a cypress while the village goats nibble among the graves, of the veiled women who preen their silks among the rocks on summer afternoons. The whole place is interfused with that intimacy of life and death, the sense of which makes the Asiatic so much more mature than the European. The one takes the world as he finds it, while the other must childishly beat his head against stone walls. It is the source of the strength and of the weakness of the two stocks.

We also love to congregate, or in Empedoclean moods to muse alone, about another old cemetery. There, on top of the steep slope behind the castle, you will often see a row of women, like love-birds contemplating the universe, or a grave family picnic. There too, especially on moonlight nights, you will not seldom hear voices up-lifted in the passionate minor which has so compelling a charm for those who know it of old, accompanied perhaps by an oboe and the strangely broken rhythm of two little drums. It is the true music for a hilltop that is called the Place of Martyrs. The victims of the first skirmish that took place during the building of the castle lie there, under a file of oaks and cypresses. At the north end of the ridge a few broken grey stones are scattered among tufts of scrub-oak that soon give way to the rounded bareness of the hillside. At the other end newer and more honourable graves, protected by railings, attend a *tekkeh* of Bektash dervishes. This establishment was founded by a companion of the Conqueror. Mohammed gave him, as the story goes, all the land he could see from the top of the hill. The present sheikh is a descendant of the founder, but I do not believe he inherited all the land he can see. The view from the Place of Martyrs is one of the finest on the Bosphorus. I am not of the company of certain travellers in the matter of that famous strait. I have seen hills with greater nobility of outline and waters of a more satisfying blue. But when one has made all due reservations in the interest of one's private allegiances the fact remains that the Bosphorus is a charming piece of water enclosed between charmingly moulded hills. It bends below you like a narrow lake as you see it from the Place of Martyrs. The northern sea is invisible; but southward the tops of islands look over the heights of Scutari, and the Marmora glimmers to the feet of a ghostly range that sometimes pretends not to be there.

Nothing could be more abrupt than the contrast between the slopes facing each other across the busy waterway, with all their picturesque detail of garden, roof, and minaret, and the plateau of which the Bosphorus is nothing but a crooked blue crack. From the Place of Martyrs it rolls desolately away to the west, almost without a house or a tree to break its monotony. Gullies cut it here and there. Patches of scrub-oak darken its surface. Sheep move slowly across it, looking in the distance like maggots in a texture of homespun. Otherwise you would never suppose that life existed there. As you watch the sun set across those great empty fields it is incredible that somewhere beyond them tilled lands and swarming cities are. Your impression is not of mere wildness, however. Two abandoned stone windmills on a far-off hill give the note of the impression. Such silence is the silence that follows upon the beating of many drums. You may sit upon that hilltop in evening light and drink melancholy like an intoxication, musing upon all the change and indifference of the world. Yet life lingers there still — life that neither indifference nor change, nor time nor ruin nor death can ever quite stamp out. Threads of water creep through some of the dry gullies, swelling after rain into noisy brooks. Above them hang patches of cultivation, dominated by the general brownness and bareness, but productive of excellent strawberries in the spring. That, too, is one of the times when the brown brightens for a little to green, while June colours whole tracts of hillside with butcher's-broom and the wild rose. And then I have said nothing of heather, of crocuses, of violets, of I know not how many flowers scattered along certain lonely lanes. On the edge of the village these are paved like streets and pleasantly arched with bay-trees. In the bottoms of the ravines, also, they have in their season quite a sylvan air. They lead to stony trails in the open where you may meet a soldier, an Albanian shepherd, or a peasant in gay jacket and baggy blue trousers, wandering from nowhere to nowhere.

But I wander too far from our village, from that larger part of it which the exigencies of space must long ago have pushed northward out of the castle close into the underlying valley. There are those who deprecate our streets, their many steps, the manner of their paving, the irresoluteness with which they proceed to their destined ends, and the desultoriness of their illumination at night. I, however, am partial to a Gothic irregularity, and I applaud the law which admonishes us not to go abroad two hours after sunset without a lantern. We do not take the admonition too seriously, but there are chances enough of breaking our necks on moonless nights to maintain a market among us for paper lanterns. These, with the candles flaring in front of sacred tombs and the casual window lamplight so pleasingly criss-crossed by lattices, make Whistler nocturnes for us that they may never know who dwell in the glare of electricity.

If I find anything to deprecate it is the tendency gaining ground among us to depart from the ways of our fathers in the matter of domestic architecture. The jig-saw and the paint pot begin to exercise their fatal fascination upon us who were so long content with simple lines and the colour of weathered wood. But the pert gables of the day are still outnumbered by square old many-windowed houses with low-pitched roofs of red tiles and corbelled upper stories inherited from the Byzantines. Under the eaves you will often see a decorative text from the Koran, framed like a picture, which insures the protection of heaven better than premium or policy. No house is too small to have a garden, walled as a garden should be, and doing more for the outsider by its green suggestions of withdrawal than by any complete revelation of its charms. Few of these pleasances do not enjoy some view of the Bosphorus. I know one such, containing a Byzantine capital that makes the cedar of Lebanon above it throw as secular a shade as you please, so cunningly laid out at length on the hillside that the Bosphorus is a mere ornamental water of a lower terrace. This Grand Canal of Constantinople enters bodily into certain thrice enviable *yalîs* on the water's edge. Their windows overhang the sea, or are separated from it merely by a narrow causeway. And each contains its own marble basin for boats, communicating with the open by a water-gate or by a canal or tunnel through the quay.

Distinctively Turkish as the flavour of our village is, we yet resemble the city and the empire to which we are tributary in the variety of our population. Of Greeks there are few. It was perhaps natural for them to flee the first stronghold of their conquerors on this side of the Bosphorus — if they ever inhabited it in any number. An Armenian quarter, however, scrambles up the north side of the valley. You can recognise the houses by their lack of lattices, and the priest by the high conical crown of his hat. There are also Albanians, Croats, Jews, Macedonians, and Montenegrins among us, in addition to nothing less exotic than a small Anglo-American colony. It dwells on the upper fringe of habitation, the American part of it being connected, principally, with the college founded by a Mr. Robert of New York.

The grey stone buildings stand on a splendid terrace above the south tower of the castle, visible from afar. And they always make me sorry that such a chance was lost for some rare person equal to the opportunity, who should have combined a knowledge of modern educational requirements with a feeling for the simple broad-eaved houses of the country and their picturesque corbels. However, there the grey stone buildings stand, ugly and foreign, but solid and sufficient, an object of suspicion to some, to others an example of the strange vicissitudes of the world, whereby above a promontory sacred once to Hermes, later to Byzantine saints, and again to Mohammed, there should fly to-day the flag of a country so distant as our own. The condition on which the flag flies is not the least picturesque of these incongruities. The proprietors from whom the first land was obtained were the holy cities of Mecca and Medina, and in conformity with the law governing such property the college bound itself to pay them, in addition to the price of purchase, a yearly tribute of some fourteen dollars.

I might speak of other public institutions flourishing in our midst: of the primary school by the water where you hear the children studying aloud while they rock back and forth over the Koran; of the Sünbüllü dervishes farther down the quay, to whom laden wood boats throw out a few sticks as they tow up the five-mile current; of the howling dervishes, and the clever ruse by which they obtained their building; of our three mosques — to say nothing of the *imam's* mother of the smallest of them, an active yet beneficent public institution in herself, who, when the American college dug foundations for a wall round a slope long beloved by the Turkish ladies, threw her ample person most literally into the breach and could only be persuaded to retire therefrom by the Ministry of Public Works. Nor should I pass over our village green, which was once a cemetery, but which is now a common meeting-place for those of us who are happy enough to live about it. Some of us spend most of our time there, in the company of our wives, our children, our horses, our donkeys, and our hens. Most notable among the habitués — at least to an alien eye — is a lady of African descent, espoused to a meek Caucasian water-carrier and the mother of an infinite chocolate-and-cream progeny. Her ardent disposition is reported to have led her through many vicissitudes, matrimonial and otherwise. On one occasion it led her to scratch out the eyes of another *habituée* of the green, over some matter of mulberries. It is a proof of the reasonableness of justice among us that when condemned to a brief term of imprisonment she first succeeded in postponing the execution of the sentence, I believe through some expectation of presenting the happy water-carrier with a new chocolate-cream, and then in causing her term to be subdivided, alternately languishing in dungeons and enjoying the society of her family until she had paid the full penalty of the law.

A larger, the true centre of our municipal life, is the *charshî*, or market-place. Very notable, to the mind of one admirer, is ours among market-places. My admiration is always divided between that crooked street of it, darkened by jutting upper stories that sometimes actually jump across it, wherein are situate the principal shops, the minor cafés, a fountain or two, and the public bath, and that adjoining portion of it which lies open to the sea. The latter certainly offers the most facilities for the enjoyment of life. Indeed, one end of it is chiefly given up to a Company for the Promotion of Happiness — if one may so translate its Turkish name — whose English steamers carry us to town, seven miles away, or to the upper Bosphorus, as quickly, as regularly, and as comfortably as any company I know. It also does much to promote the happiness of those who do not travel, through the sociable employees of its wharf and by affording a picturesque *va et vient* at almost any hour of the day. I fear, however, that it does less to promote the happiness of the boatmen who await custom at the adjacent wooden quay. They wait in those trim little skiffs, so much neater than anything of the sort we see for hire at home, which have almost superseded caïques because they hold more passengers with greater comfort. And to one who observes how much of the time they do wait, and how modestly they are remunerated for their occasional excursions, it is a miracle how they contrive to live. There is no fixed tariff. If you know the ropes you pay two and a half piastres, some twelve cents, to be rowed across the Bosphorus or to the next village. For ten they will take you almost anywhere. But they eke out their incomes by fishing. We are famous for our lobsters at Roumeli Hissar.

The boatmen, and others with them, often prefer to wait in certain agreeable resorts along that same wooden platform. The first of these is the café of the Armenian, whose corner rakes the Company for the Promotion of Happiness. He profits thereby not a little, for when we wish to take a steamer we do not always trouble ourselves to look up the time-table beforehand. The Armenian is also a barber, and in his low-ceiled room of many windows you may hear, to the accompaniment of banging backgammon boards, the choicest of conversation. The only thing I have against him is that I have to pay twice as much for my coffee as a customer who wears a girdle and a fez.

The village boatmen and their skiffs

A few doors away dwell the Albanians. You may know them by the gay stockings, red embroidered with gold, which they wear outside the tight white trousers of their country. Theirs is the dispensary of ice-cream in summer and of *mahalibi* in winter—the latter being a kind of corn-starch pudding sprinkled with sugar and rose-water. These comestibles, of which their people have a practical monopoly, they also peddle about the streets. But it is better to partake of them in their shop, surrounded by lithographic royalties and battle scenes of 1870; and best of all in front of it, sitting comfortably in a rush-bottomed chair while the never-ending diorama of the Bosphorus rolls by.

In suggestive proximity to this establishment is a Greek drug store. It might be Venetian, so impregnate is it with the sound and light of water. For situation, however, I never saw its equal in Venice. It has, indeed — especially when late sunlight warms the opposite shore — so perfect a view, the platform in front of it is so favourite a resort, the legend "La Science est Longue, mais la Vie Courte" curls with such levity about a painted Hippocrates within, that the place rather gives you the impression of an operatic drug store. The polyglot youth in charge of it stands at the door exactly as if he were waiting for the chorus on the stage outside to give him his cue; and you cannot help asking yourself whether there be anything in the porcelain jars about him.

I have spoken with unbridled admiration of our market-place and its two main branches. How shall I now speak admiringly enough of the square with which they both communicate and which unites in itself the richness of their charms? It is not a square in any geometric sense. It is a broad stone quay of irregular width, tree-shaded, awning-hung, festooned with vines and fish-nets, adorned of a flat-topped fountain whose benches are a superior place of contemplation, bordered by a quaintly broken architecture of shops, cafés, and dwellings, and watched upon by a high white minaret. It is not subject to the intermittent bustle of the Company for the Promotion of Happiness, but it carries on its own more deliberate and more picturesque activities. Here commerce goes forward, both settled and itinerant, with loud and leisurely bargaining. Here the *kantarji* exercises his function of weighing the freights unloaded by the picture-book boats at the quay. The headquarters of one of them is here, in a deep arch over the water. This is the bazaar caïque, that goes early in the morning to the Golden Horn for the transport of such

In the market-place

freight and passengers as do not care to patronise the more expensive Company for the Promotion of Happiness — a huge rowboat with an incurving beak and a high stern, to pull whose oars the rowers drop from their feet to their backs. And here is also the headquarters of the *hamals*, most indispensable of men. These are Asiatic peasants who combine with many others the offices of carts and carters in flatter towns. They carry our furniture and fuel from the water on their backs. They chop our wood, to saw it being what they refuse. They keep guard of our houses when we go away. They patrol our streets at night, knocking the hour with their clubs on the pavement and rousing us with blood-curdling yells if so much as a hen-coop burn down at the Islands twenty miles away. They likewise act as town criers; and during the holy month of Ramazan they beat us up with drums early enough in the morning to be through breakfast by the time you can tell a black hair from a white. They are a strong, a faithful, even — if you choose to expend a little sentiment upon them — a pathetic race, living in exile without wife or child, sending money home as they earn it, going to their "countries" only at long intervals, and settling there when they are too old to work for their guild.

Altogether a man might spend his days in that square and be the better for it. As a matter of fact, a surprising number of us find it possible to do so, sipping coffee, smoking cigarettes or water-pipes, and watching life slip by on the strong blue current of the Bosphorus. And as I sit there too, treated always with a charming courtliness yet somehow made to feel the vanity of thanking God that I am not as other *gyaours* are, I often ask myself how these things may be. In other parts of the world people enjoy no such leisure unless they have rents or an indifference as to going to destruction. In Roumeli Hissar we neither go to destruction nor have rents. The case may be connected with the theory that all inhabitants of Constantinople are guests of its ruler. We are not subject to military duty, we are exempt from certain burdens of taxation, and other inducements are offered those of the true faith to settle in the City of the

Sultans. I have no means of knowing how persuasive these may be, but it is astonishing how overwhelming a proportion of the less skilled labour of the place is performed by outsiders — witness the Greek shopkeepers of our village, the Albanian sweet vendors, and the *hamals*. The case at all events is not without its charm. We may not accomplish great things in the world. We may not perform memorable services for state or humanity. We may not create works that shall carry our names down the generations. But we live. We enjoy the sun, we taste each other's society, and we are little troubled for the morrow. Could life be more?

XIV

REVOLUTION

1908

Constantinople is finished! So a reactionary impressionist groaned to himself on a certain summer day — to be precise, on the 24th of July, 1908 — when the amazing truth became known that the constitution, suppressed thirty-two years before, had been re-established. Constitutions were well enough in their place, but their place was not Constantinople. A Constantinople at whose gate your Shakespeare was not taken from you as being a perilous and subversive book, a Constantinople through whose custom-house you could not bribe your way, a Constantinople which you might explore ungreeted by a derisive "*Gyaour!*" or a casual stone, a Constantinople of mosques open to the infidel without money and without price, a Constantinople wherein you were free to walk at night without a lantern, a Constantinople indifferent to passports or to ladies' veils, a Constantinople where it was possible to paint in the streets, to meet and see off steamers, to post a local letter — and, what is more, receive one — a Constantinople without a censor, a spy, or a dog, might be a Constantinople of a kind; but it would not be the true Constantinople. It could never be the impenetrable old Constantinople that lent a certain verisimilitude to stories like "Paul Patoff" and made it possible for a romantic Gladstone to be taken seriously at his most romantic moments. Violated of its mystery, laid open to the deadly levelling of Western civilisation, what could save it from becoming a Constantinople of straight streets, of pseudo-classic architecture, of glaring lights, of impatient tram and telephone bells, of the death-dealing motors that Abd ül Hamid would never allow, of the terrible tourists — the German *Liebespaar*, the British old maid, the American mother and daughter — who insist on making one place exactly like another?

Well, the Constantinople of a reactionary impressionist *is* finished. A good deal of it vanished by magic on the night of the revolution. Of the outward and visible remainder more has disappeared already than an outsider might suppose. The dogs and the beggars went very soon, followed by the worst of the cobblestones and the bumpy old bridge that every traveller wrote a chapter about; and when I took a little journey in the world after this process was well started it struck me that the streets of Paris and New York were less clean than those of Stamboul. As for the censor and the spies, if they still exist it is in a tempered form. In the meantime the telephones, the motors, the dynamos so redoubted by Abd ül Hamid, have made their appearance. And with them has come a terrifying appetite for civic improvement. The mosaics of Justinian are about to be lighted by electricity. Boulevards have been cut through Stamboul. Old Turkish houses have been torn down by the hundred in the interests of street widening. Only a miracle saved the city walls from being sold as building material. I could wish that the edifices encumbering the sphendone of the Hippodrome might be sold as building material, in order to give back to the city its supreme ornament of a sea view. Imagine what such a wide blue vision might be, seen from the heart of the town — perhaps through a dark-green semicircle of cypresses! In the meantime the Hippodrome has been made to blossom, not quite as the rose, depriving Stamboul of its one good square and threatening to hide the beauty of Sultan Ahmed's marble mosque. If the new gardens also do something to hide the Byzantino-Germanico-Turkish fountain which William II, in remembrance of a memorable visit, had the courage to erect in line with the obelisk of Theodosius and the twisted serpents of Platæa, they will not have been planted altogether in vain. But direr changes still have the people of Constantinople witnessed since their revolution night — fire, pestilence, earthquake, mutiny, war. They have even lived to hear, from streets of something less than sweet security, the nearing thunder of cannon, and to ask themselves if the supreme change were at hand, and Constantinople itself was to go.

Of all these things more has been written than is profitable to read. It is still too soon to know very much about the Young Turks — their real leaders, their real motives, their real aims, their real accomplishment. It is fairly safe to conclude, however, that they were neither the demigods acclaimed in 1908 as the saviours of their country nor the rascals execrated as its destroyers in 1912. They were, in all likelihood, men neither better nor worse than the rest of us, who found their country in an evil case and who for no shameful reason lacked the knowledge and the power to make it an earthly paradise. Yet it seems to me that history will give them credit for breaking the spell of Abd ül Hamid, that strange and tragic figure of myth who struggled to keep the thirteenth century alive in the twentieth. Nor do I see how they could have matched him otherwise than as they did, with his own weapon of secrecy. And whatever their subsequent mistakes may have been, it also seems to me that history will absolve them from much of the reproach of losing their European empire. No one can fairly blame them for wishing to make the Turk the dominant element in his own empire, and for wishing to make that empire independent of the foreigner. Neither they nor any one else, moreover, could in the long run have saved their European provinces. It is a serious

Badge of the revolution: "Liberty, Justice, Fraternity, Equality."

question whether they will succeed in saving certain of their provinces that remain — or whether their own good advises them to do so. There are influences of common blood and common tradition which no mere political influence can indefinitely withstand. In any case, I have come to look upon the Turkish revolution with other than the eye of a reactionary impressionist. It would be a reactionary impressionist indeed who put the picturesqueness of Stamboul before the good of a people — and a blind one who failed to see what there was of human colour in those dramatic events. And although time has only partially fulfilled so many generous hopes, or has turned them to bitterness, I refuse to believe that they were totally insincere. I shall always count it, on the contrary, among the most enlarging experiences of my life to have been in Constantinople in 1908, and to have seen a people at one of those rare moments when it really lives.

It is strange to recall, in the light of all that has happened since, how silently that momentous change announced itself. We knew that there were disturbances in Macedonia; but there were always disturbances in Macedonia. We gathered that there were dissensions at the Palace, for on the very day of his decoration by William II with the Black Eagle, Ferid Pasha, the Albanian Grand Vizier, fell. But there were usually dissensions at the Palace. And when, two days later, we read at the top of our morning papers a bare official announcement that the constitution had been re-established, that long-suspended constitution, the promise of which had brought Abd ül Hamid to the throne, we asked each other what it meant. Apparently no one could tell — least of all the diplomats supposed to sit at the fountain-heads of information. The most frequent conjecture was of a trick to gain time. It was only later that rumours began to run about, in the true Constantinople way, of the revolt of Macedonia; of the telegrams exchanged between Salonica and Yîldîz, and the memorable night council at which Abd ül Hamid, fainting with exhaustion and rage, acknowledged himself beaten at last; of the mysterious Committee of Union and Progress that had performed the miracle, and of the men who had gone about the country, disguised as pedlers and dervishes, feeding the hunger for liberty and the courage to demand it, and of the women who carried messages from harem to harem and so delivered them without writing, and of the revolutionary circles that flourished under the eyes of spies, subordinate to the larger circles of Constantinople, Salonica, and Paris, wherein only one or two members knew of the definite existence of another circle, and then of only one or two of its members.

When the lancers rode through the streets that Friday

morning of the 24th of July to guard the Sultan on his way to mosque, a few Greeks cheered them. The soldiers looked uneasy. Such a thing had never happened to them. That afternoon a few shopkeepers hung out their flags. The police went about zealously taking down the offenders' names. By the next day, however, the police gave up trying to keep track of the flags. The whole city flapped with them. And other strange manifestations took place. Music marched through the streets. Orators sprang up at every corner. Newspapers quadrupled their editions and burst into extras at the novelty of containing news. Hawkers everywhere sold long red badges bearing golden words that it had been forbidden to utter — Liberty, Justice, Equality, Fraternity. It was as if a cover had suddenly been taken off. For thirty years this people had been kept in constantly closer restriction, had lived under the eyes of that vast army of informers from which they were not safe even within their own doors, had been robbed one by one of all the little liberties of life so common in other countries that we think nothing of them — to visit one's friends, to gather for amusement or discussion, to read the book of one's choice, to publish one's sentiment or protest, to go out at night, to travel at will. Hundreds of thousands had grown up to man's estate knowing no other manner of life. And from one day to another they were told that it was all at an end — that they were free. Was it any wonder that at first they were dazed? Was it not rather a wonder that they did not lose their heads?

The natural goodness and peaceableness of a race that has been accounted one of butchers could have had no more triumphant proof than those trying days when the whole machinery of government was disorganised. But of the sanguinary scenes that have marked other revolutions there were none. In Salonica, to be sure, where the constitution was proclaimed one day earlier, a policeman was shot for tearing down the proclamation. Ten notorious spies were also shot in honour of the date. Their comrades had the Julian calendar to thank that the number was not twenty-three! In Broussa another spy, the infamous Fehim Pasha of Constantinople, was killed by a crowd he unwisely went out of his way to insult. In the capital, however, although the Stamboul troops were ready to occupy Pera and cut off Yîldîz, extreme measures proved unnecessary. The moderation of the revolutionists, the astuteness of the Sultan, and the character of the people combined to make the affair pass off without bloodshed. If it had not been for foreigners employed in some of the public services, who promptly set about fomenting strikes, nothing would have occurred to disturb the peace. Zeki Pasha, it is true, the man who would have repeated the Bloody Sunday of St. Petersburg, had his windows smashed. Otherwise the hostility of the people toward the ringleaders of the old régime restricted itself to cartoons of the most primitive drawing and satire, which had an enormous sale in the streets and which were ultimately suppressed by the Committee of Union and Progress. The Committee sedulously fostered the belief that the real author of the Hamidian régime had merely been the victim of his advisers.

The Bloody Sunday which might have been was the Sunday after the coup d'état, when all day long deputation after deputation marched up to the Palace in the July sun, until a hundred thousand fezzes and turbans packed the avenues of approach. They had been the day before to each of the ministers in turn, demanding their oaths to maintain the constitution. They now came to the Sultan, loyal and unarmed, but asking from him too an assurance that he would not a second time withdraw the instrument which he had been the first of his line to promulgate. The Palace guards did not resist, but within was such terror as those without had never dreamed of inspiring. The Sultan, always chary of his person, uncertain as to the designs of a mob the like of which he had never seen before, refused to show himself. He merely sent messages to the people and begged them to disperse. They would not. Then Zeki Pasha, Grand Master of Artillery, asked leave to clear the crowd away — with his cannon. Fortunately, most fortunately, the old martinet's advice was not taken. But still the Sultan did not appear. Finally, late in the evening, the last deputation of all arrived. It was composed of the more enlightened element of the population and contained members of the Committee. Like those who had preceded them, they respectfully asked to see his majesty. They were told that his majesty had retired. They insisted, with what arguments one may never know. And at last, near midnight, his majesty appeared on a balcony of the Palace and asked the people what they wished. They, amid frantic demonstrations of loyalty, said that they wished to see the imperial master who had so long been kept from them by traitors, and to hear him swear fealty to his own constitution. He replied: "My children, be certain that I shall shrink before no sacrifice for your happiness. Henceforth your future is assured. I will work with you in common accord. Live as brothers. I am overcome by the sentiments of devotion and gratitude which you show. Return to your homes and take your rest." This speech, characteristic of its maker's adroitness, satisfied the thousands who did not hear it, and they went away.

It did not satisfy the instigators of the demonstration, who later obliged the Sultan to make the desired oath on the Koran. It was his only chance to save his throne. But bitter as his surrender doubtless was, he must have had moments of compensation. One of them occurred on the succeeding Friday, when a hundred thousand people gathered again to see him go to mosque. Hours before the time of the ceremony the precincts of the Palace were invaded, and *hamals* kicked their heels from the edge of the terrace reserved for visitors with cards from their embassies. A great tree near the mosque was so full of men and boys that two or three branches cracked off. When the imperial cortège came down from the Palace there was such cheering as Abd ül Hamid, accustomed to the perfunctory "*Padishah'm chok yasha!*" of his guard, could scarcely have heard before. The monarch who all his life had been most afraid of bombs and bullets may never have been so nervous, but he stood up like a man, saluting his people with the red-and-white rosette of the constitution pinned to his shoulder. They responded in a frenzy of emotion, tears streaming from many of their eyes. After returning to the Palace the Sultan showed himself again at a balcony and spoke a few words. Could there have been only terror for him in the joyful shouting of a mob that would have torn an assassin to shreds? Could he have seen there only enemies who had overcome him by the brute force of numbers? Could he have felt only the irony of his undoing by the very schools he had created, by the very means he had taken to stamp out individual liberty?

There may be question as to whether any real generous impulse, any true glimmer of repentance, visited that old lion at bay. But there can be none as to the temper of the crowds that marched about the streets for days with flags and music, cheering the army that had freed them, cheering the Sultan who, they said, had been kept from them by traitors, cheering the orators who told them again and again of their happiness and assured them that thenceforward in the Ottoman Empire there was no distinction between Armenian, Greek, Jew, and Turk: all were Ottomans, all were brothers, all were free. It was, of course, too good to be true. Yet, even in the light of subsequent history, I persist in remembering those days as a little golden age which no one was the worse for having known. A carriage wheel was crushed in the press. The hat — or should one say the fez? — was instantly passed around, and the happy jehu was given the wherewithal to buy fifty new wheels. A shop-window, again, was accidentally broken. The shopkeeper presently had reason to wish that the crowd would break a window every day. Ladies who never before would have dared go alone through certain streets, or through any street at certain hours, went unmolested when and where they chose. Races that had lived under an armed truce, and not always that, suddenly fell on each other's necks. A cold-hearted impressionist more than once found it in him to smile at respectable old gentlemen who insisted on kissing fervent young orators on both cheeks. And when priests of different religions exchanged such salutes it was even more a case of the lion lying down with the lamb.

The scattering of the Palace camarilla was one of the most picturesque of the many picturesque events of the day. The true story of those precious rascals is a piece of the Middle Ages — or of the flourishing days of New York. Some of them were ministers, some chamberlains and secretaries, one of them no more than an Arab astrologer, who gained immense credit during the Greek war of 1897 by holding over telegrams and prophesying their contents to the Sultan. Without this star-chamber nothing was done in the empire. The council of ministers sat at the Sublime Porte, but the true cabinet sat secretly in Yîldîz Palace. If the Grand Vizier did not happen to belong to it, so much the worse for him. He

Cartoon representing the exodus of the Palace camarilla

must be prepared to see his orders countermanded and his promises rendered void. It was always possible to obtain such a result. Those who knew the ropes knew the department of each member of the kitchen cabinet, and his price. For that matter they were willing to be accommodating. They took from each according to his means. And they were not too proud to be known as the *kebayas* of the industrial guilds. One accepted two hundred pounds a month from the butchers of Constantinople, in return for leniency in the matter of inspection. Another received a handsome allowance from the corporation of bakers, who were also obliged to subsidise the police in order to prevent the seizure of undersized loaves from being too serious. A third drew a dollar for every bag of flour that came into the city. I even heard of a pasha who allowed his kitchens to be supplied with butter by a Kürdish chief. There was no possible source of revenue which these men had not tapped — public funds, private enterprises, the distribution of places, the granting of concessions. It mattered nothing to them that the country was going to ruin, the development of its incalculable resources stopped, so long as they built great palaces on the Bosphorus and fared sumptuously every day.

The constitution took them more completely than any by surprise. Accustomed to the variable climate of the court, they were prepared to fall from favour, to be exiled, or even to lose their lives. But they were not prepared for this. Not many of them were quick enough to grasp the situation. The first to do so was Selim Pasha Melhameh, a Syrian. As Minister of Agriculture, Mines, and Forests he was in the way of getting good things from people who wanted concessions. His already comfortable fortune was agreeably increased during his last winter in office by a scarcity of fuel that caused great misery among the poor of the capital. An imperial order was issued to bring down wood from the forests of the interior and sell it at a fixed price. The wood was brought down and the price fixed — by Selim Pasha. He is said to have been absent from the all-night council at which the constitution was granted. At first he would not believe the news, but when proof was given him he called for his wife and told her to pack at once. She did so with such expedition that three days later, borrowing the Italian embassy launch on the pretext of seeing off their son, who was going to his post in the Turkish embassy at Rome, they sailed on the steamer with him.

The next to leave was the notorious Izzet Pasha, the Sultan's first chamberlain. There was a mediæval character for you — that perfect gentleman and connoisseur, descended from robber Bedouins beyond Damascus, who became the greatest robber in the empire. He robbed so shamelessly, he robbed so amusingly, that an irresponsible impressionist cannot help investing him with a romantic interest. When the coup d'état took place, his Syrian wit told him that a country he had plundered for years was no longer the country for him. He accordingly bought for eight thousand pounds, in the name of a French lady, a small Greek passenger steamer worth some fifteen hundred, and prepared to decamp. When the captain learned the identity of his new owner he refused to serve him. Rather than excite suspicion by drumming up another crew, Izzet proceeded to buy another steamer, this time under the British flag. Having been bitten once, he stipulated that the owners should be paid in three instalments — two thousand pounds down, fifteen hundred when he should get away, by cash deposited with a third party, and fifteen hundred more from his first port of call. When the owners presented their cheque for two thousand pounds at Izzet Pasha's bank they were informed that the latter had withdrawn his account. Izzet Pasha expressed infinite regret at the mistake, and courteously wrote out a second cheque on a bank from which he had withdrawn his account. Before the owners had time to present that Izzet Pasha, boarding his steamer from the German embassy launch and a series of tugs, had got away with three of his four wives, in spite of the crowd that shook their fists after him from Galata quay. At the Dardanelles he was stopped. And perhaps the most novel of all his experiences was to see a handful of gold he gave to the officer keeping him under guard thrown scornfully overboard. But the English register of his boat and a commission he displayed, sending him abroad on imperial business, saved his skin. He was not heard from again till he turned up at Genoa. There, telling his captain he was going to take his family ashore for a walk, he took ticket for England. The captain waited patiently till there was nothing left on board to eat or to burn, and then he wired to his former owners. They had not received their third payment, but as the second was duly made and as they got their boat back they did not come off so badly.

The rest of the gang were not allowed to escape. They were entertained at the War Department until they began to disgorge gold and lands. Zeki Pasha gave up no more than ten thousand pounds; but Hassan Rami Pasha, who had been Minister of Marine a year, handed over some two hundred thousand. This act of penance performed, they and their colleagues were sent to Prinkipo, where, under due surveillance, they were granted the liberties of an island six miles in circumference until such time as parliament should investigate their affairs.

In contrast to the scurrying to cover of the old régime was the return of the exiles. During Abd ül Hamid's long reign, and most actively during the latter part of it, there had been a systematic clearing out of independent personalities. Men who would not hide their disapproval of the government, who could not be bought or silenced in any other way, or whom chance spies happened to report on adversely, were banished to remote parts of the empire. Others fled to countries where life was made less difficult for them. Sixty thousand exiles are said to have left Constantinople alone. And there remains the large number of those who were suppressed in unavowed ways. One of the first acts of the new government was to issue an amnesty for exiles and political prisoners. There consequently set in an immediate tide of return. It happened that the old French steamship line of the *Messagéries Maritimes* brought back most of the exiles, partly because many of them were settled in Paris, partly because of the sympathy of educated Turks and of all revolutionaries for France. So the arrival of the *Messagéries* boat became a weekly event of the city. Steamers would be chartered to go down the Marmora, crowds would blacken the Galata quay, the windows, balconies, and roofs overlooking it, the adjacent shipping, the old bridge, to welcome back with flags, music, cheers, and frantic whistles men like old Deli Fouad Pasha, mad Fouad Pasha, who prevented the massacre of Armenians in Scutari in 1896; like the Armenian Patriarch who proved too intractable at the same period; like young Prince Sabaëddin, the Sultan's nephew, who came back from Paris with the coffin of his fugitive father. But not all of these returns were joyful. There were tragic meetings at the coming of men broken by imprisonment or deadly climates — as once when a pale figure was carried from the ship in a chair, amid a silence that was broken only by some one sobbing on the quay. And there were those who returned to the quay every week, scanning the decks of arriving steamers for faces they never found.

Altogether there was matter enough for the eye of

an impressionist resentful of the demolishing of his city. Space would never suffice me to report the scenes characteristic or picturesque, the stories romantic and humorous, that could not fail to mark so great an event. The sudden outburst of literary and dramatic activity, the movement toward emancipation of the Turkish women, the honours paid by the Young Turks to the memory of the Armenians massacred in 1896, the visits of friendly deputations from Bulgaria, Greece, and Roumania, the events in the Balkans and the Austrian boycott, the manœuvres of the reactionaries, the removal of the Palace guard, the procedure of the elections, added each its note of colour. Nothing, perhaps, filled the public eye quite so obviously as the primary elections for parliament. Symbolic of what the revolution had striven to attain, this event was celebrated in each district with fitting ceremonies. One district in Stamboul solemnly brought its voting urn to the Sublime Porte on the back of a camel. Five villages on the Bosphorus, forming another district, made a water pageant that reminded one of state days in Venice. But the five great fishing caïques, with their splendid in-curving beaks, their high poops gay with flags and trailing rugs, their fourteen to twenty costumed rowers, were no imitation of other days, like the Venetian *Bissone*. Most imposing of all was the procession that carried the urns of Pera through the city in decorated court carriages, attended by music, banners, soldiers, school children, and other representative bodies to the number of several thousand. Two of these were peculiarly striking. Near the head of the procession, led by an Arab on a camel, rode a detachment of men representing the different races of the empire, each in the costume of his "country." And later came a long line of carriages in which *imams* and Armenian priests, *imams* and Greek priests, *imams* and Catholic priests, *imams* and Jewish rabbis, drove two and two in the robes of their various cults.

The opening of parliament itself, with all the circumstance that arms and majesty could lend it, marked a term for those effervescent days. The Young Turks made it a particular point that the ceremony of December 17 should be held, not in the throne-room of Dolma Ba'hcheh, as the Sultan wished, but in the place where the parliament of 1876 had been dissolved. This Palladian structure behind St. Sophia, originally built for the university and remodelled after the dissolution of the first parliament for the uses of the Ministry of Justice, contained no hall of suitable size. There was not even room in the chamber of deputies for the two hundred odd members — if they all had arrived in time for the opening. The invitations were consequently restricted to the smallest possible number: to the greater dignitaries of state, to the heads of foreign missions and their first dragomans — leaving out disappointed secretaries and wives — and to a few representatives of the press. There was perhaps more heartburning among these spoilt children of the century than among any other section of the public. Some of them had travelled great distances to attend this historic inauguration, only to be shut out of it. The press of the country naturally had the first claim. The thorny question of allotting tickets among the press of other countries was settled by giving each head of a foreign mission two tickets to dispose of as he chose. Those fortunate enough to get them were inclined to grumble at the quarters assigned them — a species of low, dark theatre box above that of the ambassadors, from which only the ten or fifteen first to arrive could see the floor. But all could see the imperial box, directly opposite. And I, for one, being no journalist, counted myself lucky to be there at all.

The first arrival of importance was that of the diplomatic corps, led by their formidable German dean, Baron Marschall von Bieberstein. Not least noticeable among them was the Persian ambassador, in a coat so thickly incrusted with gold that one could not tell what colour it was, and wide scarlet trousers and black astrakhan cap. The tall chargé d'affaires of Montenegro was also a striking figure in the national dress of his country — loose trousers thrust into top-boots, embroidered bolero and hanging sleeves, and black pill-box with red top — as was Mgr. Sardi, the Apostolic Delegate, in his flowing violet robes. Another splash of colour was presently made to the right of the tribune by the senators, in gala uniform and decorations. They are forty in number, appointed for life by the Sultan from among active or retired functionaries of state. A sprinkling of green robes of the cult was conspicuous among them. They were followed by the deputies in a body, or by as many of them as had arrived. For in the remoter parts of the empire the elections were not quite through by the time parliament, already a month late, opened. Their prevailing soberness of frock coat and fez was relieved by an occasional military uniform and by a surprising proportion of religious turbans. There were also a few Syrian or Arab head-dresses above picturesque robes of striped silk. In the meantime ministers, religious dignitaries, and certain unofficial guests of the kind known in the East as notables, had been taking their places. The ministers sat at the left of the tribune, facing the house. They were resplendent in gold lace and orders, with the single exception of the white-bearded Shei'h ül Islam in his simple white robe. Facing the ministers were the green, purple, and fawn-coloured robes of the *ülema*. On the other side of the steps of the tribune, in front of the senators, were the heads of the non-Moslem sects of the empire. Their black robes and head-dresses made a contrastingly sombre group, in which the red-topped turban of the *locum tenens* of the Grand Rabbinate and the crimson hat and veil of the Armenian Catholic Patriarch were vivid notes of colour. But the most conspicuous contrast was made by certain of the "notables" present, among whom were members of that loquacious body known as the Balkan Committee and their ladies. I do not know whether the latter appreciated the honour that was done them, alone of their sex. These *komitajis* were prudently tucked as far out of sight as possible, where, nevertheless, their wayworn British tweeds and sailor-hats did not fail to attract musing Oriental eyes, and to suggest to light-minded impressionists the scenarios of comic operas.

By noon only the president's tribune and the two boxes facing those of the diplomats and the journalists, reserved for guests from the Palace, remained without an occupant. Great doubt had been expressed as to whether the imperial box would be filled at all. If the matter had been left to Abd ül Hamid's preference the box would doubtless have remained empty. But the Committee had found a way of overcoming Abd ül Hamid's preferences, and not only did he reopen in person the parliament he had tried to suppress, but he drove all the way from Beshiktash to Stamboul to do it. He had not seen so much of his capital for fifteen years. The arrival of his brilliant cortège we did not witness from our black pen under the ceiling of the parliament chamber. We heard the fanfare of bugles heralding the approach of majesty, the bands striking up one after the other the Hamidieh March, the cheers sounding nearer and nearer till the last rose from the court below. A few glittering personages near the tribune, a deputy or two from the front row, who had gone to the windows, resumed their places. There was a general stir of expectancy, a last preening of orders and epaulets. After a few minutes a group of very literally gilded youths was ushered into the left hand of the three compartments of the imperial box. They were five of the Sultan's sons, accompanied by his cousin Abd ül Mejid Effendi. A moment later the box above them filled with members of the imperial suite. In the midst of their gold lace and jewels the black face and white eyeballs of a Palace eunuch were a characteristic note.

These personages had time to admire and to be admired of all beholders before the more august guest of the occasion arrived. In fact it was a full quarter of an hour before a new splendour of uniforms was seen to mount the stairs at the rear of the box, and the Sultan came in sight. He then made the mistake of entering the compartment reserved for his brother Mehmed Reshad Effendi and his cousin Youssouf Izzeddin Effendi, the next two heirs to the throne — who failed to honour the occasion. With earth-sweeping salaams the master of ceremonies inducted his majesty into the central compartment. There seemed to be something less than imperial ease in the hesitation with which he lingered a moment in the rear of the box. He dropped his glove, and the master of ceremonies picked it up. The dead silence that greeted him when he did step forward was a surprise to those who had witnessed European acclamations of royalty. All rose to their feet and stood with folded hands in the Oriental attitude of respect. They did, however, permit themselves to look up. The Sultan stood with his hand on his sword of empire, looking down, a figure of dignity in his plain dark military overcoat, visibly bowed by years and anxiety, yet not so grey as one might expect, keen-eyed, hawk-nosed, full-bearded, taking in one by one the faces that represented every race and region of his wide domains. The silence and the intentness of that mutual regard grew dramatic as the seconds gathered into minutes. "A wolf in a cage!" whispered some one behind me. There was too little room in the epigram for the strangeness of the scene. One could fill the silence with what one pleased of historic visions, of tragic memories, of hatreds and ambitions, of victory and defeat. But all the East was in that unyielding surrender and in that uncelebrated triumph.

The silence was suddenly broken by the voice of the Sultan's secretary, who began to read, beside the steps of the tribune, the speech from the throne. My Turkish is too small and too colloquial to take in much of so high-flown a document, but I caught references to the perfidy of Austria and Bulgaria and to the author's satisfaction in being able to open again the assembly for which thirty years ago the country had not been ripe. Twice the house broke into applause, which the Sultan acknowledged with a military salute. At the close of the reading a green-robed *mollah* offered prayer. The majority of those present listened to it, as Moslems do, in an attitude very much like that of the Greek *adorante* in Berlin, except that the hands are held lower and closer to the body. When the prayer came to an end, with a fervent responsive *amin*, the Sultan did a thing that no one had expected. He made a brief speech. But the signal had already been given, according to programme, for bands and cannon to announce the inauguration of the new era. The consequence was that few heard even the sound of his majesty's voice. In a moment more he was gone.

The entire ceremony, during which all remained on their feet, lasted less than half an hour. When it was over, those who had lost the spectacle of the Sultan's arrival made haste to secure places whence they might witness that of his departure. The view from the windows of the parliament house was one never to forget — for its own picturesqueness, for its historic significance, for its evocations of the unconquerable vitality, of the dramatic contrasts and indifferences of life. The sun was in gala mood that day, to match the mood and to bring out the predominatingly Asiatic colour of the thousands that packed the square which had been the Forum Augustæum of New Rome. Not only did they pack the square, those Asiatic thousands, and every radiating open space as far as the eye could reach; they loaded its bare trees, they filled the windows and lined the roofs overlooking it, they darkened the buttresses, the cupolas, the minaret galleries of St. Sophia. Two men even clung to the standard of the crescent at the apex of the great dome. The brown *chasseurs* of Salonica, in recognition of the part they played in the revolution, were given the honour of keeping open a narrow lane through the middle of the square. They were assisted by tall blue Anatolians of the imperial guard and by deputations with flags and inscribed banners. A gilded barouche drove into the courtyard where once had stood the Roman senate. A scarlet-and-gold coachman drove the four superb iron-grey horses, and in front of them pranced a fifth iron-grey mounted by a blue-and-silver outrider. Three buglers in black and scarlet faced the porte-cochère. At the sound of their bugles the soldiers presented arms and a band burst into the imperial march. The thin blue and brown fringe of guards undulated with the eddies of motion that surged through the pressing thousands in their frenzy to see the monarch whom they had shorn of his power. Then, surrounded by the glitter of the princes and his aides, preceded and followed by the scarlet flutter of the lancers' banderoles, the Caliph of Islam flashed away toward the column of Constantine.

XV

THE CAPTURE OF CONSTANTINOPLE

1909

WHAT could be more aggravating to a greedy impressionist than to have sat nearly two years in Constantinople, to have watched the amicable revolution of 1908, to have been one of a privileged few to assist at the reopening by Abd ül Hamid of the parliament he suppressed thirty-two years ago, and then to have been caught in an ignoble Florentine pension, among ladies passionate after pictures, when the mutiny of April 13 broke out in Stamboul? And nothing, from the meagre Italian telegrams, was more difficult to make out than the origin of that mutiny. Had the Committee of Union and Progress made the mistakes their friends had feared? Had the opposition liberals been unconsciously playing into the hands of reactionaries? Had the Sultan, who appeared to swallow the revolution in so lamblike a manner, merely been lying low? The only thing was to go back and find out, and to get what reparation one could by seeing the end of the affair — if end there were. For it must be recorded against the sagacity of impressionists, or of one particular impressionist, that he thought nothing at all might happen.

The first hint of anything to the contrary came from a *Neue Freie Presse*, obtained at a Croatian railway-station, which announced that by the 19th a Macedonian army would concentrate at Chatalja, some twenty-five miles from Constantinople. The 19th was the next day, and I was due in Stamboul on the morning of the 20th. There might, then, be sights to see on the way. I had a further hint of them after getting into the Constantinople sleeper that night at Belgrade. Two men were already in bed in the compartment, and before morning I became conscious of the porter telling one of them in Turkish that he must change for Salonica in twenty minutes. I told myself that he must be a Young Turk hurrying back from Europe to take part in — what? I had the strangest sense, as we whistled through the dark toward Nisch, of forces gathering silently for an impending drama.

We spent the next day crawling through Bulgaria, along that old highway of the empire where Janissaries march behind the sacred banner of the Prophet no more. Being no master of Slavic languages, I was dependent on our polyglot porter for news. This gloomy individual, a Greek from Pera, gathered assurance with each kilometre — and they were not few, for the philanthropic Baron Hirsch, who was paid for each one, put in as many of them as he could — that his family had been massacred. He looked for confirmation of his fears at Moustafa Pasha. We reached that humble frontier station about ten o'clock that night. There was no news, but there were soldiers of a new kind, sturdy fellows in moccasins and white leggings, who strode up and down between tracks with a businesslike air entirely different from the usual Moustafa Pasha military. I was to see more of those white leggings.

I got up early the next morning, in order to steal a march on the lavatory. The porter, gloomier than ever, assured me that I need not have taken the trouble. We had been delayed by troop trains and could not reach Constantinople much before noon. That began to look interesting. I must confess, though, that the interest paled as we stood still — and breakfastless — at a small way station for something over an hour, with no apparent reason. The reason became apparent at the station following, where we overtook a long train of freight-cars. Their freight consisted of horses, of camp baggage, and notably of soldiers, many of them in moccasins and white felt leggings bound with black. Many others wore the strong pointed slippers of the country, with the counter turned under their heels, and white felt Albanian skull-caps. All of them were friendly, curious as to a train so much more comfortable than their own, and good-humouredly willing to be photographed. A whitecap who led a party of inspection through our sleeping-car explained to his companions why I could not instantly present them with their portraits. He did a little photography himself, he told me; also that he was by profession a municipal clerk in Macedonia, although for the moment a volunteer. I asked him, in my ignorance, what side he was on and what he was going to do. "We are for liberty," he answered gravely. "We are going to kill Sultan Hamid. In Stamboul the great men sit and eat *pilaf* while we starve. We have had enough." And that was the general chorus. "Papa Hamid is finished," said a young officer whom I later met again in Stamboul. It was clear what the Macedonians thought of the situation. The Sultan had had his chance and he had lost it.

The troop train left us to meditate for two or three hours on a siding, but toward noon we renewed acquaintance with it — at Chatalja. That name had yet to become a household word. Nevertheless I looked with considerable interest at Chatalja, where the rumoured concentration should by this time have taken place, where already existed the line of fortifications that was to save Constantinople in 1912, and where of old a Byzantine wall ran from sea to sea. Of Byzantine walls however, of modern fortifications, or of concentrating armies, there was no sign. There was merely a red-brown wooden station, a dusty road, a scarce less dusty coffee-house

Soldiers at Chatalja, April 20

beyond it, a group of quarantine shanties farther away, and on a low rim of green that lifted itself against the April blue something that looked like a ruined watch-tower. For the study of this simple *mise en scène* not less than five hours were afforded us. The slightest incident, accordingly, assumed a grave importance. A plump person in shoulder-straps rattled down the dusty road in an ancient landau. Was he the generalissimo of the investing army? I later had occasion to learn that he was not. A naval officer appeared from somewhere and was fervently embraced by the officers of our troop train. He might be bringing them assurance of the loyalty of the fleet. In fact, I believe he did. Two individuals in black robes and white turbans were brought in under guard of a new kind of soldier, smart fellows in lightish blue. I was told that the priests were agitators who had been caught trying to corrupt the soldiers, while their captors belonged to the famous Macedonian gendarmerie. And after our troop train had gone another one came, gaily decorated with boughs and flags. The men were all volunteers — Albanians, Bulgars, Greeks, Jews, Vlachs. But there was nothing of the tyro in the way they carried their rifles and cartridge belts. I have no doubt that many of them were ex-brigands and *komitajis*, turned into patriots by the mutiny at Constantinople. And excellent patriots they made, poor fellows, many of whom were killed four days later in the city to which they went so light-heartedly.

So the day passed, with long stops, with short advances, with pangs of hunger which a disgusted Orient Express — itself some nine hours late — reluctantly consented to appease, with melodramatic rumours of battle, and with a final sight of soldiers making a thin black ant trail over a bare hill. Night came upon us in the green valley of Sparta Kouleh, at the end of which a gleam of the Marmora was visible, and the Bithynian Olympus ethereal with snow. A bonfire reddened the twilight in front of us, soldiers were singing not far away, frogs or tree-toads made a silver music in the distance. To what grim things, I wondered as we so mysteriously waited, did nature make this soft antithesis? At last a long train, fifty-seven empty freight-cars, rumbled out of the dark from the direction of the city. We then started on again, stopping only to take on and let off officers at way stations, and reached town, fourteen and a half hours late, at half past ten.

Expectation, after a checkered approach, had been raised to a pitch. But Constantinople proved a most singularly beleaguered city. I perceived that when I saw a couple of Macedonian officers get off the train with me. I perceived it again when I passed the customs with an unaccustomed ease and drove away through streets that gave no hint of siege. Still more clearly did I perceive it during the three long days that followed my arrival. Beleaguering there was, for rumour peopled the fields of Thrace with advancing thousands, and Hüsseïn Hüssnü Pasha, commander of operations at the front, issued manifestoes. To the garrison he offered immunity on condition of their taking a solemn oath of obedience before the Sheï'h ül Islam. To those of the populace not implicated in the late uprising he promised security of person and property. And both apparently made haste to put themselves on the right side. Deputation after deputation went out to the enemy's camp in token of surrender. The War Office made plans for provisioning the invaders. Parliament assembled at San Stefano in the shadow of the Macedonian camp, and the fleet followed suit. At the same time the air was tense with the feeling that first came to me when the porter of my sleeping-car called that unknown passenger at Nisch. What was going to happen? It was an indication of the colour of people's thoughts that the outgoing steamers were crowded during those days, and panics ran through the town like rumours. Some one would shout: "They are coming!" The streets would instantly fill with the rush of feet, the clang of closing shutters.

On Friday, the 23d, I went to *Selamlîk.* I also wrote a last will and testament before doing so, which I left with careless conspicuousness on my desk, for there was much talk of bombs and depositions. So much was there that in the diplomatic pavilion, to which I was admitted by courtesy of our embassy, no heads of missions were present. There were also fewer general spectators than usual, and they were kept at a greater distance. Otherwise the ceremony took place with its old pomp. I missed the handsome white Albanian and the blue Arab zouaves, recently expelled from the imperial guard; but the dark-blue infantry, the black-and-red marines, the scarlet-pennoned lancers, the matched cavalry of Daoud Pasha, a brown battalion of sappers, and even a detachment of the Salonica sharpshooters, marched up the hill with sounding brass. Before they had quite banked up the approaches to the Palace and the mosque the sun, breaking from morning clouds, brought out all the colour of that pageant set for the last time. Toward noon five closed court carriages of ladies drove slowly down the avenue, surrounded by solemn black eunuchs, and turned into the mosque yard. A group of officers in gala uniform took their places in line opposite the diplomatic pavilion. At their head stood Prince Bourhan ed Din, the Sultan's favourite son. His presence excited no little interest, for it had been reported that he had run away. He looked unusually pale. Suddenly the *müezin's* shrill sweet cry sounded from the minaret and the bands began to play the Hamidieh March. Then the Sultan's cortège — of brilliant uniforms on foot, of trusty Albanian riflemen, of blue-and-silver grooms leading blooded chargers — emerged from an archway in the Palace wall. Abd ül Hamid, in a hooded victoria drawn by two beautiful black horses, sat facing Tevfik Pasha, the Grand Vizier of the moment, and his son Abd ür Rahim Effendi. He looked bent and haggard, the more because his sunken cheeks were so palpably rouged. As he passed under the terrace of the diplomatic pavilion he glanced up to see if any of the ambassadors were there. The fact that none of them were was afterward said to have irritated him intensely. He did not betray it, at all events, as he passed down the avenue, saluting right and left to his cheering soldiers. After leaving his carriage at the mosque door, where his little son Abid Effendi waited quaintly in the uniform of an officer, he turned and saluted again before going up the steps.

When the bowed figure disappeared it was as if a spring were suddenly let go. Guards and spectators alike relaxed from a tension. There had been no bomb. There had been no irruption of invading armies. There had been no sign of disloyalty among troops who were supposed to have gone over to the Macedonians. Indeed, they had cheered as I never heard them except at the *Selamlîk* after the re-establishment of the constitution. It did not look very much as if Papa Hamid were finished, to quote my Macedonian officer. It looked, on the contrary, as if what an aide-de-camp whispered might be true — that Papa Hamid took the famous beleaguering as a bluff, and proposed to call it. The situation became more equivocal than ever.

In the meantime big English tea baskets were brought up the avenue, and the soldiers were served with tea, coffee, and biscuits at the expense of a paternal sovereign. Then a bugle sounded and they jumped to attention, gulping down last mouthfuls as the imperial carriage left the mosque. The Sultan returned with the same ceremony as before, except that Bourhan ed Din Effendi accompanied him. After he had entered the Palace the troops dispersed in review order, marching up one side of the avenue to the Palace gate and marching down the other. When most of them were gone the Sultan appeared for a moment at a window overlooking the terrace of the diplomatic pavilion. Again he was enthusiastically cheered.

It was for the last time. But the situation seemed to clear. That afternoon Mahmoud Shefket Pasha, generalissimo of the Macedonian forces, whom I did not see at Chatalja, issued the first of a notable series of manifestoes. He announced his assumption of command at the front and his intention to punish only those responsible for the late disturbance. One phrase attracted particular attention. He said: "Certain intriguers, in fear of punishment, have spread the rumour that the above-mentioned forces have arrived in order to depose the sovereign. To these rumours I oppose a formal denial." Every foreign correspondent in Constantinople thereupon telegraphed to his paper that the Salonica troops would make a peaceful entry into the city and that Abd ül Hamid would remain on the throne.

The next morning, Saturday, I was roused before six o'clock by a member of our country household. "I don't know," he said, "but do you hear anything?" I listened. I heard a light air in the garden trees, a pervading twitter of birds. Then it seemed to me that I heard something else in the distance, something faintly crackling, followed occasionally by something more deeply booming. It sounded like firing, and I suddenly remembered my friends of the white leggings. Yet the morning was so delicious, the sky was so soft, the garden so full of birds. By the time I got down to the wharf a few people were gathered there, talking gravely in low voices. The shots we heard did not altogether break the tension of the last few days. My friend the ticket seller gave me serious advice. "Go back to your house," he said. "Sit in your garden, and be at peace. Lead falls into the sea like rain at Beshiktash. No steamers run. They have all been sent back." I was disinclined to believe him. It seemed incredible that anything particular was happening — on such a day, after so many overtures to the Macedonians. Among those at the *scala* I saw Habib the boatman, whom all men know for a liberal and a reader of papers. "Habib," I said, "let us row to the city. It is necessary for me to go, and there seem to be no steamers. I will pay you a dollar." Habib regarded me as one might regard a lunatic for whom one entertains friendly sentiments. "*Effendim*," he replied, "what do you say? They are fighting at Yîldîz, and not for one or for many dollars will I go. What have you to do in town to-day?" I began to be rather annoyed. I had to get some films, and there was no reason why I shouldn't, if they were fighting at Yîldîz. It didn't occur to me that there could be trouble anywhere else in the town. But neither boat nor boatman could be induced to go down the Bosphorus.

I climbed Hissar hill again, to warn the rest of a town-going household of the situation and to collect recruits for a forced march of seven miles across country. They were not difficult to obtain. Three of us were starting for a last reconnaissance of the *scala*, when we heard a steamer whistle. We were just in time to jump triumphantly on board. So the croakers were mistaken, after all! The passengers were few, however. At the next station of Bebek, where a considerable English colony lives, a number of friends joined us. At the station below that the captain threw up the sponge. An up-bound steamer was there, which had turned back. We told our captain he was a fool, a coward, and as many other uncomplimentary things as we could think of, but he refused to budge. We accordingly got off and took the stony street following the shore to the city. People stared at us as Habib had stared at me. The tide of travel was all the other way. There were carriages full of Turkish women, with eunuchs on the box. There were Armenians, Greeks, and Jews of the lower classes — the last distinguishable by the furred robes of the old men — hurrying northward on foot, with babies and bundles in their arms. There were, more notably, soldiers of the garrison, singly, in groups, with or without rifles. We stopped the first we saw and asked what was up. They all declared that they knew nothing, showing much haste to be on. We afterward realised that they were running away. We saw some of them bargaining for boats to take them to the Asiatic side.

There had been no firing for some time, and the sight of rowboats so much nearer the scene of action than Hissar convinced me anew of a false alarm. The Macedonians had probably come into town at last. The Palace guard might very well have made a row. Perhaps even the Sultan had been deposed, and had objected to it. But how was it possible that there should be any general fighting? At Orta-kyöi, next to the imperial suburb of Beshiktash, six of us got in to two *sandals*. We soon separated. The boat in which I sat had not gone far toward the harbour before firing broke out again. There was no doubt about it this time. The crack of musketry, intensely sharp and sinister in the clear spring morning, would be followed by the deeper note of a field-piece. But we could see nothing. The roofs of Yîldîz nestled serene as ever among their embosoming gardens. The imperial flag still floated from its accustomed staff. Not a cloud, not a puff, indicated the direction of the firing. It was uncanny. What could have happened? We skirted the artillery magazines of Top Haneh, passed the embassy despatch-boats, and began rounding into the harbour. Suddenly the man in the stern of the boat uttered a quick "By Jove!" and ducked. A bullet had whizzed behind his ear. Another splashed the water off our bow. A third sang over our heads. I began to think that they had not been wrong at Roumeli Hissar when they advised me to sit in my garden and be at peace. I was far from being at peace and I decidedly wished that I were in my garden. The next best place seemed to be the bottom of the boat. In the face of public opinion, however, as represented by two Englishmen and a Turk, the only course left a scared impressionist was to continue taking uncomfortable impressions in as erect a posture as possible and be shot like a gentleman. The sole satisfaction I had was in meditating of my last will and testament, providently made the day before, and of its eventual discovery. But it was never discovered and none of us were laid low. While a few more bullets spattered around us, we were soon out of range alongside Galata quay.

The first thing I saw there was a pair of white leggings on guard at a gate. I went up to the sunburned soldier who wore them as to a long-lost brother, and asked for news. My reception, I regret to confess, was not too cordial. "Do not stop," admonished the Macedonian. "If you have business, do it and go. There is no danger, but the bridge is closed and boats do not run. To-morrow everything will be the same as yesterday." In one respect, at least, he was right. The bridge was closed. Access not only to Stamboul but to the great street of Galata was cut off by white leggings. There was, accordingly, no chance of making the tunnel to Pera. As my friends were divided as to their projects, I explored certain noisome alleys leading back from the quay to see if I could reach the street of steps climbing past the Genoese tower. On the way I met a party of American tourists, hurrying for their steamer in charge of an embassy *kavass*. They amusingly looked to an impressionist forgetful of his partiality for the bottoms of boats as if they doubted whether they would escape with their

Photograph by W. G. M. Edwards

Macedonian volunteers

lives. Step Street luckily proved open. The shops, however, were shut, and pedestrians were remarkably scarce. Moreover most of them wore white leggings, or grey-blue ones. Young gentlemen so apparelled, with rifles slung across their backs and cartridges festooned about them, strolled up and down the streets or lolled in front of public buildings. There was an engaging negligence about these picturesque persons, who had an air of keeping an eye on things in spite of manifold cigarettes. Rifles might pop desultorily in the distance, but there was no doubt what had happened. The Macedonians had captured Constantinople.

I went to the American Embassy to obtain details as to this historic event. I found the gate guarded by cadets of the War College and Macedonian Blues. One of the latter smoked cigarettes on the sidewalk and scrutinised every one who passed. At a sign from him an approaching group of marines was stopped and searched. A Turkish *hoja* was even more roughly handled, for his honourable cloth had been a favourite disguise for political agitators. No one suspected of carrying weapons was let by. The man in blue, it transpired, was one of many officers who escaped during the mutiny and came back with the invading army as privates, or so dressed for strategic reasons. As for news, it was remarkably meagre. The Macedonians had occupied both banks of the Golden Horn early in the morning and had encountered resistance at some of the barracks. There were conflicting reports of the first shots being due to a mistake and of treacherous flags of truce. At all events, the affair was not finished, for every now and then we heard firing. But so far as any one knew there had been no fight at Yîldîz.

What made me realise more sharply than anything else the seriousness of the affair was the further news that Frederick Moore, of the New York *Sun*, whom I had often met during the last six months, had been badly wounded. I started up Pera Street to see what I could see. More people were about by that time, but the shops were shut and no cabs or trams were running. All the embassies, legations, and consulates were guarded, like ours, by cadets and Macedonian gendarmes. Other Macedonians, they of the white caps and white leggings, they of the careless Mauser and the casual cigarette, mingled informally with the crowd. As an inhabitant of a captured city, it was interesting to note the friendliness of captives and captors. A rare shot was the sole reminder that there might be more than one side to this question. By the time I reached the vicinity of the Taxim artillery barracks, however, there were other reminders. I saw an iron shutter neatly perforated by dozens of small round holes. The windows of houses in otherwise good repair were riddled and broken. Walls were curiously pockmarked, and I saw a shell embedded in one. These phenomena were particularly visible about the local guard-house, which I was told had only just surrendered. Several stretchers passed me, carrying soldiers in contorted attitudes. A man went into the guard-house with a ridged pine coffin on his back, followed by two of the dervishes who wash the bodies of dead Mohammedans. I didn't count how many more coffins and dervishes I saw go into that guard-house.

A Macedonian Blue

I followed one of the stretchers into the adjoining French hospital, in hope of hearing from Moore. The resources of the place were evidently overtaxed, and I took the liberty of going farther to verify the information given me by a white-winged sister of charity. At a hospitable English house across the street I found Mrs. Moore. Mr. Graves, of the London *Times*, who had been reported as dead, was also there, and two English officers of the Macedonian gendarmerie. They had come up unofficially from Salonica to see how their men acquitted themselves. It seemed they and Mr. Booth, of the *Graphic*, had been with Moore that morning. They ran into the firing before they knew it, thinking, as other people did, that the action was taking place around Yîldîz. Their position was the more awkward because the Macedonians were determined to prevent the soldiers of the garrison from getting down into Pera, and there was cross-firing from side streets. The two correspondents were wounded almost at the same moment, Booth getting a bullet that grazed his scalp, and Moore being shot clean through the neck. A Greek behind him was killed, apparently by the same ball. The officers got Booth into an adjoining house, but by a regrettable misunderstanding they left Moore lying in the street, whence he was rescued by a young Greek sculptor.

The streets grew more animated until the Grande Rue de Pera assumed the appearance of a Sunday afternoon. But another aspect of the situation was presented to me when I bearded the Blues of the telegraph office for Mrs. Moore, and heard clerks politely regretting that all wires were down except those to Europe by way of Constantza. I concluded that Shefket Pasha, who did not trouble Yîldîz until he was sure of the city, proposed to leave no loophole for reactionary telegrams to the provinces. Returning to the Taxim for further reconnaissance, I was taking snapshots when shots of another kind began to snap again. They were neither near nor many, but they caused an extraordinary panic. People ran wildly back into Pera, the women screaming, the men tucking those near and dear to them under their arms or abandoning them to the mercy of the foe as their motor centres dictated. I, seeing some soldiers grin, waited in the lee of a tree. When the street was clear I went on to the artil-

Taxim artillery barracks, shelled April 24

lery barracks that had given so much trouble in the morning. The big building was quiet enough now, under the afternoon sun that made jagged black shadows in the holes torn by Macedonian shells. Beyond, at the far corner of the Taxim Garden, I saw a group of white leggings. A bugle blew, and some of them crept around the wall into the side street. As I came nearer a soldier ran toward me, brandishing his rifle. "What are you doing here?" he demanded. I replied as politely as I could that I was taking photographs. "Is this a time to take photographs?" he vociferated. "We are killing men. Go back!" If other argument were needed I had it in the form of renewed shots that banged behind him, where I could see through trees the yellow mass of Tash Kîshla. I went back less rapidly than I might have done, remembering the people who had just run away. Opposite the garden was the parade-ground of the barracks, bounded on its farther side by stables and a strip of wall behind which heads bobbed. I began to repent of my retreat, also to thirst for human companionship, and I resolved to join those comfortably ensconced spectators. As I strolled toward them across the great empty space of sun they hailed me from afar. I then perceived with some embarrassment that they wore white caps, *à la macédonienne*, and that a portentous number of rifle barrels were gaping at me. They were, in fact, reserves posted for the afternoon attack on Tash Kîshla.

I cannot say that they received me too civilly. Grace, however, was given me to appreciate that the moment was not one for civilities, especially from men who had been under action for twelve hours. I also appreciated the opportunity, urged without forms upon me, of studying their picturesque rear. Tired soldiers smoked or slept on a steep grass slope, and a mule battery lurked in the gully below. Wondering if it might not yet be possible to see what was going on, I approached a young man who stood at the door of a house behind the artillery stables and asked him in my best French if he objected to my ascending to a balcony I saw on the top story of his house. He, being a Greek, replied in his best English that he would be happy to accompany me thither. On the way up he pointed out to me, at a broken window of the opposite stable, the figure of an artilleryman, his rifle across his knees, sitting dead and ghastly against a wall. And he told me about the engagement of which he had been an uncomfortably close witness: how the Macedonians marched in from the valley of the Golden Horn early in the morning; how the first of them were allowed to pass the artillery barracks, and were even cheered; how another lot, who scrambled up the gully from Kassîm Pasha, saw a white flag flying from the artillery stables, advanced more confidently, and were met by a treacherous fire; how they then retired for reinforcements, brought up machine guns and field-pieces, and took stable, barracks, and guard-house after a nasty little fight of five hours.

They were, in fact, reserves posted for the afternoon attack on Tash Kîshla

From the balcony we had a perfect view of the last operations around Tash Kîshla. That great yellow barracks will be memorable in the annals of the Turkish revolution. Many an officer is said to have been tortured there on suspicion of being connected with the Young Turks. It was there that a detachment of the imperial guard fired on the first sharpshooters brought up from Salonica to replace them. And there a battalion of those same sharpshooters, who had been corrupted into fomenting the late revolt and who knew how little quarter they might expect from their old comrades, held out desperately, long after the other barracks had given in. The last act of the tragedy looked less real than a stage tragedy on that divine spring afternoon while we watched, as from a box at the play, the white-legged figures crouching behind their wall, the farther figures stealing up the side of a sunny road, the sortie of the last handful of sharpshooters from their shot-riddled stronghold. They took refuge in a garden before the barracks, where rifles blazed and men dropped until a desperate white handkerchief fluttered among the trees.

The surrender of Tash Kîshla — the Stone Barracks — practically completed the occupation of the city. But the tension was not over. There were yet three days of uncertainty, of waiting, of a strange sense in the air of contrast between the April sunlight and dark forces working in silence. For Yîldîz, as ever, remained inscrutable. From the top of Pera we could see, across the valley of Beshiktash, the scene of Friday's *Selamlîk*. No sign of life was visible now at the archway in the Palace wall, on the avenue leading to the mosque. Had the Sultan surrendered? Had he abdicated? Had he fled? All we knew, until the end, was that white flags floated over two of the imperial barracks and that white leggings nonchalantly appeared on Sunday morning at the Palace gates. In the meantime Shefket Pasha, the man of the hour, continued to secure his position. The redoubtable Selimieh barracks, scene of Florence Nightingale's work in Haïdar Pasha, he took on Sunday with half a dozen shells. On the same day he proclaimed martial law. No one was allowed in the streets an hour after sunset, weapons were confiscated, suspicious characters of all sorts were arrested, and the deserters of the garrison were rounded up. Thousands of them were picked out of rowboats on the Bosphorus or caught in the open country. The poor fellows were more sinned against than sinning. The most absurd stories had been spread among them: that the invaders were Christians come forcibly to convert them; that the son of the King of England intended to turn Abd ül Hamid off the throne in order to reign himself; that if taken they would all be massacred. Dazed by all that had been told them, lost without their officers, worn out by the excitement and confusion of the last ten days, their one idea was to get back to their Asiatic villages. On Monday morning several hundred of them, including the remnant of the Tash Kîshla sharpshooters, were marched away to the court martial at Chatalja. The rest, who were merely the victims of an ignorant loyalty to their Caliph, were sent to Macedonia for lessons in liberalism and road making.

I wondered whether it were by accident that the prisoners sent to Chatalja marched down the hill by which their captors had entered Pera, as preparations were being made on the same height, since named of Perpetual Liberty, for the funeral of the first volunteers killed. A circular trench was dug on the bare brown hilltop, and in it fifty ridged deal coffins were symmetrically set toward the east, each covered with the star and crescent and each bearing a fez at the head. Then a long double file of whitecaps drew up beside it, and a young officer made a spirited address. Not knowing, in my ignorance, who the officer was or much of what he said — he turned out to be the famous Nyazi Bey of Resna — I wandered away to the edge of the bluff. A few tents were still pitched there, overlooking the upper valley of the Golden Horn. Seeing a camera and hearing a foreign accent, the men were willing enough to be photographed. They were from Cavalla, they said, where an American tobacco company maintains a factory. One of them offered me

'hotograph by George Freund

Burial of volunteers, April 26

his tobacco-box in English. He had lived two years and a half in New York. When I got back to the trench the soldiers had gone and the coffins were almost covered. One officer was left, who made to the grave-diggers and the few spectators a speech of a moving simplicity. "Brothers," he said, "here are men of every nation — Turks, Albanians, Greeks, Bulgarians, Jews; but they died together, on the same day, fighting under the same flag. Among us, too, are men of every nation, both Mohammedan and Christian; but we also have one flag and we pray to one God. Now, I am going to make a prayer, and when I pray let each one of you pray also, in his own language, in his own way." With which he raised his hands, palms upward, in the Mohammedan attitude of prayer. The other Mohammedans followed his example, while the Christians took off their caps or

Photograph by W. G. M. Edwards

Deputies leaving Parliament after deposing Abd ül Hamid, April 27

fezzes and crossed themselves; and a brief "*amin*" closed the little ceremony.

By Tuesday, parliament having returned to town the day before, and having sat in secret session with no outward result, people began to say again that the Sultan would keep his throne. As the morning wore on, however, there began to be indications of a certain nature. In Pera Street I encountered a long line of open carriages, each containing two or three black eunuchs and a Macedonian soldier. The odd procession explained itself.

The eunuchs were from the Palace. Some of them looked downcast, but the majority stared back at the crowd with the detachment supposed to be of their nature, while a few of the younger ones appeared to be enjoying an unaccustomed pleasure. It was not so with a procession I saw later, crossing Galata Bridge. This was composed of the lower servants of the Palace, on foot, marching four and four between a baker's dozen of sardonic Macedonians. There was no air of palaces about them. Some were in *stamboulines,* frock coats with a military collar, that looked the worse for wear. Others wore a manner of livery, coarse black braided with white. Others still were in the peasant costume of the country. They were followed by the last of the Palace guard, shuffling disarmed and dejected between their sharp-eyed captors. A few jeers were raised as they passed, but quickly died away. There was something both tragic and prophetic about that unhappy company.

Returning to Galata, I found the approaches of the Bridge guarded by soldiers, who kept the centre of the street clear. The sidewalks were packed with people who waited — they did not know for what. More soldiers passed, with flags and bands. It began to be whispered that a new sultan was going over to Stamboul that afternoon. The rumour was presently confirmed by an extra of the *Osmanischer Lloyd,* an enterprising Franco-German paper, which was the first in Constantinople to publish the news of Abd ül Hamid's dethronement and the accession of his brother. But still people could not believe the news they had been expecting so long. They continued to wait, to see what would happen. I met some friends who suggested going to the vicinity of Dolma Ba'hcheh Palace, the residence of the heir presumptive. If he went out that afternoon we should be surer of knowing it than if we joined the crowds in the city. At the junction of the Pera road with the avenue behind Dolma Ba'hcheh we were stopped by a white-legginged Albanian with a Mauser. This tall, fair-haired, hawk-nosed, and serious young man saw no reason why we should occupy better posts than the rest of the people — happily not many — he held at bay. We accordingly waited with them, being assured by the inexorability of the Albanian and by the presence of gunners mounting guard beyond him that we should not wait in vain.

In front of us a wide paved space sloped down to the Bosphorus, pleasantly broken by fresh-leaved trees and a stucco clock-tower. To the left ran a tree-shaded perspective cut off from the water by the white mass of Dolma Ba'hcheh. Before long we saw three steam-launches pass close in front of us, making for the harbour. A few minutes later a cannon banged. Another banged after it, another, and another, till we could doubt no longer that what we had been waiting for had really happened at last. Then, before we had time to taste the rushing emotion of new and great things, a small-arm cracked in the distance. That sharp little sound caused the strangest cold sensation of arrest. More rifles cracked. People looked at each other. The soldiers began feeling for their cartridges, their eyes on their officers. As the firing became a fusillade, and drew nearer, one of the latter made a sign to our Albanian. "Go back!" commanded that young man fiercely, thrusting his musket at us. There was an instant retreat. Could it be that reactionaries had chosen this moment to make an attack on the new Sultan, that there had been a reply, and that battle was beginning again in the streets? We had not gone far, however, before we saw men shooting revolvers into the air and laughing. So we returned, not without sheepishness, to our places. We were just in time to see our Albanian discharge his rifle with the delight of a boy. The volley that followed did not last long. "Who told you to fire?" demanded the officer who had been so uneasy a moment before. "Eh, the others are firing," replied the Albanian. "Never mind what the others do," retorted the officer sharply. "We came here to show that we know how to obey orders. Now, stop firing." His soldiers did, although the city was by that time one roar of powder.

It was not long after three o'clock. We still had nearly four hours to wait before Sultan Mehmed V should land at Seraglio Point, proceed to the War Office for the first ceremonies of investiture, return to the Seraglio to kiss the mantle of the Prophet, and then drive past us to his palace. I could not help thinking of the other palace on top of the hill from which the servants had been taken that morning. The boom of saluting guns, the joyous crackle accompanying it, must have gone up with cruel distinctness, through the still spring afternoon, to the ears of one who had heard that very sound, on the supplanting of a brother by a brother, thirty-three years before. As the time wore away our Albanian grew less fierce. The light, unfortunately, did likewise, until all hope of snap-shots failed. I then took my place at the edge of the avenue. Finally, toward seven o'clock, a piqueur galloped into sight from behind the wall that hid the right-hand stretch of the street. Behind him, in the distance, rose a faint cheering. It came nearer, nearer, nearer, until a squadron of dusty cavalry clattered into sight. After the cavalry clattered a dusty brougham, drawn by two black horses, and in the brougham an elderly man with a double chin bowed and smiled from the windows as the crowd shouted: "*Padishah'm chok yasha-a-a!*"

I shouted with them as well as I could, not stopping to inquire why anything should impede the throat of an indifferent impressionist from oversea, at the spectacle of a fat old gentleman in a frock coat driving out between two disreputable columns of cavalry. They made a ter-

Photograph by W. G. M. Edwards

Mehmed V driving through Stamboul on his accession day, April 27

rific dust as they galloped away through the young green of the avenue toward the white palace — dust which a condescending sun turned into a cloud of glory.

During the days and nights of flags and illuminations that followed there were other sights to see. One of them was the *Selamlîk* of the ensuing Friday. It took place at St. Sophia, whither Mehmed II rode to pray after his conquest of Constantinople, and where popular opinion willed that a later Mehmed, after this memorable recapture of the town, should make his first public prayer. About this ceremony was none of the pomp that distinguished the one I had witnessed the week before. A few Macedonian Blues were drawn up by the mosque, a few Macedonian cavalrymen guarded the gates of the Seraglio, and they were not all in place by the time the Sultan, in a new khaki uniform, drove slowly through the grounds of that ancient enclosure. Again, on the succeeding Monday, we beheld the grisly spectacle of those who fomented the mutiny among the soldiers, and who, in long white shirts, with statements of their names and deeds pinned to their bosoms, swung publicly from great tripods at the scene of their several crimes — three at the Stamboul end of the Bridge, five in front of Parliament, and five in the square of the War Department. And the new Sultan was once more the centre of interest on the day he was girded with the sword of Osman. He went to the sacred mosque of Eyoub with little of the pageantry that used to celebrate that solemn investiture — in a steam-launch, distinguishable from other steam-launches only by a big magenta silk flag bearing the imperial *toughra.* From Eyoub he drove round the walls to the Adrianople Gate, and then through the city to the Seraglio. His gala coach, his scarlet-and-gold coachman, his four chestnut horses, his blue-and-silver outriders, and his prancing lancers were the most glittering part of that long procession. The most Oriental part of it was the train of carriages bearing the religious heads of the empire, white-bearded survivors of another time, in venerable turbans and green robes embroidered with gold. But the most significant group in the procession was that of the trim staff of the Macedonian army, on horseback, headed by Mahmoud Shefket Pasha. Not least notable among the conquerors of Constantinople will be this grizzled, pale, thin, keen, kind-looking Arab who, a month before that day, was an unknown corps commander in Salonica. His destiny

Photograph by Apollon, Constantinople

Mehmed V on the day of sword-girding, May 10

willed that hardly more than four years after that day he should even more suddenly go again into the unknown. His fate was a happy one in that it overtook him at the height of power a Turkish subject may attain, when he was at once Field-Marshal, Minister of War, and Grand Vizier, and that it left in suspense the colder judgment of his time with regard to the actual degree of his greatness. Legends and hatreds naturally gathered around such a man. I do not know whether it was true that he took the city before he was ready, with barely fifteen thousand men, on a sudden night warning that the desperate Sultan plotted a massacre for the next day. Neither was I there to see whether he actually sent back to the new Sultan his present of a magnificent Arab charger, saying that he was a poor man and had no stable for such a steed. The crucial test of the Balkan War he had no opportunity to undergo. But less than any other personality discovered by the Turkish revolution does he need the favouring kindness of uncertainty. At the moment when if he chose he might have been dictator, he did not choose. And the decision, the promptness, the tact, the strategic ability with which he grasped the situation of the mutiny and threw an army into Chatalja before the blundering mutineers knew what he was about, made for him the one clear and positive record of that confused time. They say he suffered from an incurable disease, and captured cities for distraction.

I had the honour of meeting Mahmoud Shefket Pasha a little later, in company with Mr. Booth; and I owed it to the latter's bandaged head and to the interest which the general took in the wounded journalist that I also obtained the coveted leave to visit Yîldîz. Yîldîz had so long been a name of legend that one approached it with the vividest curiosity — even though the innermost enclosure, jutting out into the park from the crest of the hill on a gigantic retaining wall, at first remained impenetrable. When at last the gates of the Forbidden City itself were opened, it was strange to discover that the Sultan who stood for all that was conservative and Oriental, who spent as he pleased the gold of the empire, who might have created anew the lost splendours of the Seraglio, had chosen to surround himself with would-be European cottages, for the most part of wood, with a profusion of gables and jig-saw carpentry. The more ornate were those intended for the reception of ministers and ambassadors. The simplest and the largest was the long, low, L-shaped structure where Abd ül Hamid lived with his extensive family. His private apartments gave a singular picture of that singular man. The rooms were all jealously latticed, even behind the fortifications of Yîldîz, and one was scarcely to be distinguished in its use from another, so full were they all of desks, screens, couches, weapons, and pianos. In one of the least ambiguous, where white chairs stood about a long table, was shown the gilt Vienna *Récamier* in which Abd ül Hamid received the notification of his dethronement. An orchestrion filled one end of the room, where also was a piano. No less than four of these instruments were in another room. Farther on were the empty safes where the old man hoarded his gold and his famous jewels, a cupboard of ugly tiles that was a mixture of Turkish *hamam* and European bath, without the luxuries of either, and a perfectly appointed carpenter's shop. It is an old tradition for the princes of the house of Osman to learn some trade, in case their *kîsmet* should suddenly require them to make their own living. One chamber had more the air of a bedroom than any other. For the Sultan rarely slept two nights in succession in the same place, or undressed to do so. On a table were two of the bullet-proof waistcoats he wore at *Selamlîk*. A handsome case of arms stood by the door. High on the walls hung some crude pictures which he perhaps painted himself. He was fond of playing with the brush. A canvas somewhere else represented a boat full of priests, standing, to whom a group of plump pink sirens beckoned from an arsenic shore. The officer in charge told us that the faces of the priests were those of Midhat Pasha and other reformers. With all their oddity, the rooms had a familiar air of habitation. Things of use and of ornament were where Abd ül Hamid dropped them the night he was taken away. Writing materials were strewn on the desks. A photograph of the German imperial family looked out of a gold frame set in brilliants. In a corner stood a table, a chair, and a footstool, all with crystal legs, where the Sultan sat in thunder-storms. The whole palace was full of small human touches of the suspicious, ignorant, lonely old man who lived there. And East and West were strangely jumbled in his well-worn furniture, as they were in his ancient empire — as they were in the visitors inquisitively trampling the carpets and fingering the belongings of the fallen master of the house.

The harem, by a characteristic piece of Oriental reserve, was not opened even by its despoilers to the gaze of the profane. But we were allowed to go into the harem garden, overlooked by the Sultan's lattices. An artificial canal wound through the middle of it. Rowboats, a motor-boat, even a small sailboat, were moored there. Under the trees stood a miniature replica of the fountain at Gyök Sou. Pigeons fluttered everywhere and water-fowl were playing in the canal, while against the wall cutting off the immense prospect the garden might have enjoyed stood cages of gaudy birds. At one spot only did a small kiosk, execrably furnished, give access to the view. Through the telescope on the upper floor Abd ül Hamid used to watch the city he dared not enter. We also saw a little theatre that communicated by a bridge with the harem. In this bonbon box of red velvet the singers and variety actors visiting the city used to be invited to perform — sometimes before a solitary spectator. King Otto of Bavaria would have found no kinship with him, though. On the wall a photograph of Arturo Stravolo, an Italian transformationist, hung beside a large and bad portrait of Verdi.

Outside this inner citadel the fabled gardens descended to the sea. Fabled they proved, indeed — as some city park, perhaps, though not so neatly kept. A driveway, fabulously dusty, led between the massive retaining wall and a miniature lake to Merassim Kiosque, a tawdry little palace in an enclosure of its own which was built for William II of Germany. I threaded a tortuous space, at one end of it not quite touching the bastion of the Forbidden City, where a small iron door in the kiosk faced a small iron door in the bastion. They had a potency, those small iron doors, upon the imagination of a romantic impressionist. Beyond stretched courts and stables, deserted save for a few last activities of departure. A eunuch was giving shrill orders to a soldier. A drove of buffaloes stood mild-eyed under a plane-tree, waiting to be driven away. A horse whinnied in the silence. A cat lay blinking in the sun, indifferent to the destinies of kings.

On a slope of thin shade farther on were grouped an ornate wooden villa, a castellated porcelain factory, kennels where a few dogs yelped miserably, and enclosures for all sorts of animals and birds. The one really charming part of the park was the ravine behind Chira'an Palace, cool with secular trees and the splash of water. Nightingales and strange water-fowl had their habitation there, and some startled colts galloped away as I descended a winding path. The look of the paths, neither wild nor ordered, made me wonder again what four hundred gardeners did at Yîldîz. I suppose they did what any gardener would do whose master never came to see his garden. Chalets and summer-houses with red seals on their doors stood among the trees. I went into an open lodge beside a gateway. A bed was torn to pieces, clothes and papers strewed the floor, a cut loaf and an open bottle stood on a shelf as if dropped there in some hasty flight.

There was a point on the hillside whence a long view opened — of domed Stamboul and cypressed Scutari reaching toward each other across an incredible blue, with dim Asiatic mountains in the background. From the height above he must often have looked out on that scene who brooded for thirty-three years, in silence and darkness, behind the walls his terror raised. So noble against sea and sky, so vastly spreading, so mysterious in its invisible activities, the city must have been as redoubtable to him as his bastioned hilltop was to the city. And I could not help imagining how, during the days so lately passed, as he watched the city that feared his power and whose power he feared, sounds must have come up to him: of the foolish firing he ordered for the 13th of April; of a more sinister firing eleven days later, when he waited for his deluded and officerless soldiers, shut up in their barracks, to save his throne; of that last firing, for him the sound of doom, proclaiming to his face the joy of the distant city that his power over it was no more.

As we went away a line of buffalo carts, piled with nondescript furniture, began to creak down the avenue where the imperial guard used to parade at *Selamlîk*. A Macedonian gendarme stood in the great arched gateway of the Palace court and checked them as they passed. Behind him a monkey sat in the coil of a black tail, surveying the scene with bright, furtive, troubled eyes.

XVI

WAR TIME

1912–1913

I. — THE HORDES OF ASIA

"THE hordes of Asia . . ." That phrase, fished out of what reminiscence I know not, kept running through my head as the soldiers poured through the city. Where did they all come from? On the night of the 3d of October the streets began to resound portentously with drums, and out of the dark the voices of criers called every man, Moslem or Christian, married or single, to leave his house and defend his country. Then the crowded transports began to stream down the Bosphorus, sometimes as many as seven or eight a day. Opposite each village the whistle blew, the men cheered, and the people on shore waved handkerchiefs and flags. When the transports came down after dark it was more picturesque. Bengal lights would answer each other between sea and land, and the cheering filled more of the silence. It somehow sounded younger, too. And it insensibly led one into sentimentalities — into imaginations of young wives and children, of old parents, of abandoned fields, of what other fields in Thrace and Macedonia.

The hordes from the Black Sea made no more than their distant impression, perhaps no less dramatic for being so; and for them Constantinople can have been but a fugitive panorama of cypresses and minarets and waving handkerchiefs. They passed by without stopping to the ports of the Marmora. Other hordes, however, poured into the city so fast that no troop train or barracks could hold them. Hundreds, even thousands, of them camped every night under the mosaics of St. Sophia. At first they all wore the new hay-coloured

Arriving from Asia

uniform of Young Turkey. Then older reservists began to appear in the dark blue piped with red of Abd ül Hamid's time. Meanwhile, conscripts and volunteers of all ages and types and costumes filled the streets. It took a more experienced eye than mine, generally, to pick out a Greek or an Armenian marching to war for the first time in the Turkish ranks. The fact is that a Roumelian or seaboard Turk looks more European than an Anatolian Christian. Nevertheless, the diversity of the empire was made sufficiently manifest to the most inexperienced eye. The Albanians were always a striking note. Hundreds of them flocked back from who knows where, in their white skull-caps and close-fitting white clothes braided with black. They are leaner and

Reserves

often taller than the Turks, who incline to be thick-bodied; fairer, too, as a rule, and keener-eyed. Something like them are the Laz, who are slighter and darker men but no less fierce. They have the name of being able to ride farther in less time than any other tribe of Asia Minor. Their uniforms were a khaki adaptation of their tribal dress — zouave-jackets, trousers surprisingly full at the waist and surprisingly tight about the leg, and pointed hoods with long flaps knotted into a sort of turban. This comfortable Laz hood, with slight variations of cut and colour, has been adapted for the whole army. I shall always remember it as a symbol of that winter war. Certain swarthy individuals from the Russian or Persian frontiers also made a memorable

Recruits

figure, in long black hairy sleeveless cloaks and tall caps of black lamb's wool, tied about with some white rag. They gave one the impression that they might be very uncomfortable customers to meet in a blind alley on a dark night. These gentlemen, none the less, wore in their caps, like a cockade, what might have seemed to the vulgar a paint-brush, but what was in reality the tooth-brush of their country. Last of all the Syrians began to appear. They were very noticeably different from the broader, flatter, fairer Anatolian type. On their heads they wore the scarf of their people, bound about with a thick black cord, and on cold days some of them would drape a *bournous* over their khaki.

Hand in hand

Just such soldiers must have followed Attila and Tamerlane, and the roving horseman who founded the house of Osman. And just such pack-animals as trotted across Galata Bridge, balking whenever they came to a crack of the draw. The shaggy ponies all wore a blue bead or two against the Evil Eye, and their high pack-saddles were decorated with beads or small shells or tufts of coloured worsted. Nor can the songs the soldiers sang, I imagine, have changed much in six hundred years. Not that many of them sang, or betrayed their martial temper otherwise than by the dark dignity of bearing common to all men of the East. It was strange to a Westerner to see these proud and powerful-looking men strolling about hand in hand. Yet it went with the mildness and simplicity which are as characteristic of them as their fierceness. One of them showed me a shepherd's pipe in his cartridge belt. That was the way to go to war, he said — as to a wedding. Another played a violin as he marched, a quaint little instrument like a *pochette* or a *viole d'amour*, hanging by the neck from his hand. By way of contrast I heard a regimental band march one day to the train to the tune of "Yankee Doodle."

At the train no more emotion was visible than in the streets. There was a certain amount of arranged band playing and cheering by command, but the men were grave and contained as ever. So were the friends who came to see them off — unless they happened to be Christians. Nothing could have been more characteristic than the groups of women, muffled in their black dominoes and generally veiled, who stood silent while the trains went out. The only utterance I ever happened to catch from them was from an old body who watched a regiment march into the station. "Let them cut," she said, half to herself and half to those about her, making a significant horizontal movement of her hand. "Let them cut!" I heard of another who rebuked a girl for crying on a Bosphorus steamer after seeing off some member of her family. "I have sent my husband and my son," she said. "Let them go. They will kill the unbelievers."

I presume similar sentiments were expressed often

enough by men. Why not, among so much ignorance, and at a time of so much resentment against the unbeliever? Yet I did not chance to hear anything of the sort. On the contrary, I was struck by what seemed to me a distinctly new temper in Mohammedans. Nazîm Pasha sounded the note of it when he proclaimed that

Demonstration in the Hippodrome

this was a political, not a holy, war, and that non-combatants were to be treated with every consideration. If the proclamation was addressed partly to Europe, the fact remains that in no earlier war would a Turkish general have been capable of making it. It may be, too, that the disdain with which the Turk started out to fight his whilom vassals helped his tolerance. Nevertheless, as I somewhat doubtfully picked my way about Stamboul, wondering whether it was quite the thing to do at such a time, the sense grew in me that the common people were at last capable of classifications less simple than their old one of the believing and the unbelieving. It did not strike me, however, that even the uncommon people had much comprehension of the cause of the war. If they had I suppose there would have been no war. "We have no peace because of this Roumelia," said an intelligent young man to me. "We must fight. If I die, what is it? My son at least will have peace." Yet there was no particular enthusiasm, save such as the political parties manufactured. They organised a few picturesque demonstrations and encouraged roughs to break the windows of the Balkan legations. But except for the soldiers — the omnipresent, the omnipassant, hordes of Asia — an outsider might never have guessed that anything unusual was in the air. Least of all would he have guessed it when he heard people exclaim *Mashallah!* as the soldiers went by, and learned that they were saying "What God does will!" So far is it from Turkish nature to make a display of feeling. The nearest approach to such a thing I saw was on the day Montenegro declared war. Then smiles broke out on every face as the barefooted newsboys ran through Stamboul with their little extras. And the commonest phrase I heard that afternoon was: "What will be, let be."

II. — RETROSPECTIVE

Did any one dream, then, what was to be? Yet one might have known. It was not a question of courage or endurance. Nobody, after the first surprise, doubted that. The famous hordes of Asia — they were indeed just such soldiers as followed Attila and Tamerlane, and the roving horseman who founded the house of Osman.

That was the trouble with them. They had not learned that courage and endurance are not enough for modern warfare. All Europeans who have dealings with the Turk know that he is the least businesslike of men. He is constitutionally averse to order, method, promptness, discipline, responsibility. Numbers and calculations are beyond him. It is impossible to imagine him as a banker, a financier, a partner in any enterprise requiring initiative or the higher organising faculties. He simply hasn't got them, or at all events he has never developed them. Moreover, there is about him a Hamlet-like indecision which he shares with the rest of Asia. He cannot make up his mind. He waits until he is forced, and then he has usually waited too long for his own good.

I could fill pages with anecdotes that were told me before the war, illustrating the endless dilly-dallying that was an inevitable part of every army contract. Soldiers were sent to the front, in consequence, with serious deficiencies in their equipment. There were not boots enough to go around, or overcoats enough, or knapsacks enough, or tents enough. Half the navy, at the beginning of winter, was in white duck, simply because blue serge comes from England and had not been ordered in time. As for ambulances and field-hospitals, there was practically nothing of the kind. Then, although the mobilisation took place with a despatch praised by foreign critics, it became evident that trains were not getting away with anything like clockwork. Regiments left hours, in some cases days, after the time appointed. And there began very early to be rumours that all was not well with the commissariat. A soldier whom I knew wrote back from Kîrk Kil'seh, ten days before the fatal battle, that he and the members of his company lived like dogs in the street, picking up food and shelter wherever they could. We heard the same thing from San Stefano, at the very gates of the capital. And at that time the general staff of the army was quartered there. They apparently had not read, marked, and inwardly digested the opinion put forth at a memorable council of war in that very town by Enrico Dandolo, Doge of Venice, in the year of grace 1203, when he said: "For he that has supplies wages war with more certainty than he that has none." Regiments arriving by boat were given money to supply their own wants, in the absence of any other provision for them. But the resources of a village were inadequate to feed an army, and many soldiers went hungry. Bread was accordingly baked for them in Constantinople, and continued to be throughout the war. Sometimes, however, a bread train would return to the city unloaded, because it had been nobody's business to attend to it. And for a while small riots took place in the capital on account of the shortage in the customary supply. The thing was the more serious because bread really is the staff of life in Turkey, and no one makes his own.

In spite of so many straws to show how the wind blew — and I have said nothing about the politics that honeycombed the army, the sweeping changes of personnel that took place no more than a month or two before the war, the mistake of sending first to the front untrained reserves and recruits who had never handled a rifle till they found themselves on the battle-field — the speed with which the allies succeeded in developing their campaign must have surprised the most turcophobe European. As for the Turks themselves, they have always had a fatalistic — a fatal — belief that they will one day quit Europe. Many times before and after the decisive battles I heard the question uttered as to whether the destined day had come. But no Turk can have imagined that his army, victorious on a thousand fields, would smash to pieces at the first onslaught of an enemy inexperienced in war. They forgot that the flower of the troops of the conquering sultans came from those very Balkan mountains.

At first the truth was held back. Long after Kîrk Kil'seh and Lüleh Bourgass and the loss of Macedonia there were men in Constantinople who did not know or could not believe the facts. The case must have been true much longer in the remote corners of Asia Minor. When the truth did come out it was crushing. The Turks had been too sure. Hardly an officer had not promised his friends post-cards from Sophia or Belgrade or Cettinje or Athens. And to have been beaten by the serfs of yesterday! But I, for one, have hardly yet the heart to say they deserved it. I remember too well a bey in civil life whom I knew, whose face two weeks of the war had ravaged like a disease, and the look with which he said, when I expressed regret at the passing of some quaint Turkish custom: "Everything passes in this world." I quite understood the Turkish girls who went away in a body from a certain international school. "We cannot bear the Bulgarians," they said. "They look at us —" It was characteristic, however, that they presently went back. One did not like, in those days, to meet one's Turkish friends. It was like intruding into a house of death. But in this house something more than life had been lost. And I pay my tribute to the dignity with which that great humiliation was borne.

I stood one day at a club window watching a regiment march through Pera. Two Turkish members stood near me. "Fine looking men!" exclaimed one — and he was right. "How could soldiers like that have run away?" The other considered a moment. "If we had not announced," he replied, "that this was not a holy war, you would have seen!" I am inclined to believe that there was something in his opinion. At the time, however, it reminded me of the young man who complained that the Turks had no peace. They were no quicker to understand the causes of their defeat than they had been to understand the causes of the war.

Not long afterward I spent an evening with some humble Albanians of my acquaintance. Being in a way foreigners like myself, they could speak with more detachment of what had happened, although there was no doubt as to their loyalty to the empire. They asked my views as to the reason of the disaster. I tried, in very halting Turkish, to explain how the Turk had been distanced in the art of war and many other arts, and how war no longer required courage alone but other qualities which the Turk does not seem to possess. I evidently failed to make my idea intelligible. Having listened with the utmost politeness, my auditors proceeded to give me their own view of the case. The one who presented it most eloquently had been himself a soldier in the Turkish army. It was under the old régime, too, when men served seven and nine years. He attributed the universal rout of the Turks less to the incompetence than to the cupidity of the officers. He believed, like his companions, and I doubt if anything will ever shake their belief, that the officers, from Nazîm Pasha down, had been bribed by the allies. What other possible explanation could there be of the fact that soldiers starved amid plenty and that Mohammedans ran — saving my presence! — from Christians? As for the European ingenuities that I made so much of — the ships, the guns, the railroads, the telephones, the automobiles, the aeroplanes — why should the Turks break their heads learning to make them when they could buy them ready-made from Europe? After all, what you need in war is a heart, and not to be afraid to die. My Albanian then went on to criticise, none too kindly, the Young Turk officer. In his day, he said, most of the officers rose from the ranks. They had been soldiers themselves, they understood the soldiers, and they could bear hardship like soldiers. The Young Turks, however, had changed all that. The ranker officers had been removed to make room for young *mekteblis*, schoolmen, who knew nothing of their troops or of war. They knew how to wear a collar, perhaps, or how to turn up their moustaches, *à la Guillaume*. But they didn't know how to march in the rain or to sleep on the ground, and when the Bulgarians fired they ran away.

I am by way of being a schoolman myself, and I blushed for my kind as I heard this tall mountaineer make our indictment. What could I answer him? I knew that in many ways he was right. The schoolmen did not understand the fighting men as the rankers had done. Then there were far too few of them — as there were too many fighting men of the kind first sent to the front, whom I saw being recruited with handcuffs. And there had not been time to establish the new order of things on a sound footing.

III. — RED CROSS AND RED CRESCENT

After the hordes of Asia that went so proudly away it was a very different horde that began very soon to trickle back. No bands accompanied them this time, and if any of them had had violins or shepherds' pipes they had lost them in the fields of Thrace. It was pitiful to see how silently, almost how secretly, those broken men came back. One would occasionally meet companies of them on the Bridge or in the vicinity of a barracks, in their grey ulsters and pointed grey hoods, shuffling along so muddy, so ragged, so shoeless, so gaunt and bowed, that it was impossible to believe they were the same men. Most of them, however, came back in the night and were not able even to shuffle. Two or three pictures are stamped in my memory as characteristic of those melancholy days. The first of them I happened to see when I moved into town for the winter, a few days after Kîrk Kil'seh. When I landed at dusk from a Bosphorus steamer, with more luggage than would be convenient to carry, I found to my relief that the vicinity of the wharf was crowded with cabs — scores of them. But not one would take a fare. They had all been commandeered for ambulance service. Near the first ones stood a group of women, Turkish and Christian, silently waiting. Some of them were crying. Another time, coming home late from a dinner-party, I passed a barracks which had been turned into a hospital. At the entrance stood a quantity of cabs, all full of hooded figures that were strangely silent and strangely lax in their attitudes. No such thing as a stretcher was visible. Up the long flight of stone steps two soldiers were helping a third. His arms were on their shoulders and each of them had an arm around him. One foot he could not use. In the flare of a gas-jet at the top of the steps a sentry stood in his big grey coat, watching. The three slowly made their way up to him and disappeared into the archway. Again, a lady who lives in Stamboul told me her own impressions so vividly that I remember them almost better than my own — of trains whistling all night long as they came in from the front, of city rubbish carts rumbling without end through the dark, and of peering out to see one under the window, full of wounded, with refugee women and children trudging behind in the rain.

After Lüleh Bourgass there was scarcely a barracks or a guard-house or a mosque or a school or a club or an empty house that was not turned into an impromptu hospital. For a moment, indeed, the resources of the city were swamped, and train loads of wounded would wait in the station for hours before any attempt could be made to unload them. Even then, thousands must have died for lack of care, for there were neither beds nor nurses enough. And it was only the more lightly wounded who came back. The others, in the general rout and in the lack of any adequate field-hospital service, died where they fell — unless the Bulgarians took pity on them. In either case no news about them was available. No casualty lists were published. I doubt if any one knew how many hospitals there were. Women would go vaguely from one to another asking for Ali or Hassan. There might be fifty Alis and Hassans in each one, or five hundred, and who was to know which from which?

In the face of so great an emergency every one, Mohammedan or Christian, native or foreigner, took some part in relief work. A number of Turkish ladies of high rank and the wives of the ambassadors had already organised sewing-circles. Madame Bompard, I believe, the French ambassadress, was the first to call the ladies of her colony together to work for the wounded. Mrs. Rockhill gave up her passage to America in order to lend her services. Although our embassy is much smaller than the others, a room was vacated for a workshop, a sailor from the despatch-boat *Scorpion* cut out after models furnished by the Turkish hospitals, and the Singer company lent sewing-machines — to any, in fact, who wanted them for this humanitarian use. Shall I add that America had a further share in these operations in that the coarse cotton used in most of the work is known in the Levant as American cloth? Lady Lowther organised activities of another but no less useful kind, to provide for the families of poor soldiers and for refugees. In the German embassy a full-fledged hospital was installed by order of the Emperor. At the same time courses in bandaging and nursing were opened in various Turkish and European hospitals. And Red Cross missions came from abroad in such numbers that after the first rush of wounded was over it became a question to know what to do with the Red Cross.

There is also a Turkish humane society, which is really the same as the Red Cross but which the Turks, more umbrageous than the Japanese with regard to the Christian symbol, call the Red Crescent. Foreign doctors, nurses, and orderlies wore the Turkish device on their caps or sleeves, and at first a small crimson crescent was embroidered by request on every one of the thousands of pieces of hospital linen contributed by different branches of the Red Cross. It is a pity that a work so purely humanitarian should in so unimportant a detail as a name arouse the latent hostility between two religious systems. Is it too late to suggest that some new device be found which will be equally acceptable to all the races and religions of the world? To this wholly unnecessary cause must be attributed much of the friction that took place between the two organisations. But I think it was only in humbler quarters that the Red Cross symbol was resented. At a dinner given by the prefect of Constantinople in honour of the visiting missions, it was an interesting thing, for Turkey, to see the hall decorated with alternate crescents and crosses. For the rest, any work of the kind is so new in Turkey that it was not surprising if some people failed to find the right note. It was entirely natural for the Turks to prefer to care for their own wounded, when they could, and to resent any implication that they were incapable of doing so. And the ignorance of tongues of the foreigners, with their further ignorance of Turkish tastes and the very doubtful human material some of them contributed, gave many just causes for complaint.

This relief-work marked a date in Turkish feminism, in that Turkish women for the first time acted as nurses in hospitals. They covered their hair, as our own Scripture recommends for a woman, but they went unveiled. Women also served in other capacities, and something like organised work was done by them in the way of preparing supplies for the sick. A lady who attended nursing lectures at a hospital in Stamboul told me that her companions, most of whom were of the humbler classes, went to the hospital as they would to the public bath, with food for the day tied up in a painted handkerchief. There they squatted on the floor and smoked as they sewed, resenting it a little when a German nurse in charge suggested more stitches and fewer cigarettes.

It was also a new thing for men to volunteer for hospital work, as a good many did under the auspices of the Red Crescent. They had charming manners, as Turks usually do; but they proved less efficient than the women, for the reason that the Turk of any breeding, and particularly the Constantinople Turk, has no tradition of working with his hands. It is not a question of snobbishness. He is in many ways more democratic than we. He treats servants on a greater equality, and the humble rise in the world even more easily than with us. But it is not the thing for him to use his hands except in sport and in war. He is far too dignified a being to carry a tray, for instance, in the presence of women or other inferiors. Add to this his natural disinclination to do anything he can get any one else to do, and you conceive the difficulties which might surround the attendance of such a helper.

Difficulties of another kind were sometimes experienced when Red Cross and Red Crescent doctors were thrown together. Medicine is a science to which the Turks rather lean, I believe, and there are excellent physicians and surgeons among them. But the excellent man, in science at any rate, is hardly appreciated in Constantinople as yet. The persuasive man has the lead of him. A foreign doctor described in my hearing the "eminent superficiality" of some of his Turkish colleagues, who had the graces and elegancies of diplomats and spoke French perfectly but who seemed to lack the plain, unvarnished, every-day essentials of surgery. And some sensitiveness or petty jealousy in them seemed to make them wish, although there was work enough for everybody, to make themselves felt wherever their foreign colleagues were at work. One of them was supposed to supervise the operations of my informant. The Turk was very agreeable, and interfered as little as possible, but reserved the right of prescribing whatever medicine might be required by the soldiers. This he did with great zeal, paying small heed to his European colleague's opinion of a case. But to ascertain that the patient took the medicine prescribed he considered no part of his duty. Whole boxes of pills and powders were regularly found under the soldiers' pillows, where they poked them as soon as the doctor turned his back.

The barracks and guard-houses allotted to some of the missions were Augean stables which required Herculean efforts to clean out. It was the more curiously characteristic because even the lower-class Turk is always cleanly. His ritual ablutions make him more agreeable at close quarters than Europeans of the same degree. I have one infallible way of picking out the Christian soldiers in a Turkish regiment: by their nails. The Turk's are sure to be clean. And in his house he has certain delicacies undreamt by us. He will not wear his street shoes indoors. He will not eat without washing his hands before and after the meal. He considers it unclean — as, after all, it is — to wash his hands or his body in standing water. Yet vermin he regards as a necessary evil, while corporate cleanliness, like anything else requiring organisation and perseverance, seems as yet to be entirely beyond him.

I heard of a case in point from one of the great barracks in which two thousand invalids were looked after by different missions. The men were plentifully supplied with everything they required, but after the war had been going on two months or so the supply of linen began to fall amazingly low. The huge establishment was in charge of an amiable old pasha without whom nothing could be done, but who was, of course, much too grand a person to do anything himself. He asked the Red Cross to furnish a new supply of linen. The Red Cross took the liberty of asking him in return if his old linen had been washed. He replied emphatically that there could be no doubt of it: the barracks contained a perfect modern laundry. Nevertheless, no clean linen was forthcoming. One of the foreign doctors, therefore, began to explore. He finally discovered the perfect modern laundry, stuffed to the ceiling with an incalculable accumulation of dirty linen, not one piece of which had ever been washed. But the amiable pasha cried "Impossible!" when he was told of these facts. And he either did not know them or refused to take official cognisance of them until two ambassadresses, whom he could not refuse, led him, one by either hand, and made him stick his exalted nose into the perfect modern laundry. Shall I add that that laundry, neither so modern nor so perfect as the pasha affirmed, was finally taken in hand and run as long as the Red Cross had need of it by the doctor who discovered it? And shall I further be so indiscreet as to add that his name was Major Clyde S. Ford, U. S. A.?

Of the Turk as patient I heard nothing but praise. And, after all, there were many more of him. I take the more pleasure in saying it because I have hinted that in other aspects of the war the Turk did not always strike a foreign critic as perfect. I had it again and again, from one source after another, that as patients the Turks were perfect — docile and uncomplaining, in many ways like great children, but touchingly grateful. It became quite the thing for one of them who could write to send a letter to the Turkish papers in the name of his ward, expressing thanks to the doctors and nurses. And I wish I had space to quote some of those letters, so charmingly were they worded, with such a Lincolnian simplicity. It must have been a new and strange thing for most of the men to have women not of their families caring for them. They took a natural interest in their nurses, expressing a particular curiosity with regard to their *état civil* and wishing them young, rich, and handsome husbands when they did not happen to be already provided with such. But I heard of no case of rudeness that could not be explained by the patient's condition. On the contrary, an English nurse told me that she found an innate dignity and refinement about the men which she would never expect from the same class of patients in her own country. They often had a child's lack of realisation why one should be allowed what another was not. They smoked much more than children should, counting more on their cigarettes than on their food. They were also naturally inclined to find foreign cooking more medicinal than palatable. But they were rarely disobedient save when spirits or opiates were prescribed them. Those they often steadfastly refused to take. Chloroform, too, they sometimes objected to, as infringing the commands of the Prophet with regard to intoxicants. Perhaps they were a little afraid of it, suspecting in their peasant's ignorance some foreign trick. I even heard of a Turkish doctor who asked a foreign surgeon to perform an operation for him, but who refused to allow an anæsthetic to be administered.

I am not fond of going to stare at sick people, but I happened for one reason or another to visit several hospitals and I brought away my own very distinct if very hasty impressions. I remember most vividly a hospital installed in a building which in times of peace is an art school. Opposite the door of one ward, by an irony of which the soldiers in the beds could scarcely be aware, stood a Winged Victory of Samothrace. Samothrace itself had a few days before been taken by the Greeks. The Victory was veiled — partly I suppose to keep her clean, and partly out of deference to Mohammedan susceptibilities. But there she stood, muffled and mutilated, above the beds of thirty or forty broken men of Asia. I shall always remember the look in their eyes, mute and humble and grateful and uncomprehending, as we passed from bed to bed, giving them sweets and cigarettes. The heads that showed above the thick coloured quilts were dressed in white skull-caps, for an Oriental cannot live without something on his hair. It is a point both of etiquette and of religion. Those who were farther on the way to recovery prowled mildly about in baggy white pyjamas and quilted coats of more colour than length. Their wearers had an admirable indifference as to who saw them. A great many had a left hand tied up in a sling — a hand, I suppose, that

Convalescents

some Bulgarian had seen sticking a gun-barrel out of a trench in Thrace. Some limped painfully or went on crutches. But it was not always because of a bullet. There were a vast number of cases of gangrene, simply from ill-fitting shoes or from puttees too tightly bound which hands were too cold or too weak to undo. There were fewer resulting amputations than would have been the case in other countries. Many of the soldiers refused absolutely to have their legs cut off. Life would be of no further use to them, they said. I heard of one who would not go maimed into the presence of Allah. He preferred to go the sooner as he was. And he did, without a word, without a groan, waiting silently till the poison reached his heart. A European nurse told me that in all her long experience she had never seen men die like these ignorant Turkish peasants — so bravely, so simply, so quietly. They really believe, I suppose. In any case, they are of Islam, resigned to the will of God. After death they must lie in a place with no door or window open, for as short a time as possible. A priest performs for them the last ritual ablution, and then they are hurried silently away to a shallow grave.

IV. — RECONNOITRING BY TAXI

The war correspondent had arrived from Pekin too late to go to the front. The front, however, seemed to be making its way as fast as it could to the war correspondent. It was near enough, at any rate, to make him feel a certain independence of permits, passes, and other pieces of paper of which the War Office was exceeding chary. What could have made the situation more patent than that a war correspondent should engage a taxicab, a common Pera taxi, striped red and black and presumably not infallible as to its mechanism, and should invite an amateur and a British resident to help him ascertain whether the Chatalja lines were as unapproachable as they were reported?

Our first plan was to strike northwest in the hope of coming out somewhere between Hadem-kyöi, the headquarters of Nazîm Pasha, and the forest region of Derkos, which local rumour had lately peopled with Bulgarians.

I may as well say first as last that this plan did not succeed. Before we were half-way to the lines our road petered out into a succession of quagmires and parallel ruts with heather growing so high between them that it threat-

Stuck in the mud

ened to scrape off the under works of the car. Into one of the quagmires we sank so deeply that only a pair of hairy black buffalo could haul us out. For an irresponsible amateur, however, the attempt had its impressions. The most abiding one was that of the Constantinople *campagna*. It undulated to the horizon so desolate in its autumn colour, so bare save for a few tawny clumps of wood, so empty and wild, that no one would suspect the vicinity of a great capital. We met almost no one. A few Greek peasants came or went to market, apparently oblivious to wars or rumours of them. Not so a convoy of Turkish refugees, toiling up a hill with all they had in the world piled under matting on ox-carts with huge ungainly wheels. We ran through one village inhabited by Greeks — Pyrgos is its name, and a famous *panayíri* is held there in August—who gave us anew a sense of the strange persistence of their type through so many vicissitudes. Among them were girls or women with big double-armed amphoræ on their shoulders that might have come out of a museum. As we rammed the furze a mile or two beyond we saw the minaret of a Turkish village, and heard a *müezin* call to noonday prayer. We heard a shot, too, crack suddenly out of the stillness. It had to do duty with us for an adventure — unless I mention a couple of deserters we met, one of whom drew his bayonet as we bore down upon him. But I must not forget the fine Byzantine aqueduct under which we stopped to lunch. As we stood admiring the two tiers of arches marching magnificently across the ravine we heard a sound of bells afar. The sound came nearer and nearer, until a string of camels wound into sight. They took the car as unconcernedly as the car took them, disappearing one by one through the tall gateway that Andronicus Comnenus built across that wild valley.

Our second attempt was more successful. It led us through Stamboul and the cemetery cypresses outside the walls, into a *campagna* flatter and more treeless than the one we had seen in the morning, but not so void of humanity. In the neighbourhood of the city the refugees made the dominant note, with their clumsy carts and their obstinate cattle and their veiled women and their own coats of many colours. Other refugees were camped on the bare downs. The children would run toward us when they caught sight of the car, laughing and shouting. For them war was a picnic. Farther out the soldiers

The aqueduct of Andronicus I

were more numerous than the refugees. Every time we met one, at first, we expected to be stopped. Some of them were driving cattle and horses into the city. Others were going out with carts of supplies. Once we overtook a dark mass of *redifs* making in loose order for the isolated barracks of Daoud Pasha — where the Janissaries used to muster for a European campaign. We knew them by their blue uniforms, piped with red, of Abd ül Hamid's time. They looked mildly at us as we charged them, and mildly made room. So did the officer who rode at their head. On the ascent beyond him we saw two men in khaki waiting for us. We concluded that our reconnaissance was at an end. But we presently perceived that the men in khaki wore red crescents on their sleeves and carried no rifles. They merely wanted to see us

Photographed by Frederick Moore

Fleeing from the enemy

pass. It was the same at a gendarmerie station a little farther on, and at the aerodrome behind San Stefano.

We found the road unexpectedly good, after the heather and quagmires of the morning. There were bad bits in it, but they only gave us occasion to bless the French syndicate that had had time to make the good ones before the war broke out. After dipping through one wide hollow we came in sight of the Marmora. A battle-ship making for the city drew a long smudge of smoke across the vaporous blue—the German *Goeben*, we afterward learned she was. On the low shore the Russian war monument of 1878 lifted its syringe dome. Through all the region behind it a faint odour of carbolic hung in the air, a reminder of the place of horror that San Stefano had become since cholera broke out. We passed a few dead cattle. A huge dog was tearing at one carcass, a creature that twilight would have made a hyena. Some new-made graves, too, had their own story to tell.

Suddenly, on the brow of a hill, we came upon the sunset picture of Küchük Chekmejeh. Below us, at the left, was a bay into which the sun was dropping. To the right stretched a shining lake. And between them ran a long bridge with one fantastically high and rounded arch that looked at its own image in the painted water. I would like to believe that that arch is the one mentioned in the epitaph of the architect Sinan and romantically likened to the Milky Way; but I believe the true arch of the Milky Way is at Büyük Chekmejeh. The village of Küchük Chekmejeh—the Little Drawbridge—made a huddle of red-brown roofs at the right end of the bridge. As we ran down to it we encountered more soldiers guarding a railway line. In front of us a cart crossed the track with an empty stretcher. Near it two men were digging or filling a grave. The village itself was full of soldiers, who also guarded the bridge. We skimmed across it, no one saying a word to us, and up into another high bare rolling country bordered by the sea.

We decided to spend the night in Büyük Chekmejeh — the Great Drawbridge — which is the Marmora end of the Chatalja lines, and in front of which the Bulgarians were supposed to be massing for a battle that might be the end of all things. Soldiers grew thicker as we ran on. Presently we found ourselves in the midst of a camp. Fires were burning between the tents and soldiers went to and fro carrying food. Then we looked down on another picture, in composition very much like the first. The bay and the lake were bigger, however, and we saw no arch of the Milky Way as the bridge went lengthwise below us. The centre of interest this time was a man-of-war and half a dozen torpedo-boats. They, and the twilight in which we saw them, and the high black shores beyond, had an unexpectedly sinister air. Nevertheless, we began slowly picking our way down toward an invisible village. Soldiers were all about us. A line of them were carrying big round platters. Another line of them sat beside the road, in what I ingenuously took to be an unfinished gutter until the war correspondent called it a trench. We began to ask ourselves questions. We also asked them of a soldier, inquiring if we should find room in the village to spend the night. He assured us that we would find plenty of room: everybody had gone away. Oh! And where were the Bulgarians? He pointed over to the black line of hills on the other side of the bay.

We decided that we would not, after all, spend the night in Büyük Chekmejeh! Our taxi, that had behaved irreproachably all day, chose that inauspicious moment to balk. While the chauffeur was tinkering with it an officer rode up and recommended him to be off as quickly as possible. That officer was the first member of his army who had addressed a question or a remonstrance to us all day. The chauffeur stated our plight. "Never mind," said the officer, as if a car were a mule that only had to be beaten a little harder to make it move, "you must go back. And you must be quick, for after six o'clock no one will be allowed on the roads." It was then half past five. And we realised with extreme vividness that we were between the lines of the two armies, and that our lamps would make an excellent mark for some Bulgarian artilleryman if he took it into his head to begin the battle of Chatalja. As a matter of fact, he obligingly waited till the next night. In the meantime the car made up its mind to go on. We sputtered slowly up the long hill, passing lighted tents that looked cosy enough to an amateur bound for the rear. But once in open country a tire gave out and we lost our half-hour of grace.

As we coasted down the hill to the bridge which should have been of the Milky Way our lamps illuminated a hooded giant in front of us. He barred the road with his bayonet, saying pleasantly to the chauffeur:

"It is forbidden, my child."

"What shall we do?" asked the chauffeur.

"In the name of God, I know not," replied he of the hood. "But the bridge is forbidden."

Personally, I did not much care. A southerly air warmed the November night, a half-moon lighted it, and while there was not too much room in the taxi for three people to sleep, still the thing could be done. The British resident, however, who had grey hairs and a family, asked to be taken to the officer in command. The gentleman in the hood did not object. The British resident was accordingly escorted across the bridge by another gentleman in a hood, who mysteriously materialised out of the moonlight, while we waited until our companion came back with his story. The point of it was that the officer in command happened to know the name and the face of the British resident, and agreed with him that, if stopping was to be done, it should have been done earlier in the day. The colonel, therefore, let us through his lines. But he gave strict orders that no one, thereafter, was to cross the bridge of Küchük Chekmejeh without a pass from the War Office.

I forbear to dwell too long upon the rest of our return. We fell once more into the hands of sentries, who were somehow softened by the eloquence of the chauffeur. We broke down again and hung so long on the side of a hill that we made up our minds to spend the night there. We fell foul of bits of road that made us think of a choppy sea; and, in turning off a temporary bridge into a temporary road, we stuck for a moment with one wheel spinning over eternity. We passed many military convoys, going both ways. Our lamps would flare for a moment on a grey hood, on a high pack-saddle, on a cart piled with boxes or sacks, and then the road would be ours again. Camp-fires flickered vaguely over the dark downs. Sometimes we would overtake a refugee cart, the head of the house leading the startled bullocks, the women and children walking behind. As we began to climb out of the last dip toward the cypresses and the city wall the road became one confusion of creaking wheels, of tossing horns, of figured turbans, of women clutching a black domino about their faces with one hand and with the other a tired child. Under the sombre trees fires burned murkily, lighting up strange groups of peasants and gravestones. And all the air was aromatic with burning cypress wood.

At the Top Kapou Gate, where Mehmed II made his triumphal entry in 1453, the press was so thick that we despaired of getting through. "It is no use," said a peasant when we asked him to pull his cart to one side. "They are letting no one in." It was true. The outbreak of cholera had made precautions necessary. A line of grey hoods stood outside the gate and kept back the carts that streamed townward more thickly than ever on the eve of Chatalja. But our infidel car was allowed to enter the city of the Caliph, although his true children, fleeing from an unknown terror, waited outside among the graves. Stamboul was almost deserted as we sped through the long silent streets, save for an occasional patrol or a watchman beating out the hour on the pavement with his club. Twice we met companies of firemen, pattering half naked after a white linen lantern, with their little hand-pumps on their shoulders. Then came the parallel lights of the new bridge, and dark Galata, and Pera that looked never so urban or so cheery after those desolate downs.

On the comfortable leather cushions of the club — somehow they made me think of the refugees among the cypresses — we told the story of our day.

"So," said another war correspondent, who had been lucky enough to see the battle of Lüleh Bourgass through the eyes of a lost dragoman, "you saw nothing at all?"

"No," I said. "Nothing at all."

V. — SAN STEFANO

It is strange how San Stefano, in spite of herself, like some light little person involuntarily caught into a tragedy, seems fated to be historic. San Stefano is a suburb on the flat northwestern shore of the Marmora that tries perseveringly to be European and gay. San Stefano has straight streets. San Stefano has not very serious-looking houses standing in not very interesting-looking gardens. San Stefano has a yacht-club whose members, possessing no yachts, spend their time dancing and playing bridge. And a company recently bought land and planted groves on the edge of San Stefano with the idea of making a little Monte Carlo in the Marmora.

Whether San Stefano was trying to be worldly and light-minded as long ago as 1203, when Enrico Dandolo stopped there with the men of the fourth crusade, I cannot say — nor does Villehardouin. Another far-come army to stop there was that of the Russians, in 1878, who left not much light-heartedness in San Stefano. In 1909 the events which preceded the fall of Abd ül Hamid turned the yacht-club for a moment into the parliament of the empire, and the town into an armed camp. Turned into an armed camp again at the outbreak of the Balkan War, San Stefano soon became a camp of a more dreadful kind.

I did not see San Stefano, myself, at the moment of its greatest horror. When I did go, one cold grey November morning, it was rather unwillingly, feeling myself a little heroic, at all events wanting not to seem too unheroic in the eyes of the war correspondent and the other friend he invited to go. I did not know then, in my ignorance, that cholera can be caught only through the alimentary canal. And my imagination was still full of the grisly stories the war correspondent had brought back from his first visit. There was nothing too grisly to be seen, however, as we landed at the pier. Chiefly to be seen were soldiers, coated and hooded in grey, as usual, who were transferring supplies of different kinds from small ships to the backs of small pack-animals. The correspondent accordingly took out his camera; But he pretended to focus it on us, knowing the susceptibility of Turks in the matter of photography — a susceptibility that had been aggravated by the war. Seeing that the men were interested rather than displeased at his operations, he went about posing a group of them. Unfortunately an enterprising young police sergeant appeared at that moment. He took the trouble to explain to us at length that to photograph soldiers like that, at the pier, with hay on their clothes and their caps askew, was forbidden. People would say, when we showed the prints in our country, "Ha! That is a Turkish soldier!" and get a wrong impression of him. The impression I got was of his size and good looks together with a mildness amounting to languor. I do not know whether those men at the pier had been through the two great battles, or whether the pest-house air of the place depressed them. A Greek who witnessed our discomfiture came up and told us of a good picture we could take, unmolested by the police, a little way out of the village, where a soldier sat dead beside the railway track with a loaf of bread in his hands. We thanked the Greek but thought we would not trouble him to show us his interesting subject.

As we went on into the village we found it almost deserted except by soldiers. Every resident who could do so had run away. A few Greek and Jewish peddlers hawked small wares about. A man was scattering disinfecting powder in the street, which the wind carried in gusts into our faces. Patrols strolled up and down, sentinels stood at doors, other soldiers, more broken than any I had yet seen, shuffled aimlessly past. We followed a street that led toward the railway. On the sea side of the line we came out into an open space enclosed between houses and the high embankment. The grass that tried to grow in this space was strewn with disinfecting powder, lemon peel, odds and ends of clothing — a boot, a muddy fez, a torn girdle. That was what was left of the soldiers who strewed the ground when the correspondent was there before. There were also one or two tents. Through the open flap of the nearest one we saw a soldier lying on his face, ominously still.

We followed our road through the railway embankment. Sentries were posted on either side, but they made no objection to our passing. On the farther slope of the bank men were burning underbrush. A few days before their fellows, sent back from the front, had been dying there of cholera. A little beyond we came to a large Turkish cholera camp. By this time all the soldiers seemed to be under cover. We passed tents that were crowded with them, some lying down, others sitting with their heads in their hands. A few roamed aimlessly in the open. The ground was in an indescribable condition. No one was trying to make the men use the latrines that had been constructed for them. I doubt if any one could have done so. Some of the soldiers, certainly, were too weak to get so far. After all they had gone through, and in the fellowship of a common misery, they were dulled to the decencies which a Mohammedan is quicker than another to observe.

Near the station some long wooden sheds were being run up, to make shelter for the men in the tents and for those who were yet to come back from Hadem-kyöi. We made haste to be by, out of the sickening odour and the sense of a secret danger lurking in the air we breathed. We crossed the track and went back into the village, passing always more soldiers. Some were crouching or lying beside the road, one against the other, to keep warm. I could never express the shrunken effect the big fellows made inside their big overcoats, with dog-like eyes staring out of sallow faces. Some of them were slowly eating bread, and no doubt taking in infection with every mouthful. Venders of lemons and lemon-drops came and went among them. Those they seemed to crave above everything. In front of the railway station were men who had apparently just arrived from

Hadem-kyöi. They were being examined by army doctors. They submitted like children while the doctors poked into their eyes, looked at their tongues, and divided them into categories. In a leafless beer-garden opposite the station tents were pitched, sometimes guarded by a cordon of soldiers. But only once did a sentry challenge us or otherwise offer objection to our going about.

We finally found ourselves at the west edge of the village, where a street is bordered on one side by open fields. This was where until a few days before hundreds, perhaps thousands, of men had lain, those with cholera and those without, the dying among the dead. The ground was strewn with such débris of them as we had seen under the railway embankment, but more thickly. And, at a certain distance from the road, was a débris more dreadful still. At first it looked like a great heap of discarded clothing, piled there to be burned — until I saw two drawn-up knees sticking out of the pile. Then I made out, here and there, a clinched hand, a grey face. A little omnibus came back from somewhere in the fields and men began loading the bodies into it. The omnibus was so short that most of the legs stuck out of the door. Sometimes they had stiffened in the contortion of some last agony. And half the legs were bare. In their weakness the poor fellows had foregone the use of the long girdle that holds together every man of the East, and as they were pulled off the ground or hoisted into the omnibus their clothes fell from them. We did not go to see where they were buried. There had been so many of them that the soldiers dug trenches no deeper than they could help. The consequence was that the dogs of the village pawed into many of the graves.

There are times when a man is ashamed to be alive, and that time, for me, was one of them. What had I done that I should be strolling about the world with clothes on my back and money in my pocket and a smug feeling inside of me being a little heroic, and what had those poor devils done that they should be pitched half naked into a worn-out omnibus and shovelled into trenches for dogs to gnaw at? They had left their homes in order to save their country. Before they had had time to strike a blow for it they had been beaten by privation and neglect. Starved, sick, and leaderless, they had fallen back before an enemy better fed, better drilled, better officered, fighting in a better cause. Attacked then, by an enemy more insidious because invisible, they had been dumped down into San Stefano and penned there like so many cattle. Some of them were too weak to get out of the train themselves and were thrown out, many dying where they fell. Others crawled into the village in search of food and shelter. A few found tents to crowd into. The greater number lay where they could through wet autumn days and nights, against houses, under trees, side by side in fields, and so died. Out of some vague idea of keeping the water uncontaminated, the sentries were ordered to keep the poor fellows away from the public drinking fountains, and hundreds died simply from thirst.

The commander of an Austrian man-of-war, hearing of this horrible state of affairs, went to see San Stefano for himself. He made no attempt to conceal his disgust and indignation. He told the authorities that if they wished to save the last vestige of their country's honour they should within twenty-four hours put an end to the things he had seen. The authorities did so: by shipping several hundred sick soldiers — prodding them with bayonets when they were too weak to board the steamer—off to Touzla, on the Asiatic side of the Marmora, where they would be safely out of sight of prying foreigners. We were told several times, both by residents of the village and by outsiders, that they were actually prevented from doing anything to help, because, forsooth, the sick men had betrayed and disgraced their country and only deserved to die. I cannot believe that any such argument was responsibly put forward unless by men who needed to cover up their own stupidity and criminal incompetence. How could human beings be so inhuman? Were they simply overwhelmed and half maddened by their defeat? And, with their constitutional inability to cope with a crisis, with the lack among them of any tradition of organised humanitarianism, were they paralysed by the magnitude of the emergency? I am willing to believe that the different value which the Oriental lays on human life entered into the case. In that matter I am inclined to think that our own susceptibility is exaggerated. But that does not explain why the Oriental is otherwise. Part of it is, perhaps, a real difference in his nervous system. Another part of it is no doubt related to that in him which has kept him behind the West in all practical contrivances. Human life was not of much account in Europe a few hundred years ago. And in the back of the Turk's brain there may be some proud Islamic view of battle and dying therein, descended from the same remote Asiatic conception as the Japanese theory of suicide. Certainly the Turk fears death less and bears it more stoically than we. Does that give him the right to think less of the life of his fellow beings?

The Austrian officer raised his voice, at least, for the soldiers in San Stefano. The first to lift a hand was a

Swiss lady of the place. Her name has been pronounced so often that I shall not seem yellow-journalistic if I mention it again. Almost every resident who could possibly leave San Stefano had already done so. Fräulein Alt, however, remained. She carried the soldiers the water from which the sentries kept them. She also made soup in her own house and took it to the weakest, comforting as best she could their dying moments. It was, of course, very little that she could do among so many. But she was the first who dared to do it. She was soon joined by another lady of the place, Frau Schneider. And presently a few Europeans from the city helped them make a beginning of relief-work on a larger scale. One of the new recruits was a woman also, Miss Graham, of the Scotch mission to the Jews. The others were Rev. Robert Frew, the Scotch clergyman of Pera; Mr. Hoffman Philip, first secretary of the American embassy; and two gentlemen who had come to Constantinople for the war, the English writer Maurice Baring, and Major Ford, whom I have already mentioned, of our own army medical staff. English and American friends and the American Red Cross contributed help in other ways and obtained that of the authorities. These half-dozen good Samaritans left their own affairs and did what they could to make a hospital out of a Greek school into which sick soldiers had been turned. It was a heroic thing to do, for at that time no one knew that the men were chiefly suffering from dysentery brought on by privation, and Red Cross missions were hesitating to go. Moreover the sanitary conditions of the school were appalling. Six hundred men were lying there on the filthy and infected floor, as well as in a shed which was the rainy-day playground of the school, and in a few tents in the yard. Some of the soldiers had been dead two or three days. Many of them were dying. None of them had had any food besides the intermittent bread of the municipality, or any care save such as Fräulein Alt had been able to give them.

I felt not even a little heroic by the time I went into the yard of this school, next the field where the heap of

Photograph by Frederick Moore

Cholera

dead soldiers lay, and saw these voluntary exiles coming and going in their oilskins. I felt rather how rarely, in our padded modern world, is it given a man to come down to the primal facts of life. This reflection, I think, came to me from the smart tan gloves which one of the Samaritans wore, and which, associating them as I could with embassies and I know not what of the gaieties of life, looked so honourably incongruous in that dreadful work. The correspondent, of course, was under orders to take photographs; but his camera looked incongruous in another way in the face of realities so horrible — impertinent, I might say, if I did not happen to like the correspondent. A soldier lurched out of the school with the gait and in the necessity characteristic of his disease. He looked about, half dazed, and established himself at the foot of a tree, his hands clasped in front of his knees, his head sunk forward on his breast. Other soldiers came and went in the yard, some in their worn khaki, some in their big grey coats and hoods. One began to rummage in the circle of debris which marked the place of a recent tent. He picked up a purse — one of the knitted bags which the people of Turkey use — unwound the long string, looked inside, turned the purse inside out, and put it into his pocket. An older man came up to one of my companions. "My hands are cold," he said, "and I can't feel anything with them. What shall I do?" We also wore hats and spoke strange tongues, like the miracle-workers within: the poor fellow thought we could perform a miracle for him. As we did not he started to go into the street, but the sentry at the gate stopped him. Two orderlies came out of the school carrying a stretcher. A dead man lay on it, under a blanket. The wasted body raised hardly more of the blanket than that of a child.

When we went away the sick soldier was still crouching at the foot of his tree, his hands clasped about his knees and his head sunken on his breast.

VI. — THE PONTIFF OF THE EAST

The incidents of the Balkan War monopolised so much interest that another incident of those days in Constantinople attracted less attention. It is, perhaps, natural that those not on the ground should have small understanding of the part the Ecumenical Patriarchate has played in the politics of Turkey. In the Levant, however, the death of His All-Holiness Joachim III, Patriarch of Constantinople and ranking prelate of the Greek Orthodox Church, was an event no less important than in the West would be the death of the Pope. And for those of his spiritual flock, as for many outside it, the disappearance, at such a moment, of that remarkable personality, together with the circumstances of his funeral, were a part of the larger aspects of the war.

The organisation of the Eastern church is far less centralised than that of the Western, and the political relations of the countries in which it holds sway have tended to keep it so. There are three other Patriarchs within the Turkish empire — in Alexandria, Antioch, and Jerusalem — while the churches of Bulgaria, Greece, Montenegro, Roumania, Russia, and Servia, as well as of the Orthodox populations of Austria-Hungary, are independent of Constantinople. One of these churches, the Bulgarian, has been excommunicated by the Patriarchate. Over two others only, those of Greece and Servia, does the Phanar maintain so much authority as to provide them with the oils for the sacrament of the Holy Chrism. But the Patriarch of Constantinople enjoys dignities accorded to no other primate of his faith, and as spiritual chief of the Greeks of Turkey he exercises much of the temporal power claimed by the Pope. The autocephalous sister churches, moreover, acknowledge his spiritual supremacy, and have usually been careful to avoid the name of patriarch in their own hierarchies. And to his throne attaches all the prestige of its ancient history. That history, reaching back without a break to the time of Constantine, has not yet found its Von

Photograph by Andriomenos, Constantinople

Joachim III, Patriarch of Constantinople

Ranke. The schism of East and West and the political as well as the religious relation of Western Christianity to Rome has caused Constantinople to be neglected by Western scholars. But if the Patriarchate can boast no such brilliant period as that of the papacy during the Renaissance, its closer association with the establishment and early development of the church, and with the lands where Christianity originated, gives it an interest which the papacy can never claim.

When the Roman Empire came to an end and every Greek Orthodox country except Russia was overrun by the Turks, the Patriarchate did not cease to play a great rôle. As a matter of fact, it began to play a greater one than for many centuries before. It would be a study worth undertaking to determine the part the Patriarchs have acted in the gradual release from Islam of Orthodox Christendom. The weapon for this release was given them by the Conqueror himself. On the 1st of June, 1453, three days after Mehmed II stormed the city, he ordered the clergy left in Constantinople to elect a successor to the late Patriarch and to consecrate him according to the historic procedure. The candidate chosen was the learned monk Gennadius, otherwise known as George Scholarius, of the monastery of the Pantocrator. This was where the Venetians had their headquarters during the Latin occupation, and the palace of the Balio which the Genoese pulled down in 1261 seems to have been a part of the monastery. Its great triple church, now known as Zeïrek Kil'seh Jami, was where the Venetians put the icon of the Shower of the Way when they stole it from St. Sophia. Other relics of the church are now in the treasury of St. Mark's. I do not know whether the portrait of Gennadius is to be seen in the Riccardi Chapel at Florence, where Benozzo Gozzoli painted his delightful fresco of the Three Kings and put so many faces of noted men of his time. One of the Three Kings is none other than John VII Palæologus, whom Gennadius accompanied in 1438 to the Council of Ferrara in an attempt to bring about the reunion of the churches. In 1452, however, Gennadius defeated the last effort to reconcile the two rites, and he became the first Patriarch under the régime which, as the catchword of the day had it, preferred the turban of the Turk to the tiara of the

Pope. In the ceremony of his investiture the Sultan played the part formerly enacted by the Greek emperor, with the sole exception of receiving the communion from

The south pulpit of the Pantocrator

the hands of the new pontiff. The Conqueror then invited Gennadius to a private audience, at which he received him with every distinction. When the Patriarch took leave the young Sultan presented him with a jewelled staff of office, and said: "Be Patriarch, and may Heaven guide you. Do not hesitate to rely on my friendship. Enjoy all the rights and privileges which your predecessors have enjoyed." He then accompanied his guest to the outer gate, ordering the highest dignitaries of his own suite to accompany His All-Holiness to the Patriarchate. Which was done, the Patriarch riding one of the Sultan's finest horses. The Conqueror afterward confirmed his words in writing, making inviolable the person of the Patriarch, and confirming the Greeks in the possession of their churches and their cult. Thus the Greek Patriarch is one of the greater dignitaries of the Ottoman Empire. He ranks immediately after the members of the cabinet, taking precedence of every Mohammedan cleric except a Shei'h ül Islam in office.

We have already seen how the Sultan made similar concessions in favour of the Latins of Galata. These two acts, purely voluntary, created the precedent for the status of non-Moslems in the Ottoman Empire. This status is one of the most peculiar features of Turkish polity. The Armenians, the Greeks, the Jews, the Levantine Catholics, and various other fractions of races and religions form each what is called in Turkish a *millet* — a nation. Each has its own spiritual head, who also exercises jurisdiction in all temporal matters of his flock that concern marriage, the family, and education. Similarly, those who are not Ottoman subjects enjoy rights and privileges which no Western country would tolerate for one moment. This is in virtue of the capitulations granted by early sultans, partly out of magnanimity, partly out of disdain. The Conqueror has been praised for his generosity and statesmanship in granting these concessions. From the Christian point of view he may deserve praise. But if I were a Turk I would be more

Photograph by Alinari Brothers, Florence

Portrait of John VII Palæologus as one of the Three Wise Men, by Benozzo Gozzoli. Riccardi Chapel, Florence

inclined to denounce his youth and lack of foresight for creating conditions that entailed the ruin of the empire. He did not, it is true, altogether create those conditions. The Byzantine emperors, who ruled an empire more diverse than his own, set the example which Mehmed II followed. But if he had shown less mercy as a conqueror or less deference as a newcomer among old institutions, if he had cleared the Christians out or forced them to accept all the consequences of the conquest, he would have spared his successors many a painful problem. He might even have assimilated a hopelessly heterogeneous population, and his flag might fly to-day on the shore of the Adriatic.

Be that as it may, the Turks lived to regret the policy of the Conqueror. The whole history of the Patriarchate during the Turkish period has been one of constant encroachment on its privileges and constant attempts to preserve them. During this long struggle not even the person of the Patriarch has always been safe. At least four have met violent deaths at the hands of the Turks. The last was Gregory V, who, in revenge for the part played by the Phanariotes in the Greek revolution, was hanged on Easter morning of 1822 in the gateway of his own palace. This gate, at the top of a re-entering flight of steps, has never since been opened. The Conqueror himself, having already seized the glorious cathedral of Eastern Christianity, so far went back on his word as to take possession of the Church of the Holy Apostles. This structure, built by Constantine and magnified by Justinian, had been an imperial Pantheon. After the loss of St. Sophia it became the seat of the Patriarchate. It is true that the Latins had sacked it in 1204, and that Gennadius had voluntarily moved his throne to the church of the All-blessed Virgin. Nevertheless, it was not precisely in accord with the Conqueror's promises when he razed to the ground the magnificent church that had been the model for St. Mark's of Venice, and built on its site the first of the mosques bearing a sultan's name. This example was so faithfully followed by his successors, that of the twenty-five or thirty Byzantine churches still in existence only one is now in Greek hands. It is only fair to add, however, that a few modern churches in Stamboul occupy ancient sites, and that the decrease of the Greek population caused others to be abandoned by their original worshippers.

The one exception I have noted is a small church in the Phanar quarter called St. Mary the Mongolian. This curious name was that of the founder, a natural daughter of Michael Palæologus. After driving out the Latins in 1261 the emperor thought to consolidate his position by offering the hand of the Princess Mary to Holagou, that redoubtable descendant of Tamerlane who destroyed the caliphate of Bagdad. Holagou died, however, while his bride was on her way to him. But the Palæologina continued her journey and married the son of her elderly fiancé. After he in turn had gone the way of his father, the princess returned to Constantinople and built her church and the monastery of which it formed a part. The Lady of the Mongols, as the Greeks called her, was the first member of her house whom the founder of the house of Osman had seen, and she treated him so contemptuously that he paid her back by capturing the city of Nicæa as a base for his future operations against the empire of her fathers. When, less than two hundred years later, the descendant of Osman took the capital of the Palæologi and built there his great mosque, he made a present of St. Mary the Mongolian to his Greek architect. So it is that the Greeks have always been able to retain possession of the church.

Joachim III, two hundred and fifty-fourth in the long line of Ecumenical Patriarchs of Constantinople, played a memorable part in the struggle between the two powers. Like his cousin of the Vatican, he was of humble family. His father was a fisherman in the village of Boyaji-kyöi, on the Bosphorus. The boy was given to the church when he was no more than twelve years old, going in 1846 with his village priest to a monastery of Mount Athos. After the death of his priest, three years later, he found a more powerful protector in the person of the Metropolitan of Cyzicus, who sent him to Bucharest in charge of the Metropolitan of that city. For in those days Bucharest was merely the capital of Wallachia, a Turkish province governed by Phanariote Greeks. In Bucharest the young ecclesiastic definitely took orders and was ordained as a deacon at the age of eighteen. Before his eventual return to Constantinople he found occasion to see something more of the world, spending not less than four years in Vienna. These *wanderjahren* made up to him in considerable measure his lack of any systematic education. In 1860 his protector became Patriarch, and the young priest was called to make part of his court. Three years later the Patriarch fell from power. But in 1864 Joachim was elected Metropolitan of Varna. The fisherman's son had already become, that is, and without the favour of his protector, a prince of the church; for the Metropolitans of the Patriarchate form a body corresponding to the College of Cardinals. Eight years later he became a member of the Holy Synod, which is the executive council of the Patriarchate, composed of twelve Metropolitans. In 1874 he was transferred to the important see of Salonica. It is rather curious that the three cities of his longest ecclesiastical residence outside of Constantinople should have passed out of Turkish hands during his lifetime, and in the order of his residence in them. He remained but four years in Salonica. In 1878, at the age of forty-four, he was elected to the throne of St. John Chrysostom.

Sultan Abd ül Hamid II had but recently come to the throne of Osman. As he took account of his empire, shaken by a disastrous war, and gathered the reins of government into his own hands, he discovered that the Orthodox Church had a stanch defender at its head. In 1884, however, Joachim III was compelled to retire. The Sultan, who was no less stanch a defender of the rights of his people as he saw them, had decreed that in all questions at law the Greek priests should no longer be subject to the Patriarchate, but should be tried like Turkish priests by the Moslem religious courts. This the Patriarch stoutly objected to; but he finally expressed his willingness to agree that in criminal cases his priests should be given up to the Turkish courts. The concession was to him a verbal one only, since it is not often that a priest becomes entangled in criminal procedure. As it involved the whole question of the rights of the Patriarchate, however, the Holy Synod refused to countenance even a verbal concession, and Joachim resigned. He then spent sixteen years in "repose," visiting the different Patriarchates of the empire and finally establishing himself on Mount Athos. He occupied there for several years the picturesque residence of Milopotamo, a dependency of the monastery of the Great Lavra. But in 1901 he was elected a second time to the Patriarchal throne, which he thereafter occupied to the day of his death.

His second reign of eleven years coincided with one of the most crucial periods in Turkish history. The early days of it were marred by such bitterness between

Greeks and Bulgarians in Macedonia that Joachim III must have been surprised himself, during the last days of his life, to see soldiers of the two races fighting together against a common enemy. He had grown up in a church that acknowledged no rival and that had formed the habit of detecting and opposing encroachments on its privileges. Not only did he live, however, to see the boundaries of the Patriarchate draw nearer and nearer Constantinople, but to hear members of its diminished flock request the right to use languages other than the Greek of the Gospels, to be served by clergy from among themselves. He had been a bishop in Bulgaria when the Turks, past masters in the art of dividing to rule, listened to the after all not unreasonable plea of the Bulgars to control their own religious affairs and still further narrowed the powers of the Patriarchate by creating a new Bulgarian *millet* with a primate of its own called the Exarch. A hundred years previously, as a matter of fact, the Bulgarians had had a Patriarch of their own at Ochrida, in Macedonia. But this brought down, in 1870, the ban of excommunication. There followed a merciless feud between the two churches and their followers which reached its height during the second reign of Joachim III. And the *odium theologicum* was imbittered by an old racial jealousy reaching far back into Byzantine history; for each church was the headquarters in Turkey of a nationalist propaganda in favour of brothers across the border.

In the meantime the revolution of 1908 created new difficulties for the Patriarchate. The Young Turks avowed more openly than the old Turks had done their desire to be rid of capitulations, conventions, special privileges, and all the old tissue of precedent that made the empire a mass of *imperia in imperio*. Joachim III, however, had profited by the lesson of his first reign. During his retirement the Patriarchate, refusing to yield to Abd ül Hamid, had answered him by closing the churches. To us this seems a childish enough protest, but it is a measure of rigour immensely disliked by the Turks on account of the discontent it arouses among the large Greek population. After holding out six years, the Sultan finally gave in to the Patriarchate, and in 1891 a species of *concordat* was drawn up between the two parties. Joachim III, accordingly, met the Young Turks more vigorously than he had met Abd ül Hamid. So vigorously did he meet them that Mahmoud Shefket Pasha, in the heat of a controversy over the military service of non-Moslems, burst out one day at the Patriarch: "I will smash the heads of all the Greeks!" The question of schools also became acute, the government demanding a supervision of Greek institutions which the Patriarchate refused to admit. And a policy of pin-pricks was instituted against all the heads of the non-Moslem communities, in a belated attempt to retake the positions lost by Mehmed II and to limit the Patriarchs to their spiritual jurisdiction. It was only after the outbreak of the Italian War and the consequent fall of the Committee of Union and Progress that normal relations with the Porte were restored.

An outsider is free to acknowledge that it was natural enough for the Turks to regret the mistakes of a mediæval policy and to wish to do what they could to unify their very disparate empire. They made the greater mistake, however, of not seeing that it was too late; that, if they were not strong enough to tear up agreements when it suited them, the only course left was to devise some frank and just federation between the different elements of the empire. On the other hand, an outsider is also free to acknowledge that the Patriarchate was, perhaps, too prone to fancy itself attacked, too ready to credit the Turks with stupidity or ill will, too obsessed by the memory of its own historic greatness. Nevertheless, the fact remains that Joachim III was a remarkable prelate. If there was anything personal in his ambition to unite the churches of the East under the ægis of the Phanar, he proved that his views had broadened since the days of the Bulgarian schism and that he held no mean conception of his rôle as the shepherd of a disinherited people. Imposing in his presence, a natural diplomat, more of a scholar than his youthful opportunities had promised, and for those who knew him a saint, he faced the cunning Abd ül Hamid like an equal monarch, never allowing himself to be cozened out of his vigilance. He did more than protect his people. He gave them weapons. He wished his clergy and his laymen to be educated, to be better educated than the masters of the land. He therefore built great schools for them, and created a press. He was not only a statesman, however. It was a matter of concern with him that his church should be alive. Many interesting questions of reform arose during his incumbency — of what would be called, in the Roman Church, Americanism. Indeed, he was sometimes taxed with being too progressive, almost too protestant. He and the Archbishop of Canterbury made overtures to each other, from their two ends of Europe, in the interest of a closer union of Christendom. I know not what there may have been of politics in this ecclesiastical flirtation.

At the outbreak of the Balkan War Joachim III was seventy-eight years old. He was none the less able to conduct the affairs of his church. No one can have taken a greater interest than he in the earlier events of that remarkable campaign. He was still alive when the

Bulgarian cannon drew so near that their thunder was audible even at the Phanar. What feelings did the sound rouse in that old enemy of the Exarchate? He must, at all events, have hoped that to him would be given the incomparable honour of reconsecrating St. Sophia. That consummation, which for a moment seemed within the possibilities, was not granted him. He died while the negotiations for an armistice were going on at Chatalja. His funeral took place on the 1st of December, 1912.

The Patriarch Gennadius, as we have seen, first took up his residence in the church of the Holy Apostles and afterward in that of the Pammakaristos — the All-blessed Virgin. There sixteen of his successors reigned in turn till 1591, when Sultan Mourad III turned that interesting eighth-century church into Fetieh Jami — the Mosque of Conquest — in honour of his victories in Persia and Georgia. Then the Patriarchate moved three times more, finally settling in 1601 in the church of St. George at the Phanar. This has been the Vatican of Constantinople for the past three hundred years. The Patriarchs have never made, at the Phanar, any attempt at magnificence. Exiled from St. Sophia, and hoping, waiting, to return thither, they have preferred to live simply, to camp out as it were in expectation, thinking their means best devoted to schools and charitable institutions. The wooden palace of the Patriarchate is a far from imposing building, while the adjoining church is small and plain. It contains little of interest save an old episcopal throne and a few relics and icons, which are supposed to have been saved from St. Sophia. Nevertheless the funeral of Joachim III was a dignified, an imposing, even a splendid ceremony. To this result the Turkish authorities contributed not a little, by maintaining a service of order more perfect than I have seen at any other state pageant in Constantinople. No one who had not a card of admission was allowed even in the street through which the procession was to pass. Along this street black masts were set at intervals, from which hung black gonfalons with white crosses in the centre, while black and white wreaths or garlands decorated all the houses. On either

Church of the All-blessed Virgin (Fetieh Jami)

side of the rising curve from the main street to the gate of the Patriarchate, students from the theological college at Halki made a wonderfully picturesque guard of honour in their flowing black robes and brimless black hats, each supporting the staff of a tall church lantern shrouded in black. Within the church even stricter precautions had been taken to prevent the dignity of the ceremony from being marred. The number of tickets issued was sternly limited to the capacity of the narrow nave, and none were granted to ladies — a severity which brought down a violent protest from the better half of Byzantium.

A Greek church sometimes impresses a Westerner as containing too many glittering things within too small a space. On this occasion the natural twilight of the interior and the black gauze in which lamps and icons were veiled toned down any possible effect of tawdriness, while the tall carved and gilded *ikonostasion* made the right background for the splendour of the ceremony. One hardly realised that it was a funeral. There was no coffin, no flowers, no mortuary candles. The dead Patriarch, arrayed in his pontifical cloth of gold and crowned with his domed gold mitre, sat in his accustomed place at the right of the chancel, on a throne of purple velvet. I was prepared to find it ghastly; but in the half light I found rather a certain Byzantine solemnity. On the purple dais at the right of the Patriarch stood his handsome Grand Vicar, in the flowing black of the church. At the left another priest stood, one of the twelve archimandrites attached to the Patriarchate, holding the episcopal staff which the Conqueror is supposed to have given Gennadius, tipped like Hermes' caduceus with two serpents' heads of gold. In front of the dais burned an immense yellow candle, symbolic of the Light of the World, which an acolyte called the Great Candle-bearer always carries before the Patriarch.

The officiating clergy, consisting of the members of the Holy Synod and a number of visiting bishops, stood in front of the *ikonostasion*, some in simple black, others in magnificent vestments of white satin embroidered with gold. The rest of the church was given up to invited guests. In stalls at the dead Patriarch's left sat the heads of the other non-Moslem communities of the empire, headed by the Armenian Patriarch and including the Grand Rabbi of Turkey, and even a representative of the Bulgarian Exarch. At the right were grouped the representatives of the Sultan, of the cabinet, and of different departments of government, all in gala uniform

The lantern-bearers

and decorations. On the opposite side of the chancel was ranged the diplomatic corps, headed by the Russian ambassador with all his staff and the Roumanian minister. Their Bulgarian, Greek, Montenegrin, and Servian colleagues, being absent, seemed at that historic moment to be only the more present. The other foreign missions, as less concerned with the Orthodox Church, were represented by two secretaries apiece. The overflow of the diplomatic corps, the officers of the international squadron then in the Bosphorus, and a number of Greek secular notabilities filled the body of the nave, in chairs which had been provided for them contrary to all precedents of the Greek Church. The spectacle was extremely brilliant, nor less so for the twilight of the church — and a strange one when one realised that it was all in honour of the old man in the purple chair, his head bowed and his eyes closed, sitting so still and white in his golden robes. But strangest of all was something unuttered in the air, that reminded me a little of when Abd ül Hamid opened his second parliament — a feeling of all that was impersonated there by robe and uniform and star, a sense of forces interwoven past extricating, a stirring of old Byzantine ghosts in this hour of death, which was also in some not quite acknowledged way an hour of victory. Joachim III would scarcely have had a more dramatic funeral if it had taken place in St. Sophia.

The ceremony was not very long. It consisted chiefly of chanting — of humming one might almost say, so low was the tone in which the priests sang the prayers for the dead. No instrumental music is permitted in the Greek rite. At one point of the office two priests in magnificent chasubles, one of whom carried two candles tied together and the other three, went in front of the Patriarch, bowed low, and swung silver censers. Then the secretary of the Holy Synod mounted a high pulpit and delivered a panegyric of Joachim III. And at last he was lifted as he was, sitting on his throne, and carried in solemn procession to his grave in the monastery of Balîklî.

I did not see the procession in any ordered picture but only as a current surging down the steps, from a door at right angles to the one where Gregory V was hanged a hundred years ago, and away between the motionless black figures with their tall lanterns — a crowded current of robes, of uniforms, of priests swinging censers, of other

The dead Patriarch

priests carrying jewelled decorations on cushions, and one who bore a silver pitcher of wine to be poured into the grave in the fashion of the older Greeks. Turkish soldiers made a guard of honour before the steps, at this pause of another Greek war. They looked up with a sort of wondering proud passivity at the figure of the dead pontiff, and the two-headed Byzantine eagle emblazoned in gold on the back of his purple throne. I did not see either the last embarking of Joachim III on the yacht lent by the government — did not Mehmed II lend Gennadius his horse? — or his triumphal progress, surrounded by the prelates of his court, through the opened bridges of the harbour, to the Marmora side of the city. We drove, instead, to the monastery of Our Lady of the Fishes, outside the walls, where the priests showed us the church darkened with crape and the grave that was not quite ready. It was an underground room rather, with tiled floor and cemented walls, and beside it lay iron girders for roofing over the top. For the Patriarchs are buried as they come to the grave, sitting, according to the ancient custom of their church.

Presently a false alarm called us to the open, where another crowd was waiting. There was still a long time, however, before the procession came into sight. We spent it in the cypress lane which leads, between Turkish cemeteries, to the monastery. Among the graves a camp of refugees from Thrace was quarantined. Twenty or thirty new mounds were near them, scattered with chloride of lime. Ragged peasants leaned over the wall, grateful, no doubt, for something to break the monotony of their imprisonment. The names of Kîrk Kil'seh and Lüleh Bourgass recurred in their talk. At last an advance guard of cavalry spattered down the muddy lane. After them came policemen, mounted and on foot, followed by choir-boys carrying two tall silver crosses and six of the six-winged silver ornaments symbolising the cherubim of the Revelation. Then all the Greeks about us began to exclaim: "There he is!" and we saw the gold-clad figure coming toward us between the cypresses on his purple throne. Until then there had seemed to me nothing ghastly or barbaric about it. I had looked upon it as a historic survival worthy of all respect. But the dignity was gone as the tired bearers stumbled through the mud carrying the heavy dais. And the old man who had been so handsome and imperious in life looked now, in the clear afternoon sunlight, weary and shrunken and pitiful. I was sorry I had come to stare at him once more. And long afterward an imagination of him haunted me, and I wondered if he were in his little tiled room at last, sitting at peace in his purple chair.

VII. — REFUGEES

They say they do not like Christians to live in the sacred suburb of Eyoub. But they are used by this time to seeing us. Too many of us go there, alas, to climb the hill and look at the view and feel as sentimental as we can over Aziyadé. And certainly the good people of Eyoub made no objection to Lady Lowther when she established in their midst a committee for distributing food and clothing and fuel to the families of poor soldiers and to the refugees. The hordes of Asia had not stopped pouring through the city on their way to the west before another horde began pouring the other way, out of Europe. Within a month there could hardly have been a Turk left between the Bulgarian border and the Chatalja lines. It was partly, no doubt, due to the narrowness of the field of operations, lying as it did between two converging seas, which enabled the conquering army to drive the whole country in a battue before it. But I cannot imagine any Western people trekking with such unanimity. They would have been more firmly rooted to the soil. The Turk, however, is still half a tent-man, and he has never felt perfectly at home in Europe. So village after village harnessed its black water-buffalo or its little grey oxen to its carts of clumsy wheels, piled thereon its few effects, covered them with matting spread over bent saplings, and came into Constantinople.

How many of them came I do not imagine any one knows. Thousands and tens of thousands of them were shipped over into Asia Minor. Other thousands remained, in the hope of going back to their ruined homes. The soldiers and the sick had already occupied most of the spare room that was to be found. The refugees had to take what was left. I knew one colony of them that spent the winter in the sailing caïques in which they fled from the coast villages of the Marmora. Being myself like a Turk in that I make little of numbers and computations, I have no means of knowing how many men, women, and children, from how many villages, swelled the population of Eyoub. I only know that their own people took in a good number, that they lived in cloisters and empty houses, that certain mosques were given up to them entirely, that sheds, storehouses, stables,. were full of them. I even heard of four persons who had no other shelter than a water-closet. And still streets and open spaces were turned into camping grounds, where small grey cattle were tethered to big carts and where people in veils and turbans shivered over camp-fires — when they had a camp-fire to shiver over. They could generally fall back on cypress wood. It always gave me a double pang to catch the aroma of such a fire, betraying as it did the extremity of some poor exile and the devastation at work among the trees that give Constantinople so much of its colour.

I have done a good deal of visiting in my day, being somewhat given to seek the society of my kind. But it has not often happened to me, in the usual course of visiting, to come so near the realities of life as when, with another member of our subcommittee, I visited the mosque of Zal Mahmoud Pasha, in Eyoub. The mosque of Zal Mahmoud Pasha is worth visiting. It was built by Sinan, and its founder, a Vizier of Selim II, was nicknamed Zal, after a famous Persian champion, because, with his own hands, he finally succeeded in strangling the strong young prince Moustafa, son of Süleïman the

Exiles

Magnificent. Like its greater neighbour, the mosque of Zal Mahmoud Pasha has two courts. They are on two levels, joined by a flight of steps, each opening into a thoroughfare of its own. And very cheerless they looked indeed on a winter day of snow, especially for the cattle stabled in their cloisters. The mosque itself was open to any who cared to go in. We did so, pushing aside the heavy flap that hangs at any public Turkish doorway in winter. We found ourselves in a narrow vestibule in which eight or ten families were living. One of them consisted of two children, a little boy flushed with fever and a pale and wasted little girl, who lay on the bricks near the door without mattress or matting under them. They were not quite alone in the world, we learned. Their mother had gone away to find them bread. The same was the case with a larger family of children who sat around a primitive brazier. The youngest was crying, and a girl of ten was telling him that their mother would soon be back with something to eat.

We lifted a second flap. A wave of warm smoky air met us, sweetened by cypress wood but sickeningly close. Through the haze of smoke we saw that the square of the nave, surrounded on three sides by a gallery, was packed as if by a congregation. The congregation consisted chiefly of women and children, which is not the thing in Turkey, sitting on the matted floor in groups, and all about them were chests and small piles of bedding and stray cooking utensils. Each of these groups constituted a house, as they put it. As we went from one to another, asking questions and taking notes, we counted seventy-eight of them. Some four hundred people, that is, were living huddled together under the dome of Zal Mahmoud Paŝha. In the gallery and under it rude partitions had been made by stretching ropes between the pillars and hanging up a spare rug or quilt. In the open space of the centre there was nothing to mark off house from house save the bit of rug or matting that most of the families had had time to bring away with them, or such boundaries as could be drawn by the more solid of the family possessions and by the row of family shoes. Under such conditions had not a few of the congregation drawn their first or their last breath.

Nearly every "house" had a brazier of some kind, if only improvised out of a kerosene tin. That was where the blue haze came from and the scent of cypress wood. Some had a little charcoal, and were daily near asphyxiating themselves. Others had no fire at all. On a number of the braziers we noticed curious flat cakes baking, into whose composition went bran or even straw. We took them to be some Thracian dainty until we learned that they were a substitute for bread. The city was supposed to give each refugee a loaf a day, but many somehow did not succeed in getting their share. A few told us that they had had none, unless from their neighbours, for five days. It struck me, in this connection, that in no other country I knew would the mosque carpets still have been lying folded in one corner instead of making life a little more tolerable for that melancholy congregation. Of complaint, however, we heard as little as possible. The four hundred sat very silently in their smoky mosque. Many of them had not only their lost homes to think of. A father told us that when Chorlou was spoiled, as he put it, his little girl of nine had found a place in the "fire carriage" that went before his, and he had not seen her since. One old man had lost the rest of his family. He had been unable to keep up with them, he said: it had taken him twenty-two days to walk from Kîrk Kil'seh. A tall ragged young woman, who told us that her *effendi* made war in Adrianople, said she had three children. One of them she rocked beside her in a wooden washing trough. It came out only by accident that she had adopted the other two during the hegira from Thrace. We wondered how, if the *effendi* ever came out of Adrianople alive, he would find his wife and his baby; for hardly one in fifty of these peasants could read or write, and no exact register of them was kept. Many of them were ill and lay on the floor under a coloured quilt. If another member of the family wanted to take a nap he would crawl under the same quilt. Is it any wonder that diseases became epidemic in the mosques? Cholera did not break out in many of them except St. Sophia, which was used as a barracks.

Lady Lowther's refugees

But in Zal Mahmoud Pasha there were at one time cases of consumption, pneumonia, typhoid fever, scarlet fever, measles, mumps, and smallpox. Five cases of the last were found under one quilt. Still, the refugees would not be vaccinated if they could help it. The only way to bring them to it was to cut off their bread. And not many of them were willing to go away or to let members of their families be taken away to hospitals. How did they know whether they would ever see each other again, they asked? A poor mother we knew, whose husband had been taken as a soldier and had not been heard of since, and whose home had burned to the ground before her eyes, lost her four children, one after the other. A neighbour afterward remarked of her in wonder that she seemed to have no mind in her head.

In distributing Lady Lowther's relief we did what we could to systematise. Having visited, quarter by quarter, to see for ourselves the condition of the people and what they most needed, we gave the head of each house a numbered ticket, enabling him or her to draw on us for certain supplies. Most of the supplies were dealt out on our own day at home. They say it is more blessed to give than to receive. I found, however, that it was most possible to appreciate the humorous and decorative side of Thrace when we received, in the coffee-shop of many windows which was our headquarters. It is astonishing how large a proportion of Thrace is god-daughter to Hadijeh or Aïsheh, Mothers of the Moslems, or to the Prophet's daughter Fatma. Many, nevertheless, reminded one of Mme. Chrysanthème and Madam Butterfly. On our visiting list were Mrs. Hyacinth, Mrs. Tulip, Mrs. Appletree, and Mrs. Nightingale. I am also happy enough to possess the acquaintance of Mrs. Sweetmeat, Mrs. Diamond, Mrs. Pink (the colour), Mrs. Cotton (of African descent), Mrs. Air (though some know her as Mother Eve), Miss May She Laugh, and Master He Waited. This last appellation seemed to me so curious that I inquired into it, and learned that my young gentleman waited to be born. These are not surnames, you understand, for no Turk owns such a thing. Nor yet, I suppose, can one call them Christian names! To tell one Mistress Hyacinth from another you add the name of her man; and in his case all you can do is to call him the son of so and so.

If we found the nomenclature of Mistress Hyacinth and her family a source of perplexity, she in turn was not a little confounded by our system of tickets. We had one for bread. We had another for charcoal. We had a third for groceries. We had a fourth and a fifth for fodder. We had a sixth, the most important of all, since it entitled the bearer to the others, which must be tied tight in a painted handkerchief and never be lost. "By God!" cried Mistress Hyacinth in her honoured idiom, "I know not what these papers mean!" And sometimes it was well-nigh impossible to explain it to her. A good part of her confusion, I suspect, should be put down to our strange accent and grammar, and to our unfamiliarity with the Thracian point of view. Still, I think the ladies of that peninsula share the general hesitation of their race to concern themselves with mathematical accuracy. Asked how many children they had, they rarely knew until they had counted up on their fingers two or three times. It is evidently no habit with them to have the precise number in mind. So when they made an obvious mistake we did not necessarily suspect them of an attempt to overestimate. As a matter of fact, they were more likely to underestimate. Other failures of memory were more surprising, as that of a dowager in ebony who was unable to tell her husband's name. "How should I know?" she protested. "He died so long ago!" When questioned with regard to their own needs they were equally vague. "I am naked," was their commonest reply. "Whatever your eye picks out, I will take." But if our eye failed to pick out the right thing, they would in the end give us a hint.

Altogether it is evident that the indirections of Mistress Hyacinth follow a compass different from our own. I remember a girl not more than sixteen or seventeen who told us she had three children. Two of them were with her: where was the third, we asked? "Here," she answered, patting herself with the simplicity of which the Anglo-Saxons have lost the secret. Yet she was most scrupulous to keep her nose and mouth hidden from an indiscriminate world. Another woman, asked about a child we knew, replied non-committally: "We have sent him away." "Where?" we demanded in alarm, for we had known of refugees giving away or even selling their children. "Eh — he went," returned the mother gravely. "Have you news of him?" one of us pursued. "Yes," she said. And it was finally some one else who had to enlighten our obtuseness by explaining that it was to the other world the child had gone. But none of them hesitated to give the rest of us an opportunity to go there too. Many women came into our coffee-shop carrying in their arms a baby who had smallpox, and were a little hurt because we got rid of them as quickly as possible.

With great discreetness would Mistress Hyacinth enter our presence, rarely so far forgetting herself as to lean on our table or to throw her arms in gratitude about a benefactress's neck. For in gratitude she abounds, and in such expressions of it as "God give you lives" and "May you never have less." With a benefactor she is, I am happy to report, more reserved. Him she addresses, according to her age, as "my child," "my brother," "my uncle," or haply "my mother and my father." I grew so accustomed to occupying the maternal relation to ladies of all ages and colours that I felt slighted when they coldly addressed me as their lord. Imagine, then, my pleasure when one of them called me her creamy boy! In the matter of discretion, however, Mistress Hyacinth is not always impeccable — so far, at least, as concerns the concealment of her charms. Sometimes, indeed, she will scarcely be persuaded to raise her veil even for a lady to recognise her; but at others she appears not to shrink from the masculine eye. One day a Turk, passing our coffee-shop, was attracted by the commotion at the door. He came to the door himself, looked in, and cried out "Shame!" at the disreputable spectacle of a mild male unbeliever and a doorkeeper of his own faith within the same four walls as some of Lady Lowther's fairer helpers and a motley collection of refugee women, many of them unveiled. But the latter retorted with such promptness that the shame was rather upon him, for leaving the *gyaour* to supply their wants, that he was happy to let the matter drop. On this and other occasions I gathered a very distinct impression that if Mistress Hyacinth should ever take it into her head to turn suffragette she would not wait long to gain her end.

The nails of Mistress Hyacinth — speaking of suffragettes — are almost always reddened with henna, I notice, and very clean. The henna often extends to her fingers as well, to the palms of her hands, and to her hair. If she happen to be advancing in years, the effect is sometimes very strange to a Western eye. There is no attempt to simulate a youthful glow. The dye is plentifully applied to make a rich coral red. In other points of fashion Mistress Hyacinth is more independent than her sisters of the West. What the ladies of Paris wear must be worn by the ladies of Melbourne, New York, or St. Petersburg. But no such spirit of imitation prevails in Thrace, where every village seems to have modes of its own. We had great difficulty in getting rid of a quantity of clothing sent out by charitable but unimaginative persons in England, who could hardly be expected to know the fashions of Thrace. Articles intended to be worn out of sight were accepted without a murmur when nothing better was to be had, such as a quilted coat of many colours that we bought by the hundred in the Bazaars, called like the Prophet's mantle a *bîrka.* But when it came to some very good and long golf capes, the men were more willing to take them than the women — until they thought of cutting them up into children's coats. Mistress Hyacinth herself scorned to put on even so much of the colour of an unbeliever, preferring the shapeless black mantle of her country, worn over her head if need be, and not quite hiding a pair of full print trousers.

The village whose taste I most admire is that of Vizeh, the ladies of which weave with their own hands a black woolen crash for their mantles, with patches of red-and-blue embroidery where they button, and with trousers of the same dark blue as the sailor collar of a good many of them. I wish I might have gone to Vizeh before the Bulgarians did. There must have been very nice things to pick up — in the way, for instance, of such "napkins" as Lady Mary Montagu described to her sister on the 10th of March, 1718, "all tiffany, embroidered with silks and gold, in the finest manner, in natural flowers." She added: "It was with the utmost regret that I made use of these costly napkins, as finely wrought as the finest handkerchiefs that ever came out of this country. You may be sure that they were entirely spoiled before dinner was over." But you, madam, may be sure they were not, for I bought some of them from the ladies of Thrace, rather improved than not by their many washings. They are technically known as Bulgarian towels, being really Turkish; but it seems to me that the tradition which persists in this beautiful peasant embroidery must be Byzantine. Mistress Hyacinth was able to make it, as well as to sell it. And to turn an honest penny she and her friends set up their funny little hand-looms in a house we hired for them, and wove the narrow cloth of their country, loosely mingled of linen or cotton and silk, and shot, it might be, with bright colours of which they had the secret.

Peasant embroidery

The consort of Mistress Hyacinth, I regret to add, seemed to show less willingness to add to the resources of the family. Perhaps it was because of an inward conviction of which I once or twice caught rumours, that as unbelievers had deprived him of his ordinary means of sustenance, we other unbelievers were in duty bound to keep him alive. For the rest he is outwardly and visibly the decorative member of the family. He inclines less to bagginess than Mistress Hyacinth, or than his brother of Asia. He affects a certain cut of trouser which is popular all the way from the Bosphorus to the Adriatic. This trouser, preferably of what the ladies call a pastel blue, is bound in at the waist by a broad red girdle which also serves as pocket, bank, arsenal, and anything else he pleases. Over it goes a short zouave jacket, more or less embroidered, and round my lord's head twists a picturesque figured turban, with a tassel dangling in

Young Thrace

front of one ear. He is a surprisingly well-made and well-featured individual — like Mistress Hyacinth herself, for that matter, and like the roly-poly small fry at their heels. On the whole they give one the sense of furnishing excellent material for a race — if only the right artist could get hold of it.

VIII. — SEMIPHILOSOPHIC FINALE

One day I stopped on the quay to watch a cheering transport steam down the Bosphorus. An old Turkish lady who happened to be passing stopped to watch it too.

"Poor things! Poor things!" she exclaimed aloud. "The lions! You would think they were going to a wedding!" And then turning to me she suddenly asked: "Can you tell me, *effendim*, why it is that Europe is against us? Have we done no good in six hundred years?"

The attitude of Europe was the crowning bitterness of the war. In the beginning, Europe had loudly announced that she would tolerate no change in the *status quo*. How then did Europe come to acquiesce so quickly in the accomplished fact? Why did Germany, the friend of Abd ül Hamid, and England, the friend of Kyamil Pasha, and France, the friend of everybody, raise no finger to help? I am not the one to suggest that Europe should have done otherwise. There is a logic of events which sometimes breaks through official twaddle — a just logic drawing into a common destiny those who share common traditions and speak a common tongue. I make no doubt that Austria-Hungary, to mention only one example, will one day prove it to her cost. Nevertheless, I am able to see that there is a Turkish point of view. And my old lady's question struck me as being so profound that I made no pretence of answering it.

I might, to be sure, have replied what so many other people were saying: "Madam, most certainly you have done no good in six hundred years. It is solely because of the evil you have done that you enjoy any renown in the world. You have done nothing but burn, pillage, massacre, defile, and destroy. You have stamped out civilisation wherever your horsemen have trod. And what you were in the beginning you are now. Your enemy the Bulgarian has advanced more in one generation than you have in twenty. You still cling to the forms of a bloody and barbaric religion, but for what it teaches of truth and humanity you have no ear. You make one justice for yourself and one for the owner of the land you have robbed. Your word has become a byword among the nations. You are too proud or too lazy to learn more than your fathers knew. You fear and try to imitate the West; but of the toil, the patience, the thoroughness, the perseverance that are the secret of the West you have no inkling. You will not work yourself, and you will not let others work — unless for your pocket. You have no literature, no art, no science, no industry, worth the name. You are incapable of building a road or a ship. You take everything from others — only to spoil it, like those territories where you were lately at war, like this city, which was once the glory of the world. You have no shadow of right to this city or to those territories. The graves of your ancestors are not there. You took them by the sword, and, like everything else that comes into your hands, you have slowly ruined them. It is only just that you should lose them by the sword. For your sword was the one thing you knew how to use, and now even that has rusted in your hand. You are rotten through and through. That is why Europe is against you. Go back to your tents in Asia, and see if you will be capable of learning something in another six hundred years."

So might I have answered my old lady — had my Turkish been good enough. But I would scarcely have convinced her. Nor would I quite have convinced myself. For while it is a simple and often very refreshing disposal of a man to damn him up and down, it is not one that really disposes of him. He still remains there, solid and unexplained. So while my reason tells me how incompetent a man the Turk is from most Western points of view, it reminds me that other men have been incompetent as well, and even subject to violent inconsistencies of character; that this man is a being in evolution, with reasons for becoming what he is, to whom Dame Nature may not have given her last touch.

In this liberal disposition my reason is no doubt quickened, I must confess, by the fact that I am at heart a friend of the Turk. It may be merely association. I have known him many years. But there is something about him I cannot help liking — a simplicity, a manliness, a dignity. I like his fondness for water, and flowers, and green meadows, and spreading trees. I like his love of children. I like his perfect manners. I like his sobriety. I like his patience. I like the way he faces death. One of the things I like most about him is what has been perhaps most his undoing — his lack of any commercial instinct. I like, too, what no one has much noticed, the artistic side of him. I do not know Turkish enough to appreciate his literature, and his religion forbids him — or he imagines it does — to engage in the plastic arts. But in architecture and certain forms of decoration he has created a school of his own. It is not only that the Turkish quarter of any Ottoman town is more picturesque than the others. The old Palace of the sultans in Constantinople, certain old houses I have seen, the mosques, the *medressehs*, the *hans*, the tombs, the fountains, of the Turks are an achievement that deserves more serious study than has been given them. You may tell me that they are not Turkish because they were designed after Byzantine or Saracen originals, and because Greeks and Persians had much to do with building them. But I shall answer that every architecture was derived from another, in days not so near our own, and that, after all, it was the Turk who created the opportunity for the foreign artist and ordered what he wanted.

I have, therefore, as little patience as possible with the Gladstonian theory of the unspeakable Turk. When war ceases, when murders take place no more in happier lands, when the last riot is quelled and the last negro lynched, it will be time to discuss whether the Turk is by nature more or less bloody than other men. In the meantime I beg to point out that he is, as a matter of fact, the most peaceable, with the possible exception of the Armenian, of the various tribes of his empire. Arab, Kürd, and Laz are all quicker with their blades. To his more positive qualities I am by no means alone in testifying. If I had time for chapter and verse I might quote more than one generation of foreign officers in the Turkish service, and a whole literature of travel — to which Pierre Loti has contributed his share. But I do not hesitate to add that this is a matter in which Pierre Loti may be as unsafe a guide as Mr. Gladstone. For blind praise is no more intelligent than blind condemnation. Neither leads one any nearer to understanding the strange case of the Turk.

To understand him at all, I think one needs to take a long view of history. When we consider how many æons man must have lived on this planet and how short in comparison has been the present phase of Western civilisation, it does not seem as if we had good ground for expressing definitive opinions with regard to Eastern peoples. A hundred years ago there was no hint in the West of the expansion that was to come through the use of steam and electricity. Three hundred years ago communications in most of Europe were not so good as, and I doubt if life and property were more secure than, they are in Turkey to-day. For some reason the Turk has lagged in his development. He is to all practical purposes a mediæval man, and it is not fair to judge him by the standards of the twentieth century.

Why it should be that men who have a common origin should have followed such different roads, and at such an uneven pace, is in many ways an insoluble problem. But it should not be, by this time, an unfamiliar one. It would rather be strange, and the world would be much poorer than it is, if humanity had marched from the beginning in a single phalanx — if the world had been one great India, or one great Egypt, or one great Greece. The Turk, then, as I have no need of insisting, is a mediæval man. And one reason why he is so may be that he has a much shorter heritage of civilisation than the countries of the West. He is a new man as well as a mediæval one. In Europe and in Asia alike he is a parvenu who came on to the scene long after every one else. It is only verbally that the American is a newer man; for in the thirteenth century, when the warlike Turkish nomads first began to make themselves known, the different states which have contributed to make America were already formed, while India, China, and Japan had long before reached a high degree of civilisation.

It seems to me that this fact might well account for much of the backwardness of the Turk. He has a much thinner deposit of heredity in his brain cells. It is conceivable, too, that another matter of heredity may enter into it. Whether civil life originated in Asia or not, it is certain that of existing civilisations the Oriental are older than the Occidental. Perhaps, therefore, the Asiatic formed the habit of pride and self-sufficiency. Then as successive tides of emigration rolled away, Asia was gradually drained of everything that was not the fine flower of conservatism. He who believed whatever is is best stayed at home. The others went in search of new worlds, and found them not only in the field of empire but in those of science and art. This continual skimming of the adventurous element can only have confirmed Asia in the habit of mind so perfectly expressed by the Book of Ecclesiastes. And the Turk, who was one of the last adventurers to emerge from Asia, impelled by what obscure causes we hardly know, must have a profound racial bent toward the belief that everything is vanity and vexation of spirit. He asks himself what is the use, and lets life slip by.

Many people have held that there is something in Islam which automatically arrests the development of those who profess it. I cannot think, myself, that the thesis has been sufficiently proved. While no one can deny that religion, and particularly that Islam, is a great cohesive force, it seems to me that people have more to do with making religions than religions with making people. The principles at the root of all aspiring life — call it moral, ethical, or religious, as you will — exist in every religion. And organised religion has everywhere been responsible for much of the fanaticism and disorder of the world. For the rest, I find much in Mohammedanism to admire. There is a nobility in its stern monotheism, disdaining every semblance of trinitarian subtleties. Its daily services impress me as being a more direct and dignified form of worship than our self-conscious Sunday mornings with their rustling pews and operatic choirs. Then the democracy of Islam and much of what it inculcates with regard to family and civil life are worthy of all respect, to say nothing of the hygienic principles which it succeeded in impressing at a very early stage upon a primitive people. At the same time there can be no doubt that Mohammedanism suffers from the fact that it was designed, all too definitely, for a primitive people. Men at a higher stage of evolution than were the Arabs of the seventh century require no religious sanctions to keep themselves clean. For modern men the social system of Islam, with its degrading estimate of woman, is distinctly antisocial. And many of them must find the Prophet's persuasions to the future life a little vulgar. The question is whether they will be able to modernise Islam. It will be harder than modernising Christianity, for the reason that Islam is a far minuter system. Is there not something moving in the spectacle of a people committed to an order which can never prevail? Even for this one little ironic circumstance it can never prevail in our hurrying modern world, because it takes too much time to be a good Mohammedan. But the whole order is based on a conception which the modern world refuses to admit. The word Islam means resignation — submission to the will of God. And there can be no doubt that the mind of Islam is saturated with that spirit. Why does one man succeed and another fail? It is the will of God. Why do some recover from illness and others die? It is the will of God. Why do empires rise or fall? It is the will of God. A man who literally believes such a doctrine has no chance against the man, however less a philosopher, who believes that his destiny lies in his own hand.

It would be an interesting experiment to see what two generations, say, of universal education might do for the Turks. By education I mean no more than the three R's, enough history and geography to know that Turkey is neither the largest nor the most ancient empire in the world, and some fundamental scientific notions. It is incredible how large a proportion of Turks are illiterate, and what fantastic views of the world and their place in it the common people hold. To nothing more than this ignorance must be laid a great part of Turkey's troubles. But another part is due to the character of the empire which it befell the Turk to conquer. If he had happened, like ourselves, into a remote and practically empty land he might have developed his own civilisation. Or if he had occupied a country inhabited by a single race he would have stood a better chance. Or if, again, he had appeared on the scene a few centuries earlier, before Europe had had time to get so far ahead of him, and before the spread of learning and an increasing ease of communications made it increasingly difficult for one race to absorb another, he might have succeeded in assimilating the different peoples who came under his sway. Why the conquerors did not exterminate or forcibly convert the conquered Christians has always been a question with me. It may have been a real humanity on the part of the early sultans, who without doubt were remarkable men and who, perhaps, wished their own wild followers to acquire the culture of the Greeks. Or it may have been a politic deference to new European neighbours. In any case, I am convinced that it was, from the Turkish point of view, a mistake. For the Turk has never been able to complete his conquest. On the contrary, by recognising the religious independence of his subjects he gave them weapons to win their political independence. And, beset by enemies within and without, he has never had time to learn the lessons of peace.

Here, I think, we come very near the root of his difficulties. Not only has he paid, not only does he continue and will he long continue to pay, the price of the invader, incessantly preoccupied as he is with questions of internal order. He created a form of government which could not last. At its most successful period it depended on the spoils of war — not only in treasure but in tribute-boys, carefully chosen for the most famous corps of the army and for the highest executive posts in the empire. This form of government was highly efficient so long as the frontiers of the empire continued to advance. But it was not self-contained, and it kept the native-born Turk from developing normal habits and traditions of government. The traditions it chiefly fostered in him were those of plunder and idleness. Much of the proverbial readiness of Turks in office to receive "presents" is less a matter of dishonesty than the persistence of a time-honoured system of making a living in irregular ways. The system is one that naturally dies out with the disappearance of irregular sources of income. There must inevitably follow, however, a painful period of forming new habits, of creating new traditions. How radical this process had to be with the Turks can scarcely be realised by a country like England, for instance, which has been able to continue for a thousand years developing the same germ of government. The Turk himself hardly realises yet how little he can build on the foundations of his former greatness. And he has been the slower to come to any such realisation because circumstances have kept up an illusion of that greatness long after the reality was gone. If England, if France, if Germany, were to be left to-morrow without a bayonet or a battle-ship, they would still be great powers by the greatness of their economic, their intellectual, their artistic life. Could the same be said of the Ottoman Empire? For a century or more that empire has continued to play the rôle of a great power simply through comparison with smaller or the mutual jealousies of greater ones. It is a long time since the Turk has really stood on his own feet. He has too often been protected against the consequences of his own acts. And, the last comer into the land he rules, he has been too ready to ignore the existence of other rights. But now, stripped of his most distant and most ungovernable provinces, enlightened by humiliation as to the real quality of his greatness, he may, let us hope, put aside illusion and pretence and give himself to the humbler problems of common life. If he sincerely does he may find, in the end, that he has unwittingly reached a greatness beyond that won for him by the Janissaries of old.

MASTERS OF CONSTANTINOPLE

Byzas of Megara founded Byzantium	*about* B. C. 658
Darius Hystaspes, King of Persia	515
Pausanias of Sparta	478
First Athenian (Delian) League	477
Sparta	440
Alcibiades of Athens	408
Lysander of Sparta	405
Spartan League	404
Thrasybulus of Athens	390
Second Athenian League	378
League of Byzantium, Caria, Chios, Cos, and Rhodes	357
Alexander the Great	334
Rome	196
The Free City of Byzantium	64
Septimius Severus destroyed Byzantium and renamed it Augusta Antonina	A. D. 196
Constantine the Great	323
Dedicated New Rome	330
Constantius II	337
Julian the Apostate	361
Jovian	363
Valens	364
Theodosius I, the Great	378
Arcadius	395
Theodosius II	408
Marcian	450
Leo I	457
Leo II	474
Zeno	474
Anastasius I	491
Justin I	518
Justinian I, the Great	527
Justin II	565

Tiberius	A. D. 578
Maurice	582
Phocas	602
Heraclius	610
Heraclius Constantine III and Heracleonas	641
Constans II	642
Constantine IV	668
Justinian II	685
Leontius	695
Tiberius III	697
Justinian II (restored)	705
Philippicus	711
Anastasius II	713
Theodosius III	715
Leo III, the Isaurian	717
Constantine V Copronymus	740
Leo IV	775
Constantine VI	779
Irene	797
Nicephorus I	802
Stauracius	811
Michael I Rhangabe	811
Leo V, the Armenian	813
Michael II, the Amorian	820
Theophilus	829
Michael III	842
Basil I, the Macedonian	867
Leo VI, the Wise	886
Constantine VII Porphyrogenitus	912
Co-emperors:	
Alexander	912–913
Romanus I Lecapenus	991–945
Constantine VIII and Stephanus reigned. five weeks in	944
Romanus II	958
Basil II, the Slayer of the Bulgarians	963
Co-emperors:	
Nicephorus II Phocas	965–969
John I Zimisces	969–976
Constantine IX	976–1025
Constantine IX (sole emperor)	1025
Romanus III Argyrus	1028
Michael IV	1034

Michael V . . . . A. D. 1042
Theodora and Zoe 1042
Constantine X Monomachus 1042
Theodora (restored) 1054
Michael VI Stratioticus 1056
Isaac I Comnenus 1057
Constantine XI Ducas 1059
Michael VII Ducas and Romanus IV Diogenes 1067
Nicephorus III Botoniatēs 1078
Alexius I Comnenus 1081
John II Comnenus 1118
Manuel I Comnenus 1143
Alexius II Comnenus 1180
Andronicus I Comnenus 1183
Isaac II Angelus 1185
Alexius III Angelus 1195
Isaac II Angelus (restored) and Alexius IV Angelus 1203
Nicholas Canabus 1204
Alexius V Ducas, Murtzuphlus 1204

Baldwin I (Count of Flanders) 1204
Henry 1205
Peter 1217
Robert 1219
John of Brienne 1228
Baldwin II 1237

Michael VIII Palæologus (fifth emperor of Nicæa; succeeded 1260) 1261
Andronicus II Palæologus 1282
Co-emperor: Michael IX 1295–1320
Andronicus III Palæologus 1328
John V Palæologus 1341
Co-emperor: John VI Cantacuzene 1341–1355
Manuel II Palæologus 1391
John VII Palæologus 1425
Constantine XII Palæologus 1448

Mehmed II, the Conqueror (seventh Ottoman sultan; succeeded 1451) 1453
Baïezid II 1481
Selim I 1512
Süleïman I, the Magnificent 1520

Selim II	A. D. 1566
Mourad III	1574
Mehmed III	1595
Ahmed I	1603
Moustafa I	1617
Osman II	1618
Moustafa I (restored)	1622
Mourad IV	1623
Ibrahim	1640
Mehmed IV	1649
Süleïman II	1687
Ahmed II	1691
Moustafa II	1695
Ahmed III	1703
Mahmoud I	1730
Osman III	1754
Moustafa III	1757
Abd ül Hamid I	1774
Selim III	1788
Moustafa IV	1807
Mahmoud II, the Reformer	1808
Abd ül Mejid	1839
Abd ül Aziz	1861
Mourad V	1876
Abd ül Hamid II	1876
Mehmed V	1909

A CONSTANTINOPLE BOOK-SHELF

Abbott, G. F.: "Turkey in Transition." 1909.
American, an (J. E. De Kay?): "Sketches of Turkey." 1833.
Amicis, Edmondo de: "Costantinopoli." 1877.
Andréossy, Comte A. F.: "Constantinople et le Bosphore." 1820.
Antoniades, E. M.: "Sainte Sophie." 1905.
Ashmead-Bartlett, Ellis: "With the Turks in Thrace." 1913.

Baedeker, Karl: "Konstantinopel und Kleinasien." 1905.
Baring, Maurice: "Letters from the Near East." 1912.
Bayet, Ch.: "L'Art Byzantin." 2d ed. 1904.
Belin, M. A.: "Histoire de la Latinité de Constantinople." 2d ed. 1894.
Bérard, Victor: "La Révolution Turque." 1909.
Beylié, L. de: "L'Habitation Byzantine." 1902.
Bode, Dr. Wilhelm: "Altpersische Knüpfteppiche." 1904.
—— "Vorderasiatische Knüpfteppiche."
Boppe, A.: "Les Peintres du Bosphore au Dixhuitième Siècle." 1911.
Brown, John P.: "The Dervishes." 1868.
Brown, P. M.: "Foreigners in Turkey." 1914.
Bury, J. B.: "A History of the Later Roman Empire." 1889.
—— Notes to Gibbon.
—— "The Ottoman Conquest." Cambridge Modern History, I, 3.
Busbecq: "Life and Letters of Ogier Ghiselin de Busbecq." Translated by C. T. Forster and F. H. B. Daniell. 1881.
Byron, George Gordon, Lord: "Childe Harold," 1812, and "Don Juan." 1824.

Cervantes, Miguel: "Don Quixote de la Mancha." 1605–15.
Choiseul-Gouffier, Comte de: "Le Voyage Pittoresque de la Grèce." Illustrated. 1782.
Choisy, A.: "L'Art de Bâtir chez les Byzantins." 1884.
Crawford, F. Marion: "Paul Patoff." 1887.
Creasy, E. S.: "History of the Ottoman Turks." 1878.

Diehl, Charles: "Études Byzantines." 1905.
—— "Figures Byzantines." 2 series.
—— "Manuel d'Art Byzantin."

Djélal Essad: "Constantinople — de Byzance à Stamboul." 1909.
Djelal Noury: "The Sultan." 1912.
Dwight, Henry O.: "Constantinople and Its Problems." 1901.
—— "Turkish Life in War Time." 1879.

Ebersolt, Jean: "Le Grand Palais de Constantinople." 1910.
—— "Églises Byzantines de Constantinople." 1914.
Edhem Pacha: "L'Architecture Ottomane." 1873.
Eliot, Sir Charles (Odysseus): "Turkey in Europe." 2d ed. 1908.
Eliot, Frances: "The Diary of an Idle Woman in Constantinople."
Epstein, M.: "The Early History of the Levant Company." 1908.
Evlia Chelibi: "The Voyages of Evlia Chelibi." Translated from the Turkish.

Falke, Otto von: "Majolica."
Farrère, Claude: "L'Homme qui Assassina."
Fazy, Edmond, and Abdul Halim Memdouh: "Anthologie de l'Amour Turque."
Finlay, G.: "A History of Greece." 1877.
Fouquet, Dr.: "Contribution à l'Étude de la Céramique Orientale." 1900.

Gallaway, James: "Constantinople Ancient and Modern." Published London, 1797.
Gardner, Alice: "Theodore of Studium."
Garnett, Lucy M. J.: "Mysticism and Magic in Turkey." 1912.
—— "The Turkish People." 1909.
—— "The Women and Folklore of Turkey."
Gautier, Théophile: "Constantinople." 1854.
Gibb, E. J. W.: "A History of Ottoman Poetry." 5 vols. 1900–8.
Gibbon, Edward: "The History of the Decline and Fall of the Roman Empire." Edited by J. B. Bury. 7 vols. 1896.
Goodell, William: "Forty Years in the Turkish Empire." 1876.
Grelot: "Rélation Nouvelle d'un Voyage de Constantinople." Illustrated. 1680.
Grosvenor, Edwin A.: "Constantinople." Illustrated. 2d ed. 1900.
Gurlitt, Cornelius: "Die Baukunst Konstantinopels." 1907-12.

Hagopian, H. H.: "Ottoman-Turkish Conversation Grammar." 1907.
Hakluyt, Richard: "The Principall Navigations, Voyages, Traffiques, and Discoveries of the English Nation . . ." 1598–1600.
Halidé Edib Hanoum: "Handan." 1913.
Hamlin, Cyrus: "Among the Turks." 1878.

Hamlin: "My Life and Times." 1893.
Hammer, Joseph von, Purgstall: "Constantinopolis und der Bosporos." 1822.
—— "Geschichte des Osmanischen Reiches." 10 vols. 1827.
—— "Histoire de l'Empire Ottoman . . ." Traduit par J.-J. Hellert. 18 vols. and atlas. 1835.
Harrison, Frederic: "Nicephorus," 1906, and "Theophano." 1904.
Hatch, Dr.: "The Organization of the Early Christian Churches." 1880.
Hawley, Walter: "Oriental Rugs, Antique and Modern." 1913.
Hichens, Robert: "The Near East." 1913.
Hutton, W. H.: "Constantinople." (Mediæval Towns Series.) 2d ed. 1904.

Jackson, Sir T. G.: "Byzantine and Romanesque Architecture." 1912.
James, Lionel: "With the Conquered Turk." 1913.
Jannaris, A. N.: "A Concise Dictionary of the English and Modern Greek Languages." 1895.
Jenkins, Hester D.: "Behind Turkish Lattices." 1912.
Johnson, Mrs. (Susannah Willard): "A Narrative of Captivity." 1796; reprinted 1907.

Knolles, Richard: "A Generall Historie of the Turks." 1603. Continuation by Sir Paul Ricaut. 1687.
Kondakov: "Les Émaux Byzantins." 1892.
Koran, The. Translated by George Sale. 1734.
Krumbacher: "Geschichte der Byzantinischen Litteratur." 2d ed. 1897.
Kúnos, Ignace: "Forty-four Turkish Fairy Tales." 1913.

La Barte, Jules: "Le Palais Impérial de Constantinople." 1861.
Lamartine, Alphonse de: "Voyage en Orient." 1835.
Lane-Poole, Stanley: "Life of Lord Stratford de Redcliffe." 1888.
—— "Oriental Coins in the British Museum." 10 vols. 1875–90.
—— "Saracenic Arts." 1886.
—— "Turkey." (Story of the Nations Series.) 1886.
Lawson, J. C.: "Modern Greek Folklore and Ancient Greek Religion." 1910.
Leclerq, H.: "Manuel d'Archéologie Chrétienne." 1907.
Le Comte, Prétextat: "Les Arts et Métiers de la Turquie et de l'Orient." 1902.
Le Hay: "Engraved Costumes of the Levant." Paris, 1714.
Lethaby and Swainson: "Sancta Sophia." 1894.
Lewis, G. G.: "The Practical Book of Oriental Rugs." 2d ed. 1913.

Loti, Pierre: "Aziyadé." 1876.
—— "Les Désenchantées." 1906.
—— "Fantôme d'Orient." 1892.
—— "Turquie Agonisante." 1913.
Lybyer, Albert H.: "The Government of the Ottoman Empire in the Time of Suleiman the Magnificent." (Harvard Historical Studies.) 1913.

Mahmud Mukhtar Pascha: "Meine Führung im Balkankriege, 1912." 1913.
Margoliouth, D. S.: "Mahommed and the Rise of Islam." 1906.
McCabe, Joseph: "The Empresses of Constantinople." 1913.
McCullagh, Francis: "The Fall of Abdul Hamid." 1910.
Melek Hanoum and Grace Ellison: "Abdul Hamid's Daughter." 1913.
Melling: "Le Voyage Pittoresque de Constantinople et des Rives du Bosphore." (Plates.) 1819.
Midhat Bey, Ali Haydar: "The Life of Midhat Pasha." 1903.
Miller, William: "The Costumes of Turkey." 1802.
Miller, William: "The Latins in the Levant." 1908.
—— "The Ottoman Empire: 1801–1913." 1913.
Millingen, Alexander van: "Byzantine Churches in Constantinople." 1912.
—— "Byzantine Constantinople: The Walls . . ." 1899.
—— "Constantinople." 1906.
Montagu, Lady Mary Wortley: "Letters." 1763 *et al.*
Mordtmann, Dr.: "Esquisse Topographique de Constantinople." 1892.
Mour, J. van: "Recueil de Cent Estampes Représentant Différentes Nations du Levant." (Plates.) 1712.
Muir, Sir William: "The Life of Mohammad."
Mumford, J. K.: "Oriental Rugs." 1901.
"Murray's Handbook for Travellers in Constantinople . . ." 1900.

Neale, J. M.: "The Fall of Constantinople."
Norden, W.: "Das Papsttum und Byzanz." 1903.

d'Ohsson, Ignatius Mouradgea: "Tableau Général de l'Empire Ottoman." Illustrated. 1824.
Oman, C. W. C.: "The Byzantine Empire." (Story of the Nations Series.) 1892.

Pardoe, Miss, and W. H. Bartlett: "The Beauties of the Bosphorus." Illustrated. 1832.
Pears, Sir Edwin: "The Destruction of the Greek Empire." 1903.

Pears: "The Fall of Constantinople." 1885.
—— "Turkey and Its People." 1911.

Racine, Jean: "Bajazet." 1672.
Ramsay, Sir William M.: "Studies in the History and Art of the Eastern Provinces of the Roman Empire." 1906.
—— "The Revolution in Constantinople and Turkey." 1909.
Redhouse, Sir James: "Turkish-English and English-Turkish Dictionary."
Rémond, Georges: "Avec les Vaincus." 1913.
Rosedale, H. G.: "Queen Elizabeth and the Levant Company." 1904.

Saladin, H., and G. Migeon: "Manuel d'Art Musulman." 1907.
Schiltberger, Johann: "Bondage and Travels." Translated by J. B. Telfer. 1879.
Schlumberger, Gustave: "Un Empereur Byzantin au Dixième Siècle." 1890.
—— "L'Épopée Byzantine." 1896–1905.
—— "Les Îles des Princes." 1884.
Sélim Bey: "Carnet de Campagne d'un Officier Turc." 1913.
Smith, Francis: "Eastern Costumes." 1769.
Stanley, Dean: "The Eastern Church." 1861.
Strzygowski: "Die Byzantinischen Wasserbehälter von Konstantinopel."
——"Orient oder Rom." 1901.

Thalasso, A.: "Karagueuz."
—— "Le Théâtre Turc." 1884.
Tinayre, Marcelle: "Notes d'une Voyageuse en Turquie." 1909.
Townsend, Meredith: "Asia and Europe." 3d ed. 1909.
Twain, Mark: "The Innocents Abroad." 1869.

Vambéry, Arminius: "Manners in Oriental Countries." 1876.
—— "The Story of My Struggles." 1904.
—— "Travels in Central Asia." 1864.
—— "The Turkish People." 1885.
Vandal, A.: "Une Ambassade Française en Orient sous Louis XV."
Villehardouin, Geoffroi de: "De la Conqueste de Constantinople . . ." Translated by Sir Frank Marzials. (Everyman's Library.)
Vincent and Dickson: "A Handbook of Modern Greek." 1904.

Wallace, Lew: "The Prince of India." 1893.
Walsh, Robert: "Constantinople and the Seven Churches of Asia." Illustrated. 1840.

Walsh: "A Residence in Constantinople." 1836.
Washburn, George: "Fifty Years in Constantinople and Recollections of Robert College." 1909.
Whitman, Sidney: "Turkish Reminiscences." 1913.
Willis, N. P.: "Pencillings by the Way." 1844.
Wratislaw, A. H., M.A.: "Adventures of Baron Wenceslas Wratislaw of Mitrowitz; what he saw in the Turkish Metropolis, Constantinople; experienced in his captivity; and after his happy return to his country, committed to writing in the year of our Lord 1599." Literally translated from the original Bohemian. 1862.

Young, George: "Corps de Droit Ottoman." 7 vols. 1905.

Zanotti, Angelo: "Autour des Murs de Constantinople." 1911.
Zeÿneb Hanoum: "A Turkish Woman's European Impressions." 1913.

INDEX

References in italics are chiefly to illustrations

Printed in Great Britain
by Amazon

45657569R00328